MARITAL TENSIONS

MARITAL TENSIONS
Clinical Studies
towards a
Psychological Theory of Interaction

Henry V. Dicks

M.A., M.D., F.R.C.P., F.B.PS.S.
Honorary Consultant, The Tavistock Clinic

Foreword by
Fred M. Sander

MARESFIELD LIBRARY

London
KARNAC BOOKS

First published in 1967 by
Routledge & Kegan Paul Limited

This edition reprinted in 1993
with their permission by
H. Karnac (Books) Ltd.
58 Gloucester Road
London SW7 4QY

A CIP catalogue record for this book is available from the British Library.

ISBN 1-85575-064-3

Printed in Great Britain by BPCC Wheatons Ltd, Exeter

CONTENTS

PART ONE

THE CONCEPTS

v

status of women; culture distance and mate
choice; the equivocal rôle of parental wishes;
effects of housing and earnings; summary

PART TWO

THE PRACTICE

5. Other models of therapy; depend on setting and social conditions; U.S. work; Prague; marital groups; the Family Planning Association model

CONTENTS

4. The lessons of marital studies; their place in central studies of human predicament; prevention of European suffering in newer industrializing societies; the positive aspects of changing sexual mores in the evolution of mankind

FOREWORD TO THIS EDITION

When Henry Dicks' *Marital Tensions* was first published in 1967, I was completing my psychiatric training at the Bronx Municipal Hospital Center, home of one of the first American family therapy training centres. Nathan Ackerman, Murray Bowen, and Don Jackson visited and conveyed the excitement of a new therapeutic model in the mental health field, one as revolutionary as psychoanalysis had been a half-century earlier. Finding psychoanalysis equally compelling, I decided to seek further training in each of these ways of viewing emotional disorders.

To my chagrin, my analytic colleagues found family therapy superficial and faddish while my family therapy colleagues viewed analysis as old hat. In trying to understand human conflicts, I saw these fields as two sides of a coin. Reading *Marital Tensions*, I was reassured at that early stage in my career that these two systems of thought were as interlocking and interdependent as our individual patients and their family members. Central to Dicks' thesis was the analytic view that past family experiences, whether real or imagined, incorporated in one's inner (i.e. unconscious) world, are replayed and transformed in everyone's current life. Repeatedly, Dicks demonstrated that for this transformation to occur, each person must ultimately 'share' these inner worlds in significant ways with the important people in their lives.

Freud was aware of these dynamics when he wrote, 'Unhappy marriage and physical infirmity are the two things that most often supersede a neurosis. They satisfy in particular the sense of guilt (need for punishment) which makes many patients cling so fast to their neuroses' (1, p. 163). Dicks would have formulated such collusive neuroses as a couple's 'shared' guilt—the need to provoke their partner, for example, to enact the punishing behaviour of one of their parents. Around the same time, in his *Introductory Lectures*, Freud noted that such external real family resistances, which might include scapegoating or

xiii

blaming another for one's suffering, were often added to his patients' internal resistances to analysis and change. Nonetheless, in his comparison of psychoanalytic treatment with a surgical operation, he asked rhetorically how such treatment could succeed 'in the presence of all the members of the patient's family, who would stick their noses into the field of operation and exclaim aloud at every incision' (2, p. 459). He added that, 'No one who has any experience of the rifts which so often divide a family . . . will be surprised to find that the patient's closest relatives sometimes [are less invested—my paraphrase] in his recovery than in his remaining as he is. When neurosis is related to conflicts between members of a family, the healthy party will not hesitate long in choosing between his own interest and the sick party's recovery' (2, p. 459). This kind of observation especially interested Dicks and would become one of the core concepts in *Marital Tensions*. Each member of a couple will avoid his own conflicts by projecting and introjecting idealized (good) and/or frustrating (bad) experiences and identifications of self and other.

Dicks joined the family therapy revolution of the mid-twentieth century by positing that the family is a system involving such reciprocal interweaving and dovetailing of inner worlds. In my own attempt towards the integration of these disciplines of psychoanalysis and family therapy (3), I came upon T. S. Eliot's 'The Cocktail Party', which anticipated the latter revolution. Dr. Harcourt Railly schedules the first joint psychiatric interview in literature saying, 'Indeed, it is often the case that my patients are only pieces of a total situation which I have to explore. The single patient who is ill by himself, is rather the exception' (4, p. 350).

The reader of *Marital Tensions* will have the pleasure of joining Dicks on his journey of discovery. Indeed, much of his book reads like a traveller's journal. He always shows an awareness of the importance of contexts in clinical work. He begins by citing the spiralling breakdown of the family in this century and the ever-present role played by socio-economic and cultural factors. He then focuses on his central concern, the psychology of his patients, evident in fresh and detailed clinical material, often from notes taken after his sessions with patients.

In this book we see him move from the original Tavistock model of two collaborating therapists working individually with spouses to the discovery of the greater power and efficiency of the joint interview (JI). There is much clinical wisdom embedded throughout this book. To cite just one example, Dicks notes that the complex interaction of individual treatment with the collusive interaction in a marriage often results in the ending of a marriage. He adds, 'Some of the most poignant encounters in this field have been with the "left out" spouses who discovered too late that by their original decision to opt out of joint therapy they are now stranded, and it *was* too late' (p. 236). Just as often, individual analytic treatment can become stalled by such collusive marital systems—a phenomenon called 'split transference' by Graller, in a rare article on marital therapy in the analytic literature (5). He advocates the addition of conjoint treatment in such situations.

The fertile climate of the Tavistock Clinic (6), where Dicks developed his ideas, was successfully emulated by the Washington School of Psychiatry, which has developed the only well-established analytic family therapy training programme in the United States (7, 8). *Marital Tensions* has been an organizing text in that programme since its inception about fifteen years ago.

The fields of psychoanalysis and family therapy were and remain curiously disengaged and unintegrated. This is unfortunate in that psychoanalytic theory remains the most comprehensive psychological theory of the human mind while remaining limited in its application to a small percentage of patients. One of the causes—and there are many—of the current crisis of psychoanalysis has been an unwillingness to deal with the analysis of transferences and resistances where they are most often encountered: in everyday family life. Dicks at one point makes clear that 'the adaptation of psychoanalytic principles to the realities of clinical life in "mass practice"' requires new techniques such as conjoint therapy (p. 227). The republication of *Marital Tensions* is most timely because there are stirrings in many quarters towards the integration of the theory and clinical practice of both individual and family therapy. This is especially appropriate in the United States, where health care generally has been so fragmented and unintegrated.

Fred M. Sander M.D

Associate Clinical Professor
Mt. Sinai Medical School

Visiting Faculty
Object Relations Family Therapy Training Program
Washington School of Psychiatry

August 1993

xv

REFERENCES

1. FREUD, S. (1919) 'Lines of Advance in Psychoanalytic Therapy.' *Standard Edition 17*, pp. 159–68.
2. FREUD, S. (1917) *Introductory Lectures on Psycho-Analysis*, Part III, Lecture 28: 'Analytic Therapy'. *Standard Edition 16*, pp. 448–63.
3. SANDER, F. (1979) *Individual and Family Therapy: Toward an Integration*. Northvale, New Jersey: Jason Aronson.
4. ELIOT, T. S. (1952) *The Complete Poems and Plays (1909–1950)*. New York: Harcourt, Brace and World.
5. GRALLER, J. (1981) 'Adjunctive Marital Therapy: A Possible Solution to the Split Transference Problem', in *Annual of Psychoanalysis* ed. by G. Pollack. New York: International Universities Press, pp. 175–87.
6. RUSZCZYNSKI, S. (Ed.) (1993) *Psychotherapy with Couples: Theory and Practice at the Tavistock Institute of Marital Studies*. London: Karnac Books.
7. SCHARFF, J. (Ed.) (1989) *The Foundations of Object Relations Family Therapy*. Northvale, New Jersey: Jason Aronson.
8. SCHARFF, D. E., and SCHARFF, J. S. (1991) *Object Relations Couple Therapy*. Northvale, New Jersey: Jason Aronson.

PREFACE

This volume has been written from a sense of obligation, as Hippocrates bids us do. It records and illustrates more fully and systematically than earlier papers the progress in theory and practice over sixteen years of the Marital Unit of the Tavistock Clinic in the National Health Service. I believe that it represents to all but a few doctors and social workers, a new approach to problems of personality in interaction and hence to mental health, and therefore should be stated as fully as possible. This book is addressed to the professions concerned with mental health, I therefore make no apology for the use of technical terms which I must assume are familiar to readers in these disciplines. I have written it as the leader and spokesman of a team who have worked out this approach together. My colleagues have hitherto been even more shy than I over communicating our experience and views in this new field in psychiatry, psychology and social case work.

I would have preferred this to have been a volume of joint authorship. As it is, I can only express my indebtedness and thanks to those good colleagues and collaborators who seem to prefer that I should have the responsibility of telling the story of shared labour and discovery.

First and foremost, I could not have begun this work without the wise and reassuring collaboration of Dr. Mary C. Luff, who, until her retirement in 1958, was my partner in establishing the essential techniques and concepts out of which the Tavistock Marital Unit could grow. I am sorry that she never consented to associate her name with any of the publications issuing from our joint work. I want here to record Mary Luff's essential part in this enterprise.

My special gratitude also goes to my three highly valued colleagues who not only replaced Mary Luff but enabled our Unit to enlarge the scope of our therapeutic work: Mrs. Judith Stephens, Mrs. Mary Williams and Miss Alison Watson, As.A.P.S.W. They are indeed pillars of the Unit, and their contri-

xvii

butions to the ideas and methods presented in this volume are very great. Their skill and interest enabled us to institute and educate ourselves in the techniques of joint therapy, and communicate them to a series of colleagues who are now making their own contributions to the subject. I want to acknowledge especially the help given by Drs. John Padel, Stanford Bourne, William Brough and Trevor Smith. It is also my pleasure to acknowledge the debt the Marital Unit of the Tavistock Clinic owes Dr. Guillermo Teruel. The presence of this remarkable observer and of his gifted wife and collaborator, Mrs. Natalie Teruel, among us on a prolonged attachment, has greatly enriched our concepts and practice. We all look for great developments in marital studies from their home base in Venezuela.

Next, I want to express my thanks to Mr. Herbert Phillipson, Head of the Clinical Psychology Services of the Tavistock Clinic, not only for his continued interest and collaboration, but also for sparing, at various stages, some of the time of his associates to help us in assessment first Mr. Gerald Staunton, then Mr. John Boreham and, later especially Dr. Peter Hildebrand, with whom certain test procedures described in Chapter X were devised. Indeed, but for Mr. Phillipson's urging this book might not have been written!

No psychiatric research can survive without good records. Our efforts would have been in vain but for the efficiency and helpfulness of a succession of secretaries: Miss Nellie Clark, Miss Doris Young, Mrs. Winifred Hunt, Miss Gillian Cole, Mrs. Barbara Thorne, Miss Olive Plowman and Mrs. Bertha Roe. To all of them I want to give thanks.

I am grateful to all those publishers and editors who have permitted me to use materials (not always obviously) from my previous writings which have appeared in the following:

(1) Dr. Thomas Freeman, *British Journal of Medical Psychology,* for
   a. 'Experiences with Marital Tensions seen in the Psychological Clinic', 1953, vol. 26.
   b. 'Object Relations Theory and Marital Studies', 1963, vol. 36.
   c. 'In Search of our Proper Ethic', 1950, vol. 23.

(2) Dr. I. Douglas-Wilson, *The Lancet,* for 'The Predicament of the Family in the Modern World', 5 February 1955.

(3) Mr. G. Green, *The Royal Society of Health Journal,* for 'Mental Hygiene in Marriage', 1957, vol. 77.

(4) The Editors, *Proceedings of the Royal Society of Medicine,* 'Sexual Problems in Marriage — The Psychodynamic Aspects',

1959, vol. 52 (Section of Psychiatry).

(5) Mr Peter Leonard, *Social Work,* for: 'World Wide Problems— Marriage Relationships in Different Cultures', October 1962.

(6) The University of North Carolina Press, for Chapter: 'Concepts of Marital Diagnosis & Therapy as Developed at the Tavistock Family Psychiatric Units, London, England,' in *Marriage Counselling in Medical Practice,* edited by E. M. Nash, Lucie Jessner and D. W. Abse, 1964.

(7) The Pergamon Press, and Dr. Philip Hopkins for Chapter: 'Fitness for Marriage' in *Psychosomatic Disorders in Adolescents and Young Adults,* 1965, edited by J. Hambling and P. Hopkins.

(8) The CIBA Foundation for Chapter: 'Intra-personal Conflict and the Authoritarian Character' in the Symposium *Conflict in Society,* edited by Anthony de Reuck and Julie Knight, published by J. & A. Churchill, 1966.

So much for my conscious borrowing and re-statement of already formulated ideas, passages and case illustrations. I have also referred to many other authors' works, and have tried to acknowledge most of these in the references in my text. But there must be some, authors or other colleagues, whose thoughts are not thus marked but which I may have unwittingly duplicated or plagiarized. To them my apologies and thanks. I do not claim to be conversant with the whole growing literature in the field of marital and family psychiatry, and it is likely that other workers, in other lands, may find in this book ideas similar to theirs. The year 1949 seems to have been the *Annus Mirabilis* for the simultaneous but unconnected beginnings of systematic study and of clinics dealing with marital pathology, not only in Britain. That year in London saw the establishment of two originally independent centres: my own and the Family Discussion Bureau, and there has been two-way traffic between us which has helped me, at any rate, both with ideas and practical work. I gratefully record my indebtedness to Mrs. Lily Pincus and her team of the F.D.B. since their accession to the Tavistock Institute of Human Relations. The two units have been the best of rivals with usefully complementary rôles, and some overlap of staff. I also want to acknowledge how much this book owes to the stimulus of the Probation Training Division of the Home Office whose enlightened policies started me on systematic thinking about my topic.

I want also to place on record the kindness of the Tavistock Clinic's administering powers in tolerating my somewhat unorthodox ways of employing National Health Service time. I refer not only to Dr. J. D. Sutherland, Medical Director, whose support and encouragement was always generous. I am thinking also of the Paddington Group Hospital Management Committee, whose members and chief officers have shown a warm concern for and confidence in the kind of work and aims the Tavistock Clinic has always stood for. Their encouraging attitude gives the lie to charges so irresponsibly made against National Health Service 'bureaucracy', and I here wish to say so gratefully.

I would also like to thank my consultant confrères of the Tavistock's Adult Department for suffering this 'cuckoo in the nest' which made my services less available for the many other calls of our primary tasks.

And lastly, to my wife my deep gratitude not only for her great share in preparing the manuscript, but also for tolerating, with other members of my family, the disruptive effect on normal living of a spare-time author.

MARITAL TENSIONS

Chapter I

INTRODUCTION

The decision to take up the investigation of disturbed marriages was one that grew slowly out of the convergence of a number of lines of interest over the years. That the subject needed study was clear. Psychiatrists and social work counsellors were confronted with the ever-increasing numbers of 'broken homes', with their trail of unhappiness—and yet nobody in Britain seemed to be doing much about trying to understand these phenomena in the light of current psychological or sociological theory. Psychiatry and psychology were less equipped to approach these cases with a coherent conceptual scheme, than the brave amateurs who were actually carrying the case loads, whether as marriage counsellors or as Probation Officers. When, after the Second World War, this case load swelled into a flood as one symptom of social change and dislocation in the wake of this cataclysm, these agencies naturally turned to us, the alleged experts, for support and help in diagnosis and therapy. They found the psychiatrists absorbed with other tasks.

A picture of the medico-psychological scene as it affected family psychiatry shortly after the Second World War can be gained from the following letters which appeared in the *B.M.J.* of 30 April 1949, under the heading of 'Marriage Neurosis'. (i) The first is by Dr. J. I. Milne of Manchester:

> 'I was glad to read Dr. R. Macdonald Ladell's condemnation (April 9, p. 635) of the indiscriminate use of E.C.T. and of the equally dreadful operation of leucotomy . . . there is a great increase in the use of E.C.T. in difficult cases without any previous attempt at psychiatry. Surely the resort to E.C.T. is a confession of failure . . . a purely mechanical operation divorced from all conception of the aims of psychology . . .' (etc.)

(ii) The second letter from Dr. L. F. Donnan of Exeter, put the positive points for the use of E.C.T. in its physiological perspective. It also stated:

1

'. . . E.C.T. in out-patient use is in danger of being used as a short cut to alteration in behaviour which leaves hidden the real distortions of relationship which are the core of a neurosis . . . It would be a pity if psychiatry took only the narrow view . . . and in this lost sight of the disturbed psychodynamics [behind the action of E.C.T.—H.V.D.] . . . If the wider outlook is not taken and enough psychotherapy . . . not given to inelastic mentalities, what we are doing is no more a "cure" than is the giving of opium to a case of Phthisis . . .'

Dr. Donnan then pleads for therapy directed at an improvement of human relationships, and ends with the words:

'Marriage is one of the largest of human relationships, and to attempt to assess and deal with the difficulties of one partner without coming to know something of the other, and without a regard to the relationship between them, is like trying to lift a log by one end only.'

These protests against psychiatric practice in the field of marriage at 'official' level came from a retired doctor and young psychiatrist. In Britain, Dr. E. F. Griffith[1] had been writing on marital relations since before the Second World War, drawing medical attention to this topic. Griffith's contribution, as I see it, was that of stressing the central importance of a full and responsible (or mature) sexual life for marital and family health; of educating the educators of the young in this field, of reconciling this point of view with religious and social ethics, and thus presenting marital relations as a way of growth and fulfilment. His work hardly changed psychiatric views. But it had an important effect in easing the acceptance by our society of both the Marriage Guidance Council and the Family Planning Association. Griffith also strengthened the trend represented by the late Sir Claud Mullins, a Metropolitan Magistrate, towards creating the marital conciliation functions and training of probation officers.

In the then expanding field of marriage counselling, the Marriage Guidance Council's theoretician Dr. David Mace may be assumed to have represented the high-water mark of its principles of therapy at about the same date.[2] In a self-confessedly hasty compilation, his thinking led him to the same conclusion as Dr. Donnan's above. He mistrusted psychiatrists. He shared the prevalent dread of the joint interview. For the rest he relied mostly on the slogan *solviter ambulando* and on the intuition of his largely amateur counsellors, who were to have consultants in medicine, psychology, law, housing, etc., to back them up. Reading Dr. Mace's statement of treatment policy and orientation one was disturbed by his reliance on clichés,

2

e.g. 'A real partnership is based on justice and loyal co-operation' (p. 132). 'If the cause [for sexual coldness] can be nailed down, something can generally be done about it. All that is needed is some change in the attitude of the marriage partner.' Dr. Mace, however, was writing a popular exposition, and he did deal with the topic as one of interaction, and of rôle failure. He advised his counsellors to have analytic training (p. 134). His was a considerable advance in comparison with medical attitudes.

It was a surprise to find that the most mature thinking and practical policy was to be found in a Memorandum issued to Probation Officers of the Home Department, who had newly entered on their matrimonial conciliation functions. I shall have occasion to refer to this Memorandum in the Chapter describing Treatment.

There was therefore here an urgent challenge from several angles to remedy the lack of expertise in a subject which cried out for it. The first, as already stated, was consumer demand. There was, after the Second World War, much better public provision for social welfare and a full employment situation which enabled the voluntary social agencies to turn from bedrock aid with money and baby-clothes to the now more explicit need for support and counsel at the level of family conflicts. In a materially secure society the luxury of attention to the socio-psychiatric problems can be afforded. These reveal themselves only when the questions of elementary subsistence and of sanitation ('freedom from want and from disease') are on the road to solution. The consumer demand thus came through both public health and social welfare channels, as part of their resources could now be devoted to an expanding interest in the mental health services. These services were, as for example at the International Congress for Mental Health, London 1948,[3] visualized not only, or even mainly, as the provision of treatment for the very sick, but rather as an endeavour to use the insights into aetiological factors derived from clinical work for 'mental prophylaxis', for W.H.O.'s 'positive health'.

Then there was the public concern at the very size of the problem. Soon after the War, the Committee under Mr. Justice Denning[4] (as the learned judge then was) reported on the need to train Probation Officers for the novel task of interposing an attempt at conciliation between warring spouses, at the level of the Magistrates' Courts, before giving legal effect to separation orders and other methods of judicial intervention in marriages. This awakening of the body politic to an alarming situation was later signalized by the appointment of the Royal Commission on Marriage and Divorce in 1951, who reported in 1956.[5] That we were indeed dealing with a disquieting social epidemic was made evident by the Commission's figures.

3

Thus, whereas in 1910 in England and Wales there were filed a total of 755 matrimonial petitions of all kinds, in 1954 there were 28,347. The crude divorce rate alone in this census rose from 0·02 per thousand in 1910 to 0·67 per thousand in 1953. Had this fabulous increase of 3,350 per cent been recorded for tuberculosis or dysentery—what a panic would have been caused, and what an outcry for most drastic measures of research and prevention.

No such parallel dramatic increase was recorded in the incidence of either mental illness or even of juvenile delinquency and crime. Somehow, one felt, the tensions and discontents of many were perhaps being worked out in this intimate field of marital relations, thereby saving other manifestations of stress. Perhaps marital strife was a kind of substitute psychiatric illness, or at least a symptom of disordered bio-social adaptation following the War? At this point there comes to mind the saying that 'When the parents have eaten sour grapes the children's teeth are set on edge'. If fifty years of clinical and research work in psychological medicine has discovered anything, it is that of the close correlation of much mental illness, psychopathy and criminality with a background history of deprivation of healthy and security-giving parental home conditions. Was it those most deprived who had been most disturbed by the upheavals? While the effect on the children of the cruder criteria of disrupted background can be already demonstrated at a high degree of probability (e.g. Bowlby,[6] Tonge and Gay[7]) few psychiatrists and psychoanalysts doubt the reality also of subtler, less objectively measurable, factors depriving children of the essential elements of love, security and understanding discipline which are the nutrients of personality growth and mental health. In the size of the post-war marital problem there could be seen a great hazard to future citizens. Yet, by comparison with the efforts directed towards some narrower problems in psychiatry, towards mending the children by guidance and education, towards delinquency and industrial relations, marital psychopathology had been virtually ignored or passed over by researchers, as if it were an incidental or marginal field of enquiry. Is it not, however, the 'other half' of these subjects—the study of the interaction of the parental pair that is behind the deprived or anxious and insecure child?

It was, therefore, likely that the knowledge and skills deriving from the psychological and sociological discoveries could find one of their most fruitful applications in the therapy and prevention of marital breakdown. Despite the profound and rapid changes which the family has undergone in recent times as the result of social and technological upheavals and the encroachment of other institutions (especially in the highly developed industrial societies of the West),

4

it still remains the irreducible unit of social organization, rooted in biological reality. Human children, certainly up to the age of adolescence, can be shown to need the experience of continued parental love, concern and example in adult behaviour. For a mother to be able to answer this need especially during the earliest years of her care for her infants, she herself needs to feel cared for and valued in her rôle, and supported by 'her man', who has his own contribution to make towards the assimilation by the children of father-love, responsibility and discipline. For this basic social unit of the stable conjugal home there is no adequate substitute. All societies have invented safeguards for this precious function by marriage customs and rituals.

The decision to make the marital field a subject for detailed study, springs, therefore, from the widely felt apprehension of danger. Perhaps the 3,350 per cent increase in divorce is after all comparable to the ravages of an epidemic. If disintegration of the cells of the social organism is growing at this rate, what chain reactions will it bring in its train for our future community? Not only in the frustrations of the wish for stability, enduring love and support of many of the partners themselves, but especially in the geometric progression of deprived children whose minds cannot trust or be trusted to make lasting and undivided emotional commitments in *their* marriages or in human relations generally. A society is only as good as the emotional state of its component individuals will allow it to be. A marked and rising proportion of broken or grossly disturbed marriages is bound to swell the numbers of conflict-torn, potentially destructive offspring to whom the world, its culture and its institutions are the enemy.

Our experience based on the observation of guilt feelings in unhappy marriage partners, of their attempts to improve their relationships and to protect their children from witnessing angry scenes and from the effects of their conflicts, leads one to think that deep down mankind is aware of the biological value of the stable, united family which also offers the spouses themselves one of the greatest and simplest foundations for a sense of personal worth and maturity. The very revolt against the difficult marriage points to a higher standard of what wedlock should be, and under what conditions men and women are prepared to maintain it. The epidemic is at present checked. We know, for example, that the divorce rate has remained fairly static since that 1953 census. The U.S.A. have also observed a reduction since the post-war peak.[8] But this does not absolve one from studying the problem which remains.

The moral challenge contained in the above-mentioned situation might, however, have remained at the level of a pious aspiration if

5

certain conceptual working tools had not also become available. These are the factors converging on the choice of studying marital stress from the other direction. It was, perhaps, some inner logic which made this field come late in the list. Before this was possible there had to be the felt social need to pay attention. This has happened. Then there must be platforms from which to take off into the unexplored space. These were now provided by growth of the relevant disciplines. These newer developments in psychodynamic concepts and sociological hypotheses about human relations had to be assimilated, and interviewing and other assessment techniques adapted to the task. And the reluctance of breaking into the sacred 'private' area had to be overcome.

The theoretical orientation of this present study, which has since developed into a normal clinical service offered by the Tavistock Clinic, is broadly psycho-analytic. Harry Stack Sullivan's definition of psychiatry as the 'operational statement of interpersonal relations' might have been invented for the study of marital interaction and its failures. Until the evolution of hypotheses relating to inter-personal processes had acquired some solid support in clinical experience, the possibility of visualizing and describing happenings in groups at technical level hardly existed. The precursors of group research and group therapy were found in the work of Moreno and the field theorists, notably Kurt Lewin, and developed into the present practices. It would have made little sense to try and explain or analyse the contents of a complicated 'group' relationship, such as marriage, in the older terms of Freud's classical personality theory. Though Freud certainly conceived the *libido* as object-seeking, this powerful drive was nonetheless visualized as essentially an effect of impersonal neuro-physiological or hormonal activity seeking to discharge its tensions and manipulating the ego to do its bidding. His was a physiological psychology of 'impulse gratification'. This might have sufficed for the study of the development of sexual attractions between two people leading to successful intercourse. But we know that, however strong the operation of the sexual drive, this is not adequate to explain or even describe the range of phenomena involved in marriage, useful though it may be to account for the genital elements in the totality of marital interaction. As I have said elsewhere, 'nervous systems do not marry nor are given in marriage . . .'[9] Such social action is the attribute of *persons*. The necessary complement to group and field concept at the level of the experience of individuals involved in such processes, was the emergence of the concept of *object relations*, associated with the work of Melanie Klein and, especially relevantly to our theme, of W. R. D. Fairbairn. Ernest Jones, in his preface to Fairbairn's book in which the new

6

theory is developed, put the matter with characteristic clarity in a nutshell:

'If it were possible to condense Dr. Fairbairn's new ideas into one sentence, it might run somewhat as follows. Instead of starting, as Freud did, from the stimulation of the nervous system proceeding from excitation of various erotogenous zones and internal tension arising from gonadic activity, Dr. Fairbairn starts at the centre of the personality, the ego, and depicts its strivings and difficulties in its endeavour to reach an object where it may find support . . .'[10]

This statement, and all that has been condensed in it shows that Fairbairn's theory has moved the ego—the whole person—to the forefront of consideration, as existing from birth and *using* instinctual forces for the attainment of its object-seeking needs. Fairbairn, like J. A. Hadfield before him, regarded the stage of infantile dependence as the starting point of all capacity to make and develop intimate human relationships, and its frustration as the beginning of psychopathology. Not the discharge of somatic tensions, but the need for others and to feel needed by them is the basis of group life. It was the impact of this way of regarding human strivings which evoked in me the imaginative courage to test these concepts on a clinical examination of married couples in difficulties. I had already made it the basis of my general approach to psycho-pathology (Dicks 1939).

A further theoretical basis for the present study was provided by the sociological concepts of *rôle performance* and of *culture patterns*. These two fruitful ideas in the behavioural sciences place the individuals under scrutiny within the context of their social environment and give many clues to possible conflicts and divergencies in partners who may have originated in widely differing backgrounds.

I define marriage as a social relationship *sui generis*. In the West it is a voluntary agreement between two persons at conscious or ego levels to enter into a contract to play certain social rôles (first of the many facets of a spouse, later of a parent) in such a way as not only to satisfy many emotional and biological needs each of the other and of their own; but also to fulfil, or conform to a tolerable degree with, the requirements and mores of the cultural background in which each partner developed, and of the changing society of which they now form a constituent unit.

The culture pattern of every society has its own set of rôle norms as well as its sanctions for its conjugal institution. The society within which the marriage exists may not be the one in which one or both spouses originated, given present conditions of geographical and social mobility. Marriage, then, has the aspect of a social system,

7

while in another aspect it is the most intimate and private relation between two persons we know. We shall pursue the potential conflict implicit between this public, responsible, legally sanctioned face of marriage and its intensely personal interactions at conscious and unconscious depths as one of the main themes of the book. We hope to show the importance for marriage of the interplay of largely unconscious developmental histories of two persons so closely confronting each other, histories during which their primary biological and social needs for finding security, dependence, sexual fulfilment and self-affirmation had been structured and modified by the influences of their earlier milieu upon their given genetic predispositions. The possibilities of conflict between the demands of a socio-cultural rôle and a given personality trying to fill that rôle will be obvious.

It follows that any attempt to comprehend marital relations will require attention to the following aspects of the given case, not necessarily in the order here adopted, or with equal emphasis on each:

1. An assessment of each partner as a separate individual.
2. An assessment of the socio-cultural factors bearing on the couple both from their separate 'past' and in the 'here and now' of their connections and position in their society and its sub-groups, as the demands of economic and societal adaptation and rôle performance.
3. An attempt to identify from the clinical phenomena the more unconscious forces which flow between the partners forming bonds of a 'positive' and 'negative' kind, a love-hate involvement.

It is this last named aspect which, in my view, constitutes the personal, psychological core of marital life, not only in the disorders of marriage, but also as the healthy, normally functioning element which bind two persons into a dyad, an integrate different from the mere sum of its parts. If this statement is considered 'mystical', I do not flinch.

Thus the adequate socio-psychological assessment of a case of marital difficulty is a complex one, even after the exclusion of organic pathology or mental disorder of a more general kind. For if, by our approach, we wish to examine the interpersonal relationship, then we must regard the dyad as the 'patient', the marriage as the 'sick person'. This is not to say that in the detailed examination of people who come mainly or exclusively for stress in their marital lives we do not also find pervasive personality defects. But such defects have mainly become organized around the marriage without

8

necessarily invading or disturbing other facets of personality functioning, e.g. the work sphere or the area of social relations. It would be misleading to say that in our clinical practice we have never had to see people who came because of their marital stress but were found to be grossly mentally ill. Of course we have. In these cases the illness had disturbed the marriage together with most other aspects of the sick partner's social adaptations. Sometimes it looked as if the marriage trouble was perhaps the chief factor triggering off a severe mental illness. It is not, however, with the type of relation where one partner is or has become a mental invalid that this book is concerned. It deals with marriages in which stress or failure in marital rôle performance is the principal finding.

It follows from the concern with the dyad that there had to be adaptations of techniques, as already mentioned. On the clinical side one had become trained by the War and its immediate aftermath to use group therapeutic settings for assessment and treatment. It was a relatively short step to limit such a group to two, and to accustom oneself to observe not only those phenomena of interaction the analytic psychiatrist meets daily in his sessions with one person, but to extend this scrutiny to 'what goes on' between the partners in the dyad and between himself and the dyad, both as individuals and as a united entity.

I take some credit in having moved the technique of the *Joint Interview* into the forefront of means of observing, learning and helping what could never be fully experienced in the single interview. The method and its variants receive fuller attention in a later part of this volume.

The skills of the clinical psychologist have not been irrelevant in helping to devise quasi-normative and comparative personality inventories and tests. Owing to budgetary and staff problems in the absence of a major research grant, these tests have remained rather tentative, and await further work by those qualified in their design and use. Readers of strictly experimental-science persuasion will find only some tentative generalizations and a conceptual framework from which they might take off to isolate manageable propositions to which rigorous research techniques could be applied. This volume is not the report on a finished research project, but a stocktaking of theory and practice at a certain point in time.

The plan is to begin with the social aspects of contemporary life as it affects married couples, and to follow it with the theoretical framework for looking at the individuals' resources *qua* marriage partners. After that I shall present the views on marital interaction evolved as the result of my team's findings which fall under the third heading of the above mentioned scheme of study.

9

In the second part of the book I shall concentrate on the more practical aspects of marital diagnosis and therapy—the application of the concepts to clinical work.

REFERENCES

1. GRIFFITH, E. F. (1946) *Modern Marriage*. London: Methuen.
2. MACE, DAVID R. (1948) *Marriage Counselling. The First Full Account of the Remedial Work of the Marriage Guidance Councils*. London: Churchill Ltd.
3. *Statement of the International Preparatory Commission to the International Congress on Mental Health* (1948) Vol. IV. London: H. K. Lewis & Co.
4. *The Denning Report* (1947) Cmd. 7024. H.M. Stationery Office.
5. *Report of the Royal Commission on Marriage and Divorce* (1956). Cmd. 9678. H.M. Stationery Office.
6. BOWLBY, JOHN (1946) *Forty-Four Juvenile Thieves*. London: Bailliere, Tindall & Cox.
7. TONGE, W. L. and GAY, M. J. (1966) 'The Late Effects of Loss of Parents in Childhood', *Brit. J. Psychiatry* (in press).
8. U.S. Public Health Service, Nat. Vital Statistics Division (1963) 'Trends in Divorce and Family Disruption'. *Preprint*, August. Washington D.C.
9. DICKS, H. V. (1947) *Clinical Studies in Psychopathology*, 2nd Edition. London: Edward Arnold.
10. JONES, ERNEST, in Fairbairn, W. R. D. (1952) *Psychoanalytic Studies of the Personality*. London: Tavistock Publications.

10

PART ONE

The Concepts

Chapter II

THE SOCIAL SETTING

It was mentioned in the Introduction that the phenomena of marital stress and breakdown required to be related to the powerful forces of social change affecting all aspects of living, not least the functions of the family. The family was called the social atom, the final recipient of all the political and economic events which rain down upon it. It was also seen as the chief attitude-forming centre of the body-politic, feeding back the lessons in human relations learnt or not learnt by countless citizens at primary level as attitudes towards the larger society. It is logical, then, to begin our study with this connection between stress and the social setting of the family. Frighi and Callieri[1] and Ashley Montagu[2] cover similar ground.

The literature of cultural anthropology describes the varieties of customs and sanctions which different societies, 'primitive' and sophisticated, have devised to safeguard the family, and to regulate sexual relationships in these communities' presumed interests. All these have explicit religious, magical and legal sanctions as binding as those which obtained until quite recently in our society. These diverse prescriptions include rules governing parental responsibilities in mate choice; ascendancy of one sex over the other, polygamy and polyandry, patrilineal or matrilineal kinship arrangements, and so forth. Another aspect of cultural variability also deserves mention: this is the regulation of premarital sexual behaviour ranging from insistence on chastity and segregation of the sexes until betrothal or marriage at one end, to wide degrees of laxity and permissiveness, even encouragement, towards premarital sexual exploration and experiment at the other end of the scale. Margaret Mead, in her *Male and Female*[3] has shown us some of these variations, which will repay careful study.

THE NORM FOR ENGLISH MARRIAGE

It is perhaps interesting that within our Tavistock Clinic cases there have been comparable variations in the patterns of the premarital

13

sex habits of the spouses and in their own and their parents' marital arrangements and rôle playing. Nothing like the uniformity which we often assume exists and which we think of as the 'norm' of a 'good marriage' is encountered in practice. One meets, for example, with considerable variations from case to case of male or female predominance, of expectations of freedom to have extra-marital sexual relations, of equality and inequality of the sexes in rôle sharing, of parental attitudes and family rôle assignments—all in people resident in Greater London, and mainly indigenous to this country.

But it should also be stated that among this wide variety of married couples adherence to the *idea* of the 'norm' is frequently observed. This is a persistent cultural ideal, especially in the age groups now over 30. Our findings for English people are in striking agreement with the survey on this and related topics reported by Geoffrey Gorer,[4] especially as it affected lower middle and upper working class attitudes. Among the desiderata of this sampled population highly valued traits of good spouses were: understanding, personableness, fidelity, thoughtfulness; a relatively low valuation of sexual prowess, physical beauty or shared interests. The men stress their requirement of maternal and housekeeping skills in wives. The norm, then, as deduced by an anthropologist from a statistically analysed sample of some 5,000 (selected at random from over 10,000) was surprisingly dull and pedestrian; but one, greatly favouring enduring, unspectacular qualities such as would give a man good cherishing and a woman a sense of security and being valued as a person.

Both our population and Gorer's showed an abhorrence of any show of aggression in self and in others—notably in their children, and stressed need for tolerance and forgiveness, even, by big majorities, in the case of the ultimate injury of sexual infidelity.

These specifications show the persistence of traditional and ethically Christian (and Jewish) values in the marital expectations of English people, part of a rigorous constriction of instinctual freedom, from which the recent obsessive preoccupation with sex books, strip-tease—as well as the teenage revolt—may be an attempted break-out. The majority feel the group norms threatened, and react with anxiety and alarm at the evidences of such sexual ferment and subversion of old decencies. Iago Galdston[5] has sketched this predicament for Americans very elegantly.

It seems to me logical to see in this clash between traditional marital mores and norms and the phenomena of breakdown in these mores a long-term effect of social change, ushered in by the technological transformation of society, usually called the Industrial Revolution, and all its sequels for the loosening of the age-old order by which family relations in our country had been regulated. Some of these sequels have been given names which sufficiently describe them; urbanization, secularization, social mobility, social deracination or atomization, emancipation of women. All these profound changes have been speeded by the accelerating tempo of technological advance since the Second World War. The mass media of communication have substituted an almost simultaneous impact of events for formerly slow, easily assimilable percolation of them, with time to ponder and shape an attitude of acceptance or rejection.

SOME FEATURES OF TRADITIONAL FAMILY STRUCTURE

It is a widely accepted contention that the culture pattern tends to lag behind social change, on which it acts as a powerful resistance. We may think of the examples of the Luddites who opposed the coming of machinery, or of the long battle of the Russian peasant against Soviet innovations. In traditional societies such as were until very recently the majority in the world, and which included the West until the Industrial Revolution, the family was in a real sense the effective unit of society, and seemed both the natural and the divinely ordained order. It was centred on the joint homestead, economically self-supporting, an integrate of economic, cultural and spiritual life. The rôles, privileges and obligations of each kind of member of the three to four generation group were clearly defined by religiously sanctioned custom and taboo. Such a family was not only a rich and meaningful milieu—it was often the *only* milieu for a life-time; home; school for all needed skills and cultural heritage; workplace and 'castle'.

The Russian writer Gladkov[6] describes his childhood in such a peasant homestead, ruled over by his old grandparents, with his father and mother and uncles and aunts, siblings and cousins living under one roof, seated at table in hierarchical order, working and praying together, the women strictly subordinated even to the youngest male—all obeying grandfather in awe and piety. There was nowhere to escape to, no industrial town in which to seek alternative work for the rebel sons. There was no freedom to move except to court the girls in the village over the hill. The brides were selected for the lads by arrangement between parents—a dowry passed. The new daughter-in-law was now under orders from her mother-in-law. They all tilled the fields, and celebrated the harvest. Opposition was put down harshly by the old man, and his adult sons, who were also his labourers, begged for forgiveness on their bended knees. For Grandfather's authority, like that of the Father-Tzar's, was from God.

15

This experience describes the timeless traditional Christian family everywhere in our world. Everybody knew his place and status, and moved within their limits. It was a narrow, perhaps oppressive but emotionally secure world, because there *was* no choice, with its possibility of conflict. It was also a world in which it was easier to work out one's loves and hates, one's ambivalences, on a variety of safe—because kindred—figures within well-understood boundaries.

THE MODERN URBAN FAMILY

We leap now to the great contrast of the modern urban family with its few children, so rapidly emerging as the shrunken successor of the kind of group described above. The values of the traditional family still persist, very palpably, in our unconscious ideal of the meaningful milieu for the growing child. This 'vestigial' shrunken 'nuclear family' has now to be the 'pint-pot' into which a whole gallon of human needs for a variety of relational learning experience has to be expressed.[7,8,9] Its basic socio-biological function, being rooted in human needs, has no chance of being abrogated, as was already indicated in the introductory chapter. So the load this small interacting group has to carry is enormous. In terms of evolution, this change has been so rapid that the deeply held culture norms have not had time to be creatively adapted to the new realities. Hence the prevalence of many contradictions, stresses and conflicts which manifest themselves as social and psychiatric problems. Modern technological society has certainly contributed both perils and demands on this tiny urban family. Education, leisure, not to mention work, and social companionship have been largely taken from its control. The children are expected to surpass the parents in education, skills and status, and therefore too often found their own families far removed in geographical and social space from the parent generation. The prevailing pattern is a one-generation couple, who, for a short while during their children's minority, became two-generation, only to revert to one-generation when the young leave the nest, for jobs and founding new nuclear families. This happens while, with the growth of new dormitory suburbs and settlements, we have over a couple of generations been housing new families amidst 'a sea of strangers'. Each family often represents the only little island of security, a sanctuary in which one can hope to be oneself. This is the meaning of isolation or atomization of society.

For many such small nuclear families living off their in-group's emotional resources, the situation would look somewhat as follows: There is the first 5–10 year phase when the young lovers, who may have met in a dance hall and married out of loneliness, are immersed

16

in the almost impersonal task of career and home-building, mating and child rearing. Like all fulfilment of natural functions, this is absorbing and rewarding for them in their new nest. (In another place we will deal with those who cannot achieve this phase.) The real difficulties begin sooner or later when this initial phase is passed. The couple now face the truly *inter-personal* aspects of the life together, which had been submerged by the *infra*-personal, or biological tasks the lack of skill in which, nevertheless, may become part of the stock of causes for disappointment. We must try to imagine the expectations of a couple who might almost literally have to be 'all in all' to each other, since their families of origin live scattered geographically, and the neighbours and workmates are just as isolationist and withdrawn as the hypothetical subjects themselves. We see this very high need for a total relationship as a demand that the mate should contain all the rôle potentials of a large ideal group norm, tolerant of and responsive to all the partial identities and facets of personality one would wish to express towards them. The monotony and lack of deep satisfaction of much modern working life, industrial as well as domestic, the pressure of the 'rat race' in other sectors of employment, and the paucity of wider social connections drive many such couples and their too few children (the marriage partners of the near future) into emotional over-dependence. The children, living very close to the parents in cramped city dwellings, participate too intensively in the stresses of the elders, who are apt to involve their over-valued children in their own conflicts, including the use of displacement and projection mechanisms, by which the children become the scapegoats or recipients of many irrational demands of their parents. The children feel this ambivalence keenly. Urban life with its real dangers from traffic, perverts and so forth, moreover make a child's adventures into independence a matter of rational anxiety on the parents' part. This becomes, in the presence of the affective factors, a continuing source of over-protection, as well as a cause for more or less unconscious resentment by the parents at the ties and restrictions imposed by young children on their own freedom of movement and on leisure pursuits *together*. This emotional high pressure system is frequently unrelieved by reliable substitutes—such as mothers or sisters of the couple who could mind the children, or lighten the load in other ways. This is the milieu in which the psychic conflicts of the adults and the children, between the needs of being loved and dependent and the striving for autonomy and self-assertion, have to be played out and assimilated.

Such is the predicament into which modern technological urban society has placed many of its families. For a fortunate minority, the loss of the old, mainly religiously-based sanctions has opened

17

opportunities for wide and varied human experiences and relationships—the 'open society' with its vista for growth, sophistication and ripening into metropolitan 'world citizens', undreamt of even a hundred years ago. In theory, this limitlessness of development now lies open to all, and this alone justifies the loss of the old securities. In practice, the transition from the 'traditional' to the autonomous nuclear family based on free choice of partner, unsupported by the wider kinship group and its strict mores, has had—is having—its own penalties and crop of failures. What else would we expect? For its success it requires very considerable stability and emotional maturity, if the parents, in their social self-containment, are to steer a middle course of consistent discipline and responsible affection towards their children, without clinging to them or trying to live vicariously through them. This presupposes an abiding capacity of the parents to find and enjoy erotic and personal satisfaction and hence solidarity with one another. Then they are likely to ward off their children's over-dependence and deep unconscious erotic demands on them, and prevent fixation and regression to these early forms of relationship.

These generalizations are, it must be stressed, about trends; trends, moreover, deduced from dealing with the families whose internal tensions have broken surface in certain ways that have brought them to the marital clinic. We must remember that even today, the divorce rate is still *only* 0·67 per thousand, if this can be taken as a rough index of more widely spread but concealed or differently manifesting stress. There are old urban communities—Cockneys, Parisians, Viennese—long adapted and secure, often with excellent kinship and social networks which are as good and yet flexible as could be wished. When one speaks of social atomization, one is thinking of more uprooted persons, newly urbanized, drawn from afar by economic and employment incentives, or re-housed in traditionless settlements, to whom my generalizations seem to apply more clearly. I can think of no better observation than that made by Dr. F. A. Bevan,[10] whose general practice lay in a rural area into which a new industrial dormitory suburb was growing, to house workers' families from a gigantic new enterprise. Three-quarters of Dr. Bevan's patients were of the long-settled rural population. It was the remaining one-quarter of the 'new' industrial families that produced 'nearly' all his cases of neurosis, juvenile delinquency and family stress. There must be in the predicament of such 'unbelonging' families factors of insecurity and consequent emotional strife based on regression in the face of this insecurity, which play an important part in the total picture.

18

THE SOCIAL SETTING

EMANCIPATION AND CHANGING STATUS OF WOMEN

When thinking about the much discussed 'social deserts' widely felt to be a big factor in women's 'suburban neurosis', one is reminded of one of the greater leaps forward of modern life—the change in the rôle of women in our society in the direction of economic and political freedom and equality with men. This sequel of the Industrial Revolution has come with breathtaking speed—almost entirely in my own life-time, together with the internal combustion engine, the cinema and wireless telegraphy!

Some would see in this alteration of the power-relations of the traditional order the chief cause for the prevalence of marital strife. It is clinically observable how frequently neither husbands nor wives themselves have yet satisfactorily assimilated this new reality and its implications for their respective rôles. There are many aspects to this. Without delving into the well-known historical background of the feminist movement, which began in the upper classes, the turning point was, without doubt, the First World War, 1914–18. Then something like total mobilization brought women into real working equality with men, and exploded many stereotyped assumptions of male prerogatives and superiorities. This is the generation of wives and mothers who had to replace the absent and dead soldier fathers in their children's lives. With this emancipation of women into economic and political power, went a corresponding fall in the assured ascendancy of their male contemporaries, by no means without rear-guard actions. Most important of all, as it seems to me, there was inevitably a great shift in the unconscious perceptions and internalizations of father-and-mother figures as power-wielders among countless children already of that generation—the parents of today's young married couples. In psycho-analytic literature this change is clearly reflected when we compare Freud's early observations on his patients of Victorian vintage, and their emphasis on the boy's dread of his father's menacing power, with the emergence of many books and papers on the psychology of women, Helene Deutsch, for example and the Suttie's analysis of 'Mother—Agent or Object',[11] documenting the technical preoccupation with this new, positive woman and her effect on family relations. I only mention in passing the apparent increase in homosexuality among males since the First World War. In the social history of the inter-War period, we note the almost exclusively female-made Family Planning movement, the change in our divorce laws, and other matrimonial legislation favouring (as indeed it should) the rights and protection of women.

The Second World War enormously accelerated the diffusion of this change, begun by the *avant-garde* intelligentsia, among broad

19

layers of middle and working class women. Many still speak of this great social evolution as a 'revolt', because of the strength of our persisting culture norm relating to the primacy of the man. The 'revolt' consists, for many women, in turning against the tasks flowing from their biological constitution and needs, because male-dominated culture had devalued these. There will be more to say on this topic later. Here I stress mainly the rôle confusion in both sexes related to the change in their relative social status, and the difficulty in adapting to this new situation. The confusion is between reality and still powerful unconscious rôle expectations from 'built in' traditional patterns based on culture lag. Parents inculcate the mores of their own parents which they have internalized. Thus, young couples married sincerely on the basis of apparently concordant 'modern' ideas and values, often experience severe disillusionment that their partner's way of interpreting his or her rôle is quite different from their own unsuspected tacit inner 'blue-print'. There is also often the depressing realization that in practice their capacities to live up to their own rôle model are deficient. Some brief examples will clarify this statement.

A young man may find himself seriously thrown off balance when his wife, who had 'looked up' to him during courtship as a bio-logical female, questions his authority which, from his background norm, he had seen his father wield. She knows, for argument's sake, more about insurance than he! How does he deal with his loss of status?

A young wife may be in great conflict between her wish to be a good mother to her baby and a welcoming cook-cherisher to her hard-working husband, and the pull back to her interesting job and freedom as a 'career girl', once her new rôle has become easy and boring.

Society adds to the confusion. On the one hand we have the Health authorities, etc., stressing a higher than ever standard of intelligent motherhood and the importance of it for the infant's health (of which psychiatry, as exemplified in these pages, is a strong protagonist). On the other hand, the Exchequer and the Labour Ministry offer great incentives to stay at work, in nice, sociable, easy jobs, by con-trast with the drudgery and loneliness of the housewife-mother, for whom the arrival of the milkman is the great event of the day, and only a few shillings of Family Allowance the reward.

It is easy to see how demanding such situations are to the rôle-playing skills of the husbands, having to combine self-assurance with real sympathy for the wives' conflictful predicaments. A far cry from the good old days, when a man, faced with 'shrewish' rebellion, would have all of Society on his side, and would have been laughed to scorn if he failed to master her!

These rôle conflicts were, and in some of our case material continue to be, most marked in the marriages contracted just before or during the last war. The unions had little chance of being consolidated, during snatches of Service-leave together in lodgings or in the homes of one of the partner's parents. Then the husband would disappear to distant theatres of war. The wife would either remain to cope with *all* the problems, including children, herself, or return to her Mother, or, if childless, be called up for war-work. Unfaithfulness apart (and it was common, and often mutually condoned), the divergent maturation and change often meant a confrontation between strangers, quite unlike the boy or girl whose picture had been cherished as a precious promise of happiness after reunion. This was one of the less publicized major effects of war in favouring regression in both sexes: in the case of the serviceman to the loyalties of the uni-sexual band of brothers, in the case of the woman to the masculinized independent rôle, or to a free, more narcissistic goodtime grass-widow. Some considerable quota in the phenomenal rise in our divorce rate was contributed by this population.

CULTURE DISTANCE AND CHOICE OF MATE

The discussion of couples who, through the vicissitudes of wartime separation, had grown apart, leads naturally to another facet of the social changes we have been considering. Social mobility, the emancipation of women, and the severe limitations on the tolerated authority of parents, have had the effect of increasing the number of marriages between men and women from widely disparate backgrounds. This does not only mean the unions between different races, now better tolerated than hitherto, contracted either on foreign service, in mixed communities or in big ports. It also, and more frequently, means the marriage of two people 'who knew nothing about each other'. This is also a feature of the 'open society', and probably in successful partnerships greatly enriches the genetic and cultural potentials of the offspring.

It is, however, clear that in these marriages there are possibilities of clashes between the culture patterns of the two partners complicating the sense of 'treason' which each may feel inwardly for stepping outside the traditional mores of their own ethnic, etc., backgrounds. In our clientele the commonest were unions between adherents of orthodox religions (Roman Catholics, Jews) and less strict, or agnostic partners—the potential conflict ignored during courtship. Other glaring contrasts, such as great class, educational and regional

21

differences, carry obvious risks of conflict. But subtler failures of communication between descendants of apparently homogeneous or similar backgrounds can still occur owing to the clash of specific intra-familial culture patterns. For example: one partner's family have always expressed their differences freely by lively, short-lived quarrelling. The other partner is wounded to the core by such unsuspected angry explosiveness. Deep-lying attitudes to each other's habits, from food to reading matter can be mobilized and resented in the mutual discovery.

What is common to these conflicts created by culture distance is the strength of 'built-in' rôle models derived from the unconscious assimilation of the patterns of rôle-playing and communication experienced in the given person's family of origin and social group. It is a special instance of the wider problem of understanding and correct response to cues from someone whose tacit assumptions one has not shared. This problem bedevils not only marriages, but industrial and race relations at many levels. If to my approach A I do not get the expected response Ai but always B, and if my respondent always gets Ai from me instead of the—to him—obvious Bi there forms a mounting situation of failed communication. This slowly changes the perception of 'the other' to a frustrating figure with whom rewarding interchange is impossible.

The difficulty is that these culture gaps are not felt to be important, and are apt to be denied, while sub-personal forces hold the field. In war, nations have become temporary allies under the compulsion of the fight for survival, only to discover, once the threat was removed, that they had conflicting interests. Similarly, courting couples under the sway of loneliness and of sexual needs, will get on fine, and ignore ('not want to know about') the differences in these deeper rôle-models, because their general sexual and social needs—such as a friend to dance and make love with, etc., loom large. It is when marriage, as I defined it on p. 7, calls on the resources and deeper-lying capacities of the parties for satisfying *personal* ways of transacting rôle-exchanges that these communication failures begin to register and mount, first in the unconscious and often denied for a long time. This theme of inhibited communication will recur frequently in these pages.

In the difficult marriage which has a component of culture distance, a rationalization for conflict is readily to hand. 'I knew I should not have married a damn foreigner!' or 'That's what happens when one is married to a b—— public-school snob!' and suchlike outbursts are frequently heard.

That there should be this attribution is again part of the traditional norms persisting in subliminal awareness of the various in-groups.

22

Ethnic, religious and social sub-groups with their distinctive cultures want to guard their precious values. Jewish parents, for example, are not more chagrined when their children marry out of the faith than Hindus when their children marry into a lower caste. While the sanctions which a kinship group can now apply against such erring offspring are more limited in our society than they used to be ('Never darken my door again'; literal expulsion and ostracism), the dispositions remain, and are duly engraved on the deeper levels of such offspring's own attitudes towards their too exogamous unions. The conflict deriving from the older practice of parental choice and agreements for suitable marriage partners for their nubile children survives even in our society. A young Air Force man exclaimed in my consulting room: 'I should have listened to my parents when they told me not to marry her—they knew best!' Parents of one side will often refuse to go to the wedding of their child because they disapprove of their choice of mate, and such feuds can continue. There are still Montagus and Capulets, and Shakespeare scarcely exaggerated the long-term impact of such pulls on the marital and pre-marital tensions in the recipients of fatefully blighting parental sanctions. The legal power of intervention by parents now exists only in the form of obtaining Court injunctions against the marriages of minors.

But this diminution of overt traditional power has not extinguished the inner interdependence between parents and their children. We have gone a long way at rational level towards subscribing to the ethical rights of the younger generation to economic independence, moral autonomy, and, consequently, freedom of marital choice. What requires to be stressed is that these 'progressive' attitudes are, as yet, difficult to reconcile with the persisting momentum of millennial theory and practice, more especially when these latter can reinforce the intense demands the modern parent makes in open or, more often, disguised form on the children. These demands are, as we saw, the typical outcome of the modern nuclear family structure, in which the marriage of the children often means a severe loss, comparable to a bereavement or an amputation. So much has been 'invested' in the children as the bearers of the unfulfilled dreams of the parents. The children must not let down these 'blue-prints'. Nor is envy and jealousy of the marrying children's flowering always absent. One recalls the cases where the mothers have been furious at their daughters' marriages, especially at social and financial levels above their own: 'You are lucky—Dad and I never had a washing machine' style of bitter attitude. On the other side are the disappointed blue-prints of the parents for 'suitable matches' in terms of status and income, which throw light on the narcissistic identifications with the children as their ideal selves, on the striving towards upward social mobility.

Thus the modern ideal of free mate choice on the basis of love (by which the parental marriage may also have happened) is often opposed by the deeply-rooted fear of freedom and anxious parental or sub-culture protectiveness masking jealousy. Such conflicts are the residues of what was once the naked power of the elders over the lives and destinies of their children under the Fourth Commandment.

It is against this universally understood resistance that the younger generation exercises its rights of apparent unfettered choice. Seen against such parental possessiveness, 'exogamy' with flagrantly different ethnic, class or cultural types, may be a protest and, deeper, the only kind of sex relation in which the young person can overcome the incest taboo from their emotionally 'overcharged' childhood. Such marriages can be the critical moment of a decisive breakaway towards autonomy. Equally, they can be a futile and regretted gesture of defiance rather than of real freedom. Contrariwise, the young man or woman who deflect their choice from the potential partner whom they 'really' loved to one more in accord with parental and traditional prescriptions, often thereby sacrifice their personal integrity and autonomy and stifle their own future growth.

At the end of this book I hope to deal with some evaluation of these changes. In the meantime there is plenty of difficulty which I have highlighted. What should be stressed in a balanced attempt at identifying the social factors in marital conflict, is not only that this forms a minority of marriages at any given time. We should also emphasize the prevalence of very strong and realistic moral norms in line with the new freedom noticeable in the youngest current adults. These are a less romantic and more responsible form of equality and sharing of tasks, and a greater fusion between the image of the 'lady' and the 'harlot'. In fact the social changes have brought about a virtual disappearance of the 'lady', since even countesses wear jeans as they do their own chores.

EFFECTS OF HOUSING AND EARNINGS

Something will be expected in a chapter devoted to social factors on the topic of poor housing, financial stress and similar unfavourable conditions in the lives of contemporary married people. Social workers, and many others accustomed to think in terms of material welfare and amenities, pin great hopes on improving these factors. Improvements are, indeed, needed for the self-respect, health and enjoyment of the good life of advanced societies. Experience in the field of family relations, nevertheless, raises doubts whether the lack of these things is a major cause of marital stress. It is true that slum conditions and poverty are sources of depression, resentment and violent reactions often directed against family members, and also create problem children. It is relevant to state that people who, in the era of full employment and the welfare state, remain in such conditions are, by and large, the dull and backward, the inadequate and feckless who mismanage *every* relationship. They lack the skills to cope with even making a budget, or knowing where to collect relief. In these problem families marital difficulties are part of a general failure, just as they would be in mental illness and psychopathy. It is likely that the 'social welfare' attitude, so magnificently developed around the turn of the century, and flowering at the time of the great economic depression, suffers from a culture lag, and cannot detach itself from the deeply engraved pictures of the hardships of the working class of that time, when the skilled and competent were as miserable as the minority who remain the genetically impaired 'problem tenth'. Not only is there no evident statistical correlation between marital trouble and income, there is evidence that the working class have more conservative and traditional attitudes towards marital obligations and mores than higher classes, and meet periods of adversity with greater flexibility as well as solidarity as couples, perhaps partly because of less status anxiety. One of the observed differences between upper and lower class marital troubles is the greater prevalence of acting out by violence, desertion and withholding of support. The upper and middle classes have more resources for camouflage and controlling acting-out. This theme will be elaborated when we come to talk about varieties of marital conflict.

We see many cases of upper middle and middle class in which slum conditions prevail, despite good incomes and status. Here the order of 'cause and effect' is reversed. Because of emotional tension, anger and vindictiveness, the spouses make no attempt to maintain a pleasant or even sanitary home, and money, its withholding by one and wasteful spending by the other, becomes a weapon of war. The wives of millionaires and film stars also fight for legal remedies when their husbands only provide grudging maintenance at levels which would seem unattainable luxury for the professional class.

Allusion has already been made to the troubles of rehousing the poor in hygienic modern settlements, without awareness of the needs for social belonging. No! material shortcomings may activate the emergence of latent family conflicts and serve as an alibi, or they can even be purposely used to punish the self or the partner, just as race or other factors in a mixed marriage can be mobilized in these ways. To me, at any rate, it is human relations, not bricks or marble halls, which must be the chief concern of the Mental Health services.

SUMMARY

In this chapter I have briefly and incompletely tried to sketch in the social background against which the great increase in the incidence of specifically marital stress and breakdown should be viewed. Whilst every era has thought of itself as living in a time of flux and change, we of the present have seen an unprecedented acceleration of urbanization and emancipation of women following upon the technological transformation of society. These upheavals, hastened by wars and revolutions, have eroded the age-old order which governed explicitly and implicitly the relations of parents and children in regard to meaningful authority and subordination, including those of mate choice. The constriction and atomization of the modern family, however, have intensified the mutual reliance of its members to yield all the satisfactions for relational security and other needs previously met by a more diversified and structured family milieu buttressed by social and religious sanctions. Thus the trend towards autonomy and independence of the young, inherent in modern society, is met by the resistance within themselves and society springing from the older, more familiar and secure order, handed down by the culture lag of generations.

In this social conflict there will be a certain proportion of people who will fail to adapt to the now more challenging, because unstructured, demands of marital rôles. It will be our purpose, from now on to endeavour to identify some of the more typical failures and 'interferences' in rôle performance, and the means for their relief.

Family stress, broken marriages full of adultery and cruelty, are not peculiar to this age. From social history we may draw the comfort that these things are now less extreme. What has changed is public tolerance towards behavioural disturbances, partly because families themselves—in-laws, brothers, uncles—no longer function as a kind of private tribunal. Partly also because of the progressive refinement of the social conscience and sensibility towards matters now felt to be within the competence of medical and social science and not accepted as inevitable aspects of original sin. Not so long ago, breakdown in marital and family relations was studiously concealed as a blot on the whole kinship group, until some explosive crisis for external intervention, often by the arm of the Law.

In the medieval order marriage seems to have been a less individualized function of the person, and possibly not invested with such high expectations. The very idea of 'happiness' from mutual sexual fulfilment was secondary to the dominant quest for salvation. The sin and expiations imposed on Adam and Eve were then the basis for the evaluation of sex rôles, enforced by the power of canonical authority.

26

THE SOCIAL SETTING

It is hard to grasp the magnitude of our social evolution, to where we can and dare objectify and study the forces which influence our own development and values. The very notion of 'human development' is post-Darwinian, and the ideas on 'the right to happiness' or on 'equality of the sexes' scarcely older. The concept of the uniqueness and value of each human soul, made in the image of God, may have ancient roots. Its implementation in social policy is of very new growth and shaky indeed. Recent history is filled with examples of highly 'regressive' attitudes towards the rights of persons, outgroups, minorities and women not only to humane treatment, but to be considered as fellow humans. It is not surprising, therefore, that the same contradictions, between respect for individual growth into equality and the archaic defensive postures of dominance and possessiveness, occur within families—husbands and wives, parents and children. These nuclear families are the microcosmic reflections of what goes on in the larger society.

REFERENCES

1. CALLIERI, B., and FRIGHI, L. (undated) *Problèmes psychiatriques du mariage comme conséquence d'un contexte culturel donné.* Multigraphed memo. Issued by the Clinic for Nervous and Mental Disorders of the University of Rome (received 1965).
2. MONTAGU, M. F. ASHLEY (1956) Chap. I, in Eisenstein, V. (Ed.). *Neurotic Interaction in Marriage.* London: Tavistock Publications.
3. MEAD, MARGARET (1950) *Male and Female—a study of the sexes in a changing world.* London: Gollancz.
4. GORER, GEOFFREY (1955) *Exploring English Character.* London: Cresset Press.
5. GALDSTON, IAGO (1958) 'The American Family in Crisis', *Mental Hygiene*, 42, No. 2, pp. 229–36.
6. GLADKOV, F. (1949) *Povest' o detstve* (in Russian). Moscow: State Publishing House.
7. DICKS, H. V. (1954) 'Strains within the Family'. In National Association for Mental Health: *Strain and Stress in Modern Living.* Proceedings of Annual Conference, London: N.A.M.H. pp. 28–37.
8. DICKS, H. V. (1955) 'The Predicament of the Family in the Modern World'. A paper delivered at the Third International Congress for Mental Health, Toronto, 1954. *Lancet*, I, 5th February, pp. 295–7.
9. DICKS, H. V. (1962) 'World-wide problems: marriage relationships in different cultures' in *Social Work*, 19, No. 4, pp. 2–7.
10. BEVAN, F. A. (1953) Verbal contribution to discussion on *Family Tensions and the General Practitioner* (by H. V. Dicks) in Section of Psychiatry, Annual Meeting of B.M.A., Cardiff.
11. SUTTIE, I. and J. (1932) 'Mother—Agent or Object?' *Brit. J. of Med. Psychol.* 12, pp. 91 ff and 199 ff.

Chapter III

THE INDIVIDUAL SETTING

Having sketched the outlines of the social predicament, I now turn to personality development in its bearing on my topic. Together, these two chapters state the assumptions and views with which I launched into the study of marital pathology and its therapy. The scope of what I want to discuss is defined by some questions put to me some years ago by Dr. John Hambling in an invitation to consider 'fitness for marriage' as part of a symposium on Adolescence.[1] These questions were: 'What is this growing up process by which the dependent child is able to acquire the emotional resources for responsible parenthood? . . . What are these resources? . . . What is emotional maturity?' To these I would add another query deriving from my definition of marriage. Can we discern the factors in men and women which make them adapted or 'qualified' to risk and succeed in making a lasting commitment to another of the opposite sex to satisfy, to a tolerable degree, the other's biological, emotional and existential needs for loving intimacy, security and interdependence in ways which will also satisfy their own like needs and generate a sense of personal worth and security from such a commitment? This way of stating the problem includes the usual expectations of our population from their marriages, touched upon in Chapter II. Such expectations or group values are contained in the recurring statements of our clients, and echoed in the report of Gorer's survey.[2] We know how diversified our society is in reality, and the likes of me do not often have access to detailed study of the couples and homes that make a success of their relationship in these terms. But our records of retrospectively lamented aspirations of those who have, in varying degree, not succeeded, and told us what they had hoped for, show much consistency and uniformity. Conflict between these conscious goals in marriage and the deeper cross currents which deflect these 'mature' and reasonable intentions, and make them founder in some 30,000 divorces alone annually, is what this book is about.

I will begin with the generalizations I work with about personality

28

development in the modern family. Much of it will be familiar ground to the reader acquainted with psychodynamic concepts, and he will be aware that my individual view-point colours the argument.

A. THE FATE OF DEPENDENCE

If my image of the intensive interdependence of the typical urban family is at all accurate, then the growing-up process in countless such families towards the desideratum of lasting commitment in marriage in my definition requires an unprecedented overcoming of emotional dependence on the family of origin. In peasant societies this was hardly required; you brought your neighbour's daughter back to live under father's roof. The urban family is almost self-liquidating by dispersal, just when in their isolation they need each other most among the frightening impersonality of modern industry and commerce, where so many must gain their livelihood. We have hitherto, as a society, assumed that the family, since it has the task, also has the emotional resources to mediate the growth of its children to selfhood so much against its own age-long traditional functions and its very existence. The transition is from a previously self-evident patriarchal *heteronomy* or extra-personal direction to an equally self-evident present-day requirement of *autonomy* of the new adults. That is, all their resources and capacities for making strong and effective emotional commitments have to be carried inside the person, without benefit of moral corseting from clear and binding group directives and sanctions, or of cushioning from supportive family groups around their nuclear marital unit. History may record that *this* change of our era was the greatest evolutionary leap of all.

The successful adaptation to modern marriage seems to require a blend of autonomy of the individual—an established sense of personal identity and ego-strength—with a preservation of the capacity for dependence. As was said, technological society puts much pressure on families to prepare their children for *in*-dependence, or at least spurious 'standing on their own feet', to earn their living far from their family or origin. This is hard enough, for it often means also a bogus-tough handling of the children's dependence needs. This is felt to be a much needed armour for the 'rat-race', where it is meant to pay off in promotion and leadership rewards. For human and marital success it is, I maintain, equally necessary to conserve and make available in adult life the toleration of the opposite qualities— tender concern for others based on one's own, still felt, dependent needs. Otherwise the 'I'm all right, Jack' posture will oust the 'love thy neighbour as thyself' aim in our community. The open, giving, because secure, personality would be replaced by the anxiously taking,

29

shut-in, suspicious personality, if the prevailing attitude of the small, closed nuclear family transmitted its defensive island mentality to its children. 'Don't play with these rough boys'; 'Don't speak to strangers'; 'You must be a big boy, and not let 'em get the better of you'; 'What's that to do with us?' 'Don't be so sloppy'; 'You are a real cry baby'. The stream of such precepts, unless finely balanced by positive fostering of loving and uninhibited initiatives towards the world will certainly produce in the child a value-system leading to conflicts between affectionate and hostile, self-preservative attitudes which reach their extreme in the 'hard-bitten' criminal or in the psychotic, utterly confused between love and hate. In lesser degree we meet it in marital interaction, as two highly typical situations will illustrate:

1. Take the insecure man who has constantly to resist and belittle the emotionality of his wife and children. We trace this to a conflict in him over his own now repressed childish demands for cherishing, which he had come to despise by identification with that aspect of his parents and later parent-figures who rejected his dependence and tenderness as being 'sissy'. In his own marital life he acts out his lack of felt love by projecting the despised part of himself on his family, combining an unconscious revenge with the rationalization that he is making them 'tough and sensible', as life will require them to be.

'Mr. Crampton', in G. B. Shaw's *You Never Can Tell* is a good illustration of this type.

2. There is the parallel case of women with a similar conflict resulting in strongly masculine conscious attitudes based on identification with a father-figure of the kind described above. Such a woman will belittle and persecute her husband to the point of psychological castration for his dependent, 'soft' qualities, and provoke him to try and master her, in the image of the hated, sadistic inner 'hero'.

In both these situations, abstracted from numerous actual cases, we see the effect on marital rôle taking of self-defeating conflicts derived from the contradictions in attitude-forming due to the anxieties and over-protectiveness of the family of origin trying to deny its own deepest needs. The partner attracts because he or she represents or promises a re-discovery of an important lost aspect of the subject's own personality, which, owing to earlier conditioning, had been recast as an object for attack or denial. At the height of the courting and mating phase, biological sexual urgency often obscures this potential source of future tension. The conscious aims and purposes of the union are later invaded by hitherto latent dispositions to re-enact an intrapsychic pattern in the new setting of the marriage, which becomes to a varying extent a projection screen for such unresolved tensions *in* the individuals.

People, then, whose interaction with others becomes recurrently disturbed to the point of need for help by doctors, priests or social workers seem to have rigidities in their personalities. This forces them to deny—be blind to—the existence of certain aspects of themselves. If they are confronted by a similar aspect of the partner's personality, this will also be ignored, not accepted, because it cannot be fitted into the subject's shrunken repertoire of personal relations. When the trait can no longer be ignored in the daily intimacy of contact, then the partner's possession of it will arouse retaliatory or punitive impulses, which may grossly distort the relationship at reality level. Marital interaction, in order to fulfil the desiderata of mutual need satisfaction, requires a flexible readiness in each partner to change their rôle behaviour in response to the other's need of the moment. One may have to be the leader and the comforter of the other's weakness and dependence at one moment. The next moment the rôles will be reversed. The erstwhile leader can now comfortably accept the other's ascendancy and one's own dependence on the partner without loss of self-respect or security. The same need for flexibility could also be demonstrated as applying to aggressive and to sexual needs: to tolerate and respond appropriately to the partner's varying moods for activity, passivity, a quarrel or a tender reconciliation. This flexibility is, of course, an aspect of the capacity to tolerate, fuse and use ambivalence—perhaps the key to the secret of *all* human relations. It is the ability to 'contain hate in a framework of love'.

B. IDENTITY AND OBJECT CHOICE

This emotional flexibility betokens a secure sense of identity—adequate ego strength. It means that the self is sufficiently at ease in varied aspects of itself, has not lost touch with its own ambivalent feelings and need not adopt a rigid defensive posture to preserve a narrow, brittle sense of selfhood. It means, also, that a person with this degree of ego-strength can bear to see the partner as different, and the self as distinct from the partner, without feeling threatened in their identity by the contrast, as our two paradigmatic cases were. In such a favourable case the relationship is enriched and enhanced in the experience of 'otherness', akin to discovery. Instead of the urge to mould and assimilate the object to the rigid pattern, there is a mutual toleration of differentiation in all the areas of interaction, from the sexual to the cultural ends of the spectrum.

The foregoing is closely related to a very important proposition, which I must now discuss. For success in marriage there must be present in each partner a clear and definite sense of *sexual identification*. This is an essential personal quality for acceptance of the different rôles each has to play along broadly masculine and feminine lines. Endocrinology offers a biological link between constitution, body-image, and sexual self-identification. What is surprising is not that women with markedly hypertrophied suprarenals, or men with a feminoid physique will tend to run true to form, but rather that within a wide range of subtle constitutional variations and somato-types the impact of nurture, childhood moulding and social pattern can be so much more effective than we would expect if biology alone was at work.

The acquisition of one's sense of identity as a male or female is naturally helped by a conforming physique—the great majority of people have this. To have such an inner certainty favours the conflict-free performance of the inescapable natural (if any are left!), culture-regulated and individually conceived marital rôles and tasks in keeping with the perception of one's identity. It is, also, surely a decisive factor in mate selection. Ambiguity of self-identity will, as it were, blur the perception of the partner, as in the two brief examples. Brittle and anxiety-laden over-compensations to mask an uncertain sexual alignment make for very insecure human relations. The secure male does not have to trumpet his virility and toughness, nor a secure female proclaim her femininity. It is the doubting, insecure man who is more likely to make aggressive sexual demands, to refuse 'demeaning' chores, such as helping with the babies, and to act in defensive derogation against women. Similarly, it is the Amazon who puts on the 'warpaint of sex appeal', to borrow von Hatting-berg's phrase,[3] or exploits the power of hysterical feminine weakness. At best, such exaggerations belong to adolescent courtship behaviour, when adult identity has not yet been achieved.

The line of demarcation between culturally attributed *sex rôle distinctions* between men and women shifts in subtle ways from generation to generation. It is subject to vogue, as in the matter of length of hair, height of heels, attire and manners. It probably also corresponds to socio-economic requirements, as we saw in the quasi-virilization of 'style' among the Women's Services and female muni-tion workers during two wars. This variation in cultural rôle ascrip-tions must not be confused with the biological, primary *sex functions*. There is no evidence that these have changed very much. 'Male and female created He them.' It is in the nature of the world that females shall bear and cherish offspring as their primary task, while males, having been impelled by that nature to fertilize them, will feel the urge to be protective to the nest and feeding ground, and hunt for the sustenance to keep the mother and young alive and safe.

Parsons and Bales[4] writing on some of these inescapable primary demands inherent in physico-social sex differences, express this idea by saying 'the father rôle is relative to the others (in the family— H.V.D.) high on power and *instrumentality*, and mother's high on power and *expressiveness*'. This means that the male parent is typically equipped to fight, hunt, build, manipulate, roaming outside the home *for* the home. The female parent gives expression more typically than her man, to tender and protective emotions, and responds to those of her offspring, staying close by them. In more contemporary terms, the man's sexual identity is linked as a rule to his implicit readiness for action, by which he achieves economic security and social-occupational status ('has standing'), is somebody to be reckoned with outside. The woman's identity is typically linked with cherishing, nourishing, maternal functions towards *his* children *for* him. Few marriages can endure when these primary biological tasks are completely denied, or even if some of the secondary rôles deriving from them are too flagrantly reversed.

There are plenty of examples of the force of this statement. I have seen marriages in which husbands with obvious bi-sexual personalities of the exploitative play-boy type had for some years floated on the high professional status and earnings of their wives. In the confusion of identities, such men treated these women with parasitic, sadistic unconcern and secret envy. Psychotherapy, by clarifying to both partners the ambiguity and jealousies in these situations, had the effect of making the man catch up with his male need for *effective* power, to become 'somebody' in his own right. In response, as the husbands acquired adequate instrumentality in Parsons' sense, so the wives grew content to become more feminine and affective, and to concede their men's rise in status, enjoying the care of their children.

Marriage, too, abhors a power vacuum. When one can play *his* part, the other can play *hers*, come into her own. The striving to attain this natural level of identities, in which the rôle and the deeper biological needs are reconciled, is surely a well-attested fact in nature, even in human beings. A woman can best fulfil her rôle as a woman when she can be the wife to a man 'who is somebody'—one sure of his sexual identity and worth, who can show achievement. Then she is prepared to surrender her self-containment, her own masculine instrumentality and detachment. It is highly unlikely that a woman can achieve full sexuality if she does not feel this condition to be present. Failure in this experience of surrender, of commitment of one to the other, will be part of my subject matter. Under present social conditions of autonomy of marital choice and legal affirmation of it in our divorce acts, people of both sexes will frequently search for partner after partner who promises to give them this experience. It will depend very much on the causes of the initial failure whether subsequent relationships really heal the void, and bring about the union, or whether the search is endless because it is always a chase after an inner fantasy-partner, who cannot be matched in reality. However, when the search is successful—often first time—there occurs an astonishing recognition and response. Each feels safe to 'be themselves', and thus confirm the other's identity. The sexual function is then not in doubt. This is the essential sequence of a durable marriage, legal or natural.

C. THE CONCEPT OF 'GENITALITY'

In classical psycho-analytic theory, with its well-known emphasis on the growth of personality through a series of developmental phases of sexuality (oral, oral-sadistic, anal, phallic), the arrival at maturity is described as the reaching of genitality. I expressed in Chapter I my reservations on the usefulness of the Freudian hypothesis of 'stages of psycho-sexual development' as a mainstay for the interpretation of inter-personal relations. Since, however, the concept of genitality has gained wide currency we should see how far it can help us to understand marital integration of two persons. Balint[5] has stated his criteria by which mature sexual love might be assessed. His writing shows that it is easier to say what it ought *not* to contain. He says:

'(a) There should be no greediness, no insatiability, no wish to devour the object, to deny it any independent existence, etc., i.e. there should be no *oral* features;

(b) There should be no wish to hurt, to humiliate, to boss, to dominate the object etc., i.e. no *sadistic* features;

(c) There should be no wish to defile the partner, to despise him (her) for his (her) sexual desires and pleasures, there should be no danger of being disgusted by the partner, or being attracted only by some unpleasant features of him, etc., i.e. there should be no remnants of *anal* traits;

(d) There should be no compulsion to boast about the possession of a penis, no fear of the partner's sexual organs, no fear for one's own sexual organs, no envy of the male or female genitalia, no feeling of being incomplete or having a faulty sexual organ, or of the partner having a faulty one, etc., i.e. there should be no trace of the *phallic* phase or of the castration complex.'

34

This is, of course, a statement of a desideratum or 'blue print'. On the positive side Balint lists only three major criteria:

(1) Idealization of the partner and the relationship (which he discards as suspect and not essential).

(2) Tenderness fused with genital desire [in the ordinary sense of the term—H.V.D.].

(3) A "genital" form of identification (which sounds tautological).

Commenting, I would concur with Balint on the dangers of idealization which, as we shall see, is often the reverse of acceptance of a realistic bond, and a defence against ambivalence and unconscious 'pre-genital' traits in Balint's sense. About the 'genital identification' Balint comments that it requires a constant vigilance to please and retain the other's love, to interpret the wishes and needs of the partner —in short to be thoroughly altruistic, cherishing and giving. This seems very close to what was said on the value aspirations of the Western ideal of marriage alluded to in these pages. To this point we shall return shortly.

I would like to give some consideration to the second of Balint's criteria of genital maturity: the fusion of *tenderness* with sexual drives. He rightly associates the word with ideas of weakness, softness and immaturity, as when speaking of tender buds or shoots of a young plant, or 'tender age' of children. Thus Balint argues that in trying to fuse tenderness towards the object with sexuality, mankind is fulfilling an archaic infantile longing to experience again, and 'forever' to prolong, the happiness of being a child, protected and cherished. He contrasts this state with the behaviour of animals, who, on reaching maturity, display no further parent–child ties except respect for strength. Such a prolongation or carry-over into biological maturity of infantile features of object attachment he links to phylogenetic clues in our morphology. Human beings resemble more closely the ape embryo than the adult ape in form. We are asked to infer that therefore they like remaining infantile. This is the rather meagre yield from Balint's analysis of genitality, in which one discerns a note of chagrin: 'That's all it amounts to', so to speak. But this wistful way of formulating the human problem of mature marital relations is immensely rewarding as a starting point for our theme.

First, we recall that in development—ontogenetic and phylogenetic —the retention of undifferentiated, multi-potential structures (cells, limbs) enhances an organism's chances of further growth and change. The earth's geological strata are strewn with the remains of species that had become over-specialized, and so turned into dead-ends of evolution. So long as soft, tender growing points are not covered by hard casing, and organs and cells not too differentiated, the organism and the species can go on unfolding. Taking the morphological analogy back into the sphere of personality, we link this idea with what was said earlier about rigid defences grown to protect 'rejected' infantile needs; with repression and fixation with their well-attested stunting effect on psychological growth. In contrast to the doctrine of 'toughness' as implying energy, we think of hardening as a feature of death, and of the powers of suppleness, of running sap able to burst hard casings, as life-giving.

A great number of both men and women in our clinical marital practice have stressed, in monotonously identical terms, that their greatest deficit in the marriage has been the spouse's lack of tenderness. They have stressed how sexually the partner was adequate, even 'wonderful'. But there was no human concern, no visible affection in the intervals between love-making, nor was the love-making personalized: 'She doesn't seem to know I am there', or 'He never calls me by name, or says nice things' during coitus, and so on. Reverting to Gorer's observation of typical needs of the marriage, and to Balint's requirement of awareness and concern for the partner's needs, I think one can begin to get a fairly consistent specification of the foundations of marriage as a mutual affirmation of the other's identity as a *lovable person*, not as a coitus machine for tension relief. The failure to fulfil this mutual need, its denial through secret fear, hate and rigidity, or its belittlement as 'sloppy', 'babyish' and so on *is* the heart of our topic. Childlike, unashamed dependence and its gratification by caressing words and actions, both immediate and in the sense of continual 'thoughtfulness' and cherishing in daily relations, is, paradoxically, what makes 'mature' unions. Following Ian Suttie,[6] I call the exclusion or rejection of dependence needs in self and partner 'the taboo on tenderness'.

D. THE CHILD IS FATHER TO THE MAN

We can now return to the question, what it is that enables the growing human being to acquire the resources for emotional maturity and responsible rôle fulfilment as a spouse and parent. The child is father to the man. As mentioned, we know a great deal about the factors making for good personality development up to adolescence, and what kind of deprivations and crises interfere with this process. Without restating at length the well-documented growth stages of the child, it can be said, without fear of serious contradiction, that the young must have in their family of origin the conditions first for satisfying, and then for surmounting, their phased natural needs. These can *only* be fulfilled by a reciprocal relatedness to human objects who respond appropriately, and so confirm the child's goal-seeking—both by acceptance and by refusal. The acceptance confirms the child's lovableness, the suitable refusal protects against its feared impulses.

The best established knowledge about such responses and inter-actions concerns those of mother and infant, in which the deepest attitudes in terms of love and hate, security and anxiety are laid down. We cannot measure the threshold beyond which a given baby fails to cope with anxiety and hate, with resulting damage to its later capacity for emotional maturation. But it is widely accepted that an infancy spent in a loving communion with a good and understanding mother, with plenty of milk, creates the basis for a relatively easy passage through later phases because the goodness of the deepest internalized objects is not in doubt. The crucial importance for later personality growth of these early 'interaction models' of childhood has been demonstrated by studies of child development. More recent psycho-analytic writing, such as Melanie Klein's[7] and Fairbairn's,[8] views this developmental process as the passage through a succession of positions of conflict and ambivalence. Beginning with undifferentiated responses of total, crude, affective experiences of 'good' or gratifying, and 'bad' or frustrating actions of objects, the infant advances through a gradual lessening of these absolute contrasts. It learns by growth of the power to test the reality of the object's responses, to recognize the real person of the mother, and so develops a tolerance of frustration and its resultant feelings. The child can now contain and accept its own and the object's ambivalence. In a healthy outcome of this complex growth-process, the forward movement of successive biological and social goal-and-object-seeking drives has not been seriously impeded by the unresolved needs of the preceding phase. When dependence and receiving, especially, can be lived out in the generous warmth and wealth of sensuous pleasure of the 'nursing communion', the first, and perhaps essential step towards a good marriage will have been taken. The model for interaction at this level for both sexes is with a cherishing, nourishing, caressing figure, whose delays and shortcomings can be tolerated. From this point grows a feeling that relations with 'outside' contain the expectation of need satisfaction. The preponderance of secure, loving out-comes of reality-testing and conflict resolution between rage and love creates in the growing individual a reservoir of *relational potential* with the human figures of his little world, by the process of internalization or introjection. The child can make the *good object's* feelings his own, both as self-valuations and as rôle models. He identifies with them, and they form his inner resources. Through them he learns 'how to love as an adult', because he has felt adult love on, and in himself. The child tolerates the struggle of ambivalent feelings within him, and in others, because he has experienced the parents' tolerance and mastery of his, and their, anger in a mainly loving way and context.

To be sure, these outcomes of the developmental conflict depend not only on the right responses of the parents, but also on the innate strength of certain instinctual needs and maturational capacities of each personality. Some parents, with some of their children, will have a more exacting task than with others in rightly interpreting these needs consistently and skilfully. A child with good parents will, even if endowed with much aggressivity and libidinal drive, build more tolerance and more flexible defences against its own feelings than one in which the early human figures heightened the child's rage and despair, and so exaggerated its reaction formations into a rigid wall. One of the constant phenomena seen in all psychotherapy, but very clearly in marital cases, is the intensity of identifications with parental feelings. It makes our clients very preoccupied with the deeper quality of inter-parental relations. At the oedipal phase especially, but not exclusively, the erotic satisfactions of the parents with one another have a profound effect. The image of the united loving father and mother, who are co-operating in the same direction to bring up their children, creates a sense of security, greatly easing the child's conflicts. Not only can infantile hate and omnipotence not drive them away, or a wedge between them. The child becomes convinced of, and reconciled to the futility of its own (in themselves natural) fantasies of stealing one parent from the other. It is also less liable to perpetuate the fantasy of parental sex life ('the primal scene'), as a violent, murderous act arousing anxiety and guilt about the child's own feelings, and about the fate of the poor, loved, suffering mother. On the contrary, serious conflicts arise if in reality parental strife and open violence, as well as sexual frustration, make the child's fantasies seem possible of fulfilment. This is not only owing to the internal processes in his mind, but frequently also because some of the parental hate, as well as erotic libido, becomes diverted towards one or more of the children in such situations. In these tense marriages, which the children experience at close range, it is not only the young who have incest-fantasies and death-wishes! This too, is a two-way process. We see the fuller meaning of 'The parents have eaten sour grapes, and the children's teeth are set on edge'. Thus it is notable that every investigator, clinical or statistical, has recorded the finding that the most significant factor for marital happiness is the possession of parents who were happily married. (The contrary is not so well validated.)

In the favourable case, in contrast with such difficult situations, the child's oedipal crisis of surrendering his erotic demands on the parents will be fairly unequivocally resolved. A good maternal object will already have been internalized to give the child its basic sense of a healthily narcissistic lovable identity. At the oedipal stage the child will have a sufficiently differentiated image of itself to feel a boy or a girl. This will be fashioned not only from observed anatomical differences, but also from cultural expectations for the two sexes. It will be fortified and learnt from empathy with the actual behaviour of the parents, with a new emphasis on the father as the instrument of law, leadership and strength. If the performances of their rôles by the parents are too alike, or even to some extent reversed (as is not infrequently seen in modern families) then there is danger of some degree of confusion in sex-identity, with an ambiguity in sexual object choice or aim as a result. It is, then, at this early stage that the main patterns of how to be a husband or wife, a father or a mother, are learnt, by direct identifications or by dynamically forged over-compensations (counter-cathexes), of the type 'I won't be pushed around like Daddy', or 'I won't give in to bullying like Mummy does'.

Still pursuing the developmental outline of the healthy person, the secure child, with a good internal mother, comes to perceive the more rugged figure of the father as included in the mother's love. The father's threatening qualities are softened. A little boy, especially, can love (cathect) him as a large-scale projection of his own identity, but more powerful, swelling the child's pride and self-regard in 'belonging' to such a Daddy. Children can safely internalize both parents as rôle models; the one as a prototype of one's own father-like, male potentials, the other as the prototype of the female potentials. There is thus available an inner blue-print of a complete human unit—half oneself, half the love object. How clearly these will be differentiated and blended is the perennial interest of psychology and art. If in reality the parents are able to meet the children's jealousies and wishes to separate them, with tolerance and assurance, the required repression of oedipal sexual fantasies and demands of the young can take place without inner disruption. The ambivalence can 'hold together'. In consequence the investment of ambivalent erotic feelings can be diverted by the children to their siblings and peer group coinciding with going out into the wider world of available new object-relations. While the oedipal phase lasts, it gives the young of both sexes not only conflict and frustration, apt to be stressed by psychopathology. It also provides a prolonged period of learning by the experience of alternating, at first unstable, cross-identifications with both parents. This offers a wide range of empathy, rejection and bias with both paternal and maternal rôles. The whole bisexual

39

repertory of loves and hates, envies and jealousies, special attitudes and flavours, can be sampled, before coming to the painful renunciation of the hopeless fantasy pretence that one will ever marry mother or father. But the sensitization and readiness to respond powerfully and erotically to an adult in their likeness will have been achieved.

Here the hate and proper rejection of the father, implicit in ambivalence, plays a most constructive part in forcing the little boy into greater self-differentiation and autonomy, while the reality experience of the everyday daddy helps the internalization of that figure as the object whom mother loves, and whose being meets with her approval, i.e. as the model for a boy's internalization, including his aggressive capacities. For a girl the rejective move leading to internalization of a loved and envied mother should be a task simpler than the boy's, the more clearly her established and parentally valued female identity shows the 'hopelessness' of taking her father's place. It then becomes easy to identify with mother's love for this man, and take the figure inside her as a model whose ways one has learnt to feel with and to be in love with. In both sexes the contents of this reservoir of unfulfilled erotic needs, if successfully repressed with the parents' help in an atmosphere of understanding and loving firmness, disappear from sight during the appropriately named latency period. If not split off into a rigid unavailable enclave whose walls are guilt and anxiety (due to parental severity, or coldness) or starved by absence of parental models to internalize, this relational potential will germinate, and grow silently until adolescence, taking unto itself additional objects from the groups the child meets in school and play. Dante's Beatrice is said to have been modelled on a little girl he met and loved when he was eight! Then, in adolescence, the new biological forces at work will rouse the disposition towards resuming the latent object-quest back into activity. The childhood repertory is briefly recapitulated in the strange and stormy ambivalencies of the teen-agers' attitudes to the parents before taking off into the new world of seeking the 'lost object' in the high adventure of crushes, intimacies, and sexual experimentation out of which mate-selection will grow.

In the less fortunate outcome, with which we have to be concerned in the mental health services, there are identifiable interferences with this evolutionary process. Even healthy development is stressful. If, then, to the experience of inevitable conflict and anxiety, there is added a parental environment which is *really* frustrating or inimical to the child's needs, these needs will be deflected from their satisfaction through the required object relation. Thus there will remain certain unresolved, not outgrown need-demands on parent-figures invested with deeply ambivalent feelings of love-hate. As is attested by direct child studies, as well as by psycho-analytic findings, these 'bad' parent-figures are internalized, and the whole 'relational potential' repressed. So it comes about that the objects invested with a great deal of hate and its inevitable guilt, are felt to be both *inside the self*, while with continuing parental rejective behaviour the hate is also felt to be *in the object* towards the self, in a cycle of intro-jection-projection. With the additional load of anxiety resulting from this cycle many children will not be able to deal except by rigidly used mechanisms of ego-defence.

Where the primary objects were experienced as so hate-arousing and dangerous to the child's survival, *splitting* of the internal object world is assumed to occur, as deduced from observations by Klein and Fairbairn. The ego's identity is according to this theory preserved by an unconscious defensive fission of parts of its inner world of objects, much as a lizard sheds its tail to a pursuing enemy. The earlier such a crisis of growth occurs, the more profound are its effects on subsequent personality development. It results, according to phase of development as well as to intensity, in more or less mas-sive impoverishment of future relational potentials of the kind sketched earlier. This potential is fixated around the split-off internal ego-nuclei locked in arrested combat with the original source of the rejection: the primary parental figures, who first evoked the flowing out towards them of dependent and libidinal needs, and did not satisfy them by requisite responses. One element—the unrequited love-need—is described by Fairbairn as withdrawing itself into a split-off enclave, which he terms the *libidinal ego*. If the split occurs very early in life, this ego part may remain exceedingly infantile—a poor little self who dare not show his presence. In this hypothesized structure reside the hidden wishes for dependence, for tenderness, for being loved. Here, also, are presumed to lie dormant the highly ambivalent sexual impulses towards the exciting-frustrating object surrounded by the wall of the incest-taboo.

In another hypothesized split-off region are contained the frustra-tion-rage arousing dangerous aspects of the relationship to the rejecting, frustrating object, which the child had to internalize in fear. To this other half of the split Fairbairn gave the name of the *anti-libidinal ego*, related to and reacting in identification with the anti-libidinal or rejecting object. This concept is akin to Freud's earlier hypothesis of the primitive sadistic super-ego, scrutinizing and persecuting the libidinal ego and creating a conflict in which the growing central ego may be pictured as ground between the upper and the nether millstone. The concept is a useful one to such a study as ours because it preserves the notion of a person who, though divided, is in warring relationship with forces in his inner world. It accounts more easily for many of the phenomena of interaction between people. It helps to explain the capacity of people to re-integrate these split portions of an initially unitary structure, and the faculty for reprojection and reintrojection of these partial 'sub-identities' in relation with external love-objects while preserving a workable amount of central ego. This hypothetical model of a central ego, from which the ambivalent, painful, relational investments have been split off, allows us to understand why so many people can grow into intellectually and socially competent adults while impoverished in their intimate object relations. It also explains why, when bio-logical sexual maturation and cultural pressures stimulate the need of such a 'well-adjusted' person for total sexual loving commitment and spontaneity, the result can be so inadequate; infantilely demanding, crude and ambivalent, hence sabotaged by the anti-libidinal ego. Alternately, the response may be to stimulate mainly the anti-libidinal complex, resulting in an anti-libidinal object attachment. This makes sense of the facts of people choosing disapproving, cold partners who arouse anxiety, guilt or sexual repugnance. The classical split into 'sacred' and 'profane' love was not fully explicable until Fairbairn's formulation. Ego-splitting as a concept illumines not only 'Freudian conflicts' but actual double lives.

E. A GENERAL VIEW OF MARITAL PATHOLOGY

To go into the full implications of this theoretical scheme for inter-preting emotional growth and the interferences with it would be to write a systematic revision of psychopathology, which Fairbairn (loc. cit.) and Guntrip[9] have gone far to accomplish. But we can suggest the nature of the defensive rigidities spoken of earlier, in so far as they appear regularly in the subjective mutual fantasy-percep-tions between marriage partners. At the earliest level, mentioned a moment ago, the demeanour towards a spouse may be deeply *para-noid*, full of mistrust of the partner's goodwill, let alone affection. The most trivial mistakes or actions feed this suspicion, in which memory stores every such act forever after. This can coexist with immense possessive jealousy and demands for 'all-in-all' incorpora-tion of the partner in the life and interests of the subject.

Here is Balint's angry, orally frustrated baby, who is afraid of total loss of the one source of satisfaction, and who must, therefore, never budge or make a false move. This behaviour need not be so extreme as just outlined. We may get alternation between it and *depressive anxiety* and guilt reactions where the relation to the ambivalent figure had reached to the development of wishing to preserve the loved person as good, and therefore taking the frustra-tion-hate into oneself, and dealing with it by excessive displays of contrition, self-abasement and restitution-making in the shape of gifts or services. Many individuals also suffer from a general inhibition of sexual and general love experience, leading them to constant doubt about the possibility of happiness, a sense of hollowness and cerebral effort to go through the motions of their lovers' or marital rôles. Such schizoid or obsessional detachment is in contrast to another form of unavailability of sexual spontaneity much nearer the surface. The splitting here takes the form of hysterical reactions often related to the physiological mechanisms serving coitus, so that the focus of the case is on impotence or frigidity.

These well-known mechanisms of defence have in common a deep fear of commitment, of giving oneself over into the keeping of another, because the deeper 'relational potential' has not advanced beyond a highly ambivalent feeling towards the significant loved figure. That figure is either too punishing and castrating (as when an anti-libidinal object is projected into it) or too uncontrolled and demanding (as when a libidinal 'exciting' object is projected), and threatens the constricted and brittle security of the central ego or self, which must therefore stay aloof, unexcited or passionless. The defences, therefore, are directed to keeping the split-off ego-fragments in repression, and the self-image safe. This means that the partners must not act in such a way as to disturb this position. They must be, and play their rôle, as one needs them to be, in order to maintain these defences. In the depressive and hysterical defences especially, we find that the partner's personality remains *idealized*. *Idealization* is, in the marital field, the link between all the above psychic mechanisms of defence. By denying the reality of ambivalent hate or anger, and by the variants of projective identification, one or both spouses attribute to the partner those bad feelings they must not own themselves, or else make the partner all good and exalted while themselves taking on the guilt and the badness. Idealization prevents the treatment of the partner as a safe, real person, and thus hinders the continuation of growth into a full mutual commitment because the 'other half' of the ambivalence is not offered for reality testing—one is, oneself, acting a false part. The less secure the relationship, the more does it have to rely on various defensive devices—e.g. the absence of aggression, or even sexuality from it! For these are felt to threaten and destroy the idealized image compulsively maintained of the relationship. We now see why Balint's idealization as a mark of 'genitality' is so suspect; it operates when sexuality is feared as a threat of attack or defilement.

This discussion has been something of a preview or conspectus of the clash of defensive mechanisms which manifest themselves in marital stress and breakdown. It amounts to stating, in special lan-

43

guage, the well-known conviction that emotionally immature persons are to be found among the unhappily married. What is gained in this restatement is our ability to understand the strange evocation of infantile relational incapacities by the rôle demands of marriage, and *mainly* or *only* in the intimacy of marital interaction, in otherwise well-adjusted successful persons. The newness begins when we apply these concepts to the *dovetailing of two such systems.*

REFERENCES

1. DICKS, H. V. (1965) Chap. 'Fitness for Marriage', in Hambling & J. Hopkins P. (Eds.) *Psychosomatic Disorders in Adolescents and Young Adults.* London: Pergamon.
2. GORER, GEOFFREY, loc. cit.
3. HATTINGBERG, H. VON (1937) *Uber die Liebe.* München: Lehmann.
4. PARSONS, T. and BALES, R. F. (1955) *Family.* Glencoe Ill.: The Free Press.
5. BALINT, M. (1948): 'On Genital Love'. *Internat. J. of Psycho-Anal.* 29. Pt. 1.
6. SUTTIE, I. (1935) *Origins of Love and Hate.* London: Kegan Paul.
7. KLEIN, MELANIE (1948) *Contributions to Psychoanalysis.* London: Hogarth.
8. FAIRBAIRN, W. R. D. (1952). loc. cit.
9. GUNTRIP, H. J. S. (1963) *Personality Structure and Human Interaction.* London: Hogarth.

Chapter IV

THE DEVELOPMENT OF THE STUDY

A. THE STARTING POINT

In Spring 1949, I accepted an invitation to advise a local branch of
the Family Welfare Association on some disturbed families. My
thinking then was still mainly in the concepts of individual psychodynamics of the analytic consulting room or clinic. Looking back,
however, the assumptions set out in the two preceding chapters were
there, for example in certain parts of my *Clinical Studies in Psychopathology*,[1] especially in the chapters 'The Play of Opposites' and
'Abnormalities of Sexual Function', and also the overall significance
of the dependence need as a factor in psychopathology.

The War of 1939–45 sharpened our awareness, as Service psychiatrists, of epidemiological and group aspects of mental behaviour and
illness. Sociological and anthropological concepts and methods
became relevant, for example, in work on the comparison of Nazi
and non-Nazi Germans, in which hypotheses developed in the field
of 'culture and personality' found fruitful application.[2] At the same
time, my colleagues in the Army's psychiatric and selection services
studied group dynamics and social dislocation, to name only those
areas which required techniques with which to handle the 'group'
structure of disturbed families and marriages, as mentioned in the
Introduction. In 1947 I found myself contributing a chapter on
'Mental Hygiene' to a symposium volume, in which again the interest
in marital interaction cropped up.[3] My membership of the inter-
professional Preparatory Commission for the International Congress
on Mental Health (loc. cit.) afforded me the support of its close
concordance with my growing sense that the quality of marital life
was a crucial factor in moulding the personalities of children, and
thus the psycho-social climate of the future. This much I had learnt
not only from psychotherapeutic practice but also by the detailed
survey of the effect of family patterns on the making of Nazis, in
contrast to non-Nazis among German prisoners of war. Similar
differences were found valid for Americans in the study of *The*

45

Authoritarian Personality.[4] An influence which unconsciously persisted through more than ten years, was that of the late H. von Hattingberg's book[5] on male–female conflict patterns. His views were well in advance of current psychiatric and psychoanalytic thought.

The point of departure was the decision to study more fully some of the problem couples seen at the F.W.A. centre under the obligation to have material to lecture about to Probation officer classes, also in 1949. The material was drawn from the 'submerged tenth', in a run-down part of London, which housed a high proportion of alien or mixed families of Mediterranean origins. These latter had no small influence in shaping one's early thinking along anthropological lines. I noted the failures of co-operation arising from the incongruity of culturally acquired rôle expectations and models in spouses from a different ethnic background. This prevented me from rushing into the stereotyped 'neurosis' hypothesis to explain their stresses. One learns most from one's earliest cases. The hypotheses or generalizations drawn from such observations tend to acquire stability, and are used on later material, 'for all they are worth'. I propose in what follows to give an account of their growth and change, which I hope fresh and critical minds will amend and refine. It may be of interest to begin with my observations and the lessons I drew from the very first case looked at from the new angle of interaction.

Case One: This couple were seen at the F.W. Centre in February 1949 because the wife* had complained to the social worker of her husband's* violence. Each was seen separately for a standard psychiatric interview. H. was 34, a romantically-handsome London Jew, shabbily elegant, the typical small-time 'spiv' of those days. He was engagingly frank, and did not try to cover up. He was the only son of a small shopkeeper: father orthodox, upright, gentle and ineffectual, 'no match for mother', who was domineering, the force in home and business. H. had to fight her to hold his end up since childhood. From age 8 he had to help in the shop and forgo games and swimming. He developed a fanatical need to become athletic and strong. By adolescence he was rebellious and intolerant of control by his parents, whom he would attack. At this point he produced, for my admiration, near-nude photographs of himself in boxing kit. In brief, he presented as a highly narcissistic, exhibitionist, 'Health and Strength' sort of man. His life, up to his military service, consisted in this kind of pursuit. He also liked being admired in flashy dance halls by the girls 'who ran after him', but he was little affected by them, except as a 'beautiful dancer'. This behaviour went with a continuing battle between him-

* In this and all subsequent cases reports 'H' will denote the husband, 'W' the wife in question.

46

self and his mother for control of the little shop. His mother died in 1939. H. said 'I loved her'. The father 'went to pieces', and died in 1940, when H. was already serving, without distinction, as a private in a supply unit—not in some *corps d'élite*, as might be supposed from his self-image. In fact his army life was marked by two tearful break-downs, at the end of which he made sure of his discharge by plunging into a canal on the day he had been re-graded A.1. following psychiatric treatment. He said 'it was either that or going back and smashing up the barracks'. His mother had tried to make him marry money, but he had kept aloof from tender involvement until now, when, alone in civil life, he met his present 'wife', whom he had never formally married, but had lived with for over five years, and by whom he had children aged 3 and 2.

Although his relation to W. had been punctuated by the same kind of violent outbursts against her when she *opposed him*, as against mother, he said he loved her dearly, and was keen to make a success of his life for her sake. Though engaged in petty dealings in Army surplus stores, he was conceited to the point of grandiosity about his gifts as a smart businessman, and his command of life. He was profoundly insecure, pathologically suspicious of W.'s fidelity, and felt the need to coerce her to his will by knocking her about. He had grave doubts of his potency with her.

Tests revealed a very low combined I.Q. on the Hartford-Shipley scale. This was attributed to some abstraction loss, which in conjunc-tion with the Rorschach responses and his total behaviour made us diagnose a psychopathic personality with paranoid features, in danger of breakdown. A brief summary made at the time reads: 'A spoilt, dependent, passive character, highly narcissistic and latently homo-sexual has made a *ménage* with an attractive, temperamental mother-substitute. Denial of his dependence and sexual inadequacy leads to sadistic exploitation and domination attempts followed by crocodile's tears and masochistic identification with her.'

W. was seen on the same day. A glamorous 'peroxide blonde' of 35, of working class Irish origin, she impressed one as a primitive, temperamental, but essentially straight woman, more mature and intelligent than H., with capacity for warm feelings both of love and hate.

W's story, seen in the light of her partner's, raised at once a host of speculation which will be discussed later. It was her father who was dominant, serious, broody, always jealous of the mother's social relations. Mother was 'respectable', but flirtatious, smart and pretty, loved music halls. When W. was 15 the mother, revolted by her husband's sexuality, left the home. The parents had never got on. Of her only sister, W. said: 'She likes Germans and Nazis—I am for

47

the Eastern and Southern types; she married a rotter.' It would seem exogamy was strongly marked.

W.'s first marriage was to a 'flashy boy' when she was 18. She was innocent and loved him and her three children deeply. Somewhat pathetically, she said she 'would not now be impressed' by such a type, but she obviously idealized him still. That he got into trouble over fraud did not worry her, for 'some crooks are kind to their children'. But he gambled, lied and deceived her, even boasted of his conquests, driving her insanely jealous. When she caught him, red-handed, with his arm round a known prostitute, she left him—and he her, for he went to prison soon afterwards. She went to work and put her (then) two children into a nursery. Later she took back her first husband, and had a third baby. But he did not mend, and this ended her marriage. Now she became depressed. She allowed her older children to be evacuated, and herself lived with her baby at mother's. Here the baby died of meningitis, and W. became so ill with grief and mourning that she let her former husband take the older children. In this condition she met H., recently also bereaved. 'I liked him, he didn't seem to be after sex; he seemed hard and hard-headed —I like such men. He seemed neglected—I started looking after him, wash his things and that. I had just lost my boy, so I looked after H. like a little boy. We became intimate—but I was disappointed and started to despise him; he seemed cold, without real desire. He was crazy about me . . . I like a man who is rough and dominates, even if he is crooked. I would have loved to have him knocking me about—I was hungry for a real man, like me [sic]. I am passionate and give all. I mistook him: I thought he was Spanish and passionate—but he was soppy and sentimental. My father is the same type as me, morose and jealous. I felt insulted: what do I lack? Aren't I desirable? So I made spiteful remarks—yes, I goaded him. Now I know I am like his mother, always on guard against liberties.' (By liberties she meant men's actions which did not show deference.) W. lost another young son by the first marriage also. He died when she was already close to H. (hence the above remark about her little boy), and H. was 'like an angel' at this time. But she had turned by then, and he then sought other women. It was since then that he had become violent—'I can't love him now—he looks hideous—dirty—when he is angry he foams at the mouth like a wolf. He is lazy, and wants everything done for him.' The change in H. had coincided with the birth of their own first child.

Shortly after this initial contact it was reported that H. had made a violent physical assault on W. in the presence of her mother, and a police court case was heard, at which she offered no evidence against him.

From this point we saw little more of them, as H. made great difficulties about attendance, and, as is usual with character disorders, did not really get enmeshed with any therapeutic agency, in-patient therapy having been advised. At that time, partly on Court advice, W. left him, leaving the younger child with him. In this condition H. was reasonably insightful and deeply contrite, weeping about losing W.

Two years later they were again together, and co-operating for a time with a child psychiatric unit over the younger child, a highly intelligent 4-year-old, confused about its oedipal alignments. The outcome was not known. Six years later the couple were both attending a Marriage Guidance centre, evidently still together.

W. had, according to her statement to me, left H. 8 or 9 times, and tried to explain her need to return to him because 'she cannot get accommodation'. 'She does not love him and has to deceive him about her feelings.'

Nor had H.'s condition undergone psychotic deterioration: he was a bit sprucer, and was making a living.

This earliest case opened one's eyes to a whole range of hitherto not explicitly recognized features of such a relationship. In the absence of a legal marriage, it could only have been a credit balance of mutual need-satisfactions over frustrations that made this couple remain in faithful bondage, despite hideous violence, denial of love, and even Court advice to part. This positive balance was not due to lasting satisfaction of sexual mutuality such as Griffith placed at the heart of enduring marital love. What were these bonds?

To begin with, this couple met and developed a mutually supportive relationship when they were both lonely and mourning the loss of major love objects; H. his parents, W. her first husband and children. From their respective positions, each at this stage seemed to offer expectancy of satisfaction of *dependence needs* to the other. In W.'s data the evidence pointed to the presence in her of fantasy projections of an idealizing nature. She had seen in H. the promise of all her needs: for a controlling, protective father-figure who would respect and not sexually demean her. His very aloofness, like her 'broody' father, fitted H.'s own ego-ideal of 'unattainability'. He was to be the passionate, romantic, Valentino-like lover, who could, at the same time, allow her to express her maternal and cherishing tendencies on him. It was an expectation of fulfilment and integration of W.'s needs for secure dependence, coupled with the promise of a tender-romantic sexual potency—very like Balint's image of the fusion of the tender with the sexual in genitality. She also felt that H. valued the glamorous aspects of her femininity derived from her

49

mother which her father had condemned. We note also that W.'s inner rôle model for her men blinded her not only at 18, but again this time; she was unable to see H. as another version of the same unstable breed as her first husband. Her verbal slip showed she had internalized a 'real man' and H. was his projection. One could not be sure what was the source of this unconscious attraction towards the delinquent, inadequate 'flashy boy'. It might have been an identification with her gay mother's protest against a dreary, serious man, expressed as an adolescent revolt against the equivalent of 'squareness' of the pre-war period. 'Wide boys' and gangsters have never lacked 'molls', whose devotion seems a blend of rebellion against the forbidding aspects of the father with secret male envy that can be lived out by projective identification with their 'boy'. It was almost certainly a *contrast figure* to the anti-libidinal father, a wish fantasy of the opposite kind: 'the crook that could be kind to his children', i.e. a loving father without the withering moral scruples.

From this sort of consideration there arose in my mind the generalization which was to be tested out on future marital cases I was now determined to study. This generalization asserts that

> *Hypothesis (1).* Many tensions and misunderstandings between partners seem to result from the disappointment which one, or both of them, feel and resent, when the other fails to play the rôle of spouse after the manner of a preconceived model or figure in their fantasy world.[6]

'Unhappiness' results because a desired and needed object-relationship in the inner world which the real, present partner is cast to implement, is not fulfilled. Instead, she is twice punished by frustration, desertion and the loss of her children. Is she compelled to repeat her mother's fate? Is she trying to do better and *not* repeat her mother's fate and does she therefore stay or come back? Is she inviting sadistic attack or neglect because her men, howsoever disguised as the opposite to her father's personality, end up as rejecting father-figures? Is this why she with somnambulistic certainty chooses men who will ensure frustration and punishment for her incestuous wishes? We can as yet only pose these highly relevant questions.

What was certain, and psychiatrically novel in 1949 was the recognition that even in the case of an inadequate paranoid psychopath, *the wife contributed her full quota of ambivalence and retaliatory motivation* to the total picture of marital stress. Classically we have always had the image of the 'disturbed patient' causing distress to his wife, family or 'environment'. Matrimonial law, no less than medicine, assumes the 'offender' and the wronged 'innocent party'.

With *Case One* in mind, I was enabled to cross this limiting boundary and *see for the first time the interacting pair as the unit of perception and study*. To anyone making this discovery, psychopathology and stress reactions cease being attributes of a single 'figure against a background', but of reaction of figure with figure, even if both are but inner fantasies to each other. The 'background' are human beings with *their* needs and fantasies impinging on, and being impinged on, by the person of the hitherto principal actor—'the patient' or the 'offender'—in a system of interacting personalities we have come to call *collusion*. Was W. really, on our evidence, only the victim, the passive object of a psychopath's violence—was she not also a dynamic agent in the field of force evoking, even courting, certain responses from H. by her own behaviour?

What could be learnt of his needs, and his expectations of W.? First and most obvious was his need for a mother-figure, which requires little comment. Indeed, it was W.'s cherishing of him which seems to have related this need to her and to overcome his adolescent narcissistic 'manliness cult', and his hostility towards women. As in W.'s own case, here he met a person showing all the *positive*, loving aspects of the ambivalently invested parent of the opposite sex (i.e. he as her father, she as his mother) minus the menace and the anti-libidinal qualities. In Fairbairn's terms, both were exciting objects to the other. Here was a sexually attractive young woman, who not only mothered him but admired his muscles and his self-image of the masterful man, giving him a great narcissistic boost, both, because of her smartness and looks and by her idealization of him. She was a fine 'piece' to show off with to the boys, and so adoring, *needing* him—indeed, inspiring him to make a success. And so it appeared to H. that this woman promised the fulfilment of his defective masculine identification resulting from the reversal of authority rôles in his parental family. Here was the missing libidinal half of his oedipal mother. He must have seen her as a projected internal figure, who felt about him just as he wanted to feel about himself. Unlike his real mother, who kept him under as she did his father, W. invested him with potency, relied on him. He rose to this trust, and was 'like an angel' when she was a damsel in distress, and he in the superior position. He could feel more as nature had intended fathers to be—just as W. saw him as a strong father-figure who could yet affirm her femininity and glamour.

In the coming together of these two persons—physically handsome, quite uneducated and without psychological sophistication—there was an epitome of what courtship and marriage are about. Each has a vision of a mate who promises the slaking of the thirst for acceptance, secure cherishing, and mutual affirmation and enhancement.

51

Both wanted stability, to give faith and devotion to their little children. It was an attempt to grow to adult stature.

The sad contrast between the meeting phase and the subsequent development was strong evidence for my hypothesis in its simple form. We may assert that H. was furious and let down when he found W. possessed views and a will of her own, which came into prominence as his inadequacy at sexual and economic levels revealed itself. This was also the trigger which caused the deflation of W.'s expectations and rôle attributions. As H. proved a man of straw, W.'s own internalized figure of her strong, anti-libidinal father, ambivalently admired and hated, was activated. She found herself sliding into dominance, defying and goading H. in shrewish testing of his strength, mixed with contempt. To H. this meant the return of the attacking and controlling mother, rekindling his smouldering hate against women who threaten his brittle ego strength and self-image. With his defective self-control he acts out primitively and childishly, and as soon as the aggressive violence is spent he is filled with tearful remorse and need to be loved and forgiven. But for W. this was not the model of the strong man. Such men do not weep. Her father was sterner. Thus her rejection of H., as we saw from her own words, was not for his violence but for his childishness and lack of authority in his attempts at mastery. How galling, too, for him not to be able to sustain one's own fantasied 'mature' rôle behaviour. This is the other half of the disappointment in the union: that it induces childish feelings and actions in oneself.

At this stage I could not find a hypothesis to account for the strange fact that, though not only W. but also the Court authorities, pressed for a separation, the couple kept re-uniting. Later, as our concepts developed, it would become apparent that the 'cat and dog' type of interaction serves the immature needs to express in the marital relation the ambivalent investments of former love-objects. The 'satisfaction' derived from such sado-masochistic symbioses are surely the opportunities to 'get even', to work-through those never-solved earlier emotional ties. Even in *Case One* one could see the *collusive bonds* for continuing their superficially so unhappy marital cohabitation as formed of several strands: the urge to possess and control the love-object in their different ways; the mutual narcissistic gain from each owning a handsome and 'flashy' counterpart; the chance, in this setting of mutual dependence, to hurt and be hurt by the partner as the displaced frustrating, hated aspects of the parents and by acting in conformity with that hated parent's behaviour. It is these deeper bonds which give the necessary dynamic to the more adult aspirations for a stable home and children to love, even under the conditions in which these people were living. Evidently, within the framework of an adult marriage the private needs for continuing the old war against the bad parent images can continue to work.

This case also made me decide to exclude, as far as possible, gross abnormalities of personality from marital studies. To gain a picture of what was peculiar to the effects of marital stress, we would have to exclude disorders in the partners that would disturb any or all human relationships. *Case One* would have been excluded by this criterion and referred to the general therapeutic services. In such conditions the priority for treating the sick partner overrides the claims of adequate investigation of the interaction which was the aim of the project. There may be more to say later on the somewhat different problem of *treating* very disturbed marriages, having established our pathological concepts. Under clinical scrutiny we seldom failed to find evidence of deeper personality difficulties. But this is not the same as established psychiatric illness.

B. THE PHASE OF PILOT STUDY

It was later in 1949, that I invited my colleague, Dr. Mary Luff,* to join me in a pilot study. At this stage we still envisaged separate full psychiatric personality assessment by one of us of each spouse as a first approach to a new case, even though we groped towards joint initial appraisal of *the couple as the unit of therapy*. To this end, with some sense of daring, we instituted the *Joint Interview*—a foursome session of both partners with both of us. The evolution of this technique, already mentioned, will be more fully described in a later chapter. Here it need only be stated that, during the pilot study, joint interview followed individual diagnostic interviews, and the decision to hold one was taken only after ensuring, by individual consultation, that cases of overt mental illness in one or both clients were excluded. An account of this phase appeared in a paper some three years later, when we had dealt with some 70 couples.[6]

The aim of the pilot study was to follow the impressions just described in Section A and to endeavour to abstract from it general propositions and hypotheses about the nature of marital bonds and their disturbances on which a rational therapy could be based. We aimed to weave the insights derived from individual case studies (including test findings) into understanding 'what the partners were doing to each other' as observed in the joint interview. In so far as the psychodynamic assessment of a stress situation tries to test the capacity to accept interpretation of the unconscious content, we interpreted when we thought wise, not primarily with therapeutic

* Mary C. Luff, M.D., D.P.M., Consultant Psychiatrist to the Tavistock Clinic 1932–58.

intent, but in order to stimulate the emergence of further material. this trial interpretation is a general technique of diagnosis I have consistently used in intra-personal, inter-personal and group situations. It can often be therapeutic in effect, and turned out to be so with a proportion of 'only diagnostic' marital cases. During the first four years we aimed at insight, at conceptualization and, hopefully, some classification of marital stress, rather than mainly at treatment. For therapy, we took on a small proportion of cases, each of us treating the partner we had interviewed on our familiar lines, with periodic conferencing to co-ordinate findings and policy. As regards data to be collected, we cast our net wide, covering the scope of Chapters II and III. At simplest level, we collected and evaluated the relevance of standard demographic variables: comparisons in ages of partners, intelligence levels, educational and social class differences. In a small proportion of cases great disparity of general intelligence, or educational achievement, or social class origins, contributed something. Overall, these were rare and not prominent in our client population. In Chapter XII there are some Tables defining these sorts of data.

What turned out to be constant and impressive was the frequency of grossly disturbed or unhappy family background in the histories given by one or both partners. This will also be commented on in Chapter XII.

At intra-personal level we made judgments about the general maturity and adaptation of our clients' relationships and effectiveness in coping with their marital as well as non-marital life situations. A list of data looked for would include capacity for libidinal gratification; frustration tolerance; activity or passivity in social and sexual relations; intensity of aggressivity and levels of guilt and defences against it; the closely related problem of ambivalence and ego-strength. As a method of eliciting such factors we used a systematic profile of the marriage I called 'areas of co-operation', which will be elaborated in Chapter X. The idea behind it is that the total field of marital life can be subdivided into fairly natural functions: sexual; affection and personal respect; child-rearing; domestic 'chores'; financial and family policy; social (friends, in-laws); cultural and leisure; religion and political values. In all these areas degrees of fit, sharing or differentiation, conflict or harmony, could be rated without raising too powerful resistance in their eliciting. The attitudes towards sharing in these areas were valuable indices of the pervasiveness of conflict or its localization to a few foci, as well as being pointers to deeper personality traits. For example, the man who hands his unopened pay-packet to his wife, and receives his weekly pocket money back from her is a different person and culture product from one who does not even tell his wife what he earns, but doles out to her a minimal housekeeping allowance. The woman who expects her husband to help in chores the moment he enters home after work, has different notions of male/female powers and privileges from the wife who encourages him to rest or pursue his hobbies in his free time.

Our concern was not so much with static data, or varieties of rôle distributions as such, sociologically interesting though this may be. It was our aim to try and dovetail these separate factors or partial aspects into a meaningful whole for each couple, as throwing light on the sources of stress. It seemed, over the series, to matter little who did the dishwashing or held the purse-strings, as compared to the different meaning the given partners gave to such functions under the pressure of their deeper feelings about the other. Any such detail in task and rôle distribution or failure could become a peg on which to hang projected feelings about domination, victimization and threat to the ego. They also revealed tellingly the differences and consequent disappointments in rôle expectancies postulated by my *Hypothesis (1)*.

This hypothesis has stood up well to further observation over the years, though it had to be supplemented by additional refinements. Thus, we soon learnt to distinguish what appeared in the data as simple displacements of the original object, usually a parent figure, to the marriage partner from investments of the partner with *expectations in apparent contrast to the original object*. In the latter cases there were often attempts to reshape the self's own rôle-interpretation. Case One had pointed up the possibility. Some illustrative case material, previously published[6] will, perhaps, help to clarify our thinking of that time.

(a) First, an example of simple displacements of rôle expectancies based on direct identifications with parental attitudes and family cultures.

Case Two: A skilled artisan of 44, married 9 years to a woman aged 41 (both first marriages), with one child of $2\frac{1}{2}$. Referred by a Probation Officer on account of violent quarrels, the partners respectively stated their complaints as follows: W.: . . . 'My husband has tried to dictate how I should run the house, and though I have been out to work full time the majority of my life, he also wants me to spend any money I have according to his ideas. Because I have not obeyed his commands, he has endeavoured to get various people to tell me to do as I am told, just like a naughty girl.' H.: 'I hope you won't mind my submitting a separate report about my trouble . . . I've waited patiently to have this childish business settled and I hope, with all my heart, that when you interview my wife and me a conclusion . . . will be arrived at that will be best for all parties, most especially the child.'

H. was a sad, serious man, studious and musical, who had during his military service in a remote area educated himself while his mates 'drank, gambled and went whoring'. His father was a police constable 'of the quiet sort', who ran his home and family by unquestioned moral authority. The mother 'had plenty to say', but the parents seemed always united in disciplining their children. H. recalls father striking mother on one dramatic occasion, after which there were no more quarrels. Mother was loving and spoiling to H., who was further cherished by three older sisters. 'It was a peaceable home with a good father to look up to.'

H. was an over-deferential, priggish man who tried to enlist our sympathies. A pacifist, he joined the Forces reluctantly, and refused rank. He was drawn to W. as a lively girl, at his firm's dances. During courtship and on leave (they married in mid-war), she never showed temper. She was 'good to him' sexually, and he remained attracted to her, even though she had gone cold, sulked and before that used to have violent tantrums when he tried to show her or help her with things. He regarded himself as the innocently injured model of courtesy and consideration. Could be obstinate, and very set in his ways. He was at a loss how to deal with his wife's open aggression, and felt guilty about having to hit her.

W.: Thin, wizened, no attempt to make herself attractive. She had been a typist, and enjoyed social mixing, but kept herself clear of sexual entanglements. Her home had been the mirror image of H.'s. The father also was quiet, but the mother completely dominated the family, exactly opposite to H.'s: three older brothers followed by W. as the 'baby'. 'Father idolized and spoilt Mother.' W. always had a fear of her dominant mother, and would cry hysterically when thwarted or punished by her. Indulged and spoilt by her father and big brothers, whom she envied. She had felt sure her marriage to H. would be a success, and prided herself she was always willing to give him sex though she had long ceased to 'feel anything'. Her original statement about H.'s dominance and meanness needs no enlargement. She confirmed our feeling of H.'s need to be always right—'to have a halo'. He begrudged her the baby, waiting for a home and a bank balance first, but now he idolized the child, and neglected W. She was angry at his expecting her to cope alone with the baby while he 'popped round' to his married sister's, whose husband treats his wife as a slave—a bad precept for him.

During our two joint interviews we heard a great deal of the nature of their relationship, and their differing expectations. The wife was

56

prepared to fight every request of his—e.g. to move an ironing board, which she placed so as to obstruct work he was doing. Next day it was .back in the same position. He complained of her untidiness, she of his meanness and 'neglect' of her. *A pattern of competition as to who can dominate, and a need to balance all points scored is revealed and pointed out.** H. claimed the bread winner calls the financial tune. W. claimed the right to her own earnings in her own account. What was remarkable during these sessions was W.'s gleeful, triumphal look, when she scored a point or heard H.'s description of her cruel wounding behaviour.

The main line of *our interpretation* after watching much of this, *is that whereas H. has tried to assert himself over W. by 'knowing better' and criticism of her shortcomings, W.'s way of asserting herself has been by contemptuous silences, which worked better in confusing him than her earlier tantrums, which he could despise as 'childish'.* At one point, when comparing the power relations of their respective parental homes, W. said H. now reminds her of the way her mother carried on; W. resents domination—no, she did not want to be like her own mother.

She cannot accept *our pointing out that this is how she has tried to get even with her husband—first by fighting as she did when a child—later by copying her mother.* H. remained throughout the uncomprehendingly rigid, avuncular, injured man, 'who wasn't criticizing, but . . .' and always 'more in sorrow than in anger'. In summary, H. was a solemn obsessional character, W. a bristling feminist, with a vicious capacity to sting and belittle. His moral rigidity could only condemn. He took it for granted that it is the husband's duty to guide and mould his 'young wife', and could only see his actions as kindly, magnanimous, and reasonedly democratic. In fact he ignored what she had to say throughout the interviews, and she got undisguised satisfaction out of his incapacity to deal with her, laughing at his elephantine self-righteousness.

We felt that the parties had lost practically all co-operation in all areas, even battling over the child, and we gave a poor prognosis of the marriage to the referring Probation Officer. A few years later we heard of their divorce. This was before we were able to offer therapy, which might or might not have changed the situation.

We inferred that at least H. in this case expected an easy continuation of the rôles he had seen his father and mother play. We had no doubt that he identified with his father as his 'quietly authoritarian' rôle model. He expected that a few sage commands and the occasional slap would maintain due wifely subordination and domestic peace. It was also obvious that W. had internalized her mother as both the

---

* To distinguish what we said to patients during interviews, our comments will throughout be printed in italics in this and subsequent Case reports.

dominant wife and as an authority to rebel against by tantrums and sulks.* This marriage had a sincere and loving beginning at mature ages and after long acquaintance. The partners had closely similar (Cockney) social backgrounds and no psychiatric history. Yet the disappointment and confusion produced by the rigidity of these unachieved rôle expectations wrecked the 'mature intentions' of this decent couple who had, under this challenge, regressed to quite childish mutual behaviour. The rigidity of their internalized family culture patterns severely limited both partners' repertoire for alternative ways of treating one another, as persons rather than as displacement figures for the parent in question. When W., in particular, failed to get her own way by childish tantrums, she switched to dealing with H. as her mother had done in dominating her household, but without achieving the desired result of an 'idolizing spoiling husband', as her father had been.

From the greatly condensed account of the case material there was omitted comment on H.'s dependence on the authoritarian father-figure, evident from his need to please me. W. had mentioned it in her statement of complaint. In his transference bearing it was clear that H. wanted a strong daddy to run to, who would bring this naughty girl to her senses (e.g. myself; before us the Probation service, and before that his in-laws). Just as W. regressed to childish hysterical fireworks to deal with H. as if he were the frustrating and would-be controlling mother instead of an indulgent daddy, so did H. himself lose confidence in his capacity to deal with her, when his unquestioned identification with his father *was* questioned.

There are, then, already two aspects of marital interaction visible in such a case as this and many similar ones. Not only is the partner seen as a replica of the incorporated parental figure (1), but the self is also compelled to act out the rôle as if he or she were the opposite parent (2). In the absence of this fantasied likeness of the partner to the wished-for compliant parent image, the deeper ambivalence towards the love object breaks surface in resentment and hate previously covered by idealization. The parties treat each other *as if* the other *were* the earlier object, and regression occurs in the means used to coerce or persuade the parent image with the old, childish resources for revenge or for gaining favour. Forbidding and rejecting qualities are attributed and evoked each by the other. It is as if the 'bad object' is shuttled to and fro in their contest which is indeed the essence of a *collusion*. In *Case Two* W. acted out her own dominance needs, but at the same time projected them in paranoid-

* This statement, and many like it, makes sense in the light of the object-relations theory which sees both the object and the ego's relation with it internalized and capable of re-projection.

hysterical fashion to H. ('He has tried to dictate', etc.) with minimal guilt. He, with more guilt and helplessness about aggression (he must have been quite afraid of his 'good' but strict father) was unable to get any satisfaction from being aggressive, and had to project most of it self-righteously into W. as the naughty child. Unable to cope with childish anger, he regresses to running, like a little boy, for support and redress to more powerful father figures, complaining and wanting them to control his shrewish wife. There will later be more to say about this 'floating projection' of unacceptable qualities among marriage partners.

The disclosure of two aspects of the internal object relation is interesting. Each partner is both: in their own rôle expectation they are the parent model, *and* the child reacting against the parent model, whose frightening aspects are used alternately in the childish behaviour against the spouse. This rigidity and limitation of rôle behaviour (instead of flexible adaptability to the needs of the real partner in the Here and Now) provides a striking illustration of the generalization I made in Chapter III about the continued power of unresolved involvement with past object relations to stunt growth and maturation.

(b) *Marriage by contrast to the parental models* was mentioned as an extension of the hypothesis of disappointed rôle expectancy. Where in *Case Two* each spouse expected to continue married life in the manner of their respective parents of the same sex, in the case I am about to quote the partners consciously do not want or intend to play the parental rôles in marriage, but have counter-identifications against these. Their parental models are repressed or denied. They are going to repair in their marriage the shame of the silly squabbling parents. In their case the let-down happens, when despite this conscious intention they become aware that they are repeating the old rejected patterns after all. Such a variant was brought home to us by an early case. I reproduce it as a milestone in our progress of hypothesis-making. It was also published in Dicks.[6]

Case Three: Two intellectuals, aged 37 and 31 when first seen, are greatly attracted sexually and by a shared interest in left-wing politics. In personality styles they are not unlike the partners of Case Two: he serious and ponderous, she lively, emotional, rebellious. The superficial symptomatology of W.'s defiant, hysterical behaviour, and H.'s sorrowful, accusing incomprehension of her naughtiness also resembles the previous case. The marital developments, however, and the backgrounds, are quite different. H. came from working class 'puritan' background, with a quiet, home-loving father whom the son

59

described 'less worthy of my respect when I was young—later I modified this'. The mother 'a personality, who dominated father and drove us all (H. and 2 sibs.) on' and gave H. a sense of 'not in the top class' though he had done well in academic life. Following a protracted illness at 14, he had to be rather cosseted. This pointed up his mother's lovingness and efficiency in running and spoiling all her family. She also found time to be a forceful Socialist-feminist, voluble, quick-tempered, despising the father's lack of political interest. 'It made me feel I wanted something stabler, not something like mother in marriage.' H. was retiring, bashful, nearly always in love; he was also interested in Left politics, but cautious, never 'whole-hogging'. He feared total commitment in love after one bad disappointment before he met W.

W. had a similar non-conformist background, with a severe patriarch scholar for a father, whose love for his five children was linked with plenty of chastisement. These whippings had been sexually exciting to W. but on the surface she became hostile and rebellious—father's black sheep, a militant Marxist atheist, etc. The gentle mother was no match for the tyrant, and her place in the family was unenviable and despised. She could not protect her daughter from being coerced to a practical training when she longed to study painting.

Meeting at a Party conference, H. and W. were sure they had found the ideal partner: similar rebellion, 'emancipated' views on un-bourgeois sexual equality, shared values, no exploitation of woman by man, leaving each other free to pursue their own interests. H. seemed so tolerant and respectful of her as a person. 'He had swept her off her feet.'

By the time we saw them three years after marriage and with a child aged 15 months, they had had to separate, as mutual anger and loss of all tender feeling had made cohabitation intolerable. W. complained that H. did not live up to the spirit of their professed values: he resented her outside life, especially after the baby came, accused her of neglecting him and the child, refused to do chores. It came to his giving an ultimatum, under which he would have her back. Her reactions to his increasing 'black moods' and disagreements were hysterical tantrums, 'just as with her family', meant to express her defiance. H. complained that he had been shocked by W.'s lack of responsibility and maternal feeling, which had dawned on him during a visit to them of his parents, who had commented on her 'bossiness' and lack of restraint. Everything she did was so 'whole-hogging' in her enthusiasm of the moment, and her hysterics filled him with gloom and contempt. He also mentioned *her* ultimatum to him: more demonstrativeness, more help and sharing. She accused him of cruelty when he 'merely' withdrew into silence under her torrent of vituperation and hysterical tempers.

This couple were seen by us over a prolonged period, including several joint interviews, during which it became clear how increasingly disillusioned both had become with the realities behind the figures they had married. These ranged from H.'s political apostasy for what were, to her, reasons of cowardice and job security, to financial and domestic sharing, in addition to the already mentioned mutual feeling of lack of love and support. H., for example, exclaimed about her saving a nest-egg for 'breaking free' with: 'That's just the trouble, what is hers is always hers, but what is mine is always ours', revealing his fear of her ruining him with her demand for equality and independence.

For W. it had become another version of struggling in vain against her father, an intolerant martinet who belittled her art, her most cherished beliefs and her striving to be somebody. For H. she had become another bossy politicizing female, but lacking the warmth and devotion of his mother; no welcoming meal, no love—even for the baby. He wasn't going to play his father's meek rôle, and have his work put in jeopardy by taking on female domestic chores and baby-minding while she went to meetings.

It was interesting to note how, with the displacement of his 'bad' mother-figure to W., H.'s political views had taken a turn to the Right, as he also rose in seniority in his job. Also interesting was how throughout this couple was, as they stated, regarded by their friends as being most well-matched: 'He is just the man for her—she needs his steadying influence.'

At this point the outcome of our long contact with the *Threes* will not be pursued. The interest lies for the moment in the support the case gives to the hypothesis of rôle expectations in apparent contrast to parental identifications. It will be recalled how H. had consciously rejected the mother as an impossible model for a wife, and had also despised his father for his meek subordination to his mother's vivid personality. Even though anyone now reading the case could, as in a bad Whodunit, see the future dénouement at once, this was not what the *Threes* could foresee. To both of them their encounter was a complete contrast to their respective parents: this vivacious, carefree girl with her disdain for tradition was matched by this progressive, leftist scholar, who respected her need for freedom. It was only slowly that H. began to see the likeness of his predicament to his father's and his own youth: being bossed by a quick-tempered juggernaut of a suffragette, such as he had always run from to seek jolly, feminine 'light-weight' girls as friends. W.'s awakening was less realistic. H.,

61

a shy, timid, withdrawn man was now endowed with her father's behaviour, when objectively it was at best a demand for maternal cherishing, at worst a rebellious sulking at this fiery young mother-substitute's attacks on his freedom. A little deeper one could also see that the initial attraction had contained the parental elements: in W.'s case the scholar, in H.'s the mother's intellectual vivacity. This, I inferred, meant that each partner had hoped for the *loved* aspects of the split parental object, without the oppressive hated aspects of their respective parents of the opposite sex.

Each of them, also, had considerable counter-identifications, or more accurately, denials of identifications with their parents of the same sex. To W. this meant a dynamic repression of her earlier masochistic gratification at being dominated and beaten by her father, resulting in an attitude 'I will not be a doormat like my mother'; a violent reaction against any show of force later by H., which her unconscious equated with the exciting aspects of father, and therefore made her frigid. To H. it meant 'I will not be dominated like my father was'. Yet as seen by us, he was repeating his defensive rebellion against his dominant mother, and at the same time *feeling*, as his father was supposed by him to feel, an essentially ineffectual, passive kind of anger. The development was as in *Case Two*—each partner reviving the defensive-aggressive behaviour which had characterized their relation to the parent figure that threatened their ego and their need for autonomy. It was the man's passivity which the wife projectively despised most because it was the part of herself she had most strongly repressed.

In the light of this case *Hypothesis (1)* receives a special rider which looks almost like inversion: *Tensions between marriage partners can result from the disappointment that the partner, after all, plays the marital rôle like the frustrating parent figure, similarity to whom was denied during courtship. This often collusive discovery leads to modification of the subject's own rôle behaviour in the direction of regression towards more childish responses to the partner. (1A)* The inversion is more apparent than real. Even in the 'marriage by contrast' (to the hated parent figure), there was the fashioning of an idealized object or rôle model by reference to rejected objects.

The idealized object is still that same love-object with its 'badness' removed by splitting or denial. It thus becomes the 'all-giving' figure sought and projectively invested in the partner, towards whom one could then also express idealized expectations of one's own rôle behaviour, denying the ego's ambivalence. This makes a straight-forward identification of the self with the parental model difficult. In the next Chapter I shall take up the further evolution of this concept. Meantime this addition to the initial hypothesis, accounted for a considerable proportion of disturbances in marriages—but not for all.

(c) *Complementariness and the Pull of Opposites.* In Chapter III allusion was made to the persecution in the marriage partner of denied or repressed parts of the self which are now projected to the partner, even though it seemed to be this 'oppositeness' to the ego's conscious self-image which had also been an important part in the attraction for the other. The encounter with situations where this explanation best fitted the dynamics of the cases, led to the construction of a second hypothesis early on.

Hypothesis (2). Subjects may persecute in their spouses tendencies which originally caused attraction, the partner having been unconsciously perceived as a symbol of 'lost' because repressed aspects of the subject's own personality.

This is not a new proposition. Not only do most people accept a general 'attraction of opposites', in marriage as well as friendships and in work. The unworldly Don Quixote needs the earthy Sancho Panza; the strong, silent man the soft outgoing woman. C. G. Jung has elaborated this pull of complementariness in human relationships. People half-jokingly speak of 'my better half'. When tolerated, it is clear that the complementarity of a functioning dyad adds considerably to its spectrum of relatedness to the world outside, and to the possibilities of psychological cross-fertilization and growth. The hypothesis just stated notes how, in the total interaction of a married couple, this mature aim and expectation is undermined by the inner split of one or both partners, laying bare the existence of unconscious transactions which run precisely counter to the social and conscious aims. One of the early cases can be cited in evidence. (Also in my 1953 paper.)

Case Four: Made a joint approach to us because of W.'s increasing frigidity and temper outbursts leading to H.'s hurt withdrawal and fear for the future of their recent marriage, originally of great passion, and regarded as a model of happiness by friends.

H. aged 28, was a white-collar technician. Orphanage-reared, he held the belief that his parents had died of hunger during the great depression. He had become a rigid Marxist, controlled and bitter against privilege, he had powerful counter-cathexes against show of anger, self-indulgence and 'sloppy sentiment'. His aim for his marriage was a reasonable, purposeful co-operation. Yet, to achieve this aim he had married a lush, over-indulged, spontaneous girl, eight years younger, from a warm, Jewish background, and was immensely fond of her. W.'s parents had lacked financial security because of the over-gentle, failure-seeking father's mismanagement, which also affected home discipline and order. It was a place of chaos, much affection, many vociferous quarrels and constant oral indulgences. Joint inter-views showed W.'s barely disguised resentment of her husband's devastating rationality and power to make her feel a demanding, contemptible baby. Behind his cold reason we could show to our satisfaction, if not to his, a great deal of aggression expressed as condescending censoriousness and sarcasm, 'more in sorrow than in anger', which robbed W. of even the satisfaction of a good row to clear the air. We learnt that H. denied her a baby 'until the house was paid for'. Her tempers represented a great threat to his beautifully planned marriage: he had brought her to us to be taught sense. He could not understand why she should have gone frigid, since he did everything right according to the book. He had difficulty in realizing our interpretation *that while he liked W.'s warmth and spontaneity, and exciting cooking too, he could not accept the other side of her orality, but had to treat her like a severe nanny treats a greedy child.*

The impressive feature of this case was H.'s need to repudiate the spontaneous, freely-feeling 'anarchic' quality of the oral infant when W. made demands for immediate satisfactions, for some relaxation of his relentless planned frugality. Here was, we confidently felt, the 'no nonsense' regime of the orphanage organizing away the rebellion of the baby in him, now projected into the marital situation.

The relation between our *Hypotheses (1)* and *(2)* merits a comment. The object-relations theory makes the contrast between the 'lost bit of himself' (his need for love from a generous giving mother) and the internalization of a forbidding, depriving anti-libidinal mother-image less absolute. His anxiety when meeting in W. such an embodi-ment of his repressed 'oral libidinal ego' showed us the split in H. between a deep longing for just such a union with this infantile part of himself through marriage, and the compulsion to act in suppression of spontaneity and gratification, which would destroy his brittle, rigid anti-libidinal ego, on which he had taken his stand in life. W.'s reaction could be interpreted on the lines of *Hypothesis (1)*: her expectation that H. was going to be an indulgent, protective parent-figure who would allow the continuation of a warm spontaneity, added to the promise of ordered reason and prudence, which she stood in need of (and which he did provide in excess) (*Hypothesis 1A*). Thus we receive an impression that a collusive bond of *comple-mentariness* was being satisfied in this marriage. It is as if each partner was aiming at the restoration of a complete personality through their union. H. was going to be the instrumental, rational 'head', giving plan and coherence to the unit. W. was going to be the expressive, affective 'heart' of the dyad. Each needed this complement. The interference with the smooth integration of this new dyadic organism came from the respective persistences of unconscious pulls towards infantile object relations, which had conditioned the splitting of ambivalent internal objects into incompatible halves. This was benign in this particular wife, who had idealized her man as a fusion of her own father's gentleness and indulgence with a 'good strict' parent such as she had lacked. Her infantility consisted of using childish temper and withdrawal of tenderness when H. failed to live up to this idealized picture. We know that her own family culture had provided a rather primitive or hysterical pattern for coping with frustration. Thus at one level she resisted the challenge of H.'s rational purposes, like a child that does not want to be disciplined, and stamps its feet when mother does not buy the ice-cream.

H.'s split has already been commented on. He could not use his great need for tenderness because the expectancy of frustration and bitter resentment was fused with it. He required his good object to be a perfectly compliant and unresisting one, over which he had complete control. Only then was it safe to feel tender. In fact, his was essentially a sadistic position.

Enough has, perhaps, been said to illustrate the concepts used during our pilot phase. With mounting case experience we were able to recognize recurrences which are embodied in the hypotheses stated above. But I must emphasize that in this, as in any field concerned with human personality in action, we never meet exact replicas. There always remains the task of applying principles to individual variabilities. The attempt to coerce the material into rigid nosological categories does violence to the specificity of human interactions. How shall we classify, for example, the following case:

Case Five: An elegant top-barman, aged 43, presented himself on account of waning potency with his wife. He was reared in a large, deprived slum family with a ne'er-do-well father, and an overworked, kind but slovenly, fat 'mum', struggling ineffectually with chaos and filth. This man determined to escape since childhood, and did so by hotel and club service, starting as bell-hop. Here he identified with upper-class clients. As part of this, he married a pretty, scented girl-beautician, and both sought status and financial security. But as she became, typically, somewhat plump, he began to feel critical. His demands on her smartness, standards of neatness and tidiness at home became more and more unfulfillable. He would react with violence if he caught her in curlers. She was easy-going and tolerant about all

65

this, a nice, attractive Cockney who basked in her good clothes and success. H. felt full of guilt and depression.[6]

The anamnesis satisfied us that this man had chosen his wife as a narcissistic protest against his slovenly mother and against his whole background. W.'s maturation into the more comfortable middle thirties was enough to re-awaken the ambivalent tie to his mother. He could not tolerate even the faintest reminder of his slum past in W., or in untidy rooms. In this case we seem to deal with a 'mixed' pathology. There is the mate-choice by contrast to the parent-figure, which, however, relentlessly pushes its way to the surface. So far we are dealing with *Hypothesis* (*1A*). But the wife in this case had the same need for status and elegance well above her own working-class past. She was not like his mother, except in class origin and in her tolerance of his nervy irritability. It seemed that we also had to invoke *Hypothesis* (*2*), of a deeper attraction to a girl of his own repudiated background, a bit of himself, who must be controlled and punished if she threatened to manifest it. Both partners had made a narcissistic object-choice, but it was the man's total intolerance of any reminder that he belonged to a dirty, slovenly mother, with all it implied, that motivated his rôle failure.

This case showed us how the internal object-relation can, from its own dynamics, compel a growing need to turn the spouse into a projection of the ambivalently-invested object even in flagrant contradiction to the real qualities of the partner's personality. In the courtship phase it determines an idealization of the partner. Later it can motivate just the opposite. When by the continual reality test of married proximity the partner fails as an idealized object, then, like a glove turning inside out, 'the other half' of the polarized ambivalence comes uppermost; the idealized relationship becomes the hated, persecuting object-relation.

Under such circumstances, behaviour towards the now denigrated or threatening object assumes the regressive patterns of such a relationship.

By the end of the pilot phase, there was strong evidence for viewing marital relations as the field of manifestation of unresolved earlier object relations par excellence: in many cases the *only* field. Marriage can 'absorb' the regressive needs and problems of the partners. If these are heightened above tolerated limits, we get an outbreak of stress—a localized neurosis, or even psychosis which can remain contained within the dyadic system. Even at this stressful level marriage can be seen to act as a natural therapeutic relationship, the partners to some extent suffering themselves to be treated by each other as scapegoats.

66

REFERENCES

1. DICKS, H. V. (1939) *Clinical Studies in Psychopathology*, 2nd edn. (1947). London: Arnold.
2. DICKS, H. V. (1950) 'Personality Traits and National Socialist Ideology', *Hum. Relat. 3*, pp. 111–54. Reprinted in Lerner D. (ed.): *Propaganda in War and Crisis*, New York: Stewart, 1951.
3. DICKS, H. V. (1948) Chap. 'Principles of Mental Hygiene', in Harris, N. G. (ed.) *Modern Trends in Psychological Medicine*, London: Butterworth.
4. ADORNO, T. W., FRENKEL-BRUNSWIK, E., LEVINSON, D. J., and SANFORD, N. (1950) *The Authoritarian Personality*. New York: Harper.
5. HATTINGBERG, H. VON (1937) op cit.
6. DICKS, H. V. (1953) 'Experiences with Marital Tensions seen in the Psychological Clinic' in 'Clinical Studies in Marriage and the Family: a symposium on methods'. *Brit. J. of Med. Psychol. 26*. pp. 181–96.

Chapter V

THE FURTHER EVOLUTION OF CONCEPTS I

A. THE COLLUSIVE MARRIAGE AND EGO BOUNDARIES

From assessment studies, to which the pilot phase was chiefly devoted, we passed on to the treatment of couples, either in individual sessions, or, latterly, in joint sessions. New problems of interpretation were created. The working hypotheses formulated early on in the development of this study were rather too broad, even if they generally explained our observations. As experience of joint therapy gained in depth, there appeared the difficult task of conceptualizing and clarifying the boundaries between parts of the ego, external object and internal object in interaction. We frequently found a confused picture about these boundaries. This confusion was not only in our minds; it corresponds to the fluidity of ego-boundaries and identities observed in disturbed marriages, and summed up by such terms as 'mutual projection', 'projective identification', 'rôle reversal', and so on. In a session with both partners this can lead to uncertainty in the observer as to which of the partners is projecting; to the strange experience of *déjà entendu*, when, within minutes of each other, the spouses, during a joint session, hurl back at each other identical paranoid projections and accusations. Another form of this blurring of personality boundaries in married couples is the sharing of feelings, either in the same phase of time or in alternating cycles. 'The illness goes round and round' from one to the other. It may pass for a while into one of their children. The latter may then become the 'presenting symptom' of the stressful family constellation. These points will be illustrated later with clinical examples. It is out of attention to these phenomena that newer insights began to emerge. One could glimpse something of the deeper unconscious bonds which could best be understood if we assumed that they were *making such couples into a unit around which some sort of joint ego-boundaries were drawn*. These attributions to each other of unconsciously shared feelings constitute the essential 'symbiotic' or collusive process. It now looked possible to answer the question as to what kept couples

68

together despite every appearance and reality of suffering and mutual destructiveness in their relationship. It will be remembered that this was one of the puzzles not easy to explain.

As I wrote in connection with *Case One* in Chapter IV, adult responsibility and parental commitments, of course, make a contribution to the motivation to stay together, or to reunite after one or more attempts at separation. These adult motives testify to the acceptance by the partners of the social norm of the reasonable marriage as a desirable end. Such people will sincerely protest their continuing love and loyalty for each other. But this highlights all the more the bizarreness of behaviour seemingly destructive of the relationship which must spring from another level of personality.

One of the most interesting recurring experiences in working with 'cat and dog' couples is their deep sense of ownership of belonging. The broadly generalized *Hypothesis* (2) which could explain behaviour of the partners in *Case Four*, foreshadowed more differentiated thinking on this theme. This stressed the need for unconscious *complementariness*, a kind of division of function by which each partner supplied part of a set of qualities, the sum of which created a complete dyadic unit. This joint personality or integrate enabled each half to rediscover lost aspects of their primary object relations, which they had split off or repressed, and which they were, in their involvement with the spouse, re-experiencing by projective identification. The sense of belonging can be understood on the hypothesis that at deeper level there are perceptions of the partner and consequent attitudes towards him or her *as if* the other was part of oneself. The partner is then treated according to how this aspect of oneself was valued: spoilt and cherished, or denigrated and persecuted. *Case Five* showed this very well in simple form. In *Case Four*, we saw the change in the husband's ambivalent behaviour towards his wife— from tender lover to severe educator, in accordance with both his need for gratification and for rejecting this need.

In classical psycho-analytic terms, his wife became his oral 'id', he himself acted as his severe super-ego.

The dynamics of these two cases could still just about be expressed in terms of Freud's earlier libido theory.

More complicated phenomena, repeatedly observed, required a more person-centred theory. One such was the loss of erotic relationship between partners, as and when they diverged after some years in their value systems (e.g. one of them ceased church membership, or changed political affiliations) which had originally been powerful bonds. The sexual withdrawal *followed* the move away of one partner from the previously shared values. We saw examples of marital stress after the 1956 Hungarian uprising which led to defections among

British communists. Such a divergence so altered the images and inter-personal communication in several of our client couples, that the faithful and the apostate ceased to be mutually lovable or sexually attractive. Sexual behaviour could thus be seen to follow interpersonal patterns—not the other way round, as would have been thought axiomatic at one time. We may say that a good object was turned into a bad object. Hints of this problem were contained in *Case Three* quoted in the last chapter. Fairbairn's views offered hope of accounting for such facts. A general outline of my version of his theoretical scheme was given in Chapter III as a basis for interpreting personal maturation towards marriage-ability (p. 41).

If, in developmental terms, a given person has not worked through and surpassed a critical conflict situation or phase with his parents in early childhood, the defensive splitting, first envisaged by Klein and elaborated by Fairbairn, can be presumed to have occurred. According to this concept, not only does the internal image of that object and the feelings surrounding it become repressed. A part of the ego itself, which is in relation with or cathects the dangerous object, must needs be split off too. *What is essential about this way of looking at mental life is that it is not feelings, not impulses as such, but affective relationships between the self and some figure outside the self which are repressed. This splitting necessarily involves also a portion of the reacting self,* which thus becomes less, if at all, available to the central ego. In this psychological theory the split off object relation remains charged with psychic energy. This energy (libido, aggression, etc.) is *psychologically* a property of the self, not of some impersonal, 'sub-psychological' generator in the suprarenals or gonads as Freud's essentially physiological theory had it. Therefore, if my split-off internal relation to a forbidden or dangerous object takes up its quota of ambivalent cathexis, and preoccupies part of me unconsciously, I have that much less investment of self to offer to an adult relationship.

B. THE SIGNIFICANCE OF IDEALIZATION

This impoverishment of the central reality-ego by the subtraction from it of relational potentials locked up in the split-off libidinal and anti-libidinal egos with their corresponding internal objects, as envisaged by Fairbairn, is not the only result. His scheme can also accommodate my *Hypotheses* (*1*) and (*2*). With its help we can better understand the *dynamics of idealization* underlying those hypotheses. It will be remembered that these hypotheses concerned the disappointment when the partner and the self failed to match the rigidly held fantasy expectations of how each should play their marital rôles. These fantasies were based on a direct or contrasting parent-image, as illustrated in *Cases Two* and *Three*. The unreal expectation that in their marriage the partners must be 'all in all' to each other, make good all defects and offer perfect gratification of all needs is, of course, idealization. I described it as the main defence mechanism in marital relations. In Freudian terms, idealization is the ego's repression of the sadistic or hate-aspect of ambivalence towards the love object, leaving only the good aspects of the object conscious. This permits an unalloyed 'pure' love to be felt. Biologically idealization serves the reproductive drive well during the courtship and mating phase, making love 'blind'. Reality-testing that follows the honeymoon may activate the return of the repressed. In Fairbairnian terms, too, it is the return of the repressed that causes the trouble. *It breaches the idealizations.* Deeper-lying and hitherto repudiated relationships of the ego to earlier objects are activated and brought into at least partial awareness in the disturbed marriage.

Guntrip[1] quoted a clinical observation which will make this point clear. On page 324 he describes the case of a man, whose love-life was split between two actual women: his wife, and a girl in the office. Mostly his wife was felt by this man to be antagonistic, persecuting and hated, while the other woman was sexually exciting. But these feelings could also be reversed, when love and attractiveness would be focused on the wife, and rejection on the office girl. Guntrip's most interesting finding for the present context was the continuous presence in that patient's fantasy of *a third figure, who did not exist in reality.* This was his 'ideal wife' perfectly supporting but in no way emotionally disturbing'. Thus in this man there were three partly dissociated structures or systems. One was an exciting, libidinal object linked to a libidinal ego, split off from the second—a rejecting, persecuting object relating to an antagonized 'anti-libidinal ego'. These partial identities, which alternated between two actual persons, were the burden which he wanted to be rid of through treatment.

Throughout his life, Guntrip reports, the patient had held to his third, ideal vision of a relationship, free from the conflictful aspects of the other two. Other relationships, such as with the father, were found to follow the same pattern. This man's expectation of marriage was one of passionless and rational good sense. This meant a deeper denial of his libidinal ego dialectically coupled to an anti-libidinal ego accepting condemnation of urgent, greedy love and dependence needs by a rejecting object.

Many hitherto obscure events and observations concerning marital interaction become clearer in the light of this concept.

(1) I first mention the astonishing degree of injured self-righteousness

in married people when their point of view is not conceded by their spouse as the obviously and universally valid one. 'If only the partner would see things my way I could be the perfect husband/wife.' There must be no variance, for idealized objects have none; they conform to the inner rôle-model.

(2) Since the idealization, by Fairbairn's hypothesis, covers the relationship between the ideal object and a central ego purged and weakened by splitting off of all disturbing elements, the ego will defensively repudiate manifestations of forbidden libidinal or other 'primary' behaviour in the real partner, who quickly becomes the scapegoat and image of the forbidden object-relation. This was already clear in *Case Five*, which receives by this theory a more coherent explanation. Only an ideal object can gain the approbation of the ideal ego with which the self is identified. It follows that the 'worse' the felt badness of the libidinal ego and its object, the more rigid will be the idealization, to the point of total exclusion, say of sex, or of any quarrelling or heat. We are probably all familiar with terrifying examples of such 'high-minded' marriages.

(3) Of special interest is the clarity given to scapegoating. In an object relations framework a scapegoat can never be wholly 'non-self', but always (as ancient sacrificial rituals already indicated) a representative *of* the self. Indeed, in religious oblation to the gods it was the most perfect human being or animal that had to be offered up—it took upon itself the bad, repudiated qualities of those who made the offering. It stresses the ambivalence residing even in the seemingly wholly hate- and paranoia-laden attitude to the bad object implied in our use of the term projection: expulsion, total rejection, even killing. Only rejected love can generate so much hate. We recall in passing the horror of men who murder intensely ambivalently loved wives. After the act the perpetrators often experience tragic awareness of what they have killed. Melanie Klein's term *projective identification* emphasises that in the repudiated object of one's projection there is a part of oneself. It is a rejected relationship potential. Alfred P. Solomon[2] uses an identical concept.

(4) There is also in this conceptual scheme a more convincing explanation than in earlier theory, of the difficult question of the compulsion to persecute or reject the people one loves best. The special feature, as already mentioned, of such apparent hate-relationships in marriage is that they occur within the framework of a compelling sense of belonging. The spouses are clear in their minds that they would not dream of treating anyone else but each other (except perhaps their children), in this way. *Case One* was a clear illustration, even though one then had no adequate hypothesis to account for

this faithful pain-laden bondage. Such a situation makes sense if we extend Fairbairn's theory to a two-body system, in which each partner feels the other to be part of themselves. This was mentioned earlier when speaking of blurred ego boundaries. In Chapter Three I drew a model of the 'ultimate' mutual commitment of two integrated persons finding in each other the security to 'be themselves' in flexible rôle changes, which allowed freedom of expression to all levels of the ego or self, implying also equal acceptance of the partner's variance and otherness. In this model ego-splitting necessitated by the continued pressures of unassimilated, rejected or rejecting internal objects would be minimal and conscious (e.g. 'There I go at you again just like mother used to' said with humour).

Paradoxically to common sense, the unconscious commitment—the mutual collusive interlocking of the partners—appears more powerful and inescapable in the kind of disturbed marriage we are now considering, than in the free and flexible interdependence of 'whole' persons. In two relatively mature people who have a wide repertoire of identifications with different inner objects at their working disposal, Balint's desideratum of 'genital identification' with the real partners' needs is available, and deep interdependence and maturation possible. In the collusive problem marriage this repertoire is not usable in a straightforward way. The activation of so much repressed childish need—for dependence, for sexual impossibilities, together with the resultant frustration rage—leads to incompatible demands on the relationship. At one level there are the conscious expectations of the ideal union already mentioned. These have the aim of keeping all 'bad' feelings out of the marriage. Here the partners have to do a lot of unconscious work 'to let the sleeping dogs lie', to deny and keep inner realities out of sight. There develops what might be called a collusive or joint resistance to change, a smooth façade of 'happiness', of perpetual sunshine without a shadow. Such unions often endure if there are inner resources (e.g. rational insight or secure repression), and living conditions to keep the fiction in being. The tensions generated then often by-pass the marital interaction, but may break surface either in psycho-somatic form, or as periodic depression; or else they appear as neurotic problems in the children, whose unconscious cannot be cheated. Such marriages are often the envy of neighbours: placid, reasonable and considerate. The partners may communicate mainly at superficial, safe uncontroversial levels. When it occurs, the breakthrough of the repressed is, in such brittle unions, often a rather tragically destructive event. The more intense and total are the collusive denials by idealization which has failed, the greater is the let-down and the force of erupting denied opposites. We see these marriages in the

Mental Health Services only when they have broken down. Child psychiatrists see them when an offspring of such a 'model' home inexplicably breaks out in psychosis or delinquency.

I mention this category of collusive marriage which is probably one of the commonest in distribution, as an illustration of the relation between the sensible aims of Fairbairn's central ego, idealization, and the tense maintenance of a precarious peace within. We may call this the joint 'false self' of the couple. The difficulty is that it is highly valued socially, because it is such a good counterfeit of Christian marriage: peaceable, sensible and worthy—just what Gorer found to be the goal of many ordinary people. It represents *in excelsis* the social conformity aspect of my earlier definition of the marital commitment, stressed at the cost of flexibility and integration of the two persons with their potentials for continuing personal development. The counterfeit element lies in the massive effort at dissociation or splitting required to keep it in being. For its success it must rely heavily on frustration tolerance and alternative sources of satisfactions available and mutually accepted as permissible within the overriding requirement of the stifling idealization mechanism. To recall Guntrip's example of the man with the threefold split object, in this form of marriage the partners act towards each other *as if* each were the 'third' or ideal image to be treated *as if* the self was identical with the ideal ego.

Some close approximations to almost complete collusive idealizations which the partners valued highly may be cited as illustrative case material to support what I have just said:

Case Six: A handsome, upper-middle-class couple are seeking help because of H.'s worsening *ejaculatio praecox*, often *ante-portas*, which is presented as the only, 'not very important' cloud in their eleven-years-old marriage. H. aged 43, W. 35. Two children of 9 and 8 conceived during foreign vacations when H. 'felt more relaxed and care-free'. H., a conventional 'English gentleman' of solid, staid family, followed his father through school, sporting distinctions and career in a respected, but tense profession, which he disliked. He dreamed of country life. Elegant and sunburnt, he looked a woman's dream man. His sexual history was of being 'not a woman's man'. Such few successes as he had had before marriage were with casual, low 'pick-ups' on war service abroad, without commitment or respect. He had been taught to respect his own class of women, and had not dared to 'demean' them by coitus. His mother was remote and beautiful, his nanny 'strict and starchy'. His one attempt at coitus with a girl of his own social circle had failed. W. shared his class background, but lost both her father and an older brother while a child, experiencing

74

financial and emotional insecurity alone with her mother, and, later, with a resented step-father. Attractive and vivacious, she had done well in her pre-marital career involving travel abroad. This led to some highly exciting and satisfying affairs with sexually competent 'naughty men'—all foreign. Despite earlier denial, at single interview it became possible for her to express strong guilt feelings about her past, of which H. knew little. For him she bade fair to merge the socially reverenced with the sexually exciting woman—a rôle which fitted her real personality well. But this is what she did not want to be when she married. After her single life, he appeared as the deliverer, without whom 'she would have gone wild'. He represented all she had missed in a father and brother. He was chivalrous, he respected her, and it was wonderful not to have sexual passes made, but to be cherished, laden with gifts, to find a 'safe anchor'. His fine physique had, however, also held out the promise of romanticized and guilt-free sexual fulfilment after marriage. This was exactly H.'s own rôle aspiration.

Some of the statements made by the partners showed the idealization. 'My wife is a most wonderful woman,' said H., 'it is unthinkable that I could ever have a row with such a lady.' In short, he put her on a pedestal, and felt very abject and disappointing to her. Gradually he had handed more and more decisions over to W. to her considerable displeasure. But not a breath of disagreement or quarrel had ever darkened their cosy mutual envelopment with tenderness. She said: 'I wanted a clean, decent Englishman—he protected me and seemed to make me a little girl.' 'I know I get nearly to screaming pitch—but I only want this man.'—'How can I fall out of love with somebody from whom I am still expecting fulfilment—it is like being perpetually engaged.' But he also must never know how much she fretted and how much irritation with his slow, fumbling diffidence she had to conceal. She made herself be a devoted mother and wife, who had to pay back all the kindness and prosperity she was enjoying by uncomplaining cheerfulness.

At a joint interview this became clear to the observer, as W. displayed her capacity to play the kind, coaxing long-suffering woman, who almost gave H.'s answers for him. Even his anxiety over financial security was twisted by her into gratitude for his concern for her. 'He insures so heavily that I shall be quite a rich widow.'

This couple were treated by two experienced therapists in single interviews for over a year. The result was practically no change: neither party could give up the collusive security which the other provided against the outbreak of either full sexual or aggressive behaviour. W. went back into an interesting job, and this helped her tenseness, not only because she could escape her boring subtopian domesticity, but because it made H. and W. move into being working team-mates. Their joint and individual resistance to their therapists is very fully documented, ranging from 'too busy' to 'slipped discs'.[3],[4]

It is clear that the idealization was nearer to cracking in W. than in H. From the intermittent success of H.'s sexual advances it can also be seen that the otherwise so superbly articulating splits were not complete. The central ego will be aware of what the adult self is missing and wants remedied. Some sexuality was, from time to time, available to H. and probably always to W., despite the shared guilt represented by the Victorian mother figures of their childhood. This guilt minimized the earthy, dirty sexual demands each could allow themselves to make on figures they had mutually elevated into giving, protecting, undemanding and never angry or unpleasant ideal selves. Both constantly protested how they regarded sex between loving spouses as 'wonderful' and 'clean'—thus extending the idealization to a cerebral abstraction of an emotionally feared and repudiated function. Each was afraid to change the way they played their own, rather stereotyped sex rôles: H. chivalrous, protective, worshipping; W. self-sacrificial, kind, long-suffering and cherishing. That some of the repressed found its way into these transactions is no matter for astonishment. Both libidinal and resentful drives came from W., who was the more independent and enterprising of the two, while some element of homosexuality and dread of the enveloping power of mother-figures on pedestals could be seen in H. Mainly, however, the idealization determined the image of the partner, and the configuration of the marriage relation itself as an idyllic undemanding state in which each could escape aggression or full libidinal gratification with its connotation of 'wildness', 'dirtiness' and so on. In this joint defence of security they had invested too much of their resources to face change. The case is also consistent with my older *Hypothesis (1)*, i.e. the attribution to the partner of idealized expectations about each other's rôle performance, based on a much needed all-giving, yet also model-setting, parent-figure. These override the real needs of the two people and have to be defensively maintained. The real needs for adult integration are sought in therapy, but cannot be faced.

Another clinical example seen during the pilot phase also illumines the strength of collusive resistance arising from idealization. This was a case of complete non-consummation—a platonic marriage.

Case Seven: A 26-year-old woman, a graduate in part-time professional work, is sent as 'the patient' because, after 2 years of marriage to her 40-year-old husband, there has been no intercourse, nor any move towards genital intimacy. This was attributed by us to her early history of fear, of rape and murder stories, bed-wetting, and general repudiation of her genitals and femininity. Her mother was hated as rejecting and domineering, whereas the father was seen as a brilliant leader in intellect and character. Test responses confirmed this idealization. W.'s relation to her father had remained adoring: she took her problems to him, but always father and she had to discuss them in a very impersonal way. She was aware that the father's sexual love went to her hated mother, of whom she recalled being jealous. She was 'docile'. Her only sibling, a younger sister, was a rebel.

Such love-making as there had been pre-maritally had always stopped at idyllic kissing; the genital area was tabooed and childbirth thought of as painful and terrifying.

H. was seen by her as a sweet, kind, older man, who gave her much security and affection, though she had hoped for more masterfulness. Their life together was 'getting happier and closer all the time', with intense sharing of highbrow interests. W. was often surprised and unbelieving that she was actually a married woman and a graduate: she still felt a little girl. There was an element of endogamy: H. was a distant kinsman, and as a child she had thought of him as a grown-up relative.

Here seemed to be enough classical psychopathology to account for the total picture. Yet it was an incomplete and even distorted picture, which could be placed in proper perspective only after also studying H.'s response to interview, and after some four joint sessions. Therefore, we continue:

H. was a boyish, gentle, shy professional man, who claimed a happy background. Both parents were old-fashioned, kindly and self-effacing. Nobody was angry: there was an unspoken taboo on heat, passion or sexuality. H. had never had any interest in meeting girls, a work-centred and hobby-ridden young man, who did badly in all competitive situations. He also stressed his knowing W. as a sweet little child 16 years earlier. She was, to him, 'a very special girl', fastidious, clever, educated, and he could not possibly force any sexual attentions on her, as this would distress her. It was really only the family who were worried why no baby was on the way, and thus prompted the investigation (in the first instance by a gynaecologist). It was distasteful to touch his wife's genitals to try and arouse her. Perhaps a baby would overcome her fastidiousness, which medical dilatation, etc., had only increased. But he had wanted this exquisite intellectual companionship, not a housewife, nor a 'coitus machine'. In the joint interviews it became clear that this man had deep fears of injuring W. if he was forceful, also that he had always avoided women for fear of venereal disease. W., however, could now say she had been strongly aroused by their pre-marital caresses, and had only stopped short for reasons of prudence and morality. In short, as we proceeded, the picture of which of the partners was squeamish, frightened, and guilty changed almost completely. H. began by seconding W.'s high moral principles, and the loathing he felt for men who indulged in dirty jokes or promiscuity, and whose minds were of the gutter. He displayed intense fear of being dragged down to this level. W. volunteered how this might be connected with H.'s dread of infections, and his fastidious cleanliness, worst on foreign travel.* This was linked with intestinal infection during war service in the Mediterranean. After this session, H., in great agitation, sought a private interview, in which he confessed he had, from the first, had a complete aversion from coitus, based on his great revulsion from all bodily odours, secretions and 'mess', and he would not wish to have treatment if it meant accepting such dirt.

After a further joint interview it was established that the onus of the non-consummation was fully shared, H. accepting more blame than W., who had been pushed forward as the 'carrier' of the marital illness. Both preferred to let the matter rest, having little except conventional motivation for changing the *status quo*. What had been achieved was insight of a shared identity of feelings, and relief for the husband from having to keep up the false front of the deeply frustrated sexual male, having to tolerate his poor little sick wife's disability.

The interest in this kind of case lies not in the psychopathology of the two personalities involved, which is amply documented in analytic literature. It is quoted as a further illustration of the dovetailing of two inner worlds in the collusive marriage: in the use made of the defence of idealization, and, in this instance, also of the *déjà entendu* experienced by the observer. What was, at one time, the condition of one partner, suddenly is seen to be as much—even more—the state of the other partner.

In one of the joint sessions with *Case Seven* the passing of the onus from wife to husband happened under our eyes, when the 'fear of damage' she had spoken of was linked by W. to H.'s fear of infection. Each was projectively endowed with the other's fears. The shared element was the condemnation for being dirty, uncontrolled children —her enuresis up to age 10, his preoccupation with excreta, 'dirty jokes' and so on. Both had split off the libidinal ego under the threat of parental rejection, which they also attributed to each other. W. had idealized her relation to her father by adopting, and identifying

---

* The British association of uninhibited sexuality and dirt with 'abroad' is strikingly illustrated! Cf. *Case Six* where H. could only function sexually when 'abroad', even with his wife.

with, the high-minded, intellectual approach she now projected to her older, uncle-like husband. He, indeed, needed just this de-sexualized, innocent child-woman (cf. Dante's Beatrice again!) whom he idealized and identified with his own ideal ego, unaggressive, fastidious, cerebral and aloof from all preoccupation with touching the unspeakable. Thus, in this shared collusive exclusion of infantile libidinal egoes from participation in their marriage of ideal selves, we could observe the blurring of ego-boundaries. H.'s panic visit expressed the joint resistance to risking the *status quo* by submitting to 'dirty psychoanalysis'. Such shared resistance can be phased between partners over time. Thus:

Case Eight: A recently married young couple in which W. was treated as an individual patient for vaginismus preventing consummation, associated with a classical snake-phobia. This condition was relieved. But soon H., in his turn, came for help with complete impotence. This was relieved, and when we felt that all was set fair—back came W. with a relapse, snake-phobia and all!

C. SHARED INTERNAL WORLDS

(1) The consideration of the function of idealization in collusive marriages has brought us to another concept important for the understanding of how, in the energy economy of a dyadic system, projective identifications distribute the conflicting elements between partners. In *Cases Six* and *Seven* this was transparently simple, because the unconscious identifications of both partners with inner rôle models of anti-libidinal objects, and the rejection of other parts of themselves were highly concordant. The *Sevens* had both split off their libidinal egoes, which had remained preoccupied unconsciously with a part-object—namely an exciting 'dirty' excretory-genital orifice which it was forbidden to play with. This part-object, so guiltily invested, must not belong to the *ME*; it must not be sought in the good object, it must be excluded from vitiating the relationship with the good object. The collusion is by anti-libidinal egoes excluding the part-object, which is covered by idealization. In the *Sixes* the relationship was more mature. It was a whole object—a bad sexual woman who could not be included, related to a bad sexual man. Here the shared object and the consequent projective identifications of each partner also fitted very neatly. In so far as Mrs. *Six* felt herself to be the bad sexual woman, she sought refuge in the good idealized man, the lost father whose religion she observed, and identified herself with this ideal man's model for a docile, dutiful daughter. In so far as Mr. *Six* rejected his own bad, sexual self, he attributed (and how rightly, at deeper level!) to his wife the expectation of his

own ideal ego—a knightly, considerate asexual man. He also projectively identified her with an image of 'ladylikeness' who, like his forbidding, starchy, aloof mother-nanny figure, must not be sullied with what might be furtively done to a low, casual 'foreign' woman. One could go on elaborating this complex to-and-fro of attributions. Yet there remained in each of them also the strong pull of the full libidinal object—the sophisticated and sexually awakened woman, pleasured by the handsome, big sporting male. These could not be killed off—only dynamically reacted against. Each promised to the other a healing of the split in their potential mature personality, yet together they also shared in avoiding the confrontation with their libidinal selves which would involve seeing the other as an exciting libidinal object, and being seen *by* the other as owning a robust primary sexual self, from the threat of which each partner was to be a refuge and saviour.

Like Guntrip's man with his three objects, the partners were deeply enmeshed in relating to one another in three such compartments: (i) an attractive sexual object who, at the same time, was felt as a (ii) rejecting object of one's sexual demands also intolerant of any frustration-anger, and who must, in consequence, be treated as (iii) ideal, above lust or potentially rage-arousing, or rejection-dealing antagonism. Each expected the other to be wholly loving, unresentful and supportive in a good-parent way.

Cases *Six* and *Seven* were quoted as instances of stable dyads depending on congruent idealization to maintain the equilibrium of the system. Yet it is not hard to see how much effort at unconscious level has to go into the repressive or splitting process to keep the required rôle performance of each partner at constant level, and to exclude the primary forces from the field. Rational regrets and appeal to medical help for this felt impoverishment and arrested maturation are feeble in comparison with the strength and rigidity of such collusive defences.

(2) The Breakdown of Mutual Idealization

Hypothesis (*1*) was derived from the weight of evidence showing that, in many disturbed marriages, the collusive defence based on idealization of the partner's and the self's rôle expectations had ceased to be effective. What happens when the repressed does return, when the goal-seeking pressures of the denied elements in the two interacting personalities increase with the progress in reality-testing as contact grows? At times these denied factors are activated from the moment of the change in social status, i.e. on the honeymoon, when the young lovers become the married couple. A terrifying sense of mortification and disenchantment is often described. This can refer to the collapse of a pre-marital sexual expectation (especially in those who had observed pre-marital abstinence from coitus), or to a feeling of being trapped, or to some trait of individual behaviour ignored by the one or actually inhibited by the other, from snoring or nailbiting to cruelty. Perhaps most remarkable for our concepts are those not infrequent cases where two people had already co-habited both sexually and spatially, and where virtually the *only* change is that from informality and some concealment to open, socially hallowed matrimony. All Hell may now break loose, as the latent anti-libidinal parental identifications are activated in the new rôle that has to be played according to the internalized models. There is a sense of all delight being over, now that one has to play 'the old man', the other the 'godly matron' of Anglican liturgy. I am not here referring to couples forced to marry, unwillingly, through pre-marital pregnancy or some other pressure on conformity and social conscience. I am discussing couples who would be called deeply committed lovers without other coercion, who had already experienced each other in such humdrum, sobering rôles as shopping, house-cleaning, etc., during their 'illicit' cohabitation. Why should these free, socially emancipated people fall into mutual recrimination, projective identifications, and their resultant tensions now they are respectably married?

Perhaps we should first ask, why they needed to decide to marry at all. The answer must surely be the shared conformity to cultural and social values, more or less strongly internalized, and ambivalently invested by people who have trouble with their parental object relations. Part of their 'courage' in being unmarried lovers was the assertion of their independence and right to individual, unfettered sexual love. An element of defiance of guilt can nearly always be demonstrated, often deeply buried. The strength of social norms, legal and conventional, is clearly very great as age brings a natural assumption of adult rôles in society. It is the entry upon such rôles which, in many people and situations, but more especially in our marital problem population, brings out the inner conflicts connected with stepping into father's or mother's shoes.

This consideration probably applies to a wide range of relational patterns between men and women who decide to marry. Where the parental marriage has been happy (as experienced by the offspring now entering upon mating) the convention and 'rightness' is not questioned, any more than a well-functioning political system invites civil disobedience or revolt. The point is that this system—whether as marital or as political model—is also *inside* as the tacit assumption of the individual (see Chapter III). Until one steps into the new social rôle one does not know what associations and feelings about it one has stored up at internal object-relations level.

Case Nine: As an illustration of the disillusionment and the return of the repressed there comes to mind a very recent marriage, between two eager young people, in which W. soon began to feel marriage '*as a kind of death*' (her words) to her personality. This threat she tried to counteract by furious concentration on writing in which she must not be interrupted, but which she felt her philistine, mundane H. was attacking and depreciating. She had a sense of unreality and dissociation from her rôle as wife. When she met an unhappy fellow-poet, who had the exact parallel in his marriage, this companionship with fantasied elopement together made her 'come alive' again. Even at first joint (and only) interview, the couple were able to volunteer that W., after marriage, had become just like her mother, who, she felt, had been 'ground down' by her father to be a domestic drudge. She recalled how her parents had often sat at table '*as a grave of silence*' (her words), and W. had, as their only child, always felt she had done something to make them angry. It also transpired that W.'s mother had been a frustrated poetess herself—while the father, apparently so depreciating of his wife's talent, could turn out better verse than hers on the rare occasions he tried! In the triangle of her primary family W. had formed a split of an adored, supportive father, and of a belittling, dour, woman-oppressing prosaic father. Her 'downtrodden' mother was the married woman with the destructive husband, now firmly projected to H. who knew before they came that 'she was re-enacting a piece of parental marriage'. Before marriage he had been able to admire and love her for her sensitive, artistic soul, but now, he said, her writing was used to attack him, and he reacted by behaviour he recognized as pompous and conventional. Before marriage he knew, also, that she would be difficult on this issue of her artistic identity versus wifely rôle. But he had been sure that love would overcome all; *his own parents had always been on the same side.* He stressed all the conventional values. H.'s trouble was his great guilt for being critical or self-assertive. This kindness and acceptance of W.'s conflict had, in fact, made him the understanding, unthreatening man who she felt would rescue her from her involvement in the parental power struggle. She married, she said, to escape this, and to do as all the girls of her circle had done—'to appease the social requirements' (her words). 'I suppose, when I have been ground down enough, I shall consent to have a baby.' . . . So he could not persist in his dear wish to be a father.

this case W. told us at first hand about her remembered ambivalence to her father. She had repressed the libidinal father-tie

(in fact this well-read young woman exclaimed 'How corny to discover one is tied up with one's father'!) in the classical Oedipal way.
Her actual father was treated by mother and daughter as a dour,
prosaic and anti-libidinal figure. Guilt had made her identify with
the mother's attitude to husbands. H. had been the premaritally
idealized figure who would *not* be like the anti-libidinal discouraging
male, but who would, as his own idealized image of marriage as a
spiritual unity of equals promised, affirm her identity as a creative
person and heal her inner split. As soon as they married, he became
her bad father instead, when he showed he also had demands and
indeed reponsibilities of a more prosaic sort—housing plans, budgets
—to make on her co-operation, and not be solely an admiring mirror
of her art. His disillusionment arose from the let-down in his (not
fully explained) need to be the all-loving unaggressive man, who, in
consequence, allowed his more expressive wife to manipulate him
into voicing, with increasing vehemence, his resentment at her treating
him as the authoritarian, philistine male (which was far from his
clinically observable personality). At interview *she* talked of spiritual
unity, he of virtue, faith and fair play.

This case is cited mainly to illustrate the abrupt switch in the
woman from idealizing her marriage and her future husband to a
replica of her mother's marital rôle, and thus also inverting her
perception of the now rôle-bound actual husband into that of her
'bad' father image. Because he could now make sexual demands
(equated with 'grinding down'), he must not be adored, but attacked,
and the threatened identity of her personality asserted against him,
as she had seen her mother do. H.'s idealization was a faithful
example of Gorer's conventional English norm. W. was continuing
the old war with a new enemy. The other man, a sort of male echo
of herself, now received the transference of the other part of the
split-object—the exciting libidinal father, whom she could adore.
It will become apparent in a later chapter that the problem of the
unassertive male and the insufficient definition of sex rôles are important factors in preventing the critical change from maiden to
woman. *Case Nine* is an illustration of my discussion on sexual
identifications in Chapter III.

In other cases where the partners had married because their
relation seemed to promise mutual rôle-playing according to the
idealized model, the breakdown of idealization proceeds more gradually. Some degree of idealization is a normal occurrence in mating.
Over the years it comes to be replaced by a more realistic, but still
quite satisfactory perception of each other when splitting and rigid
defences are within healthy limits, and hence the chosen partner is
a tolerably close approximation to the inner image. This is the

congruent maturation with its acceptance of some frustration and disappointment, offset by discovery of new latent strengths and resources in self and partner.

It should be stressed that there are different kinds of blend of idealization with mature needs. Not all idealization is of the sex-excluding or indeed aggression-excluding kind. Inhibited, introverted personalities, with powerful anti-libidinal ego controls, have voiced expectations which had strong admixtures both from the repressed libidinal needs and from what might be called ideal rôle models of maturity. They would dream of a wonderful partner and relationship, who would combine all the qualities, including romantic and sexual passion, large-hearted tolerance, and acceptance of oneself, and the capacity to quarrel in a fully satisfying way, who would, therefore, make it safe to express one's own aggression and dreamed of identity. It is the image of the 'all-in-all' relationship, in which every key fits every lock, every cue is taken up in just the way the self wants. The idealization aspect of this ultimate model lies in the exclusion of hate, monotony, etc., as well as in the *denial of the freedom of the other to deviate from the ideal image*. Possibly we may speak in such cases of clashing individual idealizations, closely related to *Hypothesis (1)*, rather than to the collusive *shared* idealization based on exclusion of deep feeling, which I have been developing here. Whereas contradictory idealizations in each partner can be broken very quickly and lead to strife, collusive or shared idealizations form a protective structure within which the semblance of an adult marriage can be lived through for a long time without seriously disturbing the slumbering inner object worlds of the partners. On the frozen tundra of Siberia enough soil thaws on the surface of the permanent ice-crust to sustain some vegetation—but it is not the place for spreading trees with deep roots.

REFERENCES

1. GUNTRIP, H. J. S. (1961) loc, cit., p. 324.
2. SOLOMON, ALFRED P. (1964) in *Workshop on concurrent psychoanalytic therapy in marital disharmony*. Mimeographed working paper at First International Congress of Social Psychiatry, London, Aug. 17–22.
3. DICKS, H. V. (1959) 'Sexual problems in Marriage: a symposium'. 'Psychodynamic aspects'. *Proc. R. Soc. Med. (Section of Psychiatry)* 52, 867–72.
4. DICKS, H. V. (1964) Chap. 'The conceptual approach to marital diagnosis and therapy developed in the Tavistock Family Psychiatric Units, London, England' in Abse, D. W., Jessner, L. and Nash, E. M. (Eds.) *Marriage Counseling in Medical Practice*. Chapel Hill: The University of N. Carolina Press.

Chapter VI

THE FURTHER EVOLUTION OF CONCEPTS II

CONFLICT IN THE DYAD

We come now to the heart of my topic. In the preceding chapters the ground was prepared for an interpretation of war within marriage revealed when the unifying forces of biological impulsion, reality, adult social norms and idealizations have lost their holding power. This explanatory framework should, strictly, be limited to the couples we see clinically. Whether it applies also to those couples who use legal means of ending their unions is not known. It can at least be said that couples who continue to live in states of severe conflict and mutual frustration, have not given up the struggle to work-through and come to terms with, their deeper object worlds. One often senses a genuine relationship underlying the now irretrievably compromised idealizations, as if the hostility-laden interaction represented the highest common denominator of object-love that the given partners, unaided, were capable of with each other, and as if they were with these means striving to recapture the lost but still cherished model that formed an essential part in their bonds. Even in the conflict-torn but continuing union, the essential contract in my definition of marriage is still honoured: such interactions must be satisfying or fulfilling some regressive, primary needs for object-love in both of them. It is the defusion of ambivalence which allows the partners to communicate their primitive, unfulfillable love needs to each other in heavily disguised or oblique ways: by sulks, revenge, in short by every device of 'representation by the opposite'. Such fireworks and suffering demonstrate the liveness of the deeper libidinal involvement. To advance the means of deciphering the code by which warring spouses hide their so much feared needs and feelings, is the aim of such a study as mine.

A case on which a team of four of us* worked over some two years, and also followed up, did a great deal to structure our insight

* Dr. Mary Luff shared with me the diagnostic interviews. Treatment was carried out by Mrs. Mary Williams and Dr. Peter Hildebrand.

85

about such marriages. This will be reported in detail, as an illustration both of our methods and of the kind of records kept. My marginal notes will be printed in brackets.

Case Ten: This was a couple aged H. 37, W. 35 at first contact. They had been married 11 years, with a son of 7. W. had a daughter of 16 by her previous marriage. This had ended in divorce, with H. as the co-respondent, but the girl, though given into the first husband's custody, was living with H. and W. The economic level was good. H. and W. both had secondary education. He was a highly qualified technician, she had skills which from time to time gave her opportunities to escape from domestic monotony. There were no major social pressures, and scarcely any disagreements on such things as finance, child upbringing, or domestic matters. (It looked a model marriage of an attractive, successful and devoted couple, and from first to last both partners had our warm counter-transference.)

The presenting complaint by both partners was H.'s blushing, which only occurred in the presence of W. and mostly when another woman of a sexually attractive kind was in the room—but not exclusively.

The step-daughter was an increasingly frequent stimulus to it. The blushing made W. very anxious and angry, and a vicious circle had developed by which H. would now anticipate her reaction and so blush, and W. would expect him to blush, and, of course, he did—and so on. From the first joint interview onwards there emerged a pattern of W. being a relentless inquisitor on every such event, with H. stalling, evading and pleading ignorance as well as no control over this 'tell-tale' reflex, which W. had made the test of his essential infidelity and lack of concern or love for her.

The history of their relationship was quite otherwise. H. and W. had been at the same co-ed school, and she had been his sweetheart from at latest age 15. He had always cherished her in his fantasy as his dream girl: attractive, seductive and vivacious, his life's mistress and wife—(a fusion of libidinal object and ideal). She was always going to be there, waiting for him, and giving him pleasure and comfort. It was W., who, under parental objections to only dating one boy, began to look farther afield. At eighteen she married an older man, while H. was in the Forces. By 19 she was a mother, and her first husband became unfaithful, but though she separated, he refused her grounds for divorce. It was H. who had waited devotedly, despite sexual affairs as a soldier, which did not touch his heart. Returning from overseas, he seized the opportunity of becoming her lover, and gladly took the onus of being cited as the co-respondent. She said: 'H. seemed like a rock after the first husband.' He was on his own, having lost his parents in an air-raid. W. now came to depend utterly on him, and demanded a lot of demonstrative affection. At this juncture H.'s attitude changed abruptly (both partners agreed). He became absorbed in his challenging civilian job, which began with an overseas assignment. From there he scarcely wrote, and W.'s disillusionment grew to mistrust—he must have another woman there, just as when he was abroad with the Forces. He had even said, before leaving, that he didn't really want her, and, on his return, he was hurtful, calling her repulsive, and slept on the sofa rather than in the marital bed. He taunted her by his obvious erotic enjoyment of pictures of nudes. But he also built up their home, gave her every penny he earned, was kind to her young daughter and to the little son born to them three years after marriage. It was this contradictory behaviour which gradually roused W. to near frenzy. His blushing began while she was pregnant, and became for her a tell-tale sign of his mental guilt. The more she suspected, and questioned, and nagged, the more evasive, cold and cuttingly belittling he became. He would go to great lengths to produce alibis about his movements, so that he could always prove her jealous persecutions groundless. By the time they consulted a social agency, who referred them to us, coitus was non-existent; their emotional relationship consisted entirely of her angry, paranoid attacks, which he would parry by a very cold and disdainful, if evasive, manner, punctuated by shouting anger and formal helplessness. If she was ill he at once became kind and solicitous. To W. this was most galling, though it kept a thread of belief in him; to all friends he was most obliging and selflessly helpful. And always the mystery of his blushing, which had become the focus of both their lives.

At this point vignettes of their greatly contrasting personalities are in place. W. was a most attractive and pretty woman, lively and very expressive (in Talcott Parsons' sense) with a good opinion of her feminine charms, low-brow tastes, a bit of a moralizer, and very demanding of the interviewer. She was the only child of young parents (her father was barely 22 years older than herself), who were 'very much wrapped up in each other, and yet did not get on'. Father was intense and violent-tempered, the mother strong-willed, very beautiful still; there were constant tensions and clashes in which W. felt quite unwanted. She had some affection from her mother, none from her father, who 'felt her a nuisance'. Both told her not to have children. Her father's indifference, if not hostility, changed abruptly to anxious concern when W. had what was clearly a passing hysterical illness (by which time he was also 12 years older!)—after saving another girl from drowning. Mainly she had been a sociable, popular teen-ager, with an evident capacity to deny anxiety and worries.

Nothing in W. suggested a psychotic make-up, except for the florid, jealous fantasies and suspicions limited to H. (She was an extrapunitive, projective personality, with limited insight).

H. was, in most ways, a complementary, opposite character. Where W. was rounded, and vivacious, he was thin, tight-lipped, shy, overcautious and cerebral in utterance, inhibited in gesture and rapport, intensive and serious in tastes and manner. In his youth, he also blushed from self-consciousness, because he felt thin and skinny, and was teased, good-naturedly, by classmates. He had a younger brother, a cardiac invalid who survived the death by bombing of both parents, severely injured, and died some years later. H.'s father was dominant, always got his own way in business and home, by a violent temper which the mother, who was older than her husband, took mildly. H. had only very dim recollections of her, as she was 'colourless'. He shared father's technical interests, and sided with him, as his objectives were such as the son could identify with. In the main he felt it was a secure home. He felt very alone when discovering his sudden bereavement. Until he married, he lived in the Service, homeless, and developed a great need for autonomy and an intolerance of being bossed. Even in his military assignments he managed to be largely his own master. But he also felt that his father's methods were too forceful, and that he could assert himself in 'better ways'.

As mentioned, he had no major love involvements outside his steady adoration of W. before marriage, and he felt he was not an adept sexual performer. He had told her before marriage of his sexual affairs. Sexually, they fitted well, but he could never approach her unless there was complete harmony. He expected from her the 'all-in-all' mate rôle, and omnipotently expected he could do anything, and not be badly thought of by her. His sexual fantasies were always about her. He had a strong sense of having let her down and disappointed her by his determination to succeed in the post-war job, and by his evasiveness and need to make his work decisions as his own master, not influenced or morally coerced by her, e.g. about going abroad, or being 'dragged round' to friends. He trusted her implicitly with money, decisions, etc., within her sphere, and as utterly loyal to him. He felt bashful about her flamboyance, and her readiness to quarrel in public—it made him hesitant to take her out. 'One would never know—if she got into a mood, the show tickets would be wasted.' He was undemonstrative, and preferred giving gifts to showing physical tenderness.

Pausing in this report on the case record, it can be said that here was a couple who gave the impression of a strong integrate. Both had not only idealized the other as the faithful one, who would be 'always there', the rock on whom to lean. They also shared the values of the co-operative marriage, and in areas external to their love-hate clinch (finance, home-making, etc.) carried it out. These were two intelligent good persons giving each other hell with scarcely any insight as to what was going on. Our discoveries together with them of what did go on at unconscious object-relations level not only helped them, but was one of the seminal experiences in clarifying our concepts of the dynamics and meaning of marital conflict.

I will now try to summarize our findings in the course of therapy,* and of a later follow-up.

During two joint interviews, preliminary to treatment decisions, many pointers to the sources of tensions became manifest. Firstly, W.'s persistent, prejudged accusations that H.'s blushing meant he wanted other women, did not want her, and only married her because of 'convention'. 'What he had done,' she said, meaning his post-marital behaviour, 'was so against my idea of him.' She was obsessionally preoccupied puzzling out what he really was. 'He was almost like a brother; I trusted him like my own flesh and blood, and when he didn't behave like my father or mother I was shattered.'

We commented that she might have seen H. as an ideal version of her combined parents, and had married such an image rather than the real H., and was therefore disappointed. (Application of my *Hypothesis (I)*). W. considered he went to extremes: not only did he not say 'I love you, I'll be back!'—no! he said 'I don't want you, I'm going.' H. explained his foreign tour as being the way back to his 'own steam' after military service; he knew that W. would oppose it, and, foolishly, to preserve his professional freedom of movement, he was tough with her. 'Yes— give her an inch and she'll take an ell,' he said. He had to shield his masculine self-respect in this way. He had long since explained this to her, but she could not accept his contrition, and dwelt on all his mis-deeds for years. W. angrily interposed 'He knew he had a duty to me—he knew I'd go to pieces if he went away', and this meant he had only married her because of their sexual togetherness before marriage.

We commented that she wanted her man to love her in her way, and he did not feel this to be compatible with his way, which included his work, ambitions, etc. Now they were punishing each other for the hurts of the past.

H. said he felt W. was an enemy to be overcome: she prevented him from finding his way to 'better things'. Much of the first joint inter-view was concerned with clarifying W.'s devouring need to 'get in' and be the 'one and only' and H.'s fear of letting her in lest she de-voured him. His way had been to deny his sexual and tender feelings

---

* Our verbal interventions, when cited, are printed in italics.

for her. *We commented at one point that the blushing must be expressive of this whole conflict, but agreed it was reasonable for W. to interpret this symptom as guilt when he saw other attractive women in her presence.* At this comment W. pricked up her ears hopefully—'Is it?' H. said he knew what was always in her mind, and so he now blushed without her having to say anything. He said that W. largely disregarded all the kind, good things he did, and insisted he gave her nothing spiritually and sexually. 'If he once kissed her in the morning—then he would always have to do it, or there would be trouble.' Both partners agreed that each, once set on a course, had to be consistent. H. saw this for both of them, though W. had always thought of herself as undemanding, happy-go-lucky, and flexible—'but was it wrong wanting him so much?' (This confirmed our earlier feeling that she had more difficulty in insight unfavourable to herself.)

We commented that W. had now come to the same point as H.: a rigid image of a hard, unloving man, just as H. thought of her as an attacking figure who demanded an unvarying level of total commitment.

'Having known me for so long she ought to know, and think that whatever I was doing was for the best,' he said. '*I trust her* implicitly.' Said W.: 'Yes, but I didn't let you down, and you are always letting me down—lying.' 'We are so different—he was always strange—he and his brother had no friends—so self-sufficient.' 'He has said "If you have a friend you owe him something"—wasn't that typical?' Of course, she said, she had disregarded this when she was young—'just his funny ways'—but now she expected the worst of him.

We commented that this meant H. could now never show her in any way that he valued her or loved her—and he had given up trying. To this W. agreed.

We gave a further interpretation that she now safeguarded herself by thinking the worst, and that this came, perhaps, from a long time ago when she had felt nobody had wanted her. Hadn't they both wanted a 'rock' to be always there, always loving, and now both feared there would be no one who cared. This made them both so alert to hurts.

This intervention brought a surprising rejoinder from W.: 'I could not bear the idea of putting myself in H.'s hands! I am now completely immune from him—I don't want him for sex, or for a companion!' 'I am not going to have it written on the wall every time a girl comes in, that that is the type he wants!—No, other things have taken his place.'

This ended the first meeting—bar arrangements for the next. W.'s parting shot was to look at the writer, and with warm feeling to say 'I wish I could take Dr. Dicks home with me!'

At this point we had established the failed mutual idealization, the continuing deeper bond of belonging but to rejecting figures, and also the marked splits in both partners, which seemed related to their respective internalization of parental attitudes. W.'s expectation of a very loving husband seemed a compensatory fantasy born of her unrequited love for her undemonstrative father, with the mother as the obvious rival, and only hysterical suffering seemed able to win him. Behind her own 'happy-go-lucky' façade was a very anxious, possessive child, with strong and rigid demands on her love-object. H.'s expectation of a permissive and security-giving wife seemed based on his identification with his father, who could behave as he liked and not be attacked by his mother. That he was, nonetheless, terrified of female castrating power and had to defend himself by denial, evasive tactics and brusque affirmation of independence was also clear.

A second joint interview added mainly evidence in favour of both partners being able to accept therapy of the insight-giving type. W. could see more of what she was contributing to the collusion: e.g. 'I am very black and white—I feel strongly or nothing. I don't reason: all I think is "is he or isn't he" (unfaithful, bad, etc.)?' They also began to be able to listen to what the other was saying. We heard more of H.'s would-be clever opportunism in trying to master W. by subtlety, and his rages when she pierced his evasions. Essentially W. showed her projectiveness: 'I know I am quick-tempered and flare. I must have peace . . . It is wonderful when we have it . . . then I tiptoe over everything because I want to keep that peace . . . but H., who has been saying "We must have peace, we must be happy, for the children . . ." —and he'll tread on it and break it all up, by exploding into a mood.' She had to admit that she blew up—but conceded only the blushing as the trigger. We learn that H. had, for a long time, been refusing home meals, and had been eating chocolate instead. The interview, this time, developed into W. talking like an anxious, perplexed mother about her difficult child—*we say so* and W. agrees 'That's how I feel he is,' a source of trouble who has altered her from a happy girl into a nagging woman. H. told us he has felt her mistrust escalating to a point where he can never be frank—a vicious circle which *he* cannot break—only *she*—she is the stronger. That was why he had to force his decision to be abroad. (On this he gave an interesting comment on his splitting and ambivalence:) 'There was a choice to be made . . . it was a round-about way of saying I'm going to do the other, to say "I don't want you", because one implies the other. You follow . . . it's diametrically opposite . . . and by saying one you are immediately naming the other. If you ask do you want this or that, you say, well, I don't want that, and the other thing automatically follows.' He admitted it was crazy to expect anyone to act like that, but he did. Nowadays, he added 'It

91

is said in just positive anger and spite.' 'It is fantastic that it can happen to you, and yet you can't do a thing about it. It's almost as if we were hypnotized . . .' It only takes a fifth of a second for W. to think—and already he is blushing and having these contradictory thoughts. She would only have to control her tongue, but he would have to learn how to control his mind . . . (As if admitting that he now has the reaction: He is labelled unfaithful, so he can't win, so he will show her he is interested in others just because that will hurt. A neat example of his projecting his own guilt feelings into her). As if in response, W. comes out with the terrible feeling of being 'unable to measure up to any girl in the room—and just because he's married and tied to me— all he can do is to blush . . .' *We suggest she may want reassurance that he still loves her by her constant attention to his state of mind*, and she agrees, but cannot any longer bring herself to put her arms round him and ask him. She now wants us to 'guarantee him' from our knowledge of men. H. assures us he has told her over and over again, but because of his contradictory behaviour neither can act on it. He tells us now she had conditioned him to act like this, and then asks why they cannot be happy. This session convinced both partners that they were in this fix together, and they agreed to therapy. (At this stage of our Unit's practice separately, with two co-operating staff members.) The interviews were to be once weekly.

W.'s findings:* April

At first session she discovered she'd be relieved if H. was really unfaithful. Blames her mother for pushing her at other men. H. was stolid and unemotional, just like her loved father. W. knew that her father loved the mother, though he never showed it. Then praised her beautiful mother, in whose gay, flighty likeness she saw the first husband, who went off with W.'s best friend. She was also shocked that he had lived with a girl before she knew him. *Her greed of owning him past, present and future, was commented on*, and she also ruefully accepted the renewed interpretation that *it was she who had deserted faithful H*. W. was subsequently able to express her sense of parental deprivation and a pervasive envy of everybody: H. for his job and brains, mother for her beauty, the therapist for her interesting life, while feeling each parent jealous of the other if W. had any attention from either. 'Others could rely on their mothers—mine would not raise a finger for me.' The next thing to emerge was W.'s flirtation with an 'old friend' when H. was away, justified in her mind by his 'deserting' her for his assignment abroad, and treating her 'like a trollop'. She stressed H.'s interest in nudes again, and insisted he must be abnormal. (There was here a clear piece of projection and

* Abstract of notes by Mary Williams, who treated W.

denigration of him, in view of her own guilt over the flirtation.) H.'s talks with his therapist had led, by this time, to his making sexual overtures to W., which she had to reject. She envies her teen-age daughter, especially as H. blushes about her when she looks seductive, while telling W. to cover up if she wears too low a de-colleté. Accepts her compulsive cattiness about her daughter's appearance. The only job she had enjoyed was that of being a man-nequin, which H. forbade.

May: After this she appeared in a little coat belonging to her daughter —as if to stress the transposition of identification, and expressed jealousy of the girl's relation to H. In fact she knew her daughter did not like her stepfather, but even the girl's ride to work in his car provoked the feeling.

She now recalled H.'s first blush occurred when he witnessed W.'s grandmother pull up her skirts and do a jig at a Christmas party. She had liked his lack of interest in women, but now realized she was included. This linked with a growing jealousy of the therapist, 'how she managed her marriage', easily interchangeable with memories of jealousy of her mother: Father had said 'You'll never be a patch on Mother'. Then 'I realize I am a child. I cannot keep anything in—never think about my feelings, they just come out. I've ridden rough-shod over H.' From this point W. could see how she had caused H.'s defensive posture: '. . . he won't eat or let me see to his clothes be-cause I've complained of being a drudge—yet he is helpful.' She also reported H.'s outburst that W. and her therapist were in league against him, when the therapist ought to be punching her. 'He nearly walked out—he can't stand the responsibility of everything going wrong. He thinks I'd have another man in a week.' (This is a telling illustration of the 'projection going from one to the other'.) 'I thought he was solid, like father, but he's not really. He dare not even hold money . . . he would spend it all. If I tell him what I am afraid of—it never works—it just completes the vicious circle. Better to keep my feelings in.' W. now had a dream: 'She was being married in Church to H. who was, however, lounging in a chair instead of taking his vows seriously as she was. She had wanted a flimsy veil, but instead wore a heavy lace affair which dragged on her. Her maternal grand-mother had crocheted it for her!' She associated this with her grand-mother being an old *queen-bee*, who says men are no good and had dinned this into her daughters: e.g. 'Fancy women having to have intercourse with men!' In W.'s maternal family men were considered a necessary evil as providers and house-helpers. 'Father objected strongly . . . and H. had said she needn't think she could behave like her mother and aunt.' W. realized this is how she had treated her first

93

husband and despised him for it. She had never felt married to him, but always wanted H. who proved a strong sexual lover, who left her exhausted. She had never managed to have an orgasm. W. now had a second dream: 'I stood up to mother and told her what a selfish, loveless, self-indulgent creature she was. Instead of being angry, mother opened her arms and said "Why did you not tell me before? Now we can put it right".' *This was interpreted as the mother-figure in herself . . . the queen-bee figure who wanted her own way and could not love unselfishly.* W. did not like this interpretation, and returned to full blame of H. as the person who had turned her into a virago (Note: this is, however, very different from her original self-image of an easy-going, fancy-free girl).

June: She now projects very crudely: 'He just employs me—I am useful for chores—never asks my advice—I am beneath contempt. One can't relax with him . . . he is always looking round corners for some horrid interpretation of what I say or do.' But she at once also confesses she is always curious to know what H. and daughter are doing, when out of sight. 'How degrading to think he is messing about with other women and I can't hold him. Such a threat to my pride—I've got to be on top.'

In the same session W. discovers that she has linked H. with her own mother. 'He's torn down the picture I had of him.' 'Dad says both H. and Mum are never at a loss for an answer, they both make it someone else's fault, and then retreat. Greek meets Greek—they never speak to each other.'

This offered an opportunity of *interpreting how W. had the same craving to 'be let in', met with the same rebuff, and had become voracious and greedy for total love, as with her mother who forbade closeness to her father, and only looked after W.'s material needs.*

W. was now able to express much depressive despair . . . H. makes her feel ashamed—of her unattractiveness, and of their pre-marital sex life. When she tries to make herself attractive he rebuffs her with 'all you think about is sex'. She feels like a 'doctored cat' who has had her litter and is on the shelf. She has been so furious with H. she has just shouted, and refused to listen to him, and he has rejected her cooking. 'He looks terrible, but I feel as hard as nails.'

This was interpreted as her consciousness of what she had done to reduce him to this state. W. was, after this, able to express a very warm sense of loving gratitude, both to her therapist and to H.'s therapist, for 'taking the burden off her shoulders'. She could see how H. and she interacted; e.g. she proposes a movie while he is washing the car. He makes feeble excuses—no, he won't go. Now she gives up the idea—and *he* says 'let's go to the flick'. Now she refuses. 'Yet he will wait ages for me at a bus stop or see me home.' W. felt moved to

94

discuss the contradictory attitudes prevailing in her paternal and maternal kinship cultures. The maternal grandfather, a feckless, gay romantic like W.'s first husband. The paternal side well-off, grandfather adored his wife, but was formal, strong and silent. She felt her own mother had been a slut who, in order to avoid rows with father, 'would hide herself and little W. so that Dad would think we'd left him'. By W.'s age 5 the mother had turned into a house-cleaning fiend, who'd force father to take his shoes off before entering.

Through sitting with H. in a restaurant, next to two old ladies, and watching him blush and stop eating because they mentioned a foreign city in which H. had had an affair during the war, W. was able to realize how shocked *she* was as well as H., over sex. Why was she when, in fact, she also looked at men and wondered what they'd be like as lovers? She hated herself for this hypocrisy. It was noticed that W. unconsciously pushed a cigarette packet up her legs as she was talking. *This was pointed out*, and led to a paroxysm of laughter and crying. The therapist said '*This is what you want—and it is creeping up without your realizing,*' followed by '*It's that old puritan preventing you from enjoying sex and makes you condemn signs of sex interest in H.*'

She was covered with embarrassment.

July: Evidently things were changing . . . H. would come and sit by her, but she would push him away, ask him not to talk because she is counting stitches in knitting, and she knows there is resentment in it. 'He only does it from calculation.' She confessed she was revolted by amorous 'older men' such as H. now was—'tarnished'. *It is put to her that here may be a source of guilt over sex—her denied sexual love for her father.* W. can accept this, for she follows it with a remark how much in love her little son is with her, and looks glowing as she says it. It is learnt that coitus has occurred several times since treatment began—but always in a half-asleep state in the middle of the night. *The opportunity occurs for interpreting the converging evidence that her taboo is due to her making H. a combined image of both rejecting parents, and she had succeeded in inducing him to act like it. Now she is guilty that he feels stranger enough to have sexual interest again.* (Now came a very important step.) W. announced H. had said he might have to make another duty trip abroad. She had responded 'I'll be jolly glad' aggressively. But he had replied 'That means you mind and want to prevent me going', and so he said he wouldn't go, and apologized for 'trying it on'. 'If he went,' said W. to the therapist, 'I wouldn't trust him an inch, but I don't care now'—to which the therapist replied '*You mean you wouldn't trust yourself if you had the chance!*'

This produced another paroxysm of laughter and the involuntary hand movement up her skirt, which was linked to her wish for, and memory of past intimacies—love scenes in cinemas and their effect on H. Now she added she enjoys H. asking her and refusing him the things he denied her for so many years. Linked to this W. recalled memories of playing 'hospitals' with detailed examination of their sex anatomy with a little girl cousin, at age 6, and being discovered by her mother, with shame and horror. 'I hate sleeping with H. in my parents' house —I don't want them to know I am a sexual being.'

Soon after this 'things were looking up' for her. She can allow for H.'s failings, though 'he needs to control everything'. She gave a frank account of how she worked herself up into tears in order to get H. to pet her (we recall her father when she was ill). 'He's like a lamb led to the slaughter. It is unscrupulous of me, but he pays no attention to me unless I act like this.'

This was interpreted as arising from her feeling that nobody loved her, so, like with her parents, she forced a semblance of love out of him which never convinced her. She now reported that he had spontaneously kissed her recently. *This was commented on as conflicting with her conviction of being unloved as proved to her by H.'s blushing, and so she now had to reject him, to punish him for being a sexual being, and in so doing she punished herself for the same reason—the unloved one was the bad sexual being.* This interpretation produced her hysterical laugh.

End August–September: On holiday with many bathing beauties about, H. did not blush, but had furious tempers, for which he apologized each time. He was also very amorous, but W. denied any enjoyment —and she was now the one to refuse. The tables had turned. She had made him promise that he should 'behave himself', and he had broken it. Slowly, by transference, idealizing her therapist as being so elegant and lady-like and herself a vulgar, blousy barmaid, it became possible to see her guilt at having a sexual nature. It was H., she said, who had brought the fish-wife out in her. She had to bathe very often because she felt unclean—wasn't she becoming like her mother—too fastidious?

It was commented that the lady and the dirty fish-wife seemed unable to acknowledge each other (but the split between libidinal and anti-libidinal egos seemed less marked). It was found that her daughter had begun sex life with her boy friend. W. produced a rather sham indignation (which covered envy by identification). But she also slapped H.'s face when he came in 15 minutes later than he had said— 'no doubt he had snatched a few minutes with some girl'.

This was interpreted as attributing to him her own sexual excitement stirred up over her daughter—she needed to prove him unfaithful to get rid of her own urges. 'My parents would have killed me if I had acted like the daughter . . . that's why I married an experienced man so young, or I could not have held out' was her reply amidst paroxysms of laughter. Her father had not wanted the marriage . . . 'Think of all the dirty women he must have had' he told her. *This was linked to her own 'dirty fish-wife' fantasies, and produced more shrill laughter.*

Mid-October–November: Now followed a break due to hospitalization for a minor leg operation. A month later W. reported a very loving, concerned H. 'who can't get her back quick enough'. She had to be careful not to take advantage—'Now he is defenceless, I am scared to hurt him. I want him to feel his manhood, but it is so easy to reduce him to pulp.' It also emerged how shy these partners remained about frank sex discussion, and how she always giggled like a schoolgirl—as if learning the 'facts of life'. She had now been able to discuss her daughter's affair with her mother, and shocked both her and herself by admitting that she, too, had felt like this as a teen-ager. Some of this 'improvement' had been motivated by a need to impress their respective therapists, and a reverse occurred in which she had again displayed envy of H.'s success in work, which had made him blush, and so raised her ire. Both partners were sending messages to have the other's kinks straightened, acting on a cross-transference. This turned out to be due to coitus with H. the night before.

A full interpretation was given of W.'s oedipal guilt; she had equated H. with her father and her mother was the perennial other woman. She asked if that was why she had felt so guilty sleeping with H. in the parents' house—it was father who made her feel most guilty. *The therapist said it was in this situation she felt the unfaithful one to her father as well as the betrayer of her mother. She wanted to be an innocent child, before sexual thoughts had spoiled the parental harmony: that's why her recent idyll with H. had been so blissful—sex had been kept out of it. As soon as they had it—trouble started.* W. agreed thoughtfully. This phase enabled W. to face her quite powerful ambivalent mother-tie, with deep resentment at being at the old lady's beck and call. She seemed relieved that she had seen through the hollow, duty-ridden relationship. She now expressed a determination to take H.'s affection for her daughter away. He was now talking a lot of sex to her—(this last projection was still active) for immediately she had spoken of this she expressed her conviction she could make any man unfaithful. 'I want to find one who can resist me!' *The therapist remarked: 'So H. has to be immune from all charms—including yours!'* W. was taken aback, and then recalled that she had often tested him deliberately by seductive clothes, and had been glad he had shown no effect. She had always thought people were taken in by appearances —she only wanted to be loved for herself, not like her mother who had captivated everyone by her beauty—even father, who knew there was 'nothing underneath'. *This was linked by the therapist to her envy first of mother and now of her pretty daughter, whom H. is supposed to be unable to resist.*

W. now developed a crop of 'angry boils' as well as depression—with H. concerned and helpful. She felt helpless and unable to cope with her household chores, unlike her mother with her 'wonderful home'. She talked of 'anger coming to a head' and 'bad blood' between her and her mother, as well as relishing H.'s concern over her boils and his growing insight. But the kinder he is the less she is able to feel sexual towards him, which is *interpreted as being part of her father-taboo.* 'He sees things my way, and he's stopped blushing', 'because he says I've altered a lot—but I haven't—he has, he's much simpler'.

December and January: She cannot accept her daughter's sexuality—'it's as if I was watching father and mother . . . mother has always been sexless to me.' (More relevantly still) W. could now face recalling her satisfaction and thrill when, after her father had lost his temper and had then become contrite, she watched mother order him about. She could, with shame, re-experience this wish to degrade and despise: 'it was worse to be the sadist than the victim'. She could really only love her H. when he was tough. W. was working through her improved closeness to her father, and could tolerate her mother's jealousy and anger at W. cold-shouldering her. She now dealt with H.'s food refusal by putting his meal into the fire. He reacted by praising her—she was learning his language! Always he had wanted his mother to stand up to father, 'that's why I chose a girl who would stand up to me'. H. has eaten his meals since, and vouchsafed her a summary of what he had learnt: From the start of their marriage he had felt inferior for not providing the material comforts he felt she expected. So he hoped that by removing himself for a time he would make W. want him, and it worked—'when he hurt she noticed him'. And the blushing made her really concentrate all her emotions on him. Because she had taunted him with being impotent and he didn't want to be unfaithful, he blushed instead. What he could not yet say was why he always needed to be approved and justified in her eyes. H. felt she did not give him the love he needed, though he knew she had it in her because she gave it to their son. W. said 'I was so wrapped up in my own needs and couldn't see this—but he made it difficult too.'

W. now had another dream: 'H. is taken to an asylum for sex lunatics. The keepers asked "Did you not see signs of it before?" and I replied I did, but no one else did. My girl cousin (one of the first blush targets) was there "inside" too.' *When this was interpreted as part of her rejection of the sexual self, and how H. and W. behave like lunatics pushing each other away for not loving each other the way each wants,* W. at once associated with playing the heavy mother rôle with her daughter. 'It's abhorrent to have the same feelings as the girl at *my* age—she needs me to be old—I want to damp her down.' *The obvious interpretation of identification with the anti-libidinal mother was made,* and W. agreed she was trying to be like mother.

February, March and April: Still she held out—her eyes fixed on H.'s blushings or childishness, but now very restless at night, wakes choking, fighting H.—'just like father says mother does every night cursing him in her sleep'. W. calls out in her sleep 'Horrible liar'. *To this the therapist comments that W. is the liar, denying her sexuality and moralizing, while H. has always to confess his badness, which is just what she puts on him. Yet she complains that H. will not make love.*

There had been more mutual explanations of why they had been so horrible to each other, and W. has developed an awareness of her resistance to change, trying to keep H. as an ogre, avoiding him, and linking it to the model of the parental marriage. He could now tell her of the terrible effect of his parents' death, and of having made W. a mother-substitute. W. now came to terms with her secret homosexual wishes when her mother would fuss over her in illness, and brought evidence of her identification with 'tough guys' from Westerns, and the respect she had for people who fight. The marital quarrels are now short-lived, intense, and it is clear W. prefers them to peace; holding back anger gives her a headache. At this stage her little son developed enuresis, and arrangements for his therapy were made.

May: H.'s attachment to her as a 'little dream girl' emerged: when she was still married to the first man, and the daughter was only 4, H. had said if he could not marry W. he'd wait for her little replica. (This was indeed the source of *both* partners' complicated feelings towards the child—he saw in her his teen-age sweetheart, she her own sexual self in relation to her anti-sexual mother-identification.) She could now work through a great deal of her envy of the trim young girl's figure, with herself as a passée 'old frump', not daring to strip before H., whose wish to 'see' she had thereby encouraged. Her one enjoyable job had been that of mannequin—very shame-laden though she was.

June and July: The marital understanding was getting much better, and H.'s blushing now occurred when W. asked him to explain things for her new job (as if she was still ordering him, or else he did not dare to be her superior). Both realized the wish for power over the other, and their shame and guilt when each fell from their high standards

99

before the other. 'Both wanted to be good and right—so the other had to be wrong.'

September, October, November and December: There were great ups and downs still, but no longer rigidity, and the partners themselves were mooting ending treatment by the end of the year, while also very afraid to lose their frank dependence on their therapists, and for W. this was also *interpreted as a danger that by herself she could ruin her now 'emptied out' H., while relapsing, out of spite, at having been abandoned by her mother-figure.* W. was now very loving and clinging towards H. who still had much doubt and ambivalence, and *it was put to her she was now treating him as a mother-figure in prospect of losing her therapist.*

A crisis blew up over the daughter being abandoned by her un-suitable boy-friend. W. had felt unable to help because of her own described involvement—the girl had run to W.'s parents. Here a most revealing talk occurred: W.'s parents said the girl would never give W. the trouble she herself had given them. Her father added 'Let's call a spade a spade; admit this kid (meaning W.) didn't have much of a life with us!' The mother tried to find excuses, and W. tried to console her. The father kissed her on leaving; but the mother did not.

The marital scene now improved very much. 'H. no longer *tried* to be helpful—he *was* helpful', and he could freely discuss his attitude to office women, including those who attracted him, sure that he loved her, and that affairs outside were crazy. Everybody had been frank, and admitted error—'You can love people then'. People were now commenting on their obvious happiness: W. had to say to H. 'The question is can we stand being happy', and he had agreed. She still had conflict about letting herself go sexually (shades of her mother's and grandmother's hate of sex and men), though verbal and physical expressions of affection were free. The children were re-ported to have benefited especially the little son, now much livelier and independent. Much of the therapy was now concerned with ending it, with W.'s ambivalence towards the therapist uppermost.

H.'s finding: April

Discoveries in H.'s treatment were slower and more subtle. An important starting point was H.'s pessimism. The incident of his first blushing was given a poignant addition: When he blushed at the grand-mother lifting her skirts up at the family party, W. had brashly drawn the roomful's attention to his reddening as if in ridicule, and he had blushed deeply ever since when conscious of his wife's observation.

* Abstracted from notes by H. P. Hildebrand, Ph.D., who treated H.

His therapist risked *an early interpretation: That the blushing was equivalent to an erection which he had in this way in front of his wife. He thus did sardonically what his wife imagined him to be doing, so that he managed to do what she did not want, hence he could be both safe and defiant.* This long shot bowled H. over: 'Christ! she has been right all these years! How am I going to face her?' By the next interview he had queried the interpretation, but gave his version of the choice between the job and W. If he had not pretended he did not care about her he could not (like Sir Philip Sidney) have won his economic spurs. So their full coming together was delayed, and even when he came back W. was jealous of his concentration on mastering his new job. *From the expressions used the therapist was able to interpret that he had deflected his sexual energies into his job,* and H. accepted it. After only two meetings he reported ability to take W. out to lunch and a less vicious feeling about her 'trying to get into him', which only drove him into himself.

May: He now transferred his negative feelings to W.'s female therapist 'who was in league with W. in accusing him of sexual wishes towards his stepdaughter'. He displayed quite paranoid feelings at this point. H. also talked of his jealousy of W.'s flirtatiousness and power to attract all manner of men. *It was interpreted that W. represented a narcissistic kind of self-extension, and that he felt very attacked by any man she talked to.* (This projective identification did not emerge at joint interviews.) By next time all the jealousy and devouring destructiveness was back in W., and he expressed sympathy with husbands goaded beyond endurance who killed their wives. This fantasy made H. very anxious indeed. He associated with childhood memories of his very angry father who lost control, an unhappy mother, and himself, a terrified witness. W. he said, also had such parents with a father who would smash plates of food in a rage. *The interpretation of this as linked to fear of what his angry wife might do, and to his blushing as a covert defiance of her castrating him,* made its mark. He next reported W. telling him all the trouble was in him—he was like her mother, preventing her realizing herself. But H. accepted that his insistence on spotless housekeeping had just this effect on her. In transference he showed his awkwardness in expressing feelings and attributed a 'strong affinity' for his therapist to his wife! (We have seen that she had a strong incognito positive transference to Dr. Hildebrand, in contrast to H.'s negative one to Mrs. Williams. The partners did not meet the other's therapist until follow-up a year later).

June and July: Inhibition of loving feelings now featured in his fuller sexual history. It was W. who, when his parents were killed in the air-raid, came to him at once and wanted him to sleep with her.

High-mindedly he declined because (she being married) it would not be right. He felt shocked by W.'s attitude. Nonetheless it was she who always made him feel in the wrong, so that he could not even give reasonable explanations of his being kept late at work to her, but let her punish him and make him feel shifty and deceitful.

September: Their summer holiday was described as successful, with W. very loving, together in a tent, and no jealousy about the 'luscious popsies' on the beach. It had all evaporated on return home, and he had been shouting at W. before she had time to do her nagging. *It was interpreted that this was what he saw 'married life' to be like, by the model of both his and W.'s parents, where the fathers shouted.* H. accepted this. He now had a bad patch of aggressive jealousy from W. over being late home, always accused of lying and going with prostitutes. She knew by 'phoning when he left the office; she met him with physical attacks. *It was put to him that he mistook the ostensible reasons for her onslaughts, when the real appeal to him was not to neglect her. Sex could only be good if they were out of their 'marital' roles: when they were at home the parental pattern, i.e. sex as a terrible battle, took possession.* 'But it was father who was the angry one—W. is just like my father! God! what does that make us now?' H. exclaimed in reply. *It was put to him that each time she showed aggression his own affectionate feelings had to be broken, he had to withdraw to protect both of them from his anger.* H. came back much happier. It was the moment when he and W. had to deal firmly with his stepdaughter's love affair, and he was surprised at the sense of closeness and unity with W. over this. It raised the problem of sexual guilt and of jealousy of the younger generation (H. and W. having been school-sweethearts), and *the therapist was able to show H. how, in transference, H. seized on the ambiguities of words employed by the therapist, just as he dealt with W. accusations—ignoring the communication behind the words.* This struck H. very forcibly: 'I've never seen this before' (i.e. the way in which he used verbal pedantry to defeat meaning and impact of words on himself, and to confound the attacker).

October: During W.'s hospitalization H. discovered his abject misery when she was not about, hence that when she was about the tension between them was part of the aliveness of their marriage. It went when they could share an external worry. He now felt more home- than work-centred, in fact had had a peaceful time with W., but a big 'rocket' at work. He laughed a lot in agreeing with *the comment that he always had to have a rocket from somebody!* Strangely, this topic led to H.'s expressing a recurrent dream and ability to ventilate his reaction to his family's death: 'not grief, but as if concrete had set inside him'.

As if in further explanation, H. described how, after a smooth week of home life, W.'s reiterated requests to take a job had made him say 'at least I shan't have to take you shopping or do any of those stupid things with you'—so different from his willing outing with her the previous week. 'She was very upset'—it was a bombshell to stop the constant questioning like 'Do you love me?' After two days, and an absence from London, they were good friends, with much better sexual relations. H. denied that *he objected to W. going out to work for fear of her flirtatiousness.*

November: The next topic was H.'s insight that he always went sour when W. enjoyed herself, e.g. over a new radiogram, which made her friendly. *It was interpreted to him that in sex the roles were reversed: he enjoyed himself, she was left sour.* H. blamed it on W.'s rejection of all contraceptives, hence a constant anxiety over pregnancy, and practice of coitus interruptus. W.'s fear of ageing, of pregnancy spoiling her figure, and of H.'s presumed sexual attraction to her daughter were much in H.'s mind; the last he repudiated with contempt.

We now reached the period when W. had been 'erupting'—but into boils. H. was able to admit his depression because she was ill. He also had a novel experience: at a party W. had accused him of looking at girls' legs—but she had later apologized, saying she was drunk. Her illness felt 'as if some part of me is ill'. He repudiated a *comment of W. being a narcissistic image of himself.* He could, together with his concern, also criticize her for being 'a bit stupid, a bit in the way, too demanding, always wanting to be the centre'. *He was given the interpretation that when W. made demands he did not reply, but chewed her up inside himself: this was all right so long as she was aggressive in return (for it showed she was alive and kicking, as it were)— but now she had stopped and developed boils, he felt he had really damaged her.* At this comment H. flushed and displayed real depression instead of a somewhat jocular defence which he had mostly used through the 5 months of interviews. He accepted how guilty he felt: 'She is everything to me, but she is like a block of concrete (note the repeated allusion to frozen emotion) on my back—she blocks everything I want to achieve', etc.

December: Within the week, still depressed and at a loss, H. could admit it was his own unbalanced stress on work and almost complete absence of time for love that had made him miss so many opportunites of making a happy marriage. It made him cold to think this (i.e. to undo the projection on to W.). He had chosen economic success instead of her dream. *The interpretation of his guilt and terror that he had damaged her was repeated,* and H. now spoke of how strange it felt to have for the first time tender feelings for W., wanting to love and cherish without having to fight her. H. and W. (who, at this point, could free herself from the compulsion to please her mother) together resisted a tiresome and expensive Christmas ritual hitherto imposed annually by W.'s mother. He felt that something was really changing in both of them. Not only did he support her show-down with her mother, but he could see her as more feminine, and became sexually 'enthusiastic' about her. They had never before chosen the little son's presents together, or made their own pattern of festivity, quite triumphant at having broken the long domination of W.'s mother. Such anger as he had shown was over W.'s continuing neglect of contraception, with one of her periodic pregnancy scares (not genuine, H.V.D.).

January: H. now volunteered more childhood history. He enjoyed the peace of his grandparents' farm, in contrast to his conflict-torn home. Much concern for his submissive mother, a wish that she'd been able to stand up to his angry, immodest, bossy father. Father had made H. embarrassed when he came into school, showing off. *It was pointed out how like his father W. seemed to him,* and H. was able to find a large number of such similarities in those two peoples' effect on him. From this theme derived an anecdote of a scene when H. took W. to a cinema. Argument arose as follows: H. 'Do you want ice-cream?' W. 'No thank you.' H. 'That means you want one' and starts to get one for her. W. 'They don't have the kind I like.' H. 'What kind *do* you like?'—whereupon he gets one of the right kind which is available, and comes back 'Here you are, get on with that!' to her, in the tone used to a spoilt, annoying child (reproduced in his tale). H. ate his ice quickly because he did not like spending time eating; but W. kept leaning over and pressing him to try a bit of her favourite flavour. 'It drove me up the wall!' He agreed *that they had both been angry with each other, and had dealt with it by over-concern with the other, but in such a way that each had to 'baby' and so belittle the other.* Yes, H. said, he had felt she was a little girl and yet how he hated it when she tried to baby him. (Now we also had the interpretation of his food refusals.) 'Nothing worse than her shoving food at me, and all the time one has to praise her wonderful cooking—she *is* a good cook, but to have to eat because of it loses your appetite—so you say "Take it away".' H. was delighted by the occasion recorded in her notes above, when W. threw his meal into the boiler. 'I felt much better for it.' (Mother had stood up to father, and H. had not been enveloped with maternal solicitude!) But while thus expressing his fear of W.'s smothering, he found how much he resented her never admiring his work though she praised it to her parents. 'If only she did—it would open the flood-gates; I would not be able to stop talking to her.' It followed that he became aware of his guilt at being impatient and inattentive to W.'s problems and interests. This led to a discussion of their mutual search of recognition for their individualities. W.'s family was prosperity oriented. H.'s standards were for achievement. But here came a profound cleavage. His father would also rush to 'promote' any initiatives the son showed, e.g. to buy the best musical instrument for him, and then force him to perform before visitors. H.'s anger was then the same as when W. pushed him to play at parties. 'I want to do things individually, not because they force me to.' (We had heard of this element in our joint interviews.)

February: The next major theme was H.'s regret that W. could not let herself go sexually. He resisted *the therapist's comment that he was, deep down, afraid of what would happen if W. really had a climax.* She had said, when at last agreeing to a contraceptive diaphragm, 'Now I can be like you—go off with anyone I please!' Though H. had laughed, he was apprehensive about sex getting out of control, had spoken of 'the sex machine' being at work between them. (Our prediction of trouble as the result of her acquiring the contraceptive proved correct.) W. had been a furious demon all that week-end. (Note: The inference made by our team was that W. had become terrified of her sexuality and temptation to promiscuity; also now she knew H. could have safe coitus with her at any time he would think of her as nothing but a sexual 'object'.)

Such was their unconscious projective bond that he would feel this projection and it thereby became his fantasy for which she would furiously attack him. This was *not* interpreted to H.

Though W. had not made so much of this incident (except to report to her therapist 'she had been misbehaving' by going to be fitted for the diaphragm), she reported H. as saying to her: 'You need not think you can blackmail me into sex just because of *that* thing'. W. said she hit the ceiling. 'I felt he was blackmailing me!' 'Having the cap was like offering myself to him. I'm only safe when I give no indication of wanting him.' Her rage came from rejection. Now she would be as he was —showing him she did not want him.

H.'s uneasiness at the change in themselves became manifest. *Instead, as it was summarized to him, of a comfortable continual quarrel, from which he could always withdraw and just let marriage occupy a little part of his life, he was now much closer.* 'Yes—shall I turn into one of those men she destroys? Because if you let W. have her head she really plays the merry devil with you, she has you on a string, you can do nothing.' 'Like W.'s father and all the men in her kin, who were set upon by these harpies if they showed independence.' (It will be recalled W. was aware of this fear in him.)

105

March: This was linked with the recent *suicide* of one of these hen-pecked uncles of W.'s which opened the way to H.'s working through his disgust with W. who could be loving to him in the midst of death. We saw an irreconcilable split in himself over her offer to sleep with him on the night his parents were killed, and how he had never accepted their death or mourned them. He also talked of the parents' great concern for his sick young brother of whom he was jealous, and who had driven him to become self-contained, aloof, independent. The death of the parents was their final desertion of him. The interpre-tation *that his parents were still very much alive in him and thus that he must go on being withdrawn and acting very independent as he did,* made a profound impression. Soon after he was able to listen to W. talking to him for an hour 'and to my surprise talking sense', as if she really understood what he felt. Shamefacedly he now went for early morning walks with her, feeling 'the park-keepers must think us goops'. But, instead of a nice breakfast, he upset her by rushing off on an earlier train to 'put in extra work'. H. accepted *the comment that when things became too loving he became too afraid of becoming dependent, and had to flee into isolation.*

H. now had a portentous dream: 'In a space rocket approaching a great golden globe. As it approached the globe split into halves, and the rocket went inside. Here was a sort of Horse Guards' parade ground with a cenotaph, and rows of chairs. He sat in the front row, and a woman with horn-rimmed glasses approached him and asked if he was alone, three times. Each time he replied "yes", but next she said "no, you are not—look around" and there he saw his (dead) brother sitting.' At this point H. awoke, weeping. *The interpretation given, in view of the just reported material, was that if (by the obvious sexual symbolism of the beginning) he entered into full intercourse with W. he would, inside her, find his parents, linked with the dead brother, still very alive—something he had not been able to face.*

H. confirmed the acceptance by saying 'Yes—the woman was Mrs. Williams (W.'s therapist—possibly as a substitute for Mr. Hildebrand. Both wore such spectacles. This dream seemed strongly confirmatory of our major hypothesis of H.'s reprojection of his internalized parents into his partner).

An almost magical incident happened immediately after the dream. He left early for work, and, driven by curiosity, went through White-hall, by the Cenotaph there, and fell into conversation with an elderly cleaning woman in a coffee shop. By the time he got to the office W. was already on the telephone making sure he wasn't out with another woman. (How psychodynamically true this was in terms of the material just presented she hardly knew yet—though she had been able to experience the 'old woman's' power in herself. It seemed to us the kind of deep maternal concern for having him safe, which was both very loving and very hateful to him.)

April and May: In the aftermath H. had some more dreams, concerned still with coitus, but now as being caught in a spider's web, hence also more rows—even about his being close to his little boy and, according to W. 'over-stimulating him'. We were now on to the child's enuresis, which enabled H. to confess he had been enuretic till 14. (From the context, the writer concluded that he got a good deal of none too angry attention from his father, and this linked to his desperate sense of guilt over his father's death before father and son could make explicit their mutual love.) Had he not disobeyed and joined the Army against father's will, he said, he would have been killed with him. As it was, it was left to father's cronies at the funeral to tell him how proud his father was of him. All the more terrifying was his confusion when W. made her loving overture to him . . . here he had not only to control himself from weeping out his misery, but also from compromising her, to protect her from herself. How frightening she was with her direct approach!

June: It was the second summer by now, and the therapist's holidays had focused H.'s dependence and resentment. *Interpretation of the ambivalence of this father transference* brought a criticism of 'nothing has changed'. *This was further interpreted as his need for nothing to change, so that he could be protected from W. by his father.* H. at the following meeting produced a youthful photograph of his father, pointing out his disagreeable sharp features. 'I thought I'd show you before I destroy it,' he said. (It was felt by us, however, that this was a premature symbolic re-burial.)

H. reported that all blushing had now ceased, there were no running fights, yet there was no real affectionate relation. If he approached W. lovingly, she would flare up in a matter of seconds, and vice-versa. *This was confidently interpreted as their great fear of regarding each other as sexual beings—sex was too frightening: the slightest advance towards each other was the prelude to doing 'something wrong'. So they rowed or disputed all day and night to prevent it, and could only flop exhausted.* This seemed to go home. He remarked on how things were always better away from home, and came also to see how they must not be seen to enjoy things together. If one was attractive, then the other might be too. This could never happen! W. was shy of 'being looked at' lovingly or of being glamorous, and he responded by not doing it.

July: The two progress reports at this point are almost identical. 'We are both crazy—but which is the crazier?' was their tenor. H. reported at a subsequent session that he had had his usual beating from W. who had called him a weak, spineless, jelly-fish baby who could not stand up for himself, because he had been too polite to a car-dealer. 'Why could he not get properly stuck into them?' This was the barrier between her and him, he said. He wanted to make contact, but could not—there was a barrier he could not *penetrate*. She always threw back the beginning at him. *This led to the question whether they had had intercourse during their teen-age courtship.* No, they petted, but agreed it would not be right, and were also afraid to—and then she had gone and married—she had dumped him, and he had been furious. He hinted it was he who had always said 'no' to coitus. *It was put to him that this was W.'s resentment: for 'not getting stuck into her', for not daring to penetrate the impassable barrier.* H. responded with interest, and remarked how, on holiday, she becomes more like a little girl, reaches out for comfort and gives a sign of love *like his father did.* Then coitus is easy. It really only needed a sign from her and things would be all right. W. had farther to go. *It was pointed out how embarrassed he became even when she just asked for support, as with her new job—for the first time in their marriage.* (We recall her report of his blushing when she asked for some technical guidance from him.)

August and September: Following a holiday, H. returned very pessimistic. W. had been awful. What was the point of coming? Evidently much hate was being worked through. W. made no bones about it, and H. was able to recognize that this represented her way of trying to impose her bursting sexuality on him. He, with his fear of his identification with the intrusive father, had to hold her off, intellectualize. Once again he saw the difference between them in terms of the night his parents died. She wanted to comfort him with her sexual love—he wanted to sit up all night with cigarettes and coffee, and talk it all out. This he now saw was how they frustrated each other. He could support W.'s fury and storms because he understood how jealous she was, not only of her daughter's affairs, but also of her widowed aunt, who was sleeping around to the indignation of the women of the family. H. felt relieved that the chips were down—now they could cope.

October: He mooted termination of treatment at Christmas. In the wake of this decision H. felt 'completely taken over by his father'—'He is dead but won't lie down'. 'I see him in all I do, in my ways of behaving and reacting.' W. would not mourn him! She was completely engrossed with a flashy girl friend who was having an affair: she and the friend changed clothes, etc. He must have looked daggers—the woman asked had she offended him? Mainly he was occupied for several sessions with working through his mourning for father, whose tenderness taboo he experienced as his own, hence also any love from father or W. as petrifying. He knew it was his character that prevented him from responding when W. was snuggling up to him. *It was interpreted to him that expressing tender feelings might bring tears, and he was terrified of being such a sissy—a lonely little boy.* H. described how they now had days of loving, then days of quarrelling, like a pendulum. He had shown great concern over a menstrual indisposition of hers. When she did not telephone while out late at work, he alerted the police, and was met finally by 'What's all the fuss?'—she was all right. He was now the one who telephoned to see if she was safe! Behind this lay her feminine protest at not being allowed to go to work owing to the 'woman's curse'. So she had just 'put the wind up him', as he had not wanted her to work and let the young son come home to an empty house. Meantime, the daughter's affair with the married man, tearfully ended, had made both partners determined to provide a better model for the girl. They both realized that the trouble had been their constant fights and bitterness which had driven the child to promiscuity.

November and December: There appeared to be much shared guilt, and a more mature adult responsibility. Their own life and sexual closeness was improving. 'Things could never go back to where they had been before,' he said. There was now a profound work-through of his loneliness—no family like W. had, only an old aunt who made him feel a small boy, and much guilt over his ailing brother whom he neglected (in fact he was on military service when this boy was ill). *His reparative guilt was linked to his experience of the good parents inside him, who had, after all, loved and been proud of him, but he had hardened himself against remembering this.* H. after this had a virtual abreaction, and was incoherent, exclaiming from time to time 'I can see where I went wrong' or 'it all makes sense'. *He was counselled to tell W. about it—'that's what wives are for'.*

In the final two visits he felt that his marriage was now good. He was mainly concerned not to become like his father in feather-bedding his son, and he laughed about it. As a piece of transference work-through H. showed great concern about the effect he must have had in upsetting his therapist's sanity. He avoided digging deeper into his lost parent relation direct, but showed how guilty and anxious he felt about the hidden damage to Mr. Hildebrand. *It was interpreted that this was his anxiety, and when people did not show any, he felt them to be 'too controlled', suffering inner turmoil as he had done.* He was not, up to the end, able to express his negative feeling at once again parting from a parent figure, but had clearly recovered his capacity to feel the good parents, lost so suddenly, who could accept his anxiety, guilt and need for support.

109

At the end of 18 months of therapy, the couple were invited to meet me, together with their respective therapists for a re-assessment. This they did with some eagerness, not least because curious to meet in reality the fantasy figures who had treated the other partner. This was a kind of 'passing-out parade' for them.

Follow-up: (Abstract of tape recording). Both felt they saw each other's point of view, and could hardly recall the interminable quarrels and tensions of 18 months ago. H. called it having shed an outer skin, and felt unable to raise steam for maintaining a grievance, though he had the impulse. W. said 'He's not perfect, and when we have a row I bang him over the head still—I s'pose I always shall. But these things aren't important any more—I just say to him "cheer up, have some tea", or else "you miserable old devil" and then we both laugh.' She recalls she used to be very 'black and white' (see her record) but now has some shades of grey. 'Before, I was always right—now I think perhaps he may be right.' H. says he need not do 'the cloak and dagger stuff' over seeing a gorgeous woman at a party. They also mention their son's changed attitude—his ability to speak about their relationship and being more assertive. Both were afraid of relapse, and felt torn between the wish to stand on their own feet and the need for our support, for sorting out the web of emotions pulling in all directions. H. had also found himself more relaxed at work, and was able to help his junior colleagues in *their* family troubles (all laugh). H. emphasized his great fear of damage or chaos in the home, which made him almost a phobic when he was out with W., who would not worry about what the children (including the naughty teen-ager) might perpetrate. The couple realized that H. remains the anxious, introvert home-bird who longs for security, while W. wants the bright lights, jealous of his introverted interests. Their slanging matches are brief and controllable, often ending in mirth. W. is able to express her continuing wish for a passionate lover, whereas she only gets breakfast in bed! He objects to hordes of friends who throng the house because W. is so friendly. To the writer, who had not seen the couple for 18 months, the change in the direction of flexible mutual acceptance, tolerance of ambivalence and of shortcomings, and the increase in frank expression of loving kindness seemed very impressive.

3 years later: Each partner seen by their respective therapists. A pregnancy scare had thrown both W. and H. into anxiety with some regression to great demandingness on her part, and consequent withdrawal on his part. However, when this was found to be an unnecessary alarm, W. recovered quickly. H. took longer, having looked forward to another child by her. He said he had been very divided, over wanting a child and protecting her from it. When it was thought

110

she was pregnant he reported that he had blushed furiously—because he still felt sexually guilty over having her as 'his beautiful blonde'. They did not return for further counselling, and the record ends here.

Discussion of findings

Here was a marriage fairly typical of the stable 'cat and dog' variety. It fell short of the worst cases of near-psychotic flavour, which are hard to budge. It was out of the experience of such inter-actions that we fashioned our more inclusive conceptual framework. The analytically experienced reader will probably find even the greatly abridged evidence of what went on during some 60 treatment sessions over 18 months, self-explanatory. I might have cited other similar cases, but I chose this one because the level of 'unconscious trans-actions' stood out clearly against the minimal contributions made by culture distance, economic or social contrasts. Their backgrounds were almost identical—down to the shared co-ed school. The contrasts in family cultures are recorded. Their distress had always been contained within their intimate relationship. I have reported the case primarily to illustrate on what sort of data the interpretations are made and the generalizations derived. For reasons of space, however, *Case Ten* must also be an illustration of our methods for Chapters X and XI.

Owing to the form of therapy then in use (of which more in the relevant chapter), there were separate accounts of each partner's progress. The therapists collaborated in frequent conferences, joined by other members of our unit. Separate accounts may help the reader unaccustomed to the focus on dyadic interaction. The data, including the therapists' contributions, nonetheless, illustrate how such concepts as fluidity of ego-boundaries, unconscious collusion and the to-and-fro of mutual projective identifications appear clinically. The report also shows how these related to the parent figures of each partner. As an exercise in constructing a dyadic model, I propose to discuss the case records in so far as they illumine these inner worlds in dynamic inter-relation.

(a) *Husband's Object Relations:* There was much to show that, initially, W. was for him an exciting libidinal figure, who fitted his pronounced voyeur tendencies. But he also never ceased to idealize her, and hence to react dynamically against this forbidden 'trollop' side of her attraction. We had evidence of this from his resistance to pre-marital sexual consummation, from his later concern to 'protect' her from being thought a flirt, from wearing risqué dresses, and finally, from his dread of her sexuality as akin to his own. This was, therefore, also a repudiation of his own excitement over her seduc-

111

tiveness. The libidinal object and the libidinal ego are suppressed or denied together.

At another level H. had expectations that W. would be a loving, all-forgiving woman like his mother, 'who was always there waiting', no matter how aggressively one treated her. This was a tabooed, idealized, guilt-arousing figure, not quite anti-libidinal, but vulnerable, damaged. This rôle-model was operating when W., after the parental death in the air-raid, tried to express her all-giving love and commitment to him in a sexual way, and he felt shocked. He wanted only motherly consolation. It became clear later that W. also carried some projections of H.'s father-figure. At first *he* was the man who would play his marital rôle like father. But at the same time he was impatient with being managed, promoted, praised and shown off. To the split in feminine object perception was added a split in the father-relation. The good, providing, protecting father he could be himself, but the dominant, identity-crushing, angry father was largely felt to be in W. It took some time for H. to realize that he wanted to 'chew her up' in fantasy, and even longer to take this bad father back into himself, and so allow his childhood father to die. After this he began to see why he was so devious, withdrawing rather than behaving as he had seen his angry father behave. This anger was in his fantasy all the more destructive because he also attributed to W. the vulnerable qualities of his mother, and wanted her to be stronger to make it safe to quarrel. But he was also thinking of her as a rejecting, anti-libidinal figure, identified with *her* mother, who pushed her husband away, kicked him, and denied him sex. So W. carried two mother-valencies as well: a suffering, gentle one and a strong castrating one. Lastly, at a still deeper level, W. was a need-object, an undifferentiated powerful parent figure, who would cherish him, but who also threatened him with devouring, with crushing his identity. This ambivalent feeling expressed itself as a refusal of W.'s meals, not only because she expected him to eat up and praise her, but because of his general taboo on tenderness and 'being babied'. That he had such an inner object inside himself was shown by his tender solicitude if W. or the children were ill. But it was a question of *them* having to be in a position of weakness and need. He must not show such infantile dependence. Yet this is just what he ultimately could admit he wanted most from her: praise and affirmation of his good self.

(b) *Wife's Object Relations:* W. had a markedly higher factor of conformity to class and cultural expectations. At this level she believed in married people living in peace, being always together, the wife sharing the man's business worries; having sex regularly, but not expecting enjoyment, sharing certain social conjugal rôles (care of children, friends, money troubles, etc.). Of her partner she expected an ideal father's rôle-playing. 'When he didn't behave like Mum and Dad I was shattered,' she said. This was clearly an idealized parental model based on a need since we learnt that her real parents behaved very like H. and W.! In so far as H. was the 'rock', reliable and 'always there', during her disintegrating marriage to a guilt-arousing playboy (i.e. an exciting libidinal object), he received, temporarily, the idealized object's transference. A large component of this was her need to matter as a person, to come first. In this respect the only-child dependence and tendency to tantrums and making a fuss as her only means of drawing the self-absorbed parents' attention and dividing them was very marked. Oral giving and generosity were the obverse of this, but her greed and devouringness of her object were very prominent. She was at one level a jealous, greedy demanding little girl. In the hopeless quest for a safe libidinal object, she wavered between father and mother, and finally internalized her mother, feeling rejected by the coveted father. Having introjected her, the mother also becomes the model of how to treat the father-figure. This involves a repudiation of the libidinal male, with the mother and 'queen-bee' grandmother enthroned as a forbidding inner 'monstrous regiment of women', to quote John Knox. This made for a curiously accurate repetition-compulsion of this pattern in her relation to H., who should have been the loving, sexual father. Instead, he became the scapegoat for her own forbidden sexuality, and the bad parent-figure, enabling her to keep her actual mother as a good object. She could recognize in treatment the sadistic pleasure of paying him out for the projected fantasied constant sexual urges, which were also her own, and for the envied parental closeness from which she felt excluded, but imagined him to have with 'other' women. She thus unconsciously re-enacted her unresolved parental triangle-situation in her marriage, that wonderful, ideal union which was to put everything right. It must be remembered that her parents were 'wrapped up in each other' in an 'égoisme à deux'. Her model was thus reality based. Not only her husband, but even her adolescent daughter became the substituted targets for her jealousy and envy of the parents' sexual love. She was for a long time identified with her inner anti-libidinal object—her mother who would not tolerate her sexual rivalry with herself.

(c) *The Collusive System in the Dyad:* Adult aims and areas of realistic co-operation apart, we could divide the marital interaction into two fields: the area of *shared* internal images, which were projected and re-projected; and, secondly, the area of *polarizations*

113

where one represented the other's lacking potentials and functions.

Dealing first with the shared elements—both partners felt themselves, at one level, to be little, needy, deprived children who 'only' wanted complete and automatic gratification by the other of even unverbalized wishes as they arose. Instead of stating and discussing these, they just felt the needs of the moment (e.g. sex, or comforting, or even response to a certain mood) from each other, and could only react with inner frustration rage and rejection when the partner did not respond to the desired cue in the appropriate way. Through the treatment reports we could see how closely they colluded to a ludicrous degree of dovetailing in the rejection of their sexual needs. They shared a highly congruent perception of an inner anti-libidinal authority. This alternated to and fro from one acting the other's anti-libidinal figure enforcing a taboo on tenderness. With growing insight they could see it as part of their own make-ups. While we may also call this to-and-fro a polarization, these changes were fleeting and temporary. The common background was provided by the *shared model* of the *marriage as a quarrel*, in which love seemed to be rejected. The most important cue-response which did not fit was, first, the unconscious identification of H. with a dominant father to whom should have corresponded a submissive, placid mother. Secondly, there was a major identification of W. with a dominant matriarch, vis-à-vis whom H. could not quite suppress his own wish for power, though consciously he rejected being an angry bully like his father. Both hated these bad parent figures, and each tried to devolve the primacy of rejection, aggression, and sexual thwarting on the other.

Perhaps the most intriguing collusion in this dyad was the great emphasis on H.'s blushing. They were intuitively right in wanting to understand and cure it, for it was one of those richly over-determined, condensed symptoms that was the neurotic focus of the whole complex transaction between the partners. H. blushed not because he was sexually interested in any given women. This was only W.'s initial need for a conventional rationalization. He blushed because he 'felt-she-felt-he-felt' her own ambivalence towards sexual fantasies, and that he was really furious with himself for letting her have such access to his secret life. To have such almost extra-sensory communication and vulnerability to each other's secret fantasy systems made them very insecure about each other's identities. When defences can be so breached without a word spoken—who, then, is captain of his or her own soul? This shared symptom was, to me, a confirmation of 'blurred ego boundaries' and a dyadic joint 'personality'. The couple expressed this in the messages to their therapists asking which was crazier. Who was the baby, who the sexual culprit? Which is my own, and which the partner's sense of guilt, opinion, decision? So long as H. blushed, W. could have the whip hand in pinning the forbidden fantasies on him. Yet they were as much hers as his. As she was able to accept ownership of her own exhibitionistic sexual needs, so his blushing receded. He then no longer had to carry a double load. We can now understand how much W. needed H. to be a *real* sexual culprit. If he were such, she would not only have had the relief of feeling that it was he, not herself, who was bad. It would also entitle her to have her own sexual impulses. Before both could accept their own 'bad', sexual and angry selves, their intensely desired love life could only use 'surface water' above the ice-crust (to recall my *tundra* image), which sufficed to maintain the formal aspects of their marriage. No wonder that both, in varying degrees, shared the fear of destruction of their separate identities. When there is so much shared projection of menacing, persecuting and scrutinizing anti-libidinal objects, then to admit one's fantasies, i.e. that the partner is really right in feeling what lies under the defensive postures, is total victory of one over the other. Yet here, also, the deeper trends were strikingly congruent. He had a voyeur streak, and had to sketch lush nudes in defiance of W. She was just such a 'lush nude', seductive, the mannequin-exhibitionist. She had to cover this up, and play the faded mother; he had to cover up that it was *she* all the time—in *both* their minds. Similarly with the shared dread of the passive, yielding woman. He did not *want* to destroy his wife, as his father had seemed to: she must be the strong, terrifying mother, who effectively fought back, and this reassured H., just as it reassured her that she would not be destroyed by her bad oedipal sexuality. Coming now to the other phenomenon, which I called *polarization* into opposites, we note first the fairly normal sex rôle-differentiation: W. expressive, highly affective; a family-integrative, hospitable, mothering woman welcoming friends, admirers, Christmas festivities and merry-making—certainly the emotional heart of the dyad. H. was high on drive for achievement and instrumental efficiency, cerebral and organizing, keen to build a good home, protective to the weak, but impatient of frivolous relaxation and women's small-talk; rather exacting and disciplinarian. Beyond this was his strong taboo on expressiveness and his need that W. should always be the 'silly little girl', whose opinions are not worth listening to, the carrier of the 'sloppy' romantic babyish qualities, and also of anarchic untidiness of the child that must be sternly reproved. Even here she had a precedent in her mother's house-pride. In his case the delegation to her of finance and many other 'masculine' functions was less a passive resignation than their delegation to the 'No. 2', to free the instrumental head of the family for more important career issues zealously

115

protected as his own. But underneath this we found, the unconscious dread of submission to this powerful, terrifying female. It will be recalled how H. exclaimed 'W. had more power than he—she need only control her tongue, he would have to control his mind'. He felt she was omnipotent, and could 'twist any man round her little finger'.

Chapter VII

PRESENT CONCEPTS

EVALUATION OF CONFLICT

A case such as has just been reported changes one's perceptions of what marital conflict is—indeed of marriage itself. At this depth of contact changing and superimposed inner object relations and corresponding ego attitudes are revealed which go beyond the scope of my earlier hypotheses. These only stated that when the idealized expectations, each of the other, break down, the partner becomes the bearer of attributes of the unconscious object-world against which idealization, and indeed the marriage, was to be the remedy.

The generalizations of our pilot phase, though valid as far as they went, were really only the starting point when confronted with such marriages as in *Case Ten*. This case displayed the sequelae of a failed idealizing process. It filled in the meaning of what, in superficial evaluation, is often called 'incompatibility'. This evaluation would have called them both 'neurotic' and 'immature', just as a boy and girl romance which they were stupid and blind enough to resume and cling to. Yes—but they also had a profound intuition that they needed and could rely deeply on each other—just as *Case One* needed one another to work through nearly all that they felt most deeply about. *Cases Six* and *Seven*, with their successful and untreatable idealizations and exclusion of deeper needs in a cosy mutual denial surely were more 'compatible'! Which of these was a 'truer' or more profound relationship—'for better or for worse'? In Chapter III, I attempted to draw a theoretical model for a complete marriage. This would permit a full and undisturbed flow of two-way communication between the conscious and unconscious parts of two people, in flexible rôle changes, with each partner able to identify with and tolerate the regressive or infantile needs of the other when occasion demanded. The nearer to this model a relationship was, the more powerful and perpetually exciting and satisfying the bonds would be. The further from it, the more would a couple need to rely on defensive exclusions of 'inflammable' material to achieve a placid, superficially

117

amiable and harmonious relation at conscious level. *Case Ten*, and similar cases could almost qualify to be called such a complete marriage! Were they not able to contain their most infantile aggressive longings within an outwardly well-run marriage? Were they not alternatingly and flexibly good father, bad father, good mother, and bad mother to each other? Were they not able to act as each other's bad conscience and sexual scapegoats, until they could hardly tell whose blush the husband was displaying?

The clarification of the difference between the dynamics of such a close but painful relationship as *Case Ten* and a 'happy marriage' is worth pursuing. The follow-up of the case helps to make the comparison. When the partners could re-internalize the parts of themselves that they had projected to their spouse, they could report a very much happier marriage than in their original statements. Perhaps I need only say that after treatment *they no longer had to use projective identifications*. They could *own* more of their previously split-off, guilt-laden libidinal and anti-libidinal egos. They had more personal autonomy and identity. This may be the chief distinction; *the 'happy' marriage can make use* of the same passionate, highly charged, loving feelings which a couple like *Case Ten* certainly shares with such a marriage but cannot admit. The *Case Tens'* pre-treatment relationship had to deny the power and validity of such feelings in themselves and in each other, and thus *exclude them* from integrated expression in their marriage. The exact patterning of the various inner bad, rejecting objects which peoples the stage of any particular marriage (and the Tens had a veritable Pantheon inside them!), is not so important theoretically as the fact of the presence and living force of such introjects from both husband's and wife's early development. These dominate the rôle behaviour, largely unseen. The dyadic configuration in *Case Ten* had all but stabilized as a pact to crush libido by aggression, to persecute and punish the despondent demanding child; to deny that each really needed the other as a good object. They could have each other, as deeply they wanted to, provided they jointly deceived the shared anti-libidinal rejecting inner objects (based on their closely similar experience of parental marriages) that they did not really badly need their primary good objects, and that they ran their own relationship in obedience *and* defiance of their fantasied models. The use of scapegoating, projection and re-presentation by the opposite constituted the repertoire of mechanisms by which this shared, skilfully collusive strategy could be kept going. The case is a good illustration of the importance of grasping the meaning of unconscious communications as the essential part of marital therapy worthy of the name.

But if there is this vital distinction, there is also a great similarity between such 'all-in-all' cat-and-dog marriages and the 'happy' deep union, which we do not see clinically, but know of, and regard as the theoretical model of the complete marriage. This would seem to lie in the capacity of the partners to express and live out in their relationship, many phases and object-relations potentials from the past. In the 'happy' marriage, unfolding into an ever richer and more satisfying secure mutual affirmation, one presumes the dyad's inner 'contents' to be of predominantly good objects or part-objects. In the problem marriage, such as *Case Ten*, the same sense of belonging gives licence to share and inflict on the partner the highly ambivalent infantile object relations which need such expressions. All this individual and shared repertoire was acted out on each other, within the boundary of a viable home, a good social façade. They stayed together because they met the requirements of my definition of marriage: they satisfied many emotional needs, while also conforming to the social mores. Even untreated, they would have been entitled to this description. Many chronically fighting couples stay together, and defy attempts to tame them or part them, because of similar belongingness and dovetailing needs. At the level of social value judgments, I would have no hesitation in rating the marriage of *Case Ten* as more living, deeper and 'truer' than the conventional whited sepulchres, in which no sleeping dog is permitted to raise his head, let alone bark.

Geoffrey Thompson[1] introducing the book in which the Family Discussion Bureau offer their contribution to this topic, writes:

> To an outside observer different marriages appear to vary widely in their degree of satisfactoriness and stability, but the more insight we obtain into the complexities of the relationship, the more we realize that the difference between "satisfactory" and "unsatisfactory" marriages is not a fundamental difference in kind . . . The same basic forces are involved in all marriages, what distinguishes one from another being the balance of the different factors . . ., their relative intensity, and the characteristic ways in which they play into one another . . .

On page 43 of the just cited book, there occurs a comment on the case of 'Mr. and Mrs. Clarke' of widest applicability to the nature of marital tensions:

> It would be difficult to find a marriage in which the problems of the two partners fitted more closely. Each seemed to be marrying a partner who offered a relationship close enough to his family pattern to be familiar, and yet sufficiently different to provide a flexibility and opportunity for growth . . . which had not existed in the parental environment . . . As it happened, this growth and development had not occurred . . .

119

The five detailed case-studies which make up the bulk of that volume, are excellent further variations on my theme, and on the dynamics of *Case Ten*.

REVIEW OF OTHER HYPOTHESES

American work around the same period as our Tavistock developments is apt to stress the concept of 'neurotic' as applied to the partners' marital fantasies and behaviour. The clinical facts justify such an epithet whether we look at the couple as individuals (which most clinicians still do) or in the aspect of their interaction. Such is, for example, the viewpoint from which Eisenstein's Symposium[2] was written. In that book there was less emphasis on the collusive, shared dyadic system than even in the earlier phases of our own work. Not surprisingly it is the social work contributors to that volume, notably the late Robert Gomberg (Chap XV, p. 269 et seq.) who come closest to the concept of interaction. The psychoanalysts writing in that book are still basing their views on the discoveries of the separate therapies of one or both partners. Ackerman[3] writing a little later gets closer to the concept of merging identities. 'Each [marital partner] yearns to complete the self through union with the other. The psychic identity of the marital couple derives from this union' (p. 21). 'Deviant behaviour . . . not merely as a projection of a fixed intra-personality distortion but also as a functional expression of emotional interplay . . .' (p. 24). It is perhaps significant that Ackerman's position is close to Harry Stack Sullivan's inter-personal hypothesis and critical of classical Freudian personality theory. Ackerman also uses the concept of the interpenetration of biological, psychological and social vectors in shaping positive and negative family group relations. He holds that Freud's historical concentration had led to a 'divorce of the inside of the mind from the outside', the emphasis on the individual to the neglect of the environing group and of social reality. This is a criticism often made not only by psychiatrists (who are, on the whole, more individual-centred), but especially by sociologists.

Two further American developments must be mentioned. The first is an outcome of the Palo Alto research into schizophrenic communication, out of which came *inter alia* the 'double-bind' hypothesis. The second is the work of Robert F. Winch and his wife Martha Winch[4] on complementariness of needs as the basis of mate selection.

Turning first to the communications theory, we find a most stimulating application of this concept to marital conflict described by Jay Haley.[5] As one would expect from a theory evolved on the evidence of schizophrenic splitting, this view begins with the statement of contradictoriness of *different levels* of messages between the spouses. This is seen already in the potential conflict generated by the very act of solemnizing their union: 'Now they are married, are they staying together because they wish to, or because they must?' I have, from my viewpoint, also commented on the change many lovers feel when the weight of social compulsion comes down after legal wedding. I interpreted it as the strongly anti-libidinally invested 'social rôle' derived from parental and religious models, being liable to oust the 'fancy-free' libidinal mutuality of the pre-marital phase. What object-relations theory would call unconscious collusion, is described by Haley in phenomenonological and behavioural terms. For example:

> When one spouse continues the marriage even though badly treated . . . a compulsory type of relationship occurs. [The wife] may begin to think he must be staying . . . because he has to, not because he wants to . . . A wife who believes that her husband stays with her because of his inner desperation . . . will dismiss his affectionate approaches as mere bribes . . . (p. 216).

We saw that the wife in *Case Ten* held just such fantasies, because of her husband's contradictory cues to her from two levels after marriage. Haley also points in the direction of our concepts when he states that, when a partner shows ability to stand alone, the other can then begin to believe in the first partner's remaining from free choice. But this dilemma only makes them more determined to prove that 'the mate will put up with anything' if they are *really* wanted, and thus they intensify the tests of all-suffering love.

Haley sees the crux of marital conflict in paradoxical communication—such as the double bind, e.g. when a husband indicates his wife should show interest and activity in sex, but repulses her when she does so as 'demanding and managing'. The wife cannot win. 'If one is asked to do something and not do it at the same time, a possible response is not *to be able* to do it—which means indicating that one's behaviour is involuntary' (p. 222). This is the slide into neurotic regression as the result of re-activation of the split between libidinal and anti-libidinal object-relations. Impotence and frigidity are obvious examples of such regression into 'I can't'. Haley is aware of the collusive and mutually dovetailing nature of neurotic interactions, though he uses the singular in describing one or another event in a spouse's mind. As other observers, Haley also discovers the solidarity of couples faced with the 'threat' of therapeutic change. Thus, wives would rather have their husbands 'bad' than weak. They will provoke sadistic or sexual acting out, and push this forward as the cause of their complaint, sooner than allow the childish dependence or inadequacy of their man to be revealed. When such an area is opened up in discussion with the therapist, anxiety or anger is aroused, demonstrating the protection the couple afford each other from having the real sensitive spots touched. Haley says: 'Usually if one mate is protective of the other there are unexpressed needs being served . . . A further aspect of protection is the confusion that occurs over who is protecting whom . . .' I would add here that these observations, which Haley supports with beautifully concise clinical examples recognizable as genotypes, point clearly to the existence of mutual projective identifications blurring individual ego-boundaries. To continue his chosen example—what is concealed when the defended area is so zealously guarded from disucssion and insight? Is it only the man's dependence and the wife's ascendancy which violate the socially accepted sterotype of rôle distribution? For our *Case Ten* Haley's observations hold, but they do not account for all that we saw going on there. The wife certainly wanted to protect her husband from her 'queen bee' castration fantasies by depicting him as the ever potent sexual transgressor and angry tyrant. But was he not equally concerned to keep up her 'queen bee' sub-identity rather than allow his own 'sadistic' sexuality to dominate her, and also protect her from her own sexual guilt and inadequacy? In Haley's conceptual framework there appears only one element in the preservation of the social façade—masking the power struggle about which side wins and 'makes the rules'. In our framework the dyad shares many and shifting mutual projective identifications, now as the libidinal ego, now as the menacing anti-libidinal parent figure, carrying the frustrated love and power needs. At another level they share awareness and aspirations of adult norms of behaviour. Both together are keeping the castrating mother-figure out, by projecting her punitive, sex-denying qualities on to each other, at the same time as being also activated by this same figure as an internal object in sleuthing out or fantasying the existence of sexual and persecuting motives in the other. I do not believe that Dr. Haley would quarrel with this further level of analysis of dyadic interaction, which adds meaning and depth to his valuable discoveries of the contradictoriness of cues or communications between people at different levels. I see the sources of these paradoxical, confusing messages and signals in the splits between the conflicting but shared ego systems delineated in Fairbairn's theory. In this way we can begin to answer Haley's question as to who protects whom in the marital collusion: each, in the first instance, their own libidinal ego from the castrating persecuting internal anti-libidinal object with whom they had identified but now re-project to the spouse. Secondly—they defend the stability of the joint legal-social personality they have created in marrying one another. In protecting the image of the partner (for example as a 'drunk' or as 'sexually inadequate' or 'slovenly', and so forth) they are in the other secretly cherishing the rejected, bad libidinal ego with its resentments and demands while *within* the dyadic system they can persecute it in an inter-personal framework. Between them and together they are a joint 'personality'. Thus, the collusive marriage, in which internal persecuting objects are shared, and polarized in dialectic fashion, may be said to represent the closest possible approximation to intra-personal resolution of conflict, to attempted integration of the splits between incompatible ego-object systems. In this way the—yes! loyal collaboration and mutual scape-goat services of the embattled partners represents a tremendous support and comfort. It is often a mutually acknowledged tireless striving after growth, even if the unconscious walled-off splits stultify this effort by the vicious circle of projections and repetition-compulsion. 'My better half' is thus a deeply revealing expression of folk wisdom! It leaves the question of what is the better half nicely vague.

Equally relevant to this study is the work on 'normal' couples by Robt. F. Winch in support of his theory of *complementary mate selection*. This theory assumes that modern marriage in Western society is based on free choice of partners, and no longer on any overt parental bargains. *Homogamy* ('like marries like') at statistical level operates through social opportunities for meeting: potential partners are more likely to encounter each other in similar backgrounds centred on neighbourhood, school, place of work, club or church. *Heterogamy* (or attraction and mating by personality contrast or complement) is related to the individual need systems of the partners. In simple form this would mean for example, that a man high on aggressiveness will tend to marry a woman high on submissiveness— she gratifying his need for dominating, and he hers for being dominated. This gets very close to my *Hypothesis* (2). Winch presents evidence moreover that a person's image of his or her spouse can embody still cherished elements of 'abandoned ego-models' (loc. cit., p. 81), or of his or her 'ideal self' (p. 86). Marriage carries the connotation of self-affirmation and the neutralization of doubt: 'at least one person thinks the self acceptable even if no one else does'. Mate selection, in brief, proceeds for Winch on the basis of each individual seeking '. . . that person who gives the greatest promise of providing him or her with maximum need gratification' (pp. 88–9). This is his operational definition of love. It is not difficult to adapt this hypothesis of conscious homogamy and deeper complementariness or heterogamy to my own definition of marriage (Chap. I). But Winch, as a good social scientist, finds by statistical testing that his theory is only approximately true. There are also other factors at work which, while not contradicting it, show that complementariness of needs is

123

but one trend in choice of mate. It would seem that in the light of our data from disturbed marriages any over-simplification is inadequate. Winch himself finds valid reason to criticize Erich Fromm's discourse on 'mature love' versus 'immature symbiosis', because maturity is so relative, and would certainly include the capacity to tolerate one's own and the partner's infantile residues. In the same way, however, Winch's own polarization of opposites, using both Jung's and Henry A. Murray's concepts of contrasted variables (e.g. 'Feeling-Thinking', or 'Succourance-Nurturance'), tends also to attribute to the 'complementarily mated' an inability to own the other half of the postulated opposite. We already know that the partner can carry a variety of the self's range of potentially available ego- and rôle identifications. It is, I would say, only in those marriages where certain rôles or ego-activities are barred as the result of antecedent intra-personal conflict, that the complementation or *apparent* mating by opposites is really marked. The dyads have *polarized* their rôles. At the level of unconscious sharing of internal objects complementarity is less clear. The promise of gratification for one's needs is at one level, and belongs to an early phase of mating. There in untested fantasy the partner is seen as the willing object of one's dominance or submission needs. But whatever the couple start with, maturation and growth, as well as the inexorable return of the repressed in the unfortunate, modify and supersede the earlier expectations, as expressed in my *Hypothesis (1)*. In a full marital relationship, the original projected idealizations and fantasy-transferences are outgrown as the reality of the other is progressively, and not without explicit or implicit conflict, accepted. In the healthy marriage the gratifications, I would hold, arise, not only in the circumstance that *at times*, and in limited ways, the partner 'vicariously gratifies' the needs of the other by being the 'lost opposite', but also in the finding of agreement of the *same* qualities as one needed to have affirmed. As in the problem of degrees of maturity, so in the question of early need systems, we are dealing with scales of intensity along a continuum, not with fixed qualities such as aggressiveness and submissiveness, or even extraversion-introversion. We must take into account the total structured personalities, as they change in time, and not the logical antithetical pairs of traits we use in our constructs. Submissive people are often unconsciously aggressive, 'cold' people have latent passions, and so on. In illustration of this point I would like to cite a case in which Winch's social homogamy and individual complementariness were fully present at the beginning, but where later the positions were almost reversed. This was one of my couples mentioned in Chapter V where ideological divergence split the marriage despite a number of typically complementary personality traits which had brought and held them together under the homogenizing umbrella of Lenin.

Case Eleven: The husband began as the wife's *beau-ideal* of a tough, dedicated youth leader, whose sadistically-tinged sexuality gratified her until she was emotionally independent enough, some 15 years later, to evaluate for herself the meaning of the Hungarian rising, which toppled not only her faith in Lenin's party, but also in the capacity of her husband to shed his party-hack's blinkers. He now became a moral prevaricator and yes-man in her eyes. She saw him as inhuman as Soviet power. It may be said that she withdrew all idealizing projections of her internalized father back into herself, and developed, almost under our eyes, a rather determined and somewhat masculine sense of her own identity. She refused to play 'Hungary' to H.'s Khrushchev—or rather she played it victoriously and gained her freedom.

To be fair, in his Chapter 13 Winch acknowledges that he had not yet studied the questions of levels (or sub-identities) of the interacting personalities, nor the changes in need patterns over time or in response to external events. His is an important contribution to our need to understand the nature of mate choice in the era of free love-marriages as against institutionalized arranged marriages, in which the personal attributes of the couple were subordinate to social rôle requirements.

FOLIE À DEUX

None of us know by what sixth sense persons of the opposite sex recognize each other as suitable for working out their complex and often internally contradictory need systems. Among such mate choices none are more surprising than the strange mutual infant-parent symbioses at the paranoid (schizoid) position in the Klein-Fairbairn sense. The dangers of loving and being loved at this primitive level are so great, and so confused with destroying and being destroyed, that the only safe thing is to act towards the libidinal object in a way which will drive the object away to escape damaging it and being damaged or even devoured. This, in effect, means a communication of hating, while all the time craving for infantile dependence and support (see Fairbairn, loc. cit., p. 25–6). The husband in *Case Ten* showed this schizoid behaviour in some degree towards his orally devouring 'little girl' wife, and later the same trend manifested in his transference relation to his therapist, whom he feared he had driven to insanity or illness by his dependent feelings about him. Even though the marriage in *Case Ten* was a long way from the classical pictures of clinical *folie à deux*, there was a strong element of what Harold F. Searles[6] has described as the 'effort to drive the other crazy' in it. Searles defines this as a predominantly unconscious ingredient in a complex pathogenic relatedness, which neither participant has the capacity to control fully. The drive consists of 'initiating any kind of inter-personal interaction which tends to foster emotional conflict in the other person—which tends to activate various areas of his personality in opposition to one another—tends to drive him crazy (i.e. schizophrenic)'. The concept was developed, like that of the 'double bind' to which it is related, from observing parent–child relations in the search for insight into the genesis of schizophrenic states. These psychic assaults by one or both parents on a child are, briefly: the questioning of the other's mental adjustment; the stimulation of sexual feelings where their gratification would be disastrous (e.g. incestuous). Related to this are the exacerbation of a conflict between the desire to mature into autonomy and the regressive desire to remain in infantile symbiosis with the parent; demanding devotion but rejecting the child's efforts to be helpful; the sudden switching from tender warmth to lashing fury—and so on. Such behaviour tends to undermine the other's confidence in his own emotional reactions and in his perception of outer reality. Searles sees such destructive behaviour as motivated by combinations of some of the following: he considers firstly that at times intense hostility can *wish* the psychic death of another—to drive the other insane. Next comes the need to externalize on to the other, in order to rid the self of one's own threatened craziness— the 'Gadarene swine' or scapegoat motif. (The partners in *Case Ten* vied with each other, at one stage, to make the other 'more crazy' than the self). Akin to this is the urge to end intolerable tension provoked by the other's psychotic relation to the self who has borne this private burden and felt the guilt of it. At other times the need is to send the other insane to draw them into companionship and sharing of one's lonely fantasy world—perhaps similar to the pervert's or drug addict's compulsion to 'infect' others. Another related motive is the misconceived wish to have the other develop too fast, to assimilate what the ego is not strong enough to stand, from worthy, but insightless, wishes to help the other to 'grow'. This is the Pygmalion theme, and probably an effect of introjection of a demanding, belittling parent–figure. More powerful, however, Searles considers to be the subtle wish to continue or recapture the gratifications of the symbiotic, primary relationships, so that growth away into individuality would become both a threat to the collusive relation and would then, itself, be considered crazy—even if it is the craziness of the boy who saw the truth about the Emperor's clothes.

I have listed these essential points of Searles' thesis, because they are directly applicable to some of the most severely symbiotic or collusive dyadic interactions outside parent–child 'schizogenic' ties.*
I hope to have shown that marital bonds, both in health and in sickness are the nearest adult equivalent to the original parent–child relationship (see also Dicks[8]). Projective identification, so prominent in the transactions of the marital dyad, belongs to the primary level of psychic function. At this early level psychotic introjections and projections have been convincingly demonstrated by child analysis as well as by studies on schizophrenics, and in adult analysands.

G. Teruel[9] has paid much attention to the strength of primary, projective bonds in marital dyads. 'The less the individual has been able to sort out his first phase of development, the more these (inner) structures are fully charged, and at the slightest provocation we have regressive behaviour . . .' He quotes material from cases studied in our Tavistock Marital unit, which supports the concept of one spouse 'carrying' or acting as the container of the other's internal object or objects, which the latter cannot contain. We saw an example of this in *Case Ten*, where the husband 'contained' his wife's sexual self embodied in his blush, while she carried his 'bad' father image as well as his dependence needs in glaring contradiction to one another. Teruel comments on the ferocity of the paranoid or depressive anxiety and hate such couples can reveal in early joint sessions to the marriage consultant.

At the opposite pole of the mutually creative and identity-confirming marriage, then, stands the marriage, equally loyal and all-inclusive, in which the primary paranoid object world comes increasingly to dominate the manifest as well as the private content and aspect of the relationship. It is to such a near or fully-psychotic *shared* world of fantasy-relations that the term *folie à deux* is appropriately applied. I have argued that there is permeability of ego boundaries, implicit in the psychological concepts of non-verbal communication, learning, identification, etc. By this concept it is possible to see how two personalities, who dovetail by sharing similar as well as contrasting primitive object-needs and anxieties, could 'mutually infect' one another to the extent that both their inner worlds come to be identical. Laing[7] wants to denote just such a process by the word 'collusion'. In the collusive dyad, says Laing, 'projection' is not just using the other as a hook to hang something on. 'He strives to find in the other, or to induce the other to become the *very embodiment* of

* R. D. Laing (in *The Self and Others*,[7]) says: 'We are using the mother–child relationship throughout simply for convenience.' He also holds that similar disruptive, double-bind communicative relations tending to the undermining of identity can go on in any dyadic interaction (p. 140).

127

that (regressive or fantasied) other, whose co-operation is required as complement of the particular identity he feels impelled to sustain.' It follows that only a partner who already possesses at least a latent complement or companion-piece to the other partner's primitive relational needs (e.g. the persecutory anti-libidinal mother of *Case Ten*), is likely to accompany the mate thus far. But some degree of falling in with the partner's infantile rôle distribution is very common. Noyes[10] in describing the phenomena of folie-à-deux as part of his discourse on paranoid states, quotes older French authors' views that in a shared persecutory system (which is the commonest form) one partner—the stronger personality—acts as the infector of the other, more submissive partner who accepts the delusional system with conviction—provided this offers some *satisfaction* (my italics) to the infected. Noyes also notes that capacity for identification must be strong, and that the 'infectee' can recover once the partners separate.*

Karl Jaspers,[11] in describing a 'folie à famille' also involving the couple's children, writes (p. 283)

'They achieved a form of understanding in a world they knew in common, in which the individual peculiarities of the separate experiences were absorbed into the common whole: "We are persecuted; whenever we encounter the outside world, the persecution is there." The clinical phenomena included a shared extensive persecutory system, infernal machines and all, and resulted finally in hospitalisation for both spouses, though it is not stated whether this resulted in the recovery of either. The children were not deeply involved.'

Shribman[14] has described a case, with suicide pact, which illustrated the kind of interaction Noyes had culled from earlier writers.

In the Tavistock we did not see any couples as ill as this, though we had application reports from referring agencies suggestive of true *folie à deux*. Such cases are not often willing to have their regressive symbiosis invaded by paranoidally perceived authorities. This would rouse dyadic resistance in excelsis. For there to be a 'case' in our sense, at least one spouse must retain some degree of personal identity. Only thus can the shred of insight which fears final existential submergence and preserves awareness of a healthier norm lead

---

* In view of my wartime work I cannot forbear to mention the analogy with the infective paranoid conviction with which Hitler evoked echoing identifications in some 35 per cent of German males, creating a *folie en masse*, because he satisfied fantasy potentials which their typical authoritarian object relations had created.[12,13]

128

to conflict, individual resistance to the partner's infection and the seeking of help.

CONCLUSIONS

The preceding chapters have presented a review of the growth and change in the concepts, other workers' and mine, with which to approach a marital problem. They have illustrated the passage from looking at married couples with certain assumptions in dynamic psychology and sociology to the making of some new hypotheses to account for the new experiences in handling the 'marriage as the patient'. I owe it to my readers to summarize this conceptual scheme as far as it has got. The result of this effort will be condensed into a series of propositions at a fairly abstract level. These are neither complete nor self-contained and independent. They do not claim to be other than a set of working hypotheses at a moment of time in a developing sphere of medico-social work. They may be of wider validity, but are here intended to refer only to marriages actually studied, i.e. in the population in and around London that has consulted us.

SUMMARY

1. Marriage as a social institution continues to be the expression of the culture's aspiration to ensure the stability, security and dignity of relational needs between the sexes and of its children. This is accepted by our clients at conscious level.

2. Marriage as a system of inter-personal relations is stable and durable to the degree that it achieves the qualities of a compound or integrated dyad from being at its start a sum of $1 + 1$. The strength and stability of this integrate depends on an overall positive balance of satisfactions over dissatisfactions for both partners, for which the term 'positive feed-back' is appropriate. This is not to be taken as implying freedom from conflict, or even 'happiness'.

3. In this interaction we can, in theory and in practice, discern *three major levels or sub-systems*, which are internally related to each other, but can vary independently, and have changing importance in maintaining the cohesion of the dyad over different phases.

(a) The *first* and most 'public' sub-system is that of socio-cultural values and norms. Although in our society selection for marriage has tended towards the valuation of autonomous commitment of the partners to each other on the principle of expected satisfaction of mutual needs, there remain the traditional norms of selection on the basis (as well as the opportunities) of social homogeneity or 'homo-

129

gamy'. Homogamy operates by sub-culture affinities of class, religion, education, race, etc., in which prospective spouses may be united by shared identifications through the parents' social status and values. Though of decreasing importance in a mobile society, homogamy at social level is a factor for initial cohesion in a certain proportion of marriages.

(b) The *second* sub-system is that of the 'central egos', which operates at the level of the *personal norms*, conscious judgments and expectations also derived from the developmental background of object-relations and social learning preceding the marriage. At this level the sub-culture element can be enriched or diluted by individual variances (even in a socially homogamous partnership) of such factors as: conscious differentiation from parent-generation models; habits and tastes; deeper rebellion, counter-cathexes, and counter-identifications vis-à-vis parental figures and values. At this point the 'heterogamy' of free choice becomes possible, and with it potential conflict in one or both partners between sub-culture pressures (now operating intra-personally) and the individuals' contrary norms and rôle expectations. The latter may be more or less adult than the sub-culture's norms, but will always be dynamically linked to the earlier object-relations by which the sub-culture's norms came to be in the individuals' field of interaction.

It is within this second sub-system of interaction that the ongoing pulls and pushes of demands of the partners on each other for rôle performance are continually testing the consistency or inconsistencies of the consciously held ego-attitudes in actual behaviour. In terms of object-relations theory these personal norms result from the vicissitudes of successive phases of personality development. As such they may be expressions of a relatively unimpeded maturation of emotional and rational capacities through the incorporation of predominantly good objects whose norms and attitudes have been uncomplicatedly identified with. This would also result in an uncomplicated personal adherence to the major social and cultural values of sub-system 1. Thus the conscious norms and rôle models may be consistent with the 'inner world' of object-relations and consequent behaviour towards the love-object.

The mating of persons with this degree of integration is likely to reveal few important contradictions between the initially attributed expectations from and towards the potential mate and the actual rôle behaviour unfolding in daily action after marriage. They will be 'really like' what the surface ego presaged. We can visualize such a marriage as being stable and offering satisfactions either by reason of absence of major rôle-demand conflicts, or by reason of the *whole-person* cathexis in the mode of conflict resolution over emerging rôle-divergencies. Within this concept there is room for both the complementarity and the similarity hypotheses of satisfactory mate selection.

It is here that such qualities of character* as flexibility and tolerance of ambivalence of self's and partner's conations and attitudes are the essential equipment for meeting the other partner's manifestations of individual identity and divergent maturation. These divergencies may be the sources of crises in adaptation and loyalty springing from ego-levels (e.g. over one spouse's diverging religious or political convictions that were an important element of shared sub-cultural heritage). Sufficient fall-off in satisfaction at this level may theoretically give rise to 'reasoned' partings, which do not result in calls for help from therapeutic services. In such cases the dyadic integration had not been completed.

The second sub-system, in so far as it works well, would correspond to Fairbairn's 'mature dependence'[16] 'characterized by a capacity on the part of differentiated individuals for co-operative relationships with differentiated objects'.

The interferences with the satisfactory interaction at this level necessitates attention to

(c) the *third* sub-system. This is the area which, in the Introductory Chapter, I called 'the unconscious forces' flowing between the partners, forming bonds of a 'positive' and 'negative' kind, often referred to as 'transactions'. It is topologically the field in which we locate the drives towards satisfaction of object-relational needs which have undergone exclusion from awareness in the course of transition from primary towards more differentiated object-seeking. According to the intensity of conflict during this development, the pathways of dynamic flow from self to object are more or less open along that developmental line, or are deflected into segregated channels or blind alleys at various phases along the line. These are the 'repressed' or 'split-off' internal ego-object relations, as envisaged by object relations theory. Their dynamic presence influences the integrity or potential contradictoriness of the central ego's perception of its own object needs and the directness with which it can perform its psychosocial rôles in seeking the object and maintaining gratifying relation with it. I hold that it is the 'mix' of the more or less unconscious interaction of object-relations in this third sub-system which governs the longer-term quality of marriages.

4. In this conceptual framework, it is possible to assess the contributions from each sub-system of each partner towards the dyadic integrate. These contributions will vary in accordance with the

* Defined by McDougall as the 'organized system of directed conative tendencies'.[15]

131

degree of consistency or conflict between the explicit social and personal value norms and rôle expectations which the partners bring to the marriage, and their two 'inner worlds' of object-relations which require satisfaction or feed-back within the dyad.

5. Within the great variety of permutations of interaction at the levels of the three sub-systems and congruence or divergence between sub-systems, I discern certain recurring patterns of dyadic adaptation to ambivalent investment of the partners ('tensions'), which in varying degree 'threaten' the stability of the relationship. It is my contention that this dyadic adaptation or homoeostasis depends on the two partners' ability to deal with the pressures in the third sub-system in one of the following ways.

(a) By congruence of all three sub-systems—including the perception of each by the other as a whole person with consequent 'benign' conflict-resolution. This was considered above under para. 3b.

(b) By the successful use of shared cultural and personal-conscious norms and values as *defences* against the deeper impulsions from the libidinal and anti-libidinal primary object-relation levels. This is collusive defence by idealization, convention, rationality, moral consensus, etc. Conflict is not allowed to arise. The defences are effective for a greater or lesser time.

(c) Contrariwise, by the collusive use of the cultural marital norms and values as a façade behind which to permit and act out the expression towards each other of elements in the primary libidinal and anti-libidinal object-relational potentials by means of projective and introjective mechanisms, for which the partners share a need. These may come into operation at once or replace the failure of defensive collusion as under 5b, after a time, and give rise to what the external observer might term 'paranoid' or 'depressive' dyadic systems, in which the satisfactions are mainly, or at least episodically, at primary, fiercely ambivalent object-relational levels. Here the 'negative' or aggression-expressing bonds of the primary object-relational attributions are often more emotionally 'rewarding' than the 'positive' or love-expressing bonds. The first and second sub-systems in this situation are maintained because in themselves supportive to the dyad, or as an arena sanctioned by the 'outside world', where the conflict (itself the satisfying feed-back for the partners) can be conducted. We do not know by what pathway or mechanism mate selection for this type of interaction operates.

6. Finally, a theoretical conjecture on the failed marriage ending in permanent separation or divorce, which has, so far, been hardly mentioned. Marriages may prove unviable at any of the three sub-system levels. It would seem necessary for at least two of the three

sub-systems postulated to function with credit-balances of satisfaction over dissatisfaction to both partners. Social affinity plus congruence of deep object-relations can withstand strong divergencies of personal norms and tastes. Strong agreements over personal norms and values plus deeper object-relations can override large cultural and social distance and incongruities. Even social homogamy and good overlap of personal norms and values can endure, provided their defensive efficacy against 'unwelcome' confrontation at deeper object levels holds. But if reality testing proves to one or both partners that the relationship was based on nothing but social affinity or meeting ground; on nothing but some shared personal interests; or on nothing but seeing a potential parent-figure or an exciting libidinal object as a guarantee against essentially infantile loneliness; then it is only a question of time before the need for a broader-based merging of lives will become felt, and, in due course, acted upon in one way or another. It is usually the case that, at this stage, the emotional content of the relationship is one of boredom, indifference and withdrawal of investment. Nothing of the self is any longer projected into the other. The institutional aspects of the cohabitation may be continued for rational or social advantages, but the marriage as interpersonal relation will be dead. The opposite to love is not hate. These two always co-exist so long as there is a live relationship. The opposite to love is indifference.

REFERENCES

1. THOMPSON, A. G. (1960), in Introduction to Pincus L. (ed.) *Marriage*. London: Methuen, p. 4.
2. EISENSTEIN, V. W. (1956) (ed.) *Neurotic Interaction in Marriage*. London: Tavistock Publications.
3. ACKERMAN, N. W. (1958) *The Psychodynamics of Family Life*. New York: Basic Books.
4. WINCH, R. F. (1958) *Mate Selection*. New York: Harper.
5. HALEY, JAY (1963) 'Marriage Therapy', *Arch. Gen. Psychiat. 8*, pp. 213-34.
6. SEARLES, H. F. (1959) 'The Effort to Drive the Other Person Crazy', *Brit. J. Med. Psychol. 32*, pp. 1-18.
7. LAING, R. D. (1961) *The Self and Others*. London: Tavistock Publications.
8. DICKS, H. V. (1963) 'Object-Relations Theory and Marital Studies', *Brit. J. Med. Psychol. 36*, pp. 125-9.
9. TERUEL, G. (1966) 'Recent Trends in the Diagnosis and Treatment of Marital Conflict', *Psyche, 20, No. 8* (In German).
10. NOYES, A. P. (1949) *Modern Clinical Psychiatry*. London: W. B. Saunders, pp. 405-6.

11. JASPERS, K. (1962) *General Psychopathology*. English. Manchester Univ. Press.
12. DICKS, H. V. (1950) op. cit.
13. DICKS, H. V. (1966) Chap. 'Intrapersonal Conflict and the Authoritarian Personality' in *Conflict in Society*. (eds.) de Reuck, A. V. and Knight, J. (CIBA Symposium July 1965). London: Churchill.
14. SHRIBMAN, I. (1958) 'A Case of Communicated Insanity: Folie à Deux', *Internat. J. of Soc. Psychiat. 4, No. 1.*
15. MCDOUGALL, WM. (1926) *An Outline of Psychology*. Third edn. London: Methuen, p. 417.
16. FAIRBAIRN, W. R. D. (1952) op. cit., pp. 145-6

PART TWO
The Practice

Chapter VIII

SYMPTOMATOLOGY I

The main objective of this book is to present and illustrate a certain approach to marital difficulties. The concepts and hypotheses with which Part One was concerned, were developed from clinical practice. From this experience grew more specific hypotheses which in turn modified our clinical work. In this part of the book I hope to describe the evolution of the diagnostic and therapeutic method in parallel with these changes. It was by design that I decided to present the development of theory first. It gives a certain framework for ordering the phenomena encountered in practice, i.e. the symptoms. The case illustrations supporting the theoretical constructions have to some extent bridged the gap and shown that it was the impact of the living material which impelled the evolution in hypothesis making.

This living material, presented by over 2,000 married couples seen over the 16 years since I began this work, is so rich and varied that only a description of each case could do justice to the full range of clinical pictures encountered. Even so, the kind of marriage that finds its way to a psychological clinic is only a selected sample of the total possibilities. There are all those marriages whose stresses get by without help like 'minor illnesses'. At the other extreme are those whose conflicts are so severe that they only want the surgical treatment of divorce or separation; and those so strongly collusive in guarding their *status quo* that they resist all pressures to seek treatment. Our work design moreover excluded couples in which one partner was alcoholic, psychotic, grossly psychopathic or overtly sexually perverted.

The manifestations of marital stress are known to everybody and form the stock-in-trade of drama and the novel. They do not need listing so much as evaluation in a coherent way. My work is concerned less with symptoms as such than with their meaning in a given relationship. For example, the periodic violence in a primitive couple has to be evaluated differently from the symptomatically similar violence which is a late expression of despair in a marital conflict among the sensitive *intelligentsia*. The floridness or reticence of

137

marital conflicts is not in itself a valid distinction in the diagnosis of the underlying dynamics. Symptoms have to be rated in a social context; by the fixity or lability of the total picture of interaction, and by the indications of presence or absence of compensatory strengths of the two persons and of the bonds between them.

To deal with the complexity and overlap in the symptomatology of marital crises, I have found it helpful to classify the phenomena under certain headings: (1) Distribution of Impact; (2) Dominance/Submission conflicts; (3) Disturbance of Sexual Function; (4) Acting-out/Containment. These may help others towards ordering their experience. They do not pretend to be anything but a working convenience.

1. DISTRIBUTION OF IMPACT

The first category is based on which member of the family group comes forward as the bearer of the stress or the illness.

(a) *One person presents*

This variant is still the commonest at the level of family doctoring; it is thus apt to result in the referral of the presenting partner to the psychiatrist. Recognition of the stress in the sick partner as essentially a manifestation of a marital interaction conflict requires a measure of diagnostic or aetiological thinking which busy general practitioners cannot be expected to do for us. That the G.P. increasingly makes that connection is an encouraging sign of the penetration of dynamic concepts into medical practice.

(i) At the somatic end of the one-body presentation common manifestations are, it need hardly be said, disturbances of sexual function. Variants of male impotence and of female frigidity, menstrual troubles or disagreeable sensations during coitus make up this fraction. From one or two cases already quoted in Chapters IV to VI it is clear that these phenomena, in the absence of organic or chemical pathology, are but the buoys marking submerged conflict. Sexual disturbance is never a diagnosis but always a symptom of conflict in the person about libidinal object-relations, in this instance projected onto the partner(s). Nobody is 'impotent'—period! They are only so vis-à-vis *another person*. The so-called completely impotent or dyspareunic can nearly always masturbate, proving the intactness of the neural pathways. If they tell us that 'they now cannot even do this' it means a final defensive self-desexualization. The reaction reminds me of the statement by a classics don, at war with the castrating mother image in his wife, that she had so reduced him that he could not even remember the Greek alphabet.

138

Sexual disturbances which will be discussed in more detail in a later section, are often masked at first contact with us by more diffuse psychosomatic symptoms comprising one or a cluster of distress signals from the whole gamut of possibilities of 'organ-jargon' (as Adler called it), by which the unconscious attaches its symbolizations from the whole to the part. I am taking as read the knowledge available in psychiatric literature about this topic as applied to individuals. It need scarcely be stated that this array of symptoms comes into play not only in marital conflicts, but is also deployed in other stress situations. If the stress is due to a passing crisis, marital or other, symptomatic treatment may be all that is needed. But persistence or recurrence calls for reappraisal in more aetiological terms—and this still needs emphasizing.

(ii) Less common are one-partner presenting symptoms of a more *psychological* kind, not necessarily devoid of somatic overtones. Thus, instead of an impotence or a dyspepsia, the complainant may bring a history of attitude change towards the marriage: of an alarming loss of affection or concern; of irritability; of sulking or withdrawal. More distressing still to decent people are added fantasies of adultery with real or imaginary substitutes, coupled with death wishes against the spouse or children. We rarely see people initially for symptoms of this 'moral' order. The depressive picture leads more often to referral to the general psychiatric service. Here the symptom is likely to be evaluated in terms of individual mental illness. The primarily marital case comes away unhelped by a diagnostic label and the currently fashionable psychotropic drug.

Loss of affection as a symptom is commoner in the 'well partner', invited for an interview after the 'presenting' partner has raised the likelihood of a dyadic conflict. We can then more readily understand why the sick partner became sick. Except for such cases, the 'non-medical' one-partner presentation is usually to seek help for the other spouse's hurtful *behaviour*. The majority are unhappy or angry wives referred from the Courts, or by social agencies. Though often accusatory, a proportion are concerned about their partner in the hope that the offending spouse is 'ill'. Only mental aberration could make the partner be so neglectful, cruel or violent in word or deed, withhold financial support, go out with other women or men, etc. At times we get lurid descriptions of veritable fiends. When the 'fiend' is seen, we usually get a totally different picture, equally distorted. These experiences began our search for concepts to explain such grossly unreal perceptions for usually we deal with averagely civilized people, above the median in intelligence. It also led to the joint interview as a method of matching the two pictures.

139

Case Twelve: Such, for example, was the presenting situation in a rural couple in their early forties who had been a passionate village Romeo and Juliet, but had, for reasons which will be described in Chapter XII, got to the point where W. pursued H. through the house in full hearing of their children and neighbours, hurling four-letter word abuse at him; denied him sex and frequently threatened suicide or desertion. Nonetheless, it was W. who had twice called the police and had also run to the Court 'because he was cruel and attacked her'. The Probation Officer would not accept her one-sided complaint and treated it as 'interaction'. The alleged fiend, H., seen by us shortly after W., was almost in despair from guilt and inferiority feelings because he did not know how to deal with this high-powered shrew. He admitted to striking her in self-defence and to stop her mounting fury. In between such episodes he would absent himself as much as possible or else glumly watch television. Their home, visited by a social worker, was a comfortable one, the children well cared for, and there was no psychiatric history except for their present condition. H., a skilled craftsman, had been a Warrant Officer air-crew in the war, while W. had run the home, the children and worked on the land bravely and ·devotedly. The separate clinical pictures were of a hysteric and reactive depressive in *relation to each other*. Both were effective and sociable persons outside their domestic conflict.

Not long ago many doctors, including psychiatrists, but not many social workers, would have treated such single-partner-presenting cases without inquiring into interaction or even interviewing the other partner. In the somatic presentation as in the behaviour case we would have talked of 'the poor chap with the frigid wife' or the 'poor woman with that dreadful husband'. There was the ill partner and there was the healthy spouse' who was at best the informant from whom we obtained our 'objective' history. It is characteristic of this category of marital case presentation that the complaining partner warns the interviewer that 'of course' the other spouse will refuse to come, or will prove very unco-operative, or pull the wool over our eyes. In practice the reverse is the case in about 98 per cent of instances. The absentee, now invited, not only redresses the balance of our one-sided view, but is often very glad that someone, at last, is concerned with his or her side of the picture. It is then that we often get the 'well partner' situation mentioned above.

In a proportion of cases, however, even if the spouse accompanies the 'sick' partner, he or she will stay 'outside' and play the detached informant who only comes to oblige the partner or the interviewer. We would expect this in view of our understanding of interaction processes by which one member of the dyad can become the 'carrier' of the stress and of most of the symptoms. But we have also learnt that the process is easily reversible if we do not fall for this misleading picture. *Cases Seven* and *Eight* taught us this. It is often the essentially iller partner who stays outside the situation.

(iii) There remains one more variant of a single 'sick' member of a conflict-torn home. That is the *child* of the warring parents. I regard it outside the scope of this book to enter into considerations of child psychiatry. In Chapter III, I gave my assumptions about the nature of a child's personality development in relation to its primary group. From these the likelihood of the offspring's emotional involvement in the parents' manifest or concealed tensions could be predicted. With the spread of object-relations theory, it becomes mandatory to assess parental interaction in the case of any maladjusted child. The Tavistock Clinic has long ago named its Children's division 'the Department for Children and Parents' to emphasize this orientation. I hope to make some further references to effects on the children of the parents' interaction in Chapter XII.

(b) *The couple presents*

The proportion of first attendances as a couple, by mutual agreement, is steadily growing. This must be due to a change in the climate of opinion under the influence of writing, of the mass media and of the known results of work by the marital counselling services. We are of course glad when the spade-work has already been done for us (e.g. by the family doctor or other referring agency) in getting recognition by the couple of the shared difficulty. In such cases we get two polarities. One type of couple will only consent to strictly confidential individual interviews, afraid to disclose to each other what may transpire. In this situation, which was complied with by the early standard method of receiving marital problem cases in nearly every clinic or centre, resistance to subsequent joint handling is a prominent symptom. With the growth of skill and insight both the clients and the professional workers have overcome some of this 'collusive' resistance to working jointly with both partners.

The opposite type is becoming more frequent: the couple *ab initio* accepts and expects a joint reception. The symptomatology, often painful, is presented to us in a resolutely shared effort at frankness. This is notably the case with the youngest age-groups of our clientele who seem able to view their problems more objectively and to have fewer respectability taboos.

It is interesting in a first joint session to observe the rapid development of an originally polite statement of differences into a heated battle between the partners. As Teruel (op. cit.) recorded in one of his cases, they may suddenly realize: 'Here we are, doctor, carrying on just as we do at home!' Within a few minutes of first meeting the new interviewer the material of such joint initial presentations can be as varied as the individual ones, and will be subsumed under subsequent headings below. What I wish to stress here is the incomparably greater vividness and reality of such a joint offering, as contrasted with the more detached individual presentation of tensions 'recollected in tranquillity'. In the joint presentation we see the symptomatology of the dyad instead of the separate, often glaringly contradictory complaints of individuals which it is difficult to blend into a valid picture of interaction diagnosis even with case-conferencing. The bearing of these matters on methods is dealt with in Chapter X.

2. DOMINANCE/SUBMISSION CONFLICTS AS PRESENTING SYMPTOMS

A second axis along which to order the symptomatology of marital trouble is by the principal or most emphasized self-descriptions of the couple, whether presented as individual or joint complaints, and most clearly displayed in joint diagnostic sessions. Outstanding here is the struggle for mastery. It could almost be said to be the key phenomenon from which all other symptoms derive. We see in such fights for ascendancy in the dyad a continuation of the old battle between a powerful 'bad' parent figure and the 'poor little self', projected and re-projected from one to the other. The partner may be attacked as if he or she were a frustrator and detractor, thus 'justifying' (displacing outwards by projection) the subject's own aggressive feelings towards the object, and warding off guilt at the failure of one's own rôle fulfilment. Only by attacking and controlling the projected powerful object that is felt to reside in the partner can the self avoid being controlled, devoured or annihilated by the other. The variations of this model in practice are many, some crude and violent, some subtle and masked. As an example of a constant ugly battle which could not be disengaged, I requote a fairly early case in our series, first published in 1953.[1] Their presentation resembled both *Case Twelve* and *Case Two*, for this is a common pattern.

Case Thirteen: This was a solid artisan couple around forty. Both had been waifs and had had a prematurely forced but intended marriage due to W.'s pregnancy. He saw his rôle as that of a gallant leader vis-à-vis a challenging but for that reason attractive girl. But his history showed a great need for a cherishing maternal woman. To the split in H. between a gentle and a masterful man, there corresponded a split in W. between a deprived girl who only wanted to be loved which she despaired of being, and a competitive and defiant tomboy who gave stroke for stroke. If H. went out because she objected to his radio, he found himself locked out. He rescinded all her disciplinary policies with the children for whose allegiance the battle was continuous. To her withdrawal of sex he replied by open association with a known loose woman. All this and much more, including verbal and physical violence, was retailed in the first joint interview, each charging the other with sadistic cruelty. During a dramatic moment, as they rose to leave, W. staggered and blanched. H. rushed to support her. When recovered she exclaimed that she had seen in his face the Devil himself (his features made him eligible for a Mephistophelian part in opera). She then told us, in a kind of abreaction, how as a girl she had been so bewitched by his sexual power that she had to seduce him 'to prove how bad he was', so as to hold it against him as a perpetual reproach. She wanted to get him down and beat him at his power game. If in the subsequent goading he reacted violently (with much guilt as a sequel) she would scream out the justification of her fantasy. If he withdrew and stayed out she could use this also as proof of his cruel neglect of his family and his perverted preference for the company of bad men and women. Each also accused the other of incestuous feelings for their children of the respective opposite sex. Yet at no time was there more wish to part than angry threats in the heat of the moment. H. held a responsible post with a large technical enterprise and was a conscientious, politically active man. In a single interview he described his wife as a 'good woman and a devoted mother' of whom he was still fond.

This case is briefly quoted not for its meaning (which is by now obvious) but as an example of dyadic symptomatology which a *first* joint attendance can reveal. It throws light on some recurring variants of the 'dominance-submission' struggle. The sub-divisions are in terms of whether the dominance is exerted as cover for repressed passivity (as could readily be seen in this and some previously cited examples), or whether passivity is used as a defence against deeper aggression and hate.

(a) *Dominant Behaviour and Rôle*

Into this sub-category fall those cases where dominant, attacking attitudes are not simple personality traits but are based on the warding off of passive submission in the self, which the partners must be compelled to adopt as *their* rôle. Each must 'get the other down'. It is like playing 'chicken'. In the male such bogus-tough behaviour is often a caricature of the culturally expected rôle stereotype. The collusive process, however, sabotages its efficacy because of the wife's unconscious recognition of it for what it is. The woman's projective identification with her internalized loved-frustrating father figure checks the man's rôle integrity against the inner model and confirms its kinship with her own identical defence against being tender or yielding and thus liable to be 'ground down' to use the phrase of the wife in *Case Nine*. Hence the bombast fails to work, the bluff is soon called.

There are many marriages in which sadistic male dominance is successful at least for a time because of another kind of woman's need to play the submissive, placidly maternal rôle vis-à-vis her dominant partner. This rôle conforms to cultural expectation and has the feed-back of his gratitude for her acceptance of his childish need for exacting love through power. We recall the naive confession of the wife in *Case One* who could love a brutal man, but not one who turned out to be weak underneath.

Women's shrewish dominance is nearly always activated by half-hearted 'passive aggressivity' of their husbands. Cheated in the satisfaction of her need for confident male rôle fulfilment, a woman will react by overt or disguised frustration rage. The unconscious now transfers the residues of still cathected rejecting or inadequate parental objects to the husband. Whether this (and the corresponding picture in the male), should be considered primary or reactive, is a matter for later assessment. The primary condition is due to a failure of adequate identification with a good female object; the reactive (or secondary) one is based on feminine frustration activating a regression to such an inner relationship latent in most people's past development. This theme was dealt with in some detail in Chapter III, while its relevance to mate-selection was alluded to in Chapter VII. Here we meet it as conditioning a frequent symptom of the disturbed marriage.

(b) *Submission and Rôle*

The second major sub-division of power conflicts is that in which aggressive feelings and need for mastery are covered by excessive gentleness and avoidance of normal anger. This syndrome was discussed in more theoretical terms under the topic of Idealization in Chapter V. Clinically such conflict avoidance comes close to obsessive-compulsive defence mechanisms shared by the partners. The long continuance of the collusion to deny and repress aggression is apt to raise the internal pressures of unconscious aggression and issue in depressive symptoms. These are the situations in which one or both partners complain of loss of zest, of contact and free communication or present with psychosomatic symptoms. Untested by expression at reality level, the aggressive impulses regress into fantasied attack on the ambivalently invested primary object. Guilt now makes a loving relationship impossible because one does not deserve or dare to relate to the projected love object against whom one also has such hateful destructive feelings. In contrast to the dominance group, these couples cannot externalize what is externalized too brutally and paranoidally by Type (a) above.

The *submissive husbands* see their wives 'on pedestals', compounded of brittleness and menacing retaliatory strength. Social values play their part in contributing a strand of knightly service to the Lady, but so do the projected and introjected hate and fear unconsciously surrounding the relation to the powerful mother figure who cannot be attacked but only propitiated. Such men will not only mention pedestals, but also speak of being 'clay in their wives' hands'. The smouldering underground heat of suppressed need for self-assertion causes periodic explosions of irritation, revolt, even violence, disproportionate to the precipitating cause. These are followed by abject guilt and restitution-making. Such outbursts cause quite undue distress to both spouses because they grossly violate their rôle norms. The man is now in 'the dog-house', more of his own than his wife's making. Characteristic of this depressive model of interaction is fear of communication, withdrawal; keeping everything dead level; attribution of disapproval to the partner or the development of a variety of compensatory activities to which the wife is no party. These range from furious overwork or angry attacks on the garden, to the pub, and to fantasied or actual search for a non-threatening, permissive woman to whom one can be a 'man'. There is frequently regression to childish sexual substitutes, such as pornography or masturbation.

If the *woman* is caught in this pattern, and has identified with a long-suffering, submissive mother rather than with a castrating 'phallic woman', then there is often a deadly absence of dynamic movement inside the partners or the relationship. For each partner the possession of power, or aggressive potential, is dangerous and destructive. Each has, as it were, come to heel and seeks only to be dutiful, in vain projecting the mastery and leadership to the other, the loved and feared parent figure whom they share and in whose service they live their joint anti-libidinal life. The fantasy meaning of the husband's passivity and withdrawal has its effects in mounting frustration rage in the wife also, especially when she is increasingly loaded with rôle-alien tasks of a masculine sort—finance, child discipline, external relations, major decision making—which her man renounces and delegates to her as 'better half'. Naturally, such smouldering anger also has its impulsive outbursts with similar

145

guilt sequelae. But female passivity, when it fuses with aggression and acquires a vengeful colouring, has different outlets from the male's. Firstly, there are more often than not the children at hand on whom to express the displaced quanta of the need to control. The emotional demandingness on which I commented in Chapter II, can now be seen at clinical level. The woman identifies the children with herself, over-valuing and 'possessing' them as bearers of her frustrated hopes and aspirations, but also exacting from them loyal affection and consideration for her hard, long-suffering rôle. From this unmet need it is only a short step to the mobilization of hysterical, phobic and hypochondriacal mechanisms. These express in varying proportions and combinations the hidden aggression and the guilt for it; the appeal to the husband and the children for succour, and the power-through-weakness motive, by which he is forced to take over what he would not do voluntarily. But in this competition the man not infrequently retaliates with even more impressive symptoms of breakdown in health by which he now threatens the very economic subsistence of the family—the last bastion of his instrumental rôle— and regresses to masochistic dependence on wife and medical services as a manifestation of 'passive aggression'. Power needs can be expressed also in competition as to which is the sickest!

Both parties may mobilize such relatives as are within reach, as allies against each other. It is often a primary complaint by one or both that the other is 'always running to Mother', or that the spouse's family interferes. The anger and bitterness of feeling the partners cannot express is thus displaced to and voiced by the hostile camps of in-laws. 'Your Mother never liked me' may be a profoundly meaningful accusation summarizing not so much the actual as the historic-dynamic interaction between the shared anti-libidinal objects containing the oedipal ties and conflicts, as well as the culture distance.

Case Fourteen: The latest case to consult me, after the above generalization was written, illustrates practically all the weapons and levels of such a shared symptomatology. A youthful, handsome couple, both aged 49, present together from choice to seek help for their lack of harmony. W. displayed—within minutes of sitting down—the full range of hysterical shrewish behaviour. This, she declared, was the 'worm turning'. W. had previously relied on her 'selfless devotion', financial help to establish H., and domestic martyrdom to expiate the guilt of her masculine envy and dominance. She spoke of her rejecting father who hated children and was always away on military duty. To please him she had joined one of the women's Services in World War II. In this context she was seduced, at 24, by a soldier of an Allied

146

nation—not even commissioned! As if to punish her the father (who knew nothing of this) died soon after. W. felt disgraced by her attractive seducer and married him to continue the unhappy rôle of the shamed but proud woman. From the first moment she expressed anti-paternal hostility to me: she supposed she had come 'to keep quiet and be lectured by a great man that she was a tiresome neurotic'. After this both H. and I had great difficulty in getting a word in edge-ways in the spate of accusations of H. for being a philanderer, for being so ambitious, only thinking of his work, which took him abroad a great deal and where he constantly met glamorous girls; how she had married beneath herself—wasn't her father a Brigadier?—how she had dreamed of a peaceful home instead of this struggle—how she hated this foreigner who did not appreciate English restraint and self-control.

The said H. it transpired, was the embodiment of correctitude and self-control. He had married out of passionate idealization of W. as an aristocratic English lady as well as for her (still obvious) vivacity and good looks. He had also idealized the loving home, in which his culture pattern was of spoilt sons and husbands expected to act very assertively and with virile panache, but really run by indulgent matriarchs. H.'s behaviour in this culture clash had been increasing withdrawal, punctuated by angry outbursts with subsequent contrition. He transferred to work which took him abroad as an escape from his wife's constant tiredness, illnesses and accusations. He had also fallen back on an elder sister through whose mouth came pitying patronage of W. and family snobbery in reverse. H. was himself a graduate with an upper class background, who had for years tolerated being treated as a boy, grateful for W.'s self sacrifice and lady-likeness. All this, greatly condensed here, emerged from one meeting.

A related pattern is formed by a competition in compulsive martyrdom of both partners to seemingly unending domestic chores and mutual service which eat up all their energies. This obsessional pseudo-co-operation becomes the chief expression of both partners' aggression and thus a perpetual battleground. It is remarkable how often such couples conspire to own impossibly dilapidated homes on the plea of the husband's inability to afford anything better, with neglected large gardens, supposedly for the children's benefit. Now there develops a war of attrition over theoretically allotted sex rôle-congruent jobs.

Case Fifteen: Such was the state of a professional class couple in their early thirties, whose doctor thought something must be done to end the deadlock of exhaustion, constant minor ailments and periodic threats of separation. They had only one child, but each made an issue of being too fatigued to get up first and take the child to school. W. accused H. of neglecting her for tinkering forever with his old car; but he held that without it the child could not be got to school. The painting, the dishes, etc., therefore all piled on her. H.'s contribution, apart from trying to make the car go, was to produce endless 'work-schedules', budgets and plans to show how thoughtful a husbandman he was. He ran from half-done task to totally unattempted task pursued by his wife's nagging that the front door lock was unmended for three months now, or the ceiling half-painted. In the small hours *he* would have to wash his office shirt. There was no time or money for any outings. Domestic patching-up took all he earned. Both were only children from spoiling, over-protective homes in which the mothers had 'done everything for them'. H. wanted a controlling mother against whom to rebel and yet to continue to be serviced by. W. was identified with just such a mother who exacted service from her father and could brook no disorder. All this was happening in the name of building the perfect home and rôle-sharing, allegedly for their child who was almost totally forgotten in the struggle of which could outdo the other in angry martyrdom and *not* rendering any help to the other.

For a vivid description of the phenomena of dominance conflicts in marriage Jay Haley's paper[2] is unlikely to be bettered.

3. DISTURBANCES OF SEX FUNCTIONS AS PRESENTING PROBLEMS

This sub-division in marital symptomatology is often thought to be THE beginning and end of the whole trouble. The preceding pages have shown why I for one cannot subscribe to this facile, pseudo-biological monofactorial explanation, with its overtones of worldly-wise cynicism and its denial of a consistent psychology of the person. The subject of sexual disturbances was briefly introduced in an earlier section of this chapter. Here I want to add some further observations which may help in more refined diagnosis and more adequate handling of cases.

Those who come with symptoms of failure, in one way or another, of a mutually satisfying and relished sex life, nearly always *consciously* desire to restore it—often only because it is part of the 'contract' and the accepted norm of the culture. There is then little deeper urgency about this desire for cure. As sub-divisions of marital cases with major sexual symptomatology we distinguish:

(i) those with overtly declared sexual malfunction, often initially assigned to one partner to carry (e.g. *Cases Six* and *Seven*);

(ii) those by whom sexual malfunction is not stressed at the intake phase, but masked with other complaints. It is readily described with little probing from the interviewer (most of the other cases quoted so far);

(iii) couples in whom periodic or even continuous sexual activity is preserved as a kind of routine in contrast to the lack of satisfaction with each other as persons, and is thus felt as shameful or demeaning.

In this section I shall deal chiefly with the (i) group, as the (ii) group is diffused over different presenting symptom categories. Before doing so, I should like to allude to the (iii) group. Dynamically, these are people with incomplete splits between adult (libidinal activity tolerating) and anti-libidinal object relations—like Guntrip's patient in Chapter V to whom his wife was at times a libidinal and at other times a rejecting object. But the adult libidinal activity need not be synonymous with adultery! It can alternate with phases of withdrawal and hate inherent in the total interaction, as we saw in *Case Ten*. In mild and insightful cases (usually not seen as patients) such a phase can be described half-humorously as 'George and I are not speaking this week', or some such statement. In more serious conflict situations it is usually only the physiological act which proceeds normally. Psychologically it lacks the satisfaction of a communion. The sexual function, as most other natural functions, can often serve immature goals: to defile, to score off each other, prove power over the other. It can be accompanied by obscene, belittling instead of loving, words and feelings, expressing part of the complex ambivalence.

Case Sixteen. Thus, in a severely disturbed marriage between a technician and his ex-nurse wife in their mid-thirties, she would frequently goad him to sexual ardour, and then at the point of penetration deny entry, attack him with words like 'You filthy beast' (not in fun) and with attempts to injure his genitals. On one such occasion he found himself stabbed with a knife hidden under the pillow. She would only consent to coitus when *she* wanted it, but he was not even then allowed to show affection or 'be nice'.

The opposite—namely male sadistic behaviour—is better known. This goes into all the much publicized variants. Beating and being beaten, tying up the woman and gloating over her 'helplessness', are the usual ones. Such sense of power alone seems to make it safe for the husband to be potent. The use of belittling, obscene words as an accompaniment to the final sex act makes it clear that the sexual union in the man's mind is not with this woman as a love object, but with a split-off image of a harlot, a slut, or a part object invested with hate and aggression. The women, nonetheless, collude in such degradation and denial of love, but pay back in contempt and dominance. We are in such cases fairly close to shared perversions, such as masochism in the woman and fetishistic or flagellatory pre-occupations in the husband, who in between such sexual episodes is often a passive, reparation-making henpecked man.

Case Seventeen: H., a company director around 45, had for years always preceded coitus by 'playful' beating and tying up of W., without her demur. A crisis occurred over the children's management when W. identified with her adolescent daughter and switched right round to sexual withdrawal and furious paranoid persecution of H. He now saw her as a sick woman—why else should she suddenly become so unreasonable over his 'harmless' love play? W.'s trans-ference to the writer betrayed her hate of sadistic father figures, whom she had hitherto tried to please in order to gain love. She poured out highly emotional writing full of preoccupation with jealousy of male power and badness, and of fantasies of herself as a poor injured, bleeding victim. We had enough data from several joint interviews to show us also that her deepest hate was, like H.'s, for a dominant, 'inhuman' mother. It was legitimate to interpret the earlier collusion in the perversion as a shared sado-masochistic identification with the powerful father punishing a degraded hated female. When H. appeared to neglect his daughter, he received the full fury of the displaced bad mother transference, and must hence-forth be treated as W. had tolerated herself to be treated symbolically, so long as she could identify during the sexual practices with her male internal object against hated torture-deserving mother figures. In the perversion H. had enacted the shared sadistic fantasies against the bad mother-figure. For the rest he was a gentle admirer of his clever wife. It took some 15 years of marriage before the sexual collusion broke and the case was presented with the symptomatology of a near-paranoid hate-filled woman maltreating and denigrating a 'kind', bland and uncomprehending husband. All men were the carriers of her own Lesbian sado-masochism.

Such a break in the hitherto tolerated collusion with its denial of hate feelings can be caused by the need for or actual occurrence, of personality growth towards a more clear-cut identity in at least one of the partners. It can also be a switch from one to another set of split inner objects, as in *Case Seventeen.*

As mentioned, the sexual act and its preparatory foreplay can become the symbols either of valuation or of denigration or damage in either or both partners' own or projected feelings. When to yield and submit has the unconscious meaning of being devoured or humiliated and de-personalized, or when the manifestations of sexual desire and its physical concomitants (e.g. female moisture) are viewed as the equivalents of excretion or of threatened loss of self-control, or greed, or repudiated sphincter erotism, then this may lead to failure by inhibition, irrespective of whether the guilt is intra-personally experienced or projected to the partner. Prudery, conservatism and lack of finesse are still plentiful despite our national new daringness in fantasy and fiction.

It is here that the complex attitudes to *contraception* and pregnancy fit in. Both partners may share the rejection of birth control appliances as being part of 'messiness', or have such a sensitive balance of libidinal and anti-libidinal trends that the pause in the unfolding of their preliminary love-making, required to fit the contraceptive, is enough to destroy erotic feeling. The rôle of being the cautious one may be assigned by the dyad to one partner, who thus 'sacrifices' his or her pleasure for the sake of the other's. This may soon develop into a battle about who has 'the dirty end of the stick', exploits the other and so on.

Similarly with the emotional attitudes to having children, which are fairly well understood and documented in psychiatric literature. It is not only many women who still believe that orgasm increases the risk of pregnancy, and that childbirth is a terrible and destructive menace. We shall see that men also can hold these views and that these influence their sexual behaviour in the direction of psycho-biological frustration and impoverishment of the dyad's shared life, e.g. by coitus interruptus. The fear of babies and all they represent in unconscious fantasy would take a whole chapter in itself, quite apart from the rational aspects of family planning. It would also cover ground already well explored by many writers.

This wealth of unconscious meanings may be given to sexual activity from the beginning of the marriage (cf. *Cases Six* and especially *Seven* in Chapter V), or may only be rekindled as the sequel of a divergence on other grounds later in the marriage. Thus one may symptomatically distinguish between *primary* and *secondary* sexual failure.

(a) *Primary sexual failure.*

This group is clinically important. In complete form, as *non-consummation* of the marriage at the time of being interviewed, it accounted for 7 per cent of our cases, with a further 8 per cent in whom it could be suspected on strength of extreme reticence, circumlocution or vagueness on the part of the couples, usually only seen once. The greater part of these had been married from 2–5 years, but some up to 15 years.

The symptomatology or history of non-consummated marriages is surprisingly monotonous, offering only a few variations on the theme of honeymoon night hysterics or anxiety on the part of the bride which the groom is 'much too nice' to override by confident mastery of the situation. This is then followed by visits to the doctor who discovers 'nothing abnormal' in the girls' genitalia, or else vaginismus and perineal muscle spasm for which a gynaecologist is asked to give dilatation with bougies. This proof of no obstruction, or possibly surgical defloration of a tough hymen, with encouragement from the doctors, sends the bride back to the *status quo* when another round with her husband renews the original situation. The visit to the doctor may well be deferred for anything up to two years, or it may never happen until the relatives begin to wonder why no babies are appearing.

The second variant and mirror image of the first is the honeymoon situation in which it is the husband who is impotent, either totally or to the extent of *ejaculatio praecox*. His wife, all prepared for a 'wonderful experience' is left crying and angry, her idealized expectations shattered and her contempt for her mate sealed for life. The third variant is one in which from the first both partners know that they are equally unable to break the taboo. None of the three variants have had coitus together before the wedding, and are often very 'virginal' characters. The first two variants are apt to present singly as stated in Section 1. Our experience of collusive dyadic interaction has, however, long since made me chary of interpreting impotence or frigidity as anything but an inter-personal problem, as also already stated. It does not follow that individual therapy is *ipso facto* ineffective—indeed it is one of the marital stress syndromes in which individual therapy may be indicated at least in one phase, as will be seen when I come to discuss treatment.*

For the first variant *Case Seven* serves as a fairly typical example. It well illustrated how a couple used the collusive mechanism of the wife covering up for her husband. It will be recalled that he began his contact with us as the aggrieved party with a dyspareunic wife, but within hours disclosed an even more severe obsessive revulsion against the genitals. The rapid disclosure of the congruence of both partners' attitudes made this case somewhat like the third variant. More commonly there is no recognition of the collusive dovetailing at the presenting stage.

* L. J. Friedman⁴ reports good results with his methods in a few interviews.

Thus *Case Eighteen:** presented as the wife's hysterical dread of consummation. This was a young couple in their early twenties married 18 months, from conventional middle-class backgrounds. She had already been the rounds of gynaecologists and resented the dilators. The wife's individual history disclosed a very strict patriarchal home, in which the daughter's virtue was supervised by a jealous, stern but loving father who inspired awe and admiration in W. He chased unwelcome suitors away, though a few hardy members of the local football team had, with the girl's connivance, breached the defences and managed to give her some exciting foretaste of what a persistent male could do—always short of coitus. When H. appeared, her father accepted him at once as the 'decent reliable' chap he looked for, with good earning prospects, and gave his blessing to their marriage. The husband was, indeed, just this sort of man, 'Sir'-ing me and presenting a thoroughly deferential 'good boy's' personality. He assured us he had nothing to reproach himself for, he had always treated her very gently and lovingly. His father had always treated his mother with the utmost solicitude, as she had 'suffered so much with her back'. He therefore could not undersand why W. was afraid of him: he would not force himself on her or wish to hurt her. His father, he said, had always punished him as a boy if he was rough or noisy, and forbidden him to worry mother. Sexually he was quite virginal at marriage.

W. both at single and in joint interviews was able to express her disappointment with H.'s meekness. She said to him 'I wish you had been stronger and had beaten all this stupidity out of me'. She also reported 'such funny' dreams she had lately had—of being chased by gangsters with guns.

The dyadic presenting symptomatology, therefore, looked rather different from the surface common-sense picture of a 'poor frightened young girl' with an 'ever so decent', understanding, eager husband thwarted by her hysteria. Dyadically, H.'s ineffectiveness and W.'s anxiety formed for us a single whole. The collusion rested on a *shared* stern father figure who had in effect driven these two to marry on an anti-libidinal basis. In W.'s case this was the model of a powerful man who compels women's submission. Her condition for being aroused was male mastery, linked to her oedipal incest taboo. Exciting libidinal objects were split off—rough boys furtively met or symbolized as gangsters, whereas the father's nominee conformed to the unexciting anti-libidinal object. H.'s conformity with this rôle and its transparent relation to his own oedipal experiences need scarcely be elaborated. His 'good' father was incorporated as

* Originally published in 'Sexual Problems in Marriage' *Proc. R.S.M.* 1959; **52**, pp. 867–72.

his ideal self in regard to sexual behaviour; his 'bad' father reacted as a deterrent anti-libidinal and anti-self-assertive figure, probably reinforcing the unconscious guilt feelings over the damaged, suffering mother. It seemed safe to infer that with this degree of negative conditioning, this young husband failed from the beginning of courtship to display mastery of the kind his wife had built into her 'blue-print' of a male. As already hinted at in general terms, especially in Chapter III, she was not going to yield to a frightened, timid creature who mistook her sexual tension and guilt for dread of being hurt. By becoming the 'patient' she covered her husband's lack of *elan*, so wounding to the *amour propre* of both partners. But even at a first interview she showed her disdain for him as well as her inability to mix idealized expectations with sexual behaviour. Once again there was the shared taboo exerted by the anti-libidinal object (chiefly of a punitive father) on the adult integration of the dyad.

One can draw up, in cases of female refusal to consummate, an ascending scale of more or less unconscious masculine identifications in the woman. At their fullest, I suppose, these would manifest as a consistent rejection of the passive feminine rôle and thus of marriage. These apart, we have all met plenty of embattled amazons in marital casework. The female needs and social pressures had been strong enough to impel the woman towards mating. Yet they were so dominated by masculine envy and competitiveness that even the possession of a vagina had to be denied. I owe to von Hattingberg[3] the description of the embattled shrew in terms of the armoured maiden, Brünhilde, upon whom her divine father, Wotan, had cast his magic spell that could only be broken by the hero (in the legend Siegfried) who did not dread the father's spear guarding his favourite daughter.* No mortal man was strong or worthy enough to gain her. This formulation of Nordic saga (best known in Wagner's setting of the 'Valkyrie') seems to be directly applicable to many cases of frigid and dyspareunic women, as for example in *Case Eighteen*, and also to such a marriage as *Case Fourteen*—an amazon caught unawares and hating the man who broke the spell. The clinical picture reveals the often complicated tie to the internalized father, which colours the girl's identity as a replica of him. In classical Freudian terminology she had not worked through her oedipal bond with the father but has introjected his sadistic penis. While the biological and social pressures impel her to make a partial surrender of this 'phallic' position, her resistance to this castrating step will evoke her secret hate and envy and denial to the man of what she had in fantasy stolen from her parents, often with the father's unconscious connivance.

* Leonard Friedman[4] has also used this figure as one of his genotypes of 'virgin wives'.

Case Nineteen: (investigated with Dr. Trevor Smith) presented in easily recognizable form both partners' collusion in maintaining non-consummation and the amazon syndrome. Though H. was about 28 and W. 22 years old, they impressed us with their almost pre-adolescent youthfulness and fair-headed charm. They had courted for 2 years and had been married 15 months: 'they just knew they were right for each other'. H. angrily repudiated the inquiry whether they had had coitus before marriage. 'He had too much respect to do that'. He described (and W. confirmed) only a little petting which faded out together with all sexual feelings as the wedding day approached. 'We became so busy with getting the home together and all the many arrangements, it left no time for sexual feelings.' It also transpired that W. was earning more money than he at their respective jobs. There was complete rôle sharing in their intense home-building and gardening activities. His personality was typical of all the husbands in this category: nice, unaggressive, polite. 'When I tried to approach her she could not bear it at all, so I stopped, because she gets so worked up, cries and makes a tremendous fuss: it got me upset too and I felt like a brute.' He was quite insightless and placed all the onus on W.'s state: 'couldn't she take something, hormones or whatever?'

W. was a most attractive elfin woman, with a slim physique and a superficially girlish personality. Her menstrual history was normal. Her discussion of sexual topics was marked by the frank objectivity of a latency child. A lively person with wide interests and a fine school record, she soon revealed the source of her symptom. 'My H. is more domesticated than me—he lost his mother young.' 'He is very protective and affectionate—I never had so much shown me . . . as a kid I was labelled "independent"—never kissed my parents.' 'When I was small, Mum was very busy looking after Grannie who was ill—she says Dad was quite hot-blooded but she was cold like me—I wasn't planned—and she didn't want other babies. When my little brother came 9 years later I ignored it all, just buried myself in books.' 'Dad was away when I was small (war service). We are very alike—so we don't get on—we don't understand each other.' 'He has old-fashioned ideas on what men and women are supposed to do. He never helped in the home. He was always critical of my school work.' 'Mum couldn't help me over sex—she knows less than I do. But she told me Dad gets the climax too soon and she is slow.' 'I don't like the penis—several times when I was young, men exposed themselves to me and I ran from them.' 'If H. had overcome my tears and fighting early on it would have been all right. Now that he has to wait for my consent it will never come.' She laughed gleefully when describing how the poor fellow had been unable to penetrate and was so un-certain of his technique—'she *tried* to help'. She had seen a TV play

155

which featured a wife still a virgin 6 weeks later—here was she herself a virgin $1\frac{1}{2}$ years later; ha! ha! A lady doctor (who referred the case to us) had taught her to understand her anatomy; followed by dilatation and even the fitting with a diaphragm. 'I had never dared explore myself there.' Yet she still felt 'she was too small' for real intercourse. It next came out that she had for years indulged in clitoric masturbation, and stimulated her erotic imagination by vivid fantasies of being a well-known strip-cartoon superman, in which she carries out science-fiction acts of daring. These dreams of being a man also occur in sleep. In her therapeutic transference she showed that her ideas of being penetrated by a man were terrifying fantasies of a sadistic old man breaking into her—in contrast to her intellectual sang-froid of the diagnostic interview. Seeing a couch in the consulting-room let loose an angry storm of speculation of what the doctor would do to her, how she had always dreaded 'something like an operation' which never happens. She disliked children, as she would have to give up her well-paid job. She wants to contribute and excel in all H. can do. She had married to be in line with her girl friends, but preferred an affectionate brother–sister relationship and some manual clitoric play, which was not repellent and animal-like, like coitus.

I think it would require wilful denial by a blinkered opponent of psycho-analytic theory to miss the interpretation of this case. Here was Brünhilde carrying her sadistic, masterful fantasy-father inside her and defying a timid mortal with mocking laughter. As Jung has often pointed out, such an unconscious 'male' is *qua* female a terrified little girl, her femaleness (despite biological normality) having remained an 'inferior', undeveloped function of her personality. Clinically, we can often distinguish frigidity (or, better, the fight against yielding in coitus) due to such 'positive' masculine identifications, from anti-libidinal ego manifestations derived from fantasied rejecting, forbidding or alternatively damaged mother-figures. These two motivations can also reinforce one another in the same person and more especially in the dyadic interaction, as in W. in this case. As a female she was identified with her cold mother and thus had to introject the father with whom she could not work through the oedipal phase.

The next case illustrates not only my second variant, i.e. the man presenting as the sexual failure, but also the reinforcing vectors just mentioned.

Case Twenty: In this non-consummated marriage of three months' duration, the husband acted as the presenting patient. The wife was another phallic amazon. H. was a gentle, scholarly man as part of a counter-identification against a show-off, possessive father 'who took all his initiative away', though he left all the disciplining and rejecting to H.'s mother. The latter was characterized as distant, and only interested in reading to him as a small boy, deputing intimate care to a formidable nanny. Then came a belated drive by his mother to compete for H.'s favour with the father ('who was more of a mother to me than Mother'), in the latency period when the son was repelled by her enveloping affection. The effect was to produce a passive, highly educated man whose sexual experiences had been limited to older women, with one of whom after her coaxing he had achieved coitus. At 23 he met his wife aged 21, a seductive, spoilt and much sought after dancer of illiterate background. She paraded both her purity and girlish idealism, and her 'hot sexual' nature to the interviewer. Behind this lay the story of her parents: a ruthless soldier forced W.'s mother to marry him when she was 16, then deserting them when the child was only 2, turning her mother forever against sex and men despite a later second marriage of convenience to a gentle, spoiling, affluent man. W. refused importunate older suitors though one such aroused her passions as a ruthless 'he-man'. She said 'He made me feel as if my body was his so it would not hurt to have him'.* But though encouraged by her young parents, she stuck to her dream: the fairy tale marriage when her future husband would make her surrender beautiful and pure. So she chose H.—least likely to perform this rôle with *elan*. 'Before my wedding I was afraid, I asked him not to do it on the first night—I shall have to get used to him in bed.' She also said 'we are like kids together and laugh a lot . . . He loves me because I am nice and pure, because I am a little girl—if I act like that he adores me. If he gets ready (for sex) I am cold; but if I am ready he cools off. I won't have it (defloration) done by doctors. I can't forgive him because he ruined my dream—so now I scream at him.'

H. described their attempts at love-making in similar terms, but added that she had the kind of hysterics which made him feel 'it was murder to persist'. He next associated that he had, amidst terrible excitement, witnessed parental coitus—and added that while towards him the parental roles were almost reversed, 'with Mother my father was always the strong one' (a good example of double bind for the son). In contrast to H., W. conveyed a sense of self-confidence and narcissistic arrogance, describing her tantalizing virginity as if she saw herself through a man's eyes, hard to get and devastating to her trail of rejected rich suitors, all of them more potent than the poor fish she had married. She did not even consider she needed help. A joint interview was abandoned. The marriage was later annulled.

---

* This fantasy seems the mirror-image of that of a man who felt his wife as his penis[5]

The Brünhilde motif, in this case with the armour of hate masked by seductiveness against the devastated males who threatened her phallic pride, needs no comment. What is socio-psychologically important is the continuity of the spectrum of castrating, phallic women extending from the 'tweedy spinster' honest man-hater to this pseudo-feminine 'cock-teaser' (the Londoners' term for this behaviour) who triumphs over men in this way, her path strewn with despised failed conquerors. Such a woman will collect suitors like Red Indians' scalps, fleeing from those who by reason of sexual confidence and panache present a real danger, and settling for the meek and mother-dominated men who project all their own repressed libido and potency fantasies into such a phallic glamour girl. To her the unthreatening gentle lover represents the promise of a more idealized and less hate-containing relationship, a lost relation-potential in herself. This is, however, almost invariably destroyed by the return of the bad, phallic father, of whose anatomy she feels a part, who remains for both partners the sought and the repudiated exciting object. The central-ego (second sub-system) level dyadic integration—such as this young couple had achieved at companion-ship level—is powerless to hold them. Their educational (first sub-system) backgrounds were incompatible.

I should now also like to illustrate the third variant of primary sexual failure—where recognition that the disability is shared precedes the initial attendance at the clinic. This shared presentation makes the collusive dyadic nature of the symptom even clearer.

Case Twenty-one: A lower middle-class couple, aged 24 and 23 when seen, consulted us as a last hope before action for annulment in view of a 2-year-old unconsummated marriage, characterized by a crescendo of bickering, tension and disillusionment to the point of exhaustion and despair. W. in her application form gave the following statement: 'Inability to consummate marriage after 2 years 4 months. Due in the first place, I believe, to fear and physical disability on my part; now due to impotence on my husband's part, and lack of desire and normal reactions on mine. Previous treatment—course of dilatory (she meant dilatation) excercises at family planning clinic—cured physically.' H. stated only his part of the failure but omitted reference to his wife's initial troubles.

After individual interviews and several joint sessions, with Mary Williams as my partner, the following report was sent to the referring psychiatrist: 'What has emerged is the tendency for mutual attribution of failure of sexual drive to the other partner. H. is one of those guilt-ridden overconscientious personalities with a terror of being aggressive or taking the lead. This does not only come from an old-fashioned hellfire puritanical background but also more narrowly from a dread of critical family authority. Whilst superficially his little wife would certainly not seem to be a menacing figure, yet, as we observed the interaction in joint interviews, he has managed to make her into a critical, belittling and rejecting figure. Not only is she a charge hand at her job with a strong mind of her own, but 'for his own good' she is trying to rearrange his needlessly hard mode of working life on a more reasonable basis, so that she can at least have something of his company. This to him feels like an attack on his honour and sense of duty to his firm. He feels attacked if she upbraids him for being late, and has taken to evade telling her if he has stopped for a drink 'with the boys' on the way. He is also nagged for building himself a super Hi-Fi set in his shed, as if avoiding her.

W. for her part shows the behaviour of a hard-to-win girl with very high demands on him. She has deeply disappointed fantasies which require her man to be tough and commanding and ardent. She also had a discouraging background in her own mother's presenting sex to her as the painful, horrible business of having babies. She has many minor phobias: of speed, going out in boats, being left alone. Thus she also feels very dependent on H.'s constant presence, to protect and reassure; in this he seems to have failed her—as she him in accompanying him in boats and cars. At the last interview we got to the point where W. was able to express this disappointment with H. as a 'strong male', because he seemed at his bosses' and everybody else's beck and call, but seemed not to care about her needing him. She felt he had not learnt how to woo her adequately (which he denied, saying she wriggled away from whatever caresses he tried—not recognizing she meant the *whole* of him devoted to her service). So now in revenge she would not let him have any sexual favours—such as allowing him even some masturbating relief. It can be said that W. has become a moulding, controlling woman for him. She has thus colluded most fittingly with H.'s own fantasies of rebellion against, and fear of such controlling figures.

We decided further treatment was marginally hopeful. Method and progress will be alluded to in a following chapter.

(b) *Secondary Sexual Failure*

I now turn to those disturbances of sexual co-operation between marriage partners which appear only after an interval before or after the wedding. During this interval coitus had been experienced as satisfactory or even intensely happy, part of the total idealization and absence of conflict we call 'love's young dream'. Whereas in primary sexual failure all conflict is displaced to the genital sphere allowing the rest of the relationship to be described as 'ideally happy' or the like, in secondary sexual failure the conflict manifests first at inter-personal level and then slowly erodes the genital function. We saw this in the example of the sexual rift following political divergence (*Case Eleven*). Another way of putting this point is that when hostility or rejection at personal level reaches a certain intensity, the sexual impulse tends to conform—first acquiring an aggressive, grudging component, later being totally extinguished in a proportion of cases. Another aphoristic generalization about symptoms of secondary sexual failure is: whereas in primary non-consummation genital activity is collusively perceived by the partners as excluded from the rigidly-held idealization of the relationship, in the secondary failures the sexual alienation may be described as a *regression* from, or reversal of, the precariously established genital function in the wake of more diffuse personal disappointment and developing hostility towards the particular partner as love-object. It is as if in the secondary cases the change from the 'all-in-all' ideal of marital relationship proceeds in the inverse manner to that of the primary cases. In the former the sexual relation for a varying period serves to disguise the deeper tensions, while in the latter the absence of tension is secured by sacrificing the sexual relation which would rouse too much anxiety.

From both types of failure and their surrounding dynamics it is permissible to infer the inverse: that where mutual sexual satisfaction continues it is the outward and visible sign of unimpaired capacity to see one another as whole persons. This capacity here outweighs the tendency to object-splitting inimical to Eros illustrated in the preceding pages. How closely the operation of sexual impulses is linked to the inter-personal relationship can be seen even in couples where genital failure in one or both is but a passing episode. While a quarrel is on, sexual attraction and potency are diminished or absent. When the quarrel is ended, sex rushes in again as the tender ritual of reconciliation. This state of affairs is universally reported by our clients. Thus, in averagely mature people the sexual response fluctuates in parallel with the total inter-personal relation and forms part of the repertoire of communication. This makes it liable to be perceived as a reassurance-symbol against fears of not being loved.

(1) We have already seen that sex can become part of the armoury in the struggle for intra-marital ascendancy and submission, and thus be used for non-sexual ends. Sadistic assertion of a 'husband's rights' can be countered by a woman's scornful and vindictive 'do your damnedest, you despicable brute, and get it over quickly', or by exploiting hysterical vaginismus or less localized forms of illness, fatigue and unresponsiveness which slowly undermine the vast

majority of men by arousing guilt and aversion, if not in finer feelings, at least by the crude erosion of their omnipotence fantasies and narcissistic vanity.

The elements of this war between the sexes are present even in the short-lived episodes just described, and the frigid rôle may be vested in either partner just as it is in the cases of primary sexual failure. In this respect the ability to remain conscious of the purposive use of sexual withdrawal or refusal as a weapon of punishment, retaliation or disparagement would seem to be healthier than repressing this purposive element and sliding into the hysterical 'I can't' of quasi-somatic illness, as discussed also by Haley (loc. cit.), and alluded to earlier. It means greater tolerance of ambivalence, and possibly a greater awareness of the need for congruence of the general personal relationship and its 'celebration' in the sexual act. To this extent the sexual function can be used as a measure of the adequacy of communication between the partners. The converse, however, need not apply. Communication can be excellent but by-pass the genital function; as in some of the primary cases of non-consummation including those on a voluntary (ethical) basis. But it is a pretty safe prediction that where communication is worsening and hostile and anti-libidinal forces are gaining ground, there sooner or later sexual co-operation will suffer in quality and slowly wither away.

There is a close parallel between liveliness and breadth of communication and degree of satisfactory mutual involvement. A good marriage between fully individualized persons can be passionate in both senses of the term: the capacity to get furious with one another as well as to enjoy a rich erotic relationship. Good quarrelling is part of a full system of communication or interaction though it may frighten more idealistic observers into persuading such couples to seek help. The couples themselves, having begun married life with more idyllic and conventional norms of rôle behaviour, may also worry what is happening to them—especially the wives. With growth of personalities such confrontations would seem to be healthy, but can be disconcerting and hence lead to a shared wish for expert assessment.

Whether such a relationship is one that the partners themselves tolerate, or alternatively leads to more angry than erotic passion and becomes merged in a chronic conflict situation probably depends chiefly on congruence of at least two of the three sub-systems of. interaction which were delineated at the end of the last chapter. It would also depend on whether the partners remain 'themselves' or regress to the pull of the projective identifications.

This makes me pause for a moment to stress that marital cases may present themselves for the first time for clinical help at *various stages*

161

in the development of their dyadic disturbance. Secondary sexual failure may be presented as the focusing symptom of the return of deeper conflict in the dyad as conceived in Part I of this book. In other cases the sex life of a marriage may be found to be essentially no better even though the partners present themselves with some other major symptomatology—e.g. personal 'incompatibility', bitter quarrels and the like. Sexual disturbance may be stressed because it has a more medical, 'non-moral' flavour in line with the contemporary emphasis on the importance of the 'normal' or 'full' sex life.*

I would also mention a category of case manifesting as sexual inadequacy which is intermediate between the primary and secondary. Typically this is a marriage of emotionally or actually young people, with strong idealizations of each other towards the anti-libidinal, high-minded austere end of the spectrum and guilt feelings about sexual matters derived from family culture. A sexual relationship is established but it can only use what I called the waters of the surface thaw while the deeper levels of libidinal life remain frozen or dormant. Often the partners value such 'respectability' and sobriety, because it conforms to their culture norm. They are glad that they have avoided pre-marital sexual experience and found each other. The women in such marriages are often unable to achieve orgasm and apt to lose interest in coitus, especially after their maternal needs are met. Their husband's attentions may be welcome only as a sign of his continuing devotion, but he has to be careful not to press his ardour for which he is apt to be called 'over-sexed', and made to feel guilty at not showing proper respect or 'being his age'. Sometimes the anti-libidinal attitude is stronger in the man. If he is working-class he may describe himself as 'not one to make a beast of himself', and fantasies of the splendours of film romance are resolutely thrust aside. These are busy, contented 'innocent' marriages until a crisis. It is not hard to see why just such dyads are extremely vulnerable to the irruption of a much more highly-charged sexuality roused by the appearance of a seductive figure vested with all the repressed fantasy qualities of the libidinal exciting object. Some evergreen Eve or experienced libidinally free man will be reacted to with elemental force because of the precariously maintained previous dyadic idealization of the 'good boy and girl' relationship. The conditions leading up to the appearance of the intruding exciting third party are usually clear on presentation of the case. There is, as it were, a period of silent incubation, characterized by worsening communication and increasing stereotypy and shallowness of shared life, which each partner feels but tends to attribute to withdrawal or rejection by the other

* Geoffrey Gorer[6] has drawn attention to the superficial change in English 'norms' towards including this as a 'cultural imperative'.

partner and regretfully accepts as 'becoming set' or middle-aged. Another pattern is the growing awareness in one partner of 'something missing' which they are too shy or guilty to talk about, leaving the spouse in a state of blithe unconsciousness that anything is wrong, and denying any lack. It is assumed that 'this is to be expected' after some years of marriage. It will be clear to the reader that I am now describing the sexual aspects of slow breakdown in the idealizing defences discussed in more theoretical terms in Chapter V. There is also overlap with the theme mentioned in Section 1 (ii) of the present chapter: when one partner has failed to maintain the original idealization on which the dyad had been established, and the other fails to be aware of this, such drying up of communication at unconscious level may be the source of neurotic or behavioural stresses in the unaware partner.

At this point the description of marital symptomatology merges into another way of classifying the phenomena—that of *acting-out* or of *containment* of the stresses within the boundaries of the dyad. I propose to discuss this topic in the next chapter, in a way which may help to link it to the legal aspects of matrimonial strife.

REFERENCES

1. DICKS, H. V. (1953) 'Experiences with Marital Tensions seen in the Psychological Clinic', loc. cit.
2. HALEY, JAY (1963) op. cit.
3. HATTINGBERG, H. VON (1937) op. cit.
4. FRIEDMAN, L. J. (1962) *Virgin Wives: A Study of Unconsummated Marriages*. London: Tavistock Publications.
5. STEIN, M. H. (1956) Chap. 'The Unconscious Meaning of the Marital Bond' in Eisenstein, V. W., op. cit., p. 65 ff.
6. GORER, G. (1966) Chap. 'Psychoanalysis in the World', in Rycroft, C. (ed.) *Psychoanalysis Observed*. London: Constable.

Chapter IX

SYMPTOMATOLOGY II:
'GROUNDS FOR DIVORCE'

As in other areas of behaviour, the failure of a system—intrapersonal or inter-personal—to contain the balance of its internal forces results in actions destructive of the integrity of the system. This breach always evokes defensive sanctions. If an incensed workman breaks his boss's windows, he renders himself liable to social penalties. But the same or greater hate may be bottled up by his manager in silent inhibition. His penalties appear as aggression turned against the self with possibly more destructive consequences for the social weal, but overtly as tensions (depression, ulcers or whatnot) redounding back on the sufferer. Society here acted through his 'superego'. In the marital sphere these dynamics are applicable.

The three great socially and legally defined ways of acting-out in marital conflicts are, of course, adultery, cruelty and desertion—and the greatest of these is adultery.

1. SEXUAL ACTING-OUT

I shall deal first with the symptoms of sexual acting-out because it takes up the theme at the end of the last chapter from the moment where failing dyadic communication had prepared the conditions for some acting-out to happen. Dynamically, I view impotence, frigidity, and other forms of withholding as 'negative' acting-out. But these are not clear to the clients and have to be decoded into their neurotic meaning. So long as dyadic tensions remain in that state, the partners can maintain some degree of denial: 'I don't know what has come over him (or her)—he is so remote—he must be ill', etc. We learnt from *Case Ten* (Chapter VI) how unsupportable this condition can be. The wife positively longed for something as understandable and concrete as infidelity in her husband, since it would free her own erotic needs and make her feelings intelligible. The husband's negative acting-out was more destructive to the marriage than if he

164

had been frankly interested in other women, and had been able to fight it out with his wife.

(a) *Adultery* when it becomes known to the spouse is the most serious threat to the great majority of marriages. It is often the last straw—the symbolic final treason. Even people of either sex who have secretly been having outside liaisons react with deep shock, anger and jealousy to the discovery that their *partner* has been doing the same. It is as if the value systems surrounding matrimony require at least one of the dyad to be identified with keeping faith. Such, moreover, is the capacity for ego-splitting that the unfaithful spouse can see one's own action as still falling within the joint boundary of the dyad, i.e. as 'not really' unfaithful, whereas the other's is. Indeed, we often see couples where this view has been shared by both partners, and the heartache denied in one way or another. I can only speak of various attitudes to adultery in couples I have examined. There have been some in which it has been taken for granted, e.g. as a devalued routine necessity, like excretion, created by the exigencies of a man's military or travelling life, and similar 'occupational hazards' in wives such as show business. But—and it is a very important 'But'—there have to be rules which when transgressed constitute the traumatic breach of faith.

The extraneous relationship has to be casual, without personal commitment to the third party. This is a 'must' in our population. The second rule may vary. At one end it runs 'So long as I know nothing about what you do out there'. At the other end we have often heard this: 'The insult wasn't that he had that tart, but that he didn't trust me enough to tell me.' Both attitudes are based on keeping faith at the personal level. The spouse who 'doesn't want to know' is concerned to maintain idealization and the sense of uncomplicated belonging which often goes with a predominantly child-parent perception of the marriage. Sexual needs in such are always played down, and the partner's split is denied. Security and cosiness are the prime desiderata, and much can be condoned so long as these are maintained. The spouse who 'must know' indicates a need for fuller dyadic communication. But this needs qualifying. It can also mean a pressure to possess, or to share in the external sex relation by identification, or to shame the erring partner by display of long-suffering parental tolerance. The knowledge can be a powerful weapon for moral blackmail and the exacting of a high price for the condonation in the war for ascendancy. Space forbids examples of all variants of even the single category of 'condoned adultery'. What I hope to show is how much the evaluation by the couple and by ourselves of sexual acting-out depends on the total dynamics of the dyadic relationship. One case must suffice.

165

Case Twenty-two: A couple sought help for a severe crisis in their previously bland and idyllic marriage of some 25 years' duration. H. in his early fifties, W. a few years his senior, with two adult children scarcely mentioned, except for W.'s statement that her daughter had ushered in the denouement by saying 'What's the matter with Daddy? —he treats you so badly.'

The profile of the relationship was of an 'innocent' marriage of two people sharing a constricting moral background of intense respectability described congruently when talking of their respective mothers whose figures influenced the story of the couple's sexual reticence and abstemiousness. 'A decent woman does not feel anything, and the man must respect this' was their implicit norm. There was some discrepancy in intelligence and maturational capacity between them. H.'s brightness led to a steep rise in socio-economic status, reflected in sophistication through contact with 'worldly' men. W. because of clinically obvious limitations could not follow him into this larger, more educated world. He secretly began to seek casual, only sexually relieving affairs outside. This regime, he felt kept him a much better, calmer husband and father and permitted him to respect W.'s implied disapproval of 'bothering' her more than occasionally. His peptic ulcer cleared up with this new policy which 'hurt nobody', least of all W. who was happy and could feel that his infrequent wooing represented his considerateness. She was then glad to oblige him—men needed that kind of thing from time to time, and she was very broadminded. Trouble began when one of H.'s mistresses came to mean a great deal to him as a person: generous, vivacious, intelligent, experienced in sex and sharing his interests. His comfortable ego split was in danger of rushing together in this new object. 'I tried so hard to see her as all the others—just good for sex', he said. Now he was in severe conflict and displayed his own unconscious need to heal the split *in* the dyad by confessing to W., out of great guilt and basic loyalty. This thing *really* threatened his marriage. It was as if he also wanted to introduce the missing libidinal object-relation into it. So he naively described how good real sex was. After being devastated and furious at this treachery, W. became depressed in the clinical sense, with feelings of inadequacy and self-hate at her own frigidity. By the time the couple came to interview the presenting picture was of a fairly cool, well controlled and on the whole complacent man who had awakened his wife to the problem, but was now making amends and showed her he meant to preserve their marriage. W. was badly confused and labile in her ambivalence.

The other woman was 'obviously more gifted' than her, yet only a harlot; H. honest and upright, yet an over-sexed villain; she herself the defender of Christian virtue and yet a poor deprived creature who

166

envied them this experience of which she could not learn the secret. Both partners agreed 'they had never been closer to each other' or communicated more freely, and wanted to work this new relationship out together. It was good, W. said, that he had told her, but dreadful to be compared with the other woman. An interesting light was thrown on the nature of the dyadic bonds when during a heated interchange ('we never used to quarrel like this!' W. said) H. suddenly felt faint and clutched his epigastrium. W. changed abruptly, searched her bag for tablets and was most concernedly maternal. An evident piece of the old pattern was revived when W. was the carrier of the anti-libidinal 'respected' mother-figure in which she visibly felt secure and adequate.

This case, by not being an extreme example illustrates several important aspects of sexual acting-out in infidelity, which need to be understood both in clinical appraisal and in handling of matrimonial cases. I have already mentioned the dyadic agreement to ignore casual sexual transgressions which do not impair the sense of mutual belonging. This attitude is clearly widespread although lip service may be paid by the 'innocent' partner to the principle of immutable sexual monogamy, whatever the factual adequacy and satisfaction in the marital genital relationship. Even in *Case Twenty-two*, despite her high conventionality and the severe blow to her *amour-propre*, W. retrospectively condoned H.'s 'offences'. His own commitment to his married ideals made him distinguish sharply between the trivial and the meaningful acts. The latter threatened the pledged loyalty and belonging of person to person—*it tore a gap in the dyadic boundary*. This boundary is always unconsciously recognized by marital dyads, though it varies greatly in its elasticity and in what it includes. Culture and norm differences may draw the boundary in rather inconsistent shapes for the two partners, not recognized until a crisis, or covered by denial.

The gap in the dyadic boundary may have unexpected results. Where the boundary was made largely of an obsolescent, maturation-inhibiting social norm tacitly accepted as a habit by both partners and personally idealized, the gap torn by one or both of them may serve to admit functions and relational potentials previously excluded. H. in the just cited case was typical of our experience that infidelity represents a need for better ego-integration by way of acting-out the libidinal object-relation excluded from the dyad. This, I think, is the reason why the unfaithful spouse, despite the customary attempts at crafty concealment, so often succeeds in letting the partner into the secret, whether by unconsciously purposive inadvertence or by courageous confession as in *Case Twenty-two*. The painful challenge

167

to the ending of a stifling collusion, indeed, frequently has the effect of making the erring partner appear in a new and more sexually exciting light. His or her pioneering effort thaws the 'injured' partner's own anti-libidinal freeze, usually together with a great deal of hate and jealousy which deepens the recognition of the partner as the needed libidinal object, and of one's own dormant sexual powers. The quietly subordinate complaisant husband, faced with an identifiable rival, at last feels his strength rising to a point where he reacts aggressively to the intruder and feels a 'new man' to the delight of his wife for whom this had been a last desperate attempt to get blood out of a stone. We may in such cases again hear the postscript: 'We have been much closer since that awful time'. Thus, it is medically permissible to speak of *benign* infidelity, which can be self-healing, even a necessary crisis in the growth process of the dyad. We may think of this kind of drama with a happy ending as a special kind of collusion, somewhat on the lines of *Case Ten* where, however, the whole situation was re-enacted with our help at a fantasy level.

In these acting-out situations we may call the third party the *transitional object*, who has the unenviable rôle of being made use of for the dyad's own deep purposes, often to disappear without trace from their further history. Yet, male or female, such transitional objects receive at first all the erupting flood of libidinal investment with its attendant idealizations and secondary elaborations from the breaking-out partner. Such poignant, searing experiences for a respectable man or woman with several children are always potentially tragic. The invasion of the dyadic as well as of the hitherto accepted ego boundary by this de-repression of the internal libidinal object system can happen with a suddenness and force which indeed justifies the marriage partner in describing the possessed spouse as ill. If there is rigidity in the anti-libidinal defences we may have to cope with suicidal depression in the adulterer. In Jungian terms such an event is called the invasion by the *anima* or *animus*, according to the respective opposite sex, to signify its relatedness to latent opposites of the conscious personality and the projective nature of the phenomenon. This is perhaps why transitional objects are so often those most easily identifiable with the childlike or the morally rejected aspects of the self and the milieu: the amoral nymphs, the sugar-babies and the caddish roués or play-boys.

But a proportion of transitional objects are provided by 'the best friend' of the deceived partner, in which case the dynamics of the 'missing part' in the dyad is even clearer. Such split love object needs sometimes create ludicrous situations for Western ethos. Not only in the swopping over of partners by friendly couples. We have seen people trying to manipulate their partners into accepting the mistress or lover either into a *ménage à trois* or at least into a 'fair share' time arrangement to be spent with the third party. These cases contain the elements of Guntrip's account of the man with the tripartite split, but acted out. We know, of course, that such arrangements exist in real life, either condoned or in secret, and that people do not bring them to us unless the dyadic 'boundary maintenance' is disturbed, however broadly drawn.

Case Twenty-three. Thus, a businessman with a frigid and rather rebellious wife fell in love with the *au pair* girl in their home. This was a special favourite with the wife, who almost pushed the girl as a sexual lightning-conductor at the husband, as well as handing over many other wifely and maternal rôles to this devoted helper who loved them both. But the boundary of the permissible was transgressed when H. actually took the girl into the marital bed. His rationalization was that it was his last trump card to try and stimulate W.'s erotic feeling via her homosexuality. This is when we had to be consulted, and the mother's help fired. The marriage has improved since then with some help, which enabled W. to mature to taking her adult rôle, having come to see that H. had understood what she needed.

As I said, the breakthrough of the need for the libidinal object can come very suddenly. In the above case, as in others, the third party may have been in the acting-out spouse's circle for months and years without any awareness of erotic feelings, as family friend, secretary, patient or home help. Nearly always the element of collusion is demonstrable or can be inferred, in many variations. These cover the spectrum from the 'innocent' partner's ambivalent projective identification with the rival, who supplies the missing link in the dyadic sex relation, to the manipulation of the situation to bring an end to a dead marriage.

The unconscious manipulation within the dyad which merits more attention is that in which one partner almost pushes the other into adultery. It becomes then the acting-out of the kind of tortuous fantasies we studied in detail in *Case Ten*. A husband with a sense of sexual and personal inadequacy uses an envied male friend into whom he projects his missing libidinal strength, much as King Gunther used the demi-god Siegfried to woo Brünhilde on his behalf in the Saga. The dynamics of such a situation show several variants, well understood from individual analysis long before marital studies were thought of. One is where the unconscious relation to the 'best friend' is a homosexual one and the projective identification is with the female enjoyment of the wife having intercourse with him. Another is where the wife, having been mainly a mother-friend to the husband, is as it were offered to another man who is the envied father figure, while the 'poor little weak' husband can only enjoy the pangs of oedipal jealousy and vicarious excitement, as if acting-out in this way his unresolved tie to the parents—and sometimes succeeding when he can at last see his wife as an attractive sexual being through another man's eyes. *Mutatis mutandis*, the same dynamics apply equally to the husband's infidelity. Thus the transitional object may be of benefit not only to one frustrated partner but also embody the 'injured' partner's repressed sexuality worked through during such a crisis. As I said, the missing libidinal object-relation is thus made available to both partners. As I write, I have a couple under observation who follow this pattern not only repeatedly, but also in alternation. They care deeply for each other and their large family. Their condoned-hated infidelities seem to function as a rejuvenation system to keep a perennial excitement about each other going.

But only some proportion of cases of adultery presenting at a marital clinic is of this benign, collusive and potentially helpful significance for the deepening of a relationship. For the greater proportion of marriages, including those whom we see, it is *destructive*. It can be the last straw in a marriage that has subsisted for a long time on a sado-masochistic rôle distribution. The presenting histories of the couples' interaction will then have a very different feel and content. They will be more like those case presentations cited under the Dominance-Submission heading above. The meaning of the adultery for both partners could only be mistaken by the very inexperienced observer for the same thing as in the collusive or benign forms.

The crucial feature of *malignant adultery* in this type of marriage is the further, possibly final, rejection or destruction of the partner as a libidinal object by the flaunting of the rival as greatly superior as a sexual mate to the spouse when the adulterous relationship comes to light. Instead of guilt and reparative feelings about the transgression of dyadic boundaries, there is callousness and indifference to consequences for the now truly injured partner. The adultery is another weapon for hurting and belittling—even for driving the injured partner crazy in Searles' terminology. This is especially so in cases where the previous collusive phase had established the dyadic interaction on the pattern of childlike, masochistically coloured dependence of one on the other so that the acting-out adulterer or adulteress knows that the partner, for emotional as well as economic reasons and for the children's sake, will not easily take self-protective or legal steps. More will be said about this under the overlapping subject of cruelty.

I do not think it necessary to cite clinical examples of this form of

170

adultery, which abound in press accounts of divorce proceedings and elsewhere. The essential points I want to make are the following. First, that the conflict-style interaction of tense marriages has a certain stability so long as the acting-out is kept within the dyadic boundary. The satisfactions come from expressing the 'negative' fraction of the ambivalence. This is still a fight on equal terms, implying that the partner is worth contending with and hence that a 'good' relationship is the aim of the struggle to coerce or mould each other to fit the respective rôle models. Adultery now means a gesture of rejection of the other *person*, and is conducted in that spirit. The rôle performance of the other is openly despised and the new lover's praised. It will be recalled that in *Case Twenty* the amazon-wife was taunting her husband with the excitement that other, better sexual males had been able to produce in her. In a case I am due to see, the wife is reported by her family doctor to be not only living with such another man but sparing the husband no detail of how much bigger her lover's penis is, and how different and superior the 'wonderful' experience of her adulterous relationship.* Analogous behaviour in men towards their wives is better documented.

Secondly, the attitude at the interview of cases that emerge as malignant or destructive adultery of one partner is one of intradyadic hate and of obvious unco-operativeness towards the potential therapist. The adulterous partners attend mainly to justify themselves and pay lip-service to social requirements. Their communications with us vary from proud acceptance of responsibility for their deed in the name of happiness for themselves and the ending of an insupportable marriage, to long histories of the shortcomings and antecedent hurts of the spouse. They often assert that their love and loyalty now belong to their lovers and their guilt is over continuing the now 'immoral' marriage with an unloved 'stranger', who means 'nothing'. The fate of the children in this kind of case seems to matter little. Either the problem is ignored, or else a wishful optimism disposes of their predicament by assuming the goodwill of the otherwise rejected other parent; or that the children 'don't know', or that in any case it is better for them not to have unhappy parents living together.

We must also distinguish between the variants of the 'worm that has turned' and is now scoring a triumph of assertion of identity and revenge against the erstwhile persecuting figure of the spouse; and the more sadistic-narcissistic adulterer who uses the transitional or new object-relation mainly as a crowning act of contempt, just because the open distress of the rejected partner makes him or her that much more despicable. It is often originally very dependent persons, cherished and encouraged by the partner *qua* parent figure, who attack

* The couple never came.

171

and discard this tutelary figure when they get the bit of social success between their teeth, or if they seek a fuller identity and can see its promise in the affirmation expected from the new love object.

The discarded partner's demeanour also merits some comment. Social values are generally on the side of the underdog, and the injured party is thus often driven to take refuge in this sub-system, and apt to stress the immorality or question the sanity of the acting-out spouse who has shattered the *status-quo*. It is often easy to see but hard to impart insight to such hurt persons, that the *status-quo* had been part of a major denial of the real dyadic dynamics which had sooner or later to break. The rigidly continued idealization of the 'partner I married' is continued side by side with manifestations of either a paranoid or a depressive attitude against the real partner and towards one's own share in the situation. Such injured partners have been throughout, or are now landed with, playing the rôle of the anti-libidinal object.

My experience of such cases, usually only seen once or twice, is that the critical acting-out by determined and destructive adultery of one partner is the climax of a dyadic collusion. This at its simplest has subsisted on the anti-libidinal rôle, say, of the wife, with the husband the dependent and subordinate partner ('the worm' now turned); or in the collusively falsified rôle of the sadistically dominant, spoilt tyrant over his long-suffering wife (who is then the worm who turns). It is more difficult here to demonstrate to the reader the subtle manipulative processes by which the erring partner is driven into adultery in order to give the injured partner the proud satisfaction of pinning social and legal guilt on the other and losing no time in preparing the divorce petition or separation writ. More often there is a less frank and more regressive phase when the injured partner is the hurt, rejected child, with commensurate hate and retaliatory fantasies. From this come many real and dramatized acts of counter-acting out: disappearing with the children, telephoning or calling on the rival or the rival's parents, attempted suicides, hysterical violence and so forth. Much dog-in-the-manger resistance to releasing the partner out of revenge comes into this, even where no rigid religious principles dictate the counter-action. The paranoid quality of the assertion of the right to legal possession often spills over into the psychiatric interview in which the injured spouse charges us with the omnipotent task of bringing the adulterer back to reason and affection—'that's all I want'. In the case of women there is, as everyone must concede, the real element of domestic and financial security which is less cogent for most men. But traumatized, dependent male cuckolds will equally demand a restoration of their domestic and nurtural comforts and rights. One finds oneself in such cases in the thick of a primitive talon-law atmosphere in which the deeper object-relations hidden under the now worn-out surface of idealizations are, alas, faithfully mirrored by matrimonial legal concepts. To the would-be helper the poignant situations are those in which betrayed spouses have their moment of truth too late, and for the first time become aware of what their rigid unseeing denial of the partner's and hence of their own changing needs has contributed to the situation.

Some of these situations can be retrieved or at least mitigated. This is especially so in marriages in which such acting-out by one or both partners is episodic. These fall somewhere between the benign and the destructive categories, and psychiatric assessment can differentiate these. The same forces are at work but the fact of repeated conciliation and resumption of full marital relations after quite lengthy and deep-going affairs with a third party favour the benign diagnosis. Often, these intermediate cases consult us for the first time after a lengthy history of 'intermittent' adultery (often coupled with desertion), because the last or current episode has produced a qualitative change (perhaps like that in *Case Twenty-two*), or age and diminished flexibility have lowered tolerance for boundary trouble.

It is a short step from this to two further variants in the symptomatology of sexual acting-out. One is the predicament of a married man or woman suspended for years on end just about mid-way between two love-objects—the spouse and another. We do not see those who manage this split successfully and for that reason can keep their two love-lives apart, usually on tissues of lies. The individuals concerned may consult us in the hope of cutting the Gordian knot—as for example an artist of some eminence who presented in a mild depressive state. He soon involved me successively in seeing his wife, his No. 1 mistress and his No. 2 mistress all of whom he managed to keep in ignorance of the continuing sexual rôles of the other two, though they were all socially acquainted. He expected me to decide for him with which lady his true happiness and future lay. We see mainly those cases in which the dyad as such is alerted and the original collusive boundary agreement disturbed, often by the impatience of the third party (who usually has the poorest deal) to get legitimized or force an end to the split life. Here it is no longer appropriate to speak of a transitional object, and the drive to cure in the principal is usually low, often because the other partner deep down condones the arrangement by reason of a corresponding ego split towards the divided partner or some other limitation of demand on them which suits them. In such cases it is strong conformity pressures, rather than emotional suffering, that bring people to seek 'adjustment' to social norms.

The second variant, in contrast to the just mentioned faithful allegiance to two love objects, is the compulsive promiscuity pattern, which we only see clinically if it is known by, objected to and hurts the other partner. In this we again have a multiplicity of patterns. One end of the spectrum consists in seeking out prostitutes or play-boys (as the case may be) representing the need for irresponsible, 'dirty' masturbatory indulgence from which the legitimate spouse 'on the pedestal' has to be protected (like *Case Twenty-two*) often against their own needs which have to be denied owing to the collusive rôle allocation. Another sort has the aim to prove one's sexual powers and to collect so many scalps as a reassurance against fears of inadequacy and castration or latent homosexual trends. This also goes for both sexes. Yet another fraction, nearer the other end of the spectrum, are concerned to find the ideal, idyllic, tender love uncontaminated by sordid everyday chores and denied by a critical too sober spouse of equal stature. Since the motivation is both infantile and therefore unattainable, and ideal and therefore also unattainable, this activity is doomed to perpetual frustration and a new search, as each successive transitional object displays his or her human ambivalence and so is 'no better' than the spouse. The prodigal now returns to base, before a new venture.

(b) *Other aspects of sexual acting-out* have been found to be as hurt-ful, if not more so, than infidelity with another person of the opposite sex to whom the injured parties have often had to concede good qualities: 'She is much more intelligent than me', or 'He is a much smarter chap than I am', etc. This *can* be accepted as the perhaps even slightly admired act of a 'whole person', and is, despite all that has been said, consistent with 'adult realities' in a wicked world. Much more insulting are the regressive continuation or recurrence of infantile acting-out which have some of the features of a com-promise between 'not being unfaithful' and yet withdrawing one's libidinal investment from the partner. In the first place one is thinking of the horror with which a spouse discovers that his or her partner refrains from loving intercourse but masturbates—the worse the more openly it happens. This is an affront to the identity of the partner, a rejection and a let-down of the projected inner image of their love-object in both of them. This and related activities—e.g. a preoccu-pation with pornography, visits to strip-tease shows (in this case always by husbands) have been the presenting symptoms for a number of couples. The consultations have been usually engineered by the wife, with the shame-faced or brazenly recalcitrant husband being brought in by us and telling us the story of his wife's bossiness, nagging or frigidity, with clear indications of her rôle as an anti-libidinal object. The provocative flirtation of either partner at parties, followed by ice-cold rejection of the other back at home, comes into this category too. So does the inordinately differential treatment of one of the children as against the spouse, provoking the kind of jealousy and sense of rejection we saw in *Case Thirteen*. Wives can produce the same effect also, as we have noted in a near-*folie à deux* case, by their adoration of a pet dog whom they obviously rate higher than their husband. They thus flaunt how much tenderness and devotion they are capable of giving to a really docile object, stinging the husband into violent paranoid retaliations.

We have now arrived at the next major heading under which to describe some of the essential phenomena of acting-out: cruelty.

2. CRUELTY

While this legal and everyday term should be clear in meaning, this is not by any means so in marital cases. The case material in these pages has described many instances of sadistic aggressive and demeaning behaviour of spouses towards each other. In only one— *Case No. 1* (not even legally married) was the issue of parting because of cruelty mooted, but not proceeded with by the 'injured' woman. Thus, the question when aggressive and persecuting behaviour becomes cruelty is as a rule only answerable in the mind of the recipient. The modern interpretation of the concept of cruelty by the judiciary includes 'mental' hurt. Even so it is rare for a man to win his divorce decree on the grounds of his wife's cruelty. Possibly this is due to the ignominy attaching to the public image of a male driven to seek this remedy by a female in contradiction to the rôle stereotype. In our experience the scores for cruel behaviour are about even, if we exclude heavy physical injury. *Case Sixteen* goes some way to correct even this last clause. The husband frequently attended us bandaged or bruised, quite apart from the attacks on his genitals he reported. It never occurred to this man to seek any legal remedy, nor to *Cases Twelve* or *Thirteen*, with their florid acting-out behaviour of ruthless provocation and belittlement by the wives and 'end of tether' retaliatory outbursts of physical violence by the husbands. In *Case Twelve* this sequence led the *wife* to seek court protection from the husband's reactions, which, later in joint interview, she could admit she provoked and expected. It is, therefore, not the existence of violence or aggressive behaviour as such which necessarily constitutes the hurt causing one partner to formulate the charge of cruelty in explicit terms. In the selected group of cases who come for help, the awareness that such behaviour *may* threaten the dyad has usually not reached such a formulation, even though the adjective 'cruel' may properly be used by them or by observers in describing a spouse's behaviour in a given context. The symptomatology described in marital Court actions is no different from what we meet in the consulting room. Swearing, hitting, locking out, refusal of help and comfort, nagging, belittlement, boycotting by silence, withdrawal of all sexual contact, undermining the partner's authority and image with the children, as well as the positive sexual acting-out behaviour dealt with above, are the stock-in-trade of our clients' dyadic self-descriptions as they are of divorce petition affidavits.

Dyadic interaction and collusion can include a wide variety of rôle distributions. Sexual frigidity and withholding can be part of an idealized, split system in which one partner is assigned the rôle of the anti-libidinal object, the other being the libidinal object. The product forms a total dyadic 'personality'. In the same way the angry, uncontrollable behaviour of one or both spouses can be a necessary polarized rôle in a shared and to that extent satisfying parent–child marriage, as we saw for example in *Case Ten*. In Russian humour there is the saying attributed to the village wife—'You have stopped beating me—don't you love me any more?'

What then is the dynamic change which turns a sado-masochistic relation into a 'case of cruelty' in one partner's mind? We get some light on this change by comparing cases who consult us as a last desperate step of self-justification before parting, with those who feel that they still 'belong' to each other and want to make the relationship more adult together. One example was *Case Seventeen* in which the couple had for years colluded in a tying-up ritual as a preliminary to coitus. A *change in the wife's perception* of the husband from a stern father to a persecuting mother figure meant a withdrawal of uncritical libidinal cathexis, a distancing from him. This standing aside broke the tacit collaborative agreement by which hitherto both partners had satisfied their dovetailing ambivalent inner object-relations (Sub-system Three) in their rôle distribution. The wife regressed to the paranoid relation with the early mother.

Case Eleven—the couple who split up after a change in political ideology had begun the process of transgressing dyadic boundaries at Sub-system One and Two level—points in the same direction. It was a similar stepping outside and looking at one's partner and one's own rôle through different eyes. In view of the importance of this issue I will cite a further illustration of how a dominance/submission conflict is turned into a 'cruelty case'.

Case Twenty-four: A couple in their late thirties who had been married for some 16 years, childless on the insistence of H. It was W. who was seeking help for the saving of the marriage, on account of H.'s final act of cruelty to her: asking W. not only to accept his adultery but to entertain the mistress, and punishing W.'s objections as hostile, narrow-minded obstructiveness which was incompatible with her 'really' loving him.

This was originally an 'all-in-all' marriage between two only children, both orphaned, who met in an Art School and developed a very loving symbiosis, including a good sexual relation, of mutual support in their parallel and often shared careers and value system. W. retrospectively, realized she had accepted H.'s uncontrollable tempers and fitful violence as the way men were, as part of a spaniel-like devotion to her precious gifted man. H. was brought to an interview by us unwillingly and displayed the resistance which masqueraded as an intellectual contempt for psychiatry. He merely hoped we might change W. back to the nice sensible girl she had been until recently. Briefly, I learnt that he combined a need of her as a compliant mother with a scapegoat for his own hostility—just as later it appeared that W. had projected all her own aggression into H. and colluded in provoking it by 'being stupid' or irritating him over trifles. Her militancy now was as much of a surprise to her as to him. The acts of violence, the peremptory orders to her, withering scorn and near-murderous throttling if she failed, etc., had scarcely changed over the years. But in the light of the final straw of callous sexual rejection in favour of a 'new' woman these were suddenly constellated by the now consciously critical wife as 'cruelty'—which indeed she had no difficulty in proving subsequently in the divorce court.

The dyadic boundary was breached first, once again, at the level of diverging values. W. remained the artist of 'high integrity'. H., sick of the struggle, succumbed to a tempting offer to turn 'commercial' and thereby became involved in flashy and opulent social circles. Each now looked at the other from the distance of different norms and social groups, and each despised the other's values: H. scorned W.'s little-girl idealism, W. hated H.'s selling his soul to mammon. This divergence threw W. into alternating depression and attempts at going with him. She re-internalized and discovered this aggression in herself. Her more logical and subtle retaliations became a source of great insecurity to him. She now managed to make him feel a vile apostate and a silly little boy. Violence was his only means of trying to maintain his erstwhile Svengali-like control over her. He could not understand how she had become a veritable she-devil of contempt and obstruction in his important new life. He had even contemplated suing *her* for cruelty and denial of conjugal rights. The flaunting of his new flashy, socially important girl-friend (who it appeared adoringly basked in his patronage) was a seal on his newly-found métier, but the final straw to W. which broke the collusion of a boy-and-girl relationship which H. had outgrown and W. had to struggle to abandon but was finally glad to shed. H. soon ceased his grudging contact with us. This helped W. to have therapy for her own sake, partly to overcome her mourning for the lost object. It involved accepting her own hate and 'masculine' drive, based on her deeper father-tie, suppressed because of her great need for being loved by somebody after her father's death, regardless of the cost to her identity. She could own her quite powerful dominance and autonomy needs, once she ceased attributing them to H.

In the light of such a case, I would hypothesize that it is transgression of the dyadic boundary that is the psychological cruelty, whether the act be violence, adultery or—as we shall see—desertion. This has the effect on the partner similar to the loss of the object with its attendant mourning and depression. It brings a re-introjection of object invest-ment, swelling the ego-cathexis and sense of separate identity. Whether this results in growth or permanent personality injury by regression cannot always be predicted. At any rate, it frees the injured partner to use means which were barred by dyadic cross-identification.

The more subtle and masked aggression of the apparently injured partner in a sado-masochistic dyad must be emphasized. Every attack and humiliation on them is projectively a vicarious acting-out for the hate they cannot own but can only suffer. Thus the more atrociously the actor-out behaves, the more guilt-free can be the triumph of the victim. The cue by which the acting-out to the point of no return is unconsciously set off may well be the dawning awareness of the actor-out that the victim is no longer in the game, that the collusive identification is withdrawn. The former now becomes wildly insecure. With a limited relational repertoire this triggers the further escalation of cruel behaviour which had become the habitual mode of inter-action while the submissive partner was colluding. A *Mr. Seventeen* or *Mr. Twenty-four* can only see the wife's new response as crazy, because it confronts him suddenly with the kind of threatening retaliatory power which his own sadistic drive has been employed to control in his love object as perceived from the paranoid position. The primitive threat of losing the compliant object is a threat to the brittle ego-defences of the actor-out. He is now impelled to test the limits of his omnipotence, which in the last analysis is double-edged, as all primitive ego-drives. We can see the 'escalation' as a regression to the level of behaviour described by Searles mentioned in Chapter VII. This is the need to control the uncompliant object by incorpora-tion, to make it safe as part of the self. This is equivalent to at least existential destruction of the object. In this context it is the no-longer-compliant object who in self-defence is rejecting the actor-out.

178

The latter now feels desperately paranoidally betrayed and alone, his bankrupt relational technique ineffective. This is why rightly society views the spouse of such a relationship in real danger and sanctions protection by leaving the matrimonial home or by injunctions against molestation. The sadist cannot live with or without his victim.

The cruelty issue arises in two kinds of case. One is where the power-submission balance is too unequally polarized, as in the Svengali-Trilby model, in which nothing short of the threat of existential obliteration will create in the dependent partner the qualitative change from collusion to withdrawal and self-assertion. The other kind of case is that in which there has been a near-equal struggle for ascendancy. It is in these that the distancing of one partner by the process of divergent growth ends the mutual satisfaction at sub-system three level, and thus forces the regression to primitive retaliatory acting-out, in the hitherto collusively 'aggressive' or dominant partner. It is my impression that in the second variant the cruelty issue is only crystallized by resort to adultery as the additional weapon in a limited armoury.

The transition from the phase of dyadic interaction of the dominance/submission conflict, to the phase of the break in the process where the dominant partner's acting-out acquires for the spouse the quality of cruelty, was shown in a couple only seen once. The interest also lies in the shift of 'power' from one partner to the other.

Case Twenty-five: A family doctor asked me to assess the following issue: An administrator of 48 married ten years to a woman nearly twenty years younger, with 3 children under 8. The presenting situation was that W. was holding over H.'s head the threat of leaving him and taking the baby with her. This followed a gradual evolution of dominance/submission conflict over the handling of the children. W., according to H., had been hard on them, chiding and correcting rather than loving and encouraging. H.'s response to this ongoing situation had been to make it up to the children, competing as the 'kinder' parent for their love with W. but only able to sulk, never to discuss joint parental policy with her. He impressed me as priggish and morally superior about W. as a woman and mother. H. (seen alone) volunteered that he had experienced the difference on himself. Father was a stern Victorian who 'was respected rather than loved'. Mother was just the opposite—soft and loving. 'Perhaps I am a little soft with the children in return.' There was thus discernible an identification with a good mother and a repudiation of a 'bad' father in himself, as it were a conspiracy of mother and child against the persecuting, belittling figure. This must have been H.'s model for marriage: a devoted

179

mother keeping the aggressive father from attacking the family. H. said 'W. was really lucky to marry me—she came from such an unhappy home.' W.'s background was described as a strict matriarchy —the model now being repeated in the present clients' home. Her father was allowed to sell in the jointly-owned shop, but the orders and policy came from the nagging mother who only criticized, making W.'s father act 'like a cabbage' when with her and take no interest in his daughter. In contrast H. felt himself to be a 'real' husband. (We felt he was trying to outmother his wife.) 'I only lived for the *children* and *home*' (note the wife was left out!). He had created a nice love nest as he thought in a house in a wood where he would have his idyll with a devoted little child-wife. He retrospectively realized that he took W. (who was only 19 when they married) for granted, made a fine garden and 'left her with the TV.' With the coming of children W. changed and began to resent her marriage and domestic ties, having been snatched from her career training and stuck into a lonely house. She felt disapproved of and sabotaged by H. when she enacted her own mother's rôle towards the children, while he tried to cajole and mould her to the pattern of his own mother, identifying with his children and also demanding constant gratitude for rescuing his 'little wife' from an unloving home. Thus W. felt angry and trapped, her maternal rôle undermined and belittled, but its effects on him undiscussed, because he was determined not to 'hurt her' by criticism which was yet implied in all his handling of the children as it had been in master-minding his young wife.

A recent move to a more inhabited neighbourhood led an observant neighbour to remark sarcastically to W.: 'You *are* a dutiful little wife!' This triggered W.'s acting-out, at first by becoming brutally outspoken. She began to show a conflict between an alarming awareness of her internalized nagging mother 'I know I am a neurotic bitch and a rotten wife and mother', and a relation to the useless, downtrodden father: 'You crushed my affection—it is all a mistake—I married too young—they all say what a wonderful husband you are but I know you don't care about *me*' etc. From this developed a crescendo of putting H. 'in the dog-house' as he termed it. He reacted by panic and emotional paralysis. 'I realized how much I was losing—so I tried to mend. I even became less affectionate to the children—they didn't seem any the worse for it.' In bed, though she never refused sex, she would show her disdain. He would find her defiantly ensconced with a book and a cigarette. 'I have a horror of forcing myself on her,' he said. 'She has reproduced the exact conditions of her parents' home: her father just a cipher, flashing back angry retorts to the mother's nagging . . . I can't even do that.'

The next twist in the screw that W. applied was to flaunt a mutual

180

acquaintance, a flashy middle-aged man whom H. despised, as her new admirer. So afraid was H. of losing her that he not only agreed to *carte blanche* in her relations with this man; he docilely entertained him, lent him money and his car neither of which the gentleman found it necessary to return. H. had to console himself with the thought that W.'s liaison was 'purely platonic' and that his rival was acting 'most circumspectly'.

This case had not yet assumed the delineation of a 'cruelty issue'. The husband had not given up his idealization and denial. Nobody however could be in any doubt that W.'s actions were what common sense would call cruel and vindictive. But we can also see that H.'s contradictory cues over the preceding years were part of the picture. The retribution is heavy for omnipotent men whose love-object is an adoring young girl, whom, Pygmalion-like, they hope to mould to their ideal image, once her investment in the collusion is withdrawn.

3. DESERTION

This major category of acting-out is nearly always found in conjunction with the other two. Without having kept count, I have the impression that desertion for the better pursuit of adultery is the commonest reason for leaving the matrimonial home. Desertion, especially if coupled with cessation of financial support, or equivalent female obligation towards home maintenance as a living milieu for the family, is equally an act of cruelty whether by vengeful malice or childish irresponsibility and flight. But it also occurs, so to speak, in a 'pure' state, uncomplicated by other forms of cruelty or by adultery on the part of the deserter. Some discussion of 'pure' desertion may be worthwhile.

Before developing these thoughts, one should exclude first those 'walk-outs' of one partner which can only be called healthy reactions to intolerable stress resulting from the acting-out, or its equivalents, on the part of the other spouse. These are defence reactions in response to violence or humiliation, even if exaggerated by inner fantasy. The Law Courts, as we know, make this distinction and do not allow such a withdrawal by the injured party to prejudice the success of their legal action. In fact such a forced step is regarded as part of the injury. The subtler complicity at Sub-system Three level is quite another matter and may closely resemble the kind of antecedent interaction conducive to, or even provocative of, the acting-out from which the superficially 'innocent' partner is now escaping, leaving the responsibility of driving them away on the 'bad' partner.

Desertion also has many variants, as regards its meaning for the dyad and as regards the phase in the developing inter-personal rela-

181

tion at which it occurs. Thus it is possible to distinguish degrees of
benign desertion by a rough estimate of the content of hate and of
other infantile emotions in the act.

Perhaps the commonest variant in a recently past period of history
was that simple panic which makes a young bride run straight back
to her mother after the honeymoon when the physical realities of sex,
carefully denied pre-maritally by idealization, were suddenly and
clumsily presented by the husband now out to assert his rights and
his virility. Not many such cases have come into the Tavistock's
field, but they occur in the less sophisticated layers of the population.
With belatedly sensible parents co-operating with a basically insightful husband such early flight reactions can be reversed, even if
never quite lived down. Some such young brides—and some husbands
too—never return.

The next commonest is a periodic disappearance of one partner,
nearly always in response to a quarrel or similar hurt to the deserter's
amour-propre and values. All the gradations of such temporary with-
drawals fall far short of legal 'desertion', and are acts inside the
dyadic boundary. The least is walking out of the room and slamming
the door, sulking in a bedroom. The next step is leaving the house
and walking or driving the streets but returning within hours 'feeling
better'. Beyond this comes the walk-out with a small suitcase and a
message where the deserter has gone. ('You'll find me in the Club', or
'Am at Mother's—no use coming for me', etc.) More vengeful are
the walk-outs with a threat of suicide, or where especially in the case
of a wife, the youngest or the favourite child, or even all the children,
have gone with her and no address given, and where messages, if
any, are calculated to arouse maximal guilt and anxiety, as they
usually succeed in doing. A typical message is: 'This is the end, don't
try to find us'. This might be the response of a man to another session
of all-night nagging and accusation (the wives in *Cases Ten* and *Twelve*
were virtuosi in this), or more frequently the acting-out of an
exasperated woman with a mounting sense of neglect. It can occur
early in marriage, and with (by average norms) slight provocation
when the rôle expectations of both partners include spoiling, ever-
considerate behaviour, i.e. a high degree of idealization with low
frustration tolerance. A generalized picture of such a case would be
of a wife resenting the husband's outside interests and demanding
more assiduous demonstration that she comes first or else is insulted.
The husband would assert his independence and fight against her
becoming a persecuting mother figure by sticking to his rights: to a
night out with the boys, or his night-school, or just pleasing himself.
On the n-th occasion of being home late without warning the wife
may have gone in one of the ways above sketched, and his fantasy of

her as the 'always there' permissive love-object receives a rude shock.

This type of temporary desertion, then, may be an impulse or a calculated gambit in the dominance/submission struggle to test out whose rôle expectation and whose rules of interaction shall prevail. So long as the sense of an unbroken dyadic boundary holds, the separation and distance created often has the desired effect. Indeed some couples, as we know, agree to temporary separation without legal and social consequences, in order to cool down and regain perspective. There are often early and continuous communications from the deserter, as solicitous and tender as those of the happiest spouses when separated by circumstances. The man who has sworn never to come back, telephones the same night from his hide-out and inquires about everything, sends more money than normally, etc. It is as if he were saying: 'When the real you is not present, I can be a model husband in the abstract'. This, incidentally, holds good for a large part of marital behaviour in idealized object relations that have broken on reality testing. It is not unusual to hear of repeated episodes of temporary desertion now by husband, now by wife at various times; both being miserable without the other and rushing back into reconciliation. With the hostile, persecuting aspect of ambivalence satisfied or autonomy affirmed, the loving side of the interaction can again prevail until the next crisis. Marital clinics would not be asked to see those who had been able to make good use of such events. It is those whose pattern of interaction is close to a split between the two sides of ambivalence and who in consequence are apt to swing between destructive or paranoid feelings and loving reparative drives whom we are asked to help.

Unfortunately, the phase at which the helping professions are called in may be the point of no return, the *n*-th time plus one. This is when the true socio-legal or *destructive* desertion is born. It happens when the satisfaction there may have been in the sado-masochistic collusion in Sub-system Three has worn too thin after repeated reality-testing, in comparison with the needs of the maturing ego and its requirements in Sub-system Two. It means that the deserter staying away has withdrawn what was left of the investment of the abandoned partner who has given up the quest for the wayward object in the absconding partner and says 'Stay away—that's it'. It is important to stress again that by this time there is likely to be a new object investment by one or both partners, whether we hear of it or not. It is common to hear: 'Oh yes, I have a boy/girl friend, but of course my husband/wife had already left me'.

Desertion, as will be obvious, is only in one aspect a form of acting-out. Psychologically, it can be argued, there is in walking-out something passive like a withdrawal from the contest. It is a sitting-apart sulk writ large, and as such may contain the component of avoidance of hot, violent strife with its threat of implementing destructive fantasies. It can equally mean an expression of dissociation from a despised and rejected part of oneself projectively identified with the partner, whether this be the dependent, clinging libidinal ego or the punitive anti-libidinal ego. In both aspects it can be said to be a compromise between wanting to hurt and yet not 'really' hurting. Its most finally destructive effect, however, is when it means that the commitment to the conquest of the abandoned partner is not worth it—a last act of personal cruelty, perhaps the only reply a defeated person can make who does not want to kill.

In practice, malignant desertion of the permanent and determined kind is thus nearly always part of cruelty or adultery of both. 'Pure' desertion is the resort of the fugitive from either his own aggression or from the real or fantasied domination of the other which the deserter has despaired of being able to withstand without loss of identity. *Constructive Desertion* is the legal term given to this more passive or withdrawing aspect of rôle behaviour, in which the frontier with mental cruelty is very ill-marked, and which can be found by the Court even in the absence of leaving the home. Where shouting and swearing would be cruelty, sulking silence might be either, but an unconcerned nightly absence in the pub or a withdrawal from common work and play without explicit rancour might be constructive desertion. Thus, if the spouses in *Case Three* had formulated a legal complaint, the husband could have claimed constructive desertion, as his wife denied him her sexual and domestic rôles, preferring her party-work to even giving him meals. She could have charged him with cruelty as he was angry, sulky and belittling. In *Case Twelve* the husband could have charged mental cruelty, the wife constructive desertion since the husband had 'abdicated all but the economic contribution to the common life of the dyad. More extreme cases could be cited.

4. GENERAL COMMENTS

In Chapter II I alluded to certain forms of acting-out by primitive personalities because they had few ego resources with which to 'buffer' their impulses, and I also mentioned more sophisticated people 'who should have known better', but who vented their hate and rebellion on the partner and the children by gross neglect of hygiene, amenity, even nutrition, as part of adult rôle abdication. One has been asked to sort out, for example, the confused marriage of a qualified accountant in rising professional demand who spent nearly all his waking hours at clients' offices, leaving his wife to cope with his own affairs, in such a muddle that the home was often besieged by creditors, sometimes the bailiffs. At other times there would suddenly be a new fur coat or a piece of jewellery for her while the children's worn-out shoes could not be replaced for lack of cash. It is as if the conflict between adult and undisciplined child in both partners had to be parcelled out in such a way that at one level the man was the trusted adviser on finance and his wife an ever-demanding child dependent on his money-omnipotence, but at another level he was the muddling, useless child relying on the maternal figure in his wife to fight his battles and nourish the family as best she could. Or there is the case of a dapper, debonair salesman who would go home nightly to the chaos of unwashed dishes, undisciplined children and decaying food in the larder which had finally drawn the intervention of the health authorities in the slum conditions his wife daily reproduced and he tolerated. He was the sophisticated façade, she the 'dirty Id' of the relationship, except when they went out together, dressed elegantly, in their car.

From a large series of cases I have drawn the impression that acting-out limited to intra-dyadic events, with good adult performance of rôles and social functions outside, can range from the psychopathology of everyday life to the grossly psychopathic. The study of intra-marital, i.e. adult intimate object-relations, raises interesting problems on the nature of psychopathy. It would seem justifiable to think of psychopathic behaviour in terms of bad-object-relations. These may be focused on one special person, or be more diffusely projected to whole groups or situations. I have already discussed the significance of the 'return of repressed bad objects' into the dyadic interaction, after the failure of idealization and other defences. Acting-out this new pressure saves the psychic effort of new defences and lessens anxiety. In this it resembles psychopathy or behaviour disorder in general. Repression and strong ego-control on the other hand save the greater pain of guilt feelings and social consequences. Differences in degree of ego-differentiation and in subculture norms of a given couple account for the ease or difficulty in controlling acting-out behaviour. These factors distinguish the prevalent symptomatology of marital cases seen in a unit like the Tavistock's from that seen by, e.g., probation officers in slum areas.

5. CONTAINMENT

We have now to look at those interactions in which major acting-out is resisted, because fraught with excessive guilt and a sense of betrayal of ideals and values, where even the fantasies of such actions lead to elaborate defences and over-compensations. These span a wide range. Aggression is turned inwards against the self in exaggerated submissiveness and martyrdom, or it manifests in psycho-somatic, neurotic or depressive symptomatology which compels the partner's anxiety and solicitude. A simpler mechanism is at work in constant need for reparative activity: we know about the mink coat as a sop to guilt feelings even where no other woman intrudes. Then there are the already amply discussed marriages in which there must be no heat or argument, all evaluated as destructive by the couple. This 'sparing' of the partner, which means a denial of ambivalence, is perhaps the common middle ground of communication failure from which spring both the just mentioned over-compensations as well as the gathering pressures towards quasi-involuntary acting-out. In Chapter V these points were covered from a theoretical angle when speaking about idealization and its effects on dyadic interaction. I doubt if I could usefully add more than a small handful of variations on this theme by way of illustrative cases. My point in creating the category of 'containment' was to differentiate it from its opposite —acting-out with its public social and legal consequences. Acting-out usually means one partner's escape from the pain of repression at the existential expense of the other. Containment means a more equal or shared burden of such pain. Granted the existence of underlying rigidity in the rejection of ambivalence, containment may carry risks as serious to health and maturation for the partners and their offspring as the more dramatic and socially condemned mode of acting-out of the tensions resulting from object-splitting.

Along the axis acting-out versus containment there are many variants and models of marital interaction by which the dyadic boundary is kept intact or slowly enlarged or contracted. Some, perhaps the most satisfactory, proceed by small and flexible alternations between agreement to contain or leave well alone and moderate acting-out. This will consist of a challenge to confront a contentious issue by discussion that may lead to heat, withdrawal and rapprochement. Others proceed by larger, more crisis-like fluctuations marked by more tense containment broken by more explosive and hurtful acting-out. The criterion of the benignity or malignancy of such interactions is the affirmation versus the denial of each other's identities, or in common parlance respect and acceptance of the person of the partner. No one can permanently continue in a dyadic relationship when they have awakened to its incompatibility with their sense of worth. This would hold true even for those partners in marriage whose ideal selves or rôle interpretations are very rigidly held ('proud and unbending') or those who contrive to play their rôle in a largely self-destructive way. Ethical principles, economic necessity or social conformity may compel the preservation of the form, but the dyad as a living organism ceases to exist.

Chapter X

INVESTIGATION AND DIAGNOSIS

1. INTRODUCTORY

In an account of relatively new methods and skills it is always easier to describe the rationale and theory than their applications in practice. It is only possible to present a *model*, which is sometimes attained even though always aimed at. The methods have to be learnt by doing the job. Between the lines of the preceding chapters a reader with experience in psychiatric case-taking from a psycho-dynamic viewpoint will already have gathered the principles and something of the evolution of our techniques of investigation of marital conflict situations.

To begin at the beginning, my colleagues and I regard it as of greatest importance to safeguard, as well as to be seen to safeguard, the privacy and the susceptibilities of our clientele. Where a couple are presumed to have agreed that it is their relationship which needs investigation, and to have consented to some joint attendances at the clinic or consulting rooms, we still require this to be made explicit by them. In their eagerness to send us cases of marital discord, family doctors and psychiatric consultants often *assume* such consent to joint interviewing and the like, when in fact the decision to consult a marital clinic together had not been worked through with both clients. By the time they are sent their appointments or actually attend us such couples can be in a state of bewilderment and resistance. Surprisingly this is true also for the one-partner presentation. The sick person is unaware of the unconsciously assigned rôle and wants 'treatment' for the illness. It is therefore necessary to make the purpose and focus of our approach clear to the couple and elicit their consent at ego-level to what may be felt by them a humiliating and unpleasant prospect of having to seek help in intimate affairs and of washing their dirty linen before strangers. After all, if they did not already feel so much guilt and resistance to intra-dyadic communication they would not be coming to us. Even with consent 'in principle' we may find the phenomena touched on in Chapter VIII

187

under the heading 'Distribution of impact' requiring our appraisal and decision before any further work is done. Indeed, the resistance displayed in one way or another at the very moment of entry into a relationship with the caseworker can be the most revealing of what we observe of the state of the marriage. In a small minority of cases, with insufficient preparation by the referring doctor or agency it may be *all* we are allowed to observe, for the couple may decide there and then 'They've come to the wrong place'—'They are not mad, thank you'—or 'I thought my wife (or husband as the case may be) was going to have *treatment*', and so on.

Some couples who have experienced previous disappointing contact with a non-medical agency or worker, are reassured by being now referred to real doctors. Others prefer their predicament to be outside the medical field. The discussion of this issue on possible health service policy will be taken up in the final chapter. For ourselves, we aim at a good level of communication with the couple's family doctor, even where they themselves for various good or bad reasons have not chosen to effect their referral through him. But if the choice lies between our respect for the clients' wish for privacy even from their other medical attendants, and the risk of a breach of medical collaboration, we choose the former.

On similar grounds we categorically refuse to give evidence in any divorce proceedings that our clients, past or present, may become involved in. We cannot later appear in court for one side when we have worked with both. Only by this being clear can any sense of security be created in potential clients' minds that we shall respect their confidences in all circumstances. Legal respect for marriage counsellors' work supports this stand.

Inside the unit it is essential to have medical and psychiatric expertise in the stage of investigation and diagnosis as well as during treatment, with a consultant taking full clinical responsibility for the contributions of his juniors and his non-medical colleagues—the social workers and clinical psychologists. This is secured not only by sharing cases, but also by conferences and, where required, supervision.

In the account that follows it will be assumed that we are dealing with couples who have consented to sharing in the process of assessment of their problem, unless otherwise explained in the text. The work of securing such consent may have been done for us by the referring consultant, general practitioner or social agency. But sometimes we have to do it ourselves, e.g. a new case in general out-patients which is judged by one of our own consultants to fall into our field. This usually only requires a courteous letter inviting the absent spouse to help us by allowing us to hear his or her side of the story.

Such cases always mean a start by separate first interviews. Some of our group in recent years have deplored this, for reasons which will be discussed in this and the next chapter.

2. THE AIMS OF INVESTIGATION

The object of any medical investigation is to make a diagnosis which at least in theory should then enable the physician to select and implement the treatment appropriate to the condition he has decided is present. In this selection a prognosis is also implicit—for before advising a remedy one has to make an estimate of its efficacy for the particular state. Even in the traditional fields of scientific organic medicine, let alone in psychiatry, we are as yet some distance from being able to live up to this model. In all illness, but in the psychiatric field especially, agreement among us about diagnosis in terms of a classifiable 'disease entity' is still subject to doubt and dispute. It is not only the idiosyncratic behaviour of patients, but also the diagnostic criteria chosen by psychiatrists which prove unamenable to the rigorous demands of unvaryingness. What, then, should be our aim in this new uncategorized field of medico-socio-psychological exploration corresponding to the diagnostic medical model? In Chapter IV I described the status and aims of this book, as somewhere between the pioneers who defined the area and proclaimed it ripe for study, and the real researchers who, following up our generalizations from massive case experience, will create valid diagnostic and prognostic categories of 'dyadic interaction' phenomena.

In investigating a *given case*, we would be concerned to elucidate the *meanings* of marital behaviour for husband and wife separately and together in terms of our conceptual framework. We take a cross-section of present 'Here and Now' marital symptomatology as our material, and try to see it as the point to which the dyad has come in its passage together through time. That is, we also attempt to construct a historical profile of the separate lives and of the marriage before and after meeting, courting and marrying. By this we hope to derive some estimate of the strengths of the bonds in all three Sub-systems (culture affinity, ego-norms and unconscious interchange), their congruities or conflicting pulls. From these we aim to form judgments on the lines set out in Chapter IV (pp. 53–55) which have gradually changed in emphasis but not in general design since the pilot phase there described.

The emphasis has shifted from a rather full assessment of each partner as an individual *before* making inferences about their interaction, to the other way round. We now aim throughout at appraisal of the dyadic communication and intactness, together with more

189

concentration on the level of maturity of Third Sub-system inter-change. With growing experience we have found that the relevant items of personal history emerge unsolicited with such an approach. I should add here, as I will repeat in the next chapter, that this shift of emphasis, which by-passes much personal detail, is the result of self-training through the groundwork that we did in earlier phases, and should not be attempted without considerable sophistication in analytic work with individuals and groups as well as experience in the earlier approach to marital work.

At the stage of assessment or investigation, then, we seek to make a decision whether the dyadic boundary exists, whether the two partners are still libidinally involved with each other however pain-fully and immaturely. If it does then the meanings for them of what they do to each other remain vital, they react to each other, they even present a united front against the interviewer. This means for us a decision to treat. Alternatively, our aim is also to eliminate from therapy, except for purposes of study and self-education, those couples who are no longer a dyad but who have at all but formal level 'disengaged'. This is as far as the diagnostic phase allows matters to be taken.

What diagnostic categories exist in my mind so far I hope to discuss towards the end of this chapter. Analysts have been criticized by more 'disease entity-minded' colleagues for not making diagnoses until the end of treatment. To the latter, diagnosis is, as it were, an independent and completed mental process, when the symptom-picture has yielded the decision to assign a given condition into an already described category within a classification. A label has been given as if this was static, the disease being something superimposed and external to the person. This is not the place to argue the philo-sophy of psychiatric epistemology. It must suffice to say that I cannot work in that frame of reference when dealing with the dynamics of marriages. For me the end of investigation and assessment lies as yet in the literal meaning of the word: *dia* = through or into; *gnosis* = recognition or knowledge: insight. The ordering of the insights is gained by observing the phenomena as they change over time and interaction with me, with the help of the conceptual scheme developed in Part One of this book. The book itself is a groping precursor to a systematic ordering of marital, dyadic genotypes which are as yet hardly defined. Indirectly then, our investigations, as we see recurrences of similar patterns of dyadic mate-selection and be-haviour, will go into the making of a new system of classification with its own vocabulary and categories. Before such a taxonomy can have any meaning, the dynamics of dyadic interchange must become as familiar as mental conflict in an individual. At present psychia-

190

trists are far from unanimity even in interpreting the events in so common a condition as 'classical' claustrophobia!

3. WHAT DATA DO WE SEEK?

In my introductory chapter I defined the aspects of marital relations, which I thought it necessary to study. These included the assessment of the partners as individuals; the relations of the couple to their social and cultural backgrounds and their current social affiliations and norms as conditioning their conceptions of their respective rôles; and last but not least an attempt to gain insight into the more unconscious communications or 'transactions' in their relationship which I feel to be the distinctive contribution the analytically trained psychiatrist has to offer.

a. *The intra-personal data*

The essentials of what we look for in individuals have already been set out in Chapter IV. They are the data that any psychiatrist or trained case-worker would wish to have about his patient or client if he used the kind of concepts presented in Chapter III. Their results on assessment have been illustrated by case histories throughout this text. There is, naturally, a bias of attention towards data bearing on each partner's perception of the other partner, and on the nature and developmental level of the cathexis of the partner as a love object. It follows that there is an attempt also to assess the prevalent defence mechanisms utilized by the individual. We try to estimate the degree of paranoid versus depressive feelings, with their typical projection and introjection; splitting and denial, obsessional reparative drives, idealization and so forth. Some of these enter into all human transactions at deeper levels. It is a question of degree and of rigidity of a given mechanism's presence which will stamp a given clinical picture as significant. This is probably as near as we get to an assessment in classical psychiatric categories of hysterical, phobic, obsessional, depressive, paranoid, or schizoid personality types. If we make a more formal diagnosis in terms of mental illness in one or both spouses then we also stop the investigation as a marital problem and take steps for appropriate therapy of the individual.

The history of past object relations and the profile of childhood screen memories is used to try and relate the present ego-involvements in the dyad and its rôle requirements to the genesis of the rôle-models derived from the parental social background and culture which are now deployed or combated in the marriage. At times, as mentioned, we have thought it wise in 'triangular situations' also to interview the third party—often very revealing.

191

b. *The dyadic culture pattern*

I have in Chapter IV described in general terms what we look for in the assessment of the marriage as a functioning unit in socio-psychological terms. I mentioned the usefulness of getting an adequate cross-section of each partner's attitudes and values in relation to 'areas of co-operation' including various rôles inside and outside the home. During the pilot and research phase these areas were systematically inquired into and the data recorded, including at one point the use of a special questionnaire to be described later in this chapter. My aim was to provide a sociological as well as a psychodynamic picture, since married couples have to adapt to outer social and economic realities and preserve their joint as well as individual identities in the world. This is the inquiry into what I called 'Sub-systems I and II'. The study of these conscious everyday aspects was often a source of insight into the deeper feelings and resistances in the marriage since the sub-systems interpenetrate. It does not detract from the objective nature of the social rôle 'variables' elicited if during their elicitation a trained observer also glimpses the unconscious meanings such ordinary activities may assume. A good illustration was *Case Fifteen* with their tortured competition in unfulfilled chores. What we seek is an understanding of *how*, and in what areas of marital co-operation, the overt culturally accepted rules and the tacit agreements deriving from all echelons of social value systems come into conflict with the private inner worlds of the couple. P. G. Herbst[1] has proposed how the two levels might be combined and has devised a notation. Elizabeth Bott[2] has prepared the way by her study of rôle-interpretations and values in ordinarily harmonious couples.

Our data are built up on a foundation of standard placement of the couple on a socio-economic scale from information on parental as well as client's occupational, educational and income levels. We used also conscientiously to assess the intelligence levels. These, as mentioned, were so rarely of significance that we now no longer include them in our routine. The potentials and achievements are nearly always clinically obvious. It requires no special tests to confirm the finding, say, in a couple of lowly origins who tell us that the husband is now head of a large plant, but his wife cannot cope with his present social contacts and refuses to act as the hostess in his Georgian mansion. *Case Twenty-two* had some of the elements of this situation.

c. *The unconscious dyadic transaction*

Most of the preceding pages have been filled with the description and commentary on this level of data from Sub-system Three, with

Case Ten as the fullest account of the kind of information we seek to obtain. I consider this area to be the core of marital conflict situations requiring diagnosis (in my sense). It is the inner world of the partners with its fantasy systems that colours the meanings they give to the various items of their social connections and rôle requirements. *Cases One, Five, Fourteen, Twenty-one* and *Twenty-two* are examples of the kind of generalization possible at the diagnostic stage. In *Case Ten* I was also careful to report separately the findings and judgments at the phase of investigation, to show how these phenomena and our interpretation of them were confirmed or changed during therapy and after.

4. HOW DO WE COLLECT DATA?

This question is the most essential as well as the most difficult and debatable of the whole topic. It cuts deep into the unresolved contrasts of theory and method in psychiatry and psychology. For it can be claimed by those who question the validity of the psychoanalytic way of seeing and doing things with case-material, that we are biased rather than scientifically objective in our selection of data and that we influence the verbal and non-verbal behaviour of our clients by this bias. This is not denied. Other schools of thought (organicist, genetic, psycho-biological, neo-behaviourist, phenomenological or whatever else) implicitly or explicitly have *their* biases or basic assumptions and do the same in their selection and stress on certain clinical 'facts' and their evaluation. What follows is a condensed statement of how my colleagues and I have set about examining our cases, given the theoretical bias which informs this book.

Not surprisingly we have relied above all on clinical interviewing, supplemented at times by information supplied by the referring agency, such as family doctors, probation officers or other informants. At various phases it has also been possible to add a 'research' component of test procedures capable of being scored and treated numerically. We take care of the more formal aspects of the data by write-in forms, in which ages, occupations, length of marriage, previous marriages, number of children, etc., as well as a written statement of the problem bringing the person to seek help are recorded by the clients themselves. For a long time we also made use of the 'statement of particulars' which is required of all new patients at the Tavistock Clinic and which, filled in, gives a good factual picture of parental background, social and economic events, schooling, career record, leisure pursuits, social and cultural interests and religious affiliation.

193

a. *Interviewing*

As already mentioned, especially in Chapter IV, we relied for a long time on an initial assessment procedure for each partner separately. These individual interviews differ little, if at all, from those analytical psychiatrists would use at a first consultation with any patient. This method is, after all, the basic tool of our trade. Our training would make us careful not to impose a pattern of question and answer, for that would be likely to falsify the result. Rather do we lean back and invite the patient to talk about his problem in his own way, with as little interference as possible with the spontaneous flow and content of his communication. Sometimes this can be fully achieved, with our patient entering into a mental state of free association beginning with the presenting symptoms. At other times there has to be some intervention by us. This must be done knowingly, bearing in mind Sullivan's definition of psychiatry as 'the operational statement of inter-personal relations'. The first type of interference is an interpretation of our counter-transference to the patient's transference perceived by us. This may have to happen very early in the encounter if the transference—shyness, suspicion, anger—blocks communication. To command an inhibited person to relax, or to become irritated, impatient or contemptuous is unprofessional conduct. To be aware what the patient feels in the difficult situation and to be able to tell him that we understand why this is happening, is not only correct professional conduct—it is also a helpful and reassuring action which in most cases will now set his communicative powers and needs free.

The second kind of intervention is used when the spontaneous flow of statements has stopped. We may call this the switch from present to past: to history after a taste of the Here and Now. We still preserve our non-directive attitude, but invite the patient to enlarge on something he has said about his family or other background. The request for amplification is made in general terms, such as 'It would be interesting to hear more about that' or 'Would you please clarify what you meant when you said so-and-so'. But one might have to be more direct to open up earlier history, by asking if the feelings or other presenting complaint had antecedents, or what early life was like.

The third kind of interference has already been mentioned. These are interpretations which have the double purpose of testing our *ad hoc* working hypotheses formed during a diagnostic interview, and also to test the capacity of the potential patient for contacting painful areas of his personality, i.e. for insight. This kind of 'trial interpretation' as it related to transference blocking the interview was mentioned a moment ago. It can be used also as a stimulus to a release of memories and feelings, or as an assay of touchiness, guilt and anxiety. It can also be substituted for the questions relating to earlier historical material. The skills in timing, wording and stressing such interpretative probes have to be learnt the hard way—on actual case material after one's own training analysis or analogous experience, aided by supervision, by tape recordings and one-way screens. Any one little example of what one actually does could be misleading without the context and the emotional rapport that set the stage for venturing an interpretative probe at a given moment during an interview.

This method of interviewing could be called non-structured, but not unfocused. We have a mental schedule of what we want to know but we leave its 'filling in' to the spontaneous flow of communication. Surprisingly often we get an adequate picture for a meaningful diagnosis.

If, as during our intensive research phase, we wanted to have detailed data on the 'areas of co-operation', this might be done at the end of the main interview. It involved a change of atmosphere, as if saying to the client: 'Let us now take a good look how you manage the marriage together', and then openly cover the schedule or else let him or her describe the daily and weekly round. In this phase there is no objection to countless questions by the interviewer, on the lines of 'Who washes the dishes as a rule?' or 'How often do you visit your in-laws?' or 'Do you like the same films/radio/TV shows?' and so forth. This, however, is no longer our practice—we get enough evidence on less detail, for we have learnt to recognize the trends. It was good exercise in learning to discriminate types of interaction and rôle expectations. But we are not sociologists who study rôle-behaviour as such.

Even excluding such a special addendum, the first interview never takes less than $1\frac{1}{2}$ hours, often longer. It is, of course, done for each partner, and not infrequently has to be followed by a second interview. In my own work and that of my team of colleagues at the Tavistock Clinic, these long and searching 'depth interviews' represented the solid foundation of our experience of marital attitudes in the two individuals concerned. They were, nonetheless, the preliminaries to the *Joint Interview* about to be described in its stages of evolution. I have dwelt in some detail on the form and procedure of the single interview because it is the model on which the joint interview itself was developed, and also because necessity, such as one-person presentations and other factors still makes it a very commonly used tool in this work. The Family Discussion Bureau (F.D.B.) have preserved this method of the individual worker, with one for each

195

marriage partner, as their standard reception procedure. Their policy has been to start as they mean to go on: the case worker who is expected to take on the therapy also does the diagnostic interview, so that this latter can, from the beginning of the contact with the client, be handled as a therapeutic 'trial' session. The build-up of the dyadic interaction diagnosis has to be done by detailed conferencing between the pair of case workers. With such an aim there can be less emphasis on Sub-systems I and II during assessment as the therapist will expect to collect the data on the more social and overt structure of the marriage as he goes along. There can also be more trial interpretation, especially at transference level, for its effects can be taken up in treatment, unless there is a long time gap.

This consideration is important. When Mary Luff and I were the only two workers doing our pilot investigation which covered diagnosis of individuals, followed by our observations of interaction in joint interviews, which were in turn succeeded for some years by individual therapy and worker-conferences on a similar model to the F.D.B.'s, our conduct of diagnostic interviews was influenced by whether we were able to take on the therapy or not. The growth of the Unit and the greater number of cases referred to it meant that the receiving consultants had to assign an increasing proportion of assessed and suitable couples for therapy by colleagues. *Case Ten* is a typical example of the assessment procedure following this plan. In such cases the diagnostic interviews should aim at minimizing transference involvement, even if they do not succeed in excluding them. It will be recalled that *Mrs. Ten* left our joint interview with the half-joking words 'I wish I could take Dr. Dicks with me'—an impressive initial transference statement of her need for the parental libidinal object, which dominated her subsequent therapeutic sessions as it had her marital behaviour. In marital cases no less than in psychotherapy in general, the initial interviewer almost always receives the 'fullest' transference, whether expressed or not. Thus referral to another figure for therapy is often perceived by the patients as a rejection, however much they may rationally accept the reality factors necessitating such a step. We therefore have to take some care to close an assessment interview with a therapeutic clarification of this issue by appropriate interpretation, in which there is no place for praise of the skill and superiority of the worker to whom the patient will be referred or returned, for it will have a hollow mocking sound for him.

b. *The Joint Interview*

I have indicated that this instrument for marital diagnosis and therapy is a central feature of my work, though I claim no priority

196

in its invention. Here I want to describe how it has evolved through time to its present uses.

At the pilot stage the joint interview (JI for short) was invariably a foursome of both doctors and the couple, held after the individual interviews and psychological testing (of which more below) by independent observers. We therefore already had fairly adequate information and views on the personal profiles of the partners and could always confer to decide whether a JI would be likely to aggravate or assist this condition. Around 1950 the JI was reckoned to be a risky step. Balint, for example, in a verbal communication, held JI to be an 'explosive situation'. Ackerman[3] mentions similar warnings not to become involved in triangles—admittedly he referred to one worker holding a JI with a couple. In 1953[4] I described our JI aims and method as follows:

> Such sessions usually last around two hours, and are sometimes repeated on one, or more rarely, several occasions. Our attitude . . . is that of relatively passive observers, the situation being allowed to develop spontaneously, but with interpretations and clarifying remarks being offered as and when that seems wise. The setting of the session has thus been exploratory and diagnostic but also motivated on both sides by the therapeutic aim of making the emerging material available for the parties to understand and work through. We have endeavoured to gain and communicate insights about what each partner's difficult behaviour is intended to convey to the other, and out of what past or present experiences and impulsions that behaviour was fashioned. As a therapeutic technique we have attempted to replace the time-honoured method of advice and exhortation by one of clarification; as it were, saying to the parties, 'You see now that you are behaving towards your partner in such-and-such ways because of such-and-such needs in yourself' in the presence of the spouse. Any demands by the parties to be told what to do or to place the burden of advice or decision on our shoulders have been interpreted and referred back to the clients. Often such an interpretation of dependence has been the starting-point of insight.
>
> The phenomena observed are naturally very complex and rich in content, the full recording of which is not as yet adequate . . . the typical situation develops somewhat as follows: one or other of the spouses (often the wife 'by courtesy') states their complaints about husband or wife, which may be a rehash of, or at times significantly different from, their original statements at individual interview. There may follow the exposition of the counter-statement by the second spouse. As a rule these are sedate speeches

197

with good control of feelings, but often one may at this stage begin to see the tensions rising, as by fidgeting, blushing, interruptions and rebuttals, with glances at the doctors conveying such meanings as 'You see what I am up against', contempt, real distress or amused incredulity.

There may now follow a pause of silence or direct appeal to us to give advice, dealt with as already stated. Points of such behaviour, or of the attitudes revealed are now commented on by us; as for example: 'We notice that you, Mrs. X. feel your silences, which you fall into, to be a sort of hopeless despair at not making your husband understand; he, on the other hand, as you have heard, feels they are a way of punishing him', etc. Or, in another development of the situation: 'We have heard you both interpreting your reactions to all these trivial incidents, as you call them, in two quite different ways. Let us try and see why you feel it to be so important to score off each other in this way', etc. These attempts to focus the discussion on somewhat deeper levels might be followed by resistances, often in the form of each spouse bringing more material and detail to support their own point of view.

Somewhere at this point the mutual heaping of charge upon charge results in a switch from addressing the doctors to direct conversation between the spouses. This is perhaps the most important part for the observers and yields the richest insights for subsequent clarifying and interpretative comments which can, on strength of less inhibited behaviour, be made about what is happening between the parties 'here and now'. With the individual case histories in mind one can interpret fairly quickly and obtain a relief of tension and a consent to the interpretation at feeling level from both parties. While we often interpret to one party while the other listens, and then shift our comments to the other party, it is probably better to reserve such interventions by the psychiatrists until a piece of 'interaction' is clear and can be put to them as such. For example: 'Listening to you, it sounds as if you are both terribly afraid of letting your love feelings come out towards each other. You, Mr. X., from what you have told us (facts and phantasies (a), (b) and (c)) are clearly looking upon taking the initiative in saying nice things to your wife as a kind of weak, childish yielding for which you have felt you would be laughed at and which is out of keeping with the whole way in which you were brought up to regard a man's rôle; therefore it seems to you that in showing this weakness you are delivering yourself up to this woman's power, etc. Instead you carp at her to try and make her think you are very strong. You, Mrs. X., not realizing what has held your husband back, interpret his behaviour as in some way disapproving of you, and so you have despaired of getting the loving advance out of him. He makes you feel angry and depressed, and you punish him by going cold on him, etc. He seems more like a threatening kind of authority than the nice man you wanted to make love to you. Yet you can both see now how you have aroused in each other these old fears and hates of being rejected which you had experienced (points of history (d), (e), (f)). So now you fence for positions to show one another that you don't need the other', etc.

This type of interpretation may be as simple as the above or more complex, bringing in other aspects such as guilt and aggression as the case may demand. It is often a case of more piecemeal interpretations in which the insights of the observers valuably supplement each other, both in language chosen and in adding or in clarifying meanings. In a number of cases we do not reach this level at all. By a kind of unspoken consensus which develops among fellow workers it emerges that the attitudes of the parties would make such intervention useless as a mere piece of intellectual communication. A kind of 'leave well alone' sense warns us to refrain.

The reaction of the parties to interpretation, their own capacity for insight, their emotional genuineness and warmth show up very clearly in these situations. It is often after an interpretation of the above-cited type that material relating to intimate sexual life becomes available and hitherto unrevealed facts and memories emerge, often as spontaneous bits of personal history which the other spouse may greet with a surprised 'Why have you never told me?'—in sympathy or in anger. These are again used in amplification of the interpretative comments . . .

'Action paragraphs' usually emerge towards the end of a joint session. (Here I described possible P.S.W. aid in regard to housing, etc.) . . . A spouse who had hitherto regarded himself or herself as the 'normal' victim of the other's troublesome behaviour may ask for treatment. Both parties may wish to come again, or else 'wait and see' the working out of the new viewpoints which the session has brought. Lastly, a fair number will go away with little if any lightening of their problems. From these people one usually gets the most profuse expressions of gratitude for having failed to disturb the *status quo*.

Second and subsequent joint sessions may or may not proceed in much the same way, with either greater frankness or greater resistance. We have not so far had experience of carrying joint sessions with a given couple on over a prolonged series of interviews. Rather have we tended to see the spouses again separately in the belief that such things as face-saving, aggressive phantasies or intimate past sexual history which might have to be dealt with as part of the aftermath of joint sessions, would be worked through more easily in individual interviews. Or, as already stated, one or both partners are referred to the regular treatment services of the clinic, not necessarily by one of us . . .

This remains a very fair account of our methods and attitudes at that time. It was rather condensed for purposes of a paper to be delivered, and it left out some aspects on which comment may be useful. In the first place, note the presence of both the original interviewers, who were forearmed with individual case histories. In the same paper I stated that we thought it wise 'to have for each party one doctor who . . . knows their side of the case well'. But, as I recorded at the time, there was also the need for mutual support of a colleague with whom to share the management of these often highly charged sessions, to exchange rôles—one interpreting, the other observing content. This was especially important during the pilot phase with its 'research and development' component. It could be followed with immediate conferencing and discussion of the shared experience. From the transference point of view it had the advantage of matching a married couple by another 'dyad' who could and did serve as parent figures. These factors make the 'foursome', after individual interviews, a good methodological step in training personnel for this work. There are also obvious advantages for a marital unit having a staff accustomed to work together, sharing concepts and perceptive to each other's trends of thought, just as in tennis regular doubles partners are better than scratch pairs.

Secondly, the above-cited description scarcely highlighted the amount of aggression that was often released in such JIs. Teruel's report referred to in Chapter VIII, of the couple who were soon saying 'Here we are carrying on just as we do at home' is a familiar experience. It is as if the warring dyad feel safe to offer a sample of their interaction while permissive figures are 'holding the ring'. And even though this is, as they tell us, no new way of behaving, the presence of, and the interpretative comment by, the therapists during such an experience can be very new and change-promoting indeed. During such a confrontation, when one of the parties may weep or flee from the room, we gain much direct insight into what they try to do to each other; into the power balance; which is the attacker and which the hurt 'withdrawer'; the ways in which ambivalence is expressed or withheld. The 'heaping of charge upon charge' of which I wrote in 1953, and the counter-attacks of the other, are presumably the explosive elements that we were warned against and which case-workers not trained analytically find it hard and painful to ride out.

I have difficulty still with such painful situations, and have to summon all my recollected experience to withstand the wish to cut them short or to pour oil and sweet reason on these hurtful contretemps. It is, however, not only diagnostically important to tolerate and participantly suffer such experiences. It is often the beginning of therapy for the couple to find parent figures (which by this time one is for them) *able* to accept the reality of such feelings, to 'survive' them without rejection and to remain there to interpret. It is my constant experience that such a storm blows itself out and is followed by lightening of tension and a display of more positive feelings of the couple for each other. This may occur without oil being poured, when we have remained passive observers throughout. The only additional intervention that is occasionally needed is to persuade the partner who is about to leave the room in tears or rage to come back, preferably with an appropriate interpretation suited to the situation. During the 'positive' phase of a JI there is often a spontaneous inquest on what has just happened with a retrospective, generalizing trend which not only shows us the areas of interaction in which the partners are vulnerable to regressive perceptions of the other's behaviour, but also how they have developed their dyadic tensions. 'He seemed ideal until one day . . .' is not an infrequent kind of statement.

The third point in the 1953 description of JI method is the telescoping of therapeutic with investigational moments. At the end of the paper I said that we had not by then initiated any longer-term therapy. Being a therapeutic and not primarily a research unit, and trained as we were, there was a compelling motivation in both Dr. Luff and myself 'to do something' to help couples who in the main came for assessment and then returned to their sources of referral, e.g. the Probation Service. The Tavistock ethos of 'no research without therapy' was added to the diagnostic probe of testing our clients' capacity to make use of 'trial interpretations'. In the next chapter I hope to show that such mixed 'assessment-cum-therapeutic trial' JIs were at times critically helpful to the couples, to their referring case-workers (fully reported of course) or to subsequent therapy by ourselves, quite apart from what we learnt through using them. There is no gainsaying, however, that *qua* 'scientific' research technique this original JI was a very 'impure' instrument. No form of human interaction between a medical figure (doctor, p.s.w., etc.) and a patient in distress can be the same process as a physicist reading a gauge. What is important in the JI (as in the single interview) is that we use our own feelings generated by the situation as part of the assessment procedure —but do not let them leak out unawares. The issue is not between detachment and involvement, but between *objectivity in the presence of involvement* as against undisciplined acting-out of unrecognized

201

involvement by the would-be 'scientific' observer towards the object of his observation.

Changes in JI. With growing experience of the trends and regularities in the course of most JIs, and with an eye on the economics of psychiatric manpower, I took the next steps: first of 'risking' the dreaded triangle situation, and later in making the JI the *first* consultation, before any individual assessments or other aids to diagnosis were used. It had already become clear that in the kind of couples we were asked to see, in increasing numbers, the explosive, potentially damaging elements direly predicted by other workers, were very rare. Nor did I any longer feel so greatly in need of a partner's presence at JI, much as I relied on post-interview conferencing and evaluation by my colleagues. While the 'individual assessment followed by JI assessment, then diagnostic decision' pattern remained the standard practice, I steadily experimented with facing couples alone, having assessed them individually alone.* It is an evolution through which some of my collaborators in the later years of the development of the Tavistock Marital Unit have passed. I found it echoed from the U.S. in the views of Nathan Ackerman (op. cit.) who on page 268 of his book states:

> 'When neurotic family pairs need psychotherapy, the most efficient form of integration of the psycho-therapies would seem to be achieved in the mind of a single therapist.'

Necessity, as well as curiosity, is the mother of invention. Like Ackerman (who had also been apprehensive about 'involvement in triangles') we found that with increasing programmes and numbers the very timing of foursomes and of the periods required for conferencing and collaborative efforts of this kind became too onerous or was honoured more in lip service than in reality. The individual of riper experience could work alone and be his own control, but if required could ask for supervision or present his problem to a unit conference after seeing a couple alone diagnostically (and in the course of continuing therapy as this developed). I found no great difference in the 'feel' or unfolding of a JI between the foursome and the threesome, even if of necessity the solo-interviewer has to carry a more ambivalent or split transference. In the foursome it was at times possible to observe how a dyad would either split their transferences according to the original pairing of one doctor with one of them, or treat one of us as good and safe and the other as the rejected

---

* Here the tennis analogy breaks down. We have yet to see a single player chosen to play 'doubles' in the Davis Cup matches!

or weak team-member. This did not always continue the single inter-view pattern, but sometimes reversed it. In the JI threesome one has to become both these figures for the couple, except where they have had previous disappointing experience of a marriage counsellor. This person from the past is then apt to be cast as the joint 'bad object' during the JI. 'He did not even bother to hear both sides, but just told George I was to blame for his state', etc.

Looking back, it is clear now that the decision to undertake the solo handling of JIs by some of us was an effect of our advance in defining the important part that *collusion* and dyadic boundaries play in marriage, as presented in Chapters V to VII. Most germane to the change in diagnostic technique was the evidence, illustrated by *Case Ten*, of such collusion centreing on an unconsciously *shared object*. If they shared such an object, it seemed appropriate to have them share one person in the interview situation. Every analyst knows that, though he may be a youngish male, he can be perceived in transference as an old mother figure or what not. This applies especially to treatment, but the phenomenon is observed also in the diagnostic stage. In the ordinary way any patient will expect to be seen for consultation by *a* doctor. Except for a tiny minority of people who happen to know about the reception procedure at the F.D.B. or our own earlier version, couples equally expect to be received by the doctor to whom they are referred. JI obviates the problem of allotting one partner to a colleague, for the first individual assessment. This second team member is liable to be perceived as a second fiddle and the partner who 'draws' him may develop corresponding jealousy or resentment. In the initial JI with *one* interviewer the shared object-transference will necessarily be directed only at him. We eliminate some insights by doing away with initial individual interviews. These are often so arranged by the partners that whichever spouse is seen first can be felt to have prejudiced the consultant in his or her favour. The rivalry is then more obvious during the JI when both partners feel that the interviewer is privy to secrets of the other which have not been shared by them. Our strict rule—really a Hippocratic principle—not to disclose what each partner has said to us in single interview to the other partner, heightens this transference of paranoid anxiety.

On balance it seemed simpler to minimize these 'iatrogenic' projec-tive situations and meet as far as possible only those inherent in the dyadic object-relations when faced with *the* helper. We had devised the original organization mainly for mutual support and education and out of the continuity of the psycho-analytic tradition which decrees the sacrosanct privacy of the one to one therapeutic relation-ship. To have the JI at all constituted the major departure! Grotjahn,[5] in a slightly different context, supports this viewpoint. On page 35 he states:

> Sigmund Freud, I am sorry to say did not believe in family therapy. Once he said: If you combine the resistance of your patient with the resistance of your patient's husband (or wife), you are lost; don't do it. Freud was a representative of negative family therapy; he was in favour of excluding the family . . . This attitude is understandable at the time when Freud was preoccupied with . . . understanding the unconscious of his individual patients; it is now time to proceed from there.

I took this step—with the usual caution—and we began to see our client-couples by JI from the beginning, postponing or altogether omitting the individual diagnostic assessments. The caution was to essay this new departure by preserving the foursome method of interviewing. It is comforting to have a companion when exploring new and uncharted terrain. This, and the possibility of retrospective discussion and evaluation were more important than the conviction that the couple would do better by seeing two of us together, except to teach us something further on object-splitting (e.g. through the 'second fiddle' situation). Soon we dispensed with foursome reception, and several of us have now used the joint interview(s) by one consultant as the basis for assessment and decision about therapy and prognosis over some 6 or 7 years. At the time of such a JI we are in possession of only what information the clients have vouchsafed on their application forms, and the referring doctor or social work agency may have supplied.

This is the streamlining to which I alluded when discussing the aims of diagnosis. We lose the differentiated early personality profiles of the two partners. We gain in clarity of focus on the dyadic interaction phenomena which are most quickly manifested in the JI. We eliminate the doubtfully efficient method of constant conferencing at our end and simplify the artifically heightened 'iatrogenic' rivalry in the couple by having one shared object for it. Dr. G. Teruel[6] has argued convincingly on the superiority of the 'new method' of solo JIs in diagnosis and therapy of marital conflict. Though he prefers the familiar concept of a 'group', to the concept of the 'dyad', he agrees with me that marriage *is* a new 'compound' entity. The principle of the JI reception procedure he advocates accords closely with my model of interviewing. In his 1964 paper Teruel writes as follows:

> For me this procedure of having to come together for the first interview is essential. As already stated, if they form a 'group'

they should come as a group . . . I emphasize the point of the *joint interview* . . . because I feel that with it both partners realize that their marriage is a serious matter where both share the responsibility of its present conflict.

After describing the expectant, non-active attitude he adopts (with the exception of the possible transference interpretation I also use to overcome blocking of communication) Teruel continues:

There is usually an embarrassing silence and then they begin to manipulate each other and the observer. They may direct themselves to me as individuals, or try to speak to each other, or fight each other, or ask me questions, etc. Everything here is important and I have come to the conclusion that if one is in a quiet and receptive mood . . . the information that begins to make itself clear is astounding . . . sometimes I note certain reactions when a clear pattern emerges . . . I may say: 'I have noted that when Mr. X does or says such and such a thing, Mrs. X does such and such a thing; now, what you have shown in front of me, is it the sort of thing that takes place outside this room . . .?' If one is clear about the observations the answer is usually a positive one. With this I do not mean that I 'interpret' to create a 'change' in them . . . It is a 'notation' to make them know that I understand things they have *not* said but have *acted out* in my presence, and with this information in mind it is easier to elicit from them more information of the same sort.

Teruel helped us also by drawing our attention to the vividness with which, even during these initial JIs, the outlines of the collusive process based on a *shared internal object* appear. This is analogous to the dream a patient frequently offers at a first consultation which foreshadows the entire neurotic conflict in condensed 'cartoon' form. The concept of such sharing of internal objects was established in our working hypotheses by such experiences as treating *Case Ten*. Teruel continues:

As the interview proceeds and no 'interference' from the observer-interviewer is created, a particular phenomenon takes place . . . What I have called, for convenience's sake, the 'emergence of the dominant internal object', which both partners seem to share inside themselves in the marriage . . . Once a 'dominant internal object' appears spontaneously . . . I follow it with the greatest care and see how it evolves in the course of the interview. Here I feel I am already dealing with unconscious material, . . . with their internal world (Sub-System Three—H.V.D.).

205

He uses the technique I have already described to try and help this emergence if it has not occurred spontaneously. That is, when the spontaneous, uninterrupted flow has dried up, we ask the couple to tell us something about their background. We agree that this is a second-best to the unaided phenomenon. The search for the unconscious parental figures inside the patients is the motive for any enquiry after 'childhood history'. Nobody is naive enough to believe that such information will yield significant sociological facts, but as projections or screen memories these data help us in defining the personal and inter-personal dynamics of our patients.

This kind of diagnostic interviewing is not suited to beginners. As I pointed out in the introduction, it requires experience in and familiarity with analytic therapy and concepts, especially the application of these to group phenomena—a kind of content analysis of inter-personal communication. Among the events that make the greatest demands on one's experience and skill are those of the transference, including the joint dyadic resistance by the couple. I will cite Teruel again in this context:

> There have been occasions when the couple have pushed me into the rôle of referee in a football match, as if my only attribute were to blow the whistle and for them to kick each other.

Here Dr. Teruel shows less welcome for the display of dyadic candour in presenting him with the hate-clinch of their relationship as a diagnostic datum than I do! It seems to me the greatest mark of confidence when people are able to do this.

> Above all I try to keep . . . from paying too much attention to one member . . . and even less, siding with him or her . . . The only time when there is nothing left but to interpret is when one gets a couple who immediately stick together to attack the interviewer, or keep up an anger-ridden long silence, or try to spoil the interview . . .

In this last passage Teruel not only summarizes the complexity of this method and the counter-transferences aroused in the interviewer, but also the very early and diagnostically revealing manifestations of dyadic resistance, based on the shared collusive defences against verbalizing their deeper problems which make rational discussion of their disappointed idealizations and adult empathy for each other so difficult. The method of the JI in experienced hands seems the obvious way of eliciting these phenomena. The regressive behaviour towards each other of often educated and attractive individuals in the presence of a shared ambivalent 'helper' can best be sampled and evaluated in this setting.

c. *Supportive Psycho-Diagnostic Methods*

In the pilot and in the subsequent research phase, we cast our net widely to obtain reliable data. Had we continued as a grant-aided research team, we would have undertaken some statistical work on these in order to give contrasting clinical situations and genotypes the beginnings of normative differentiation. We hoped also to derive new hypotheses from the scrutiny of figures. We were fortunate at the Tavistock in having a clinical psychological service whose sympathies and training make them sensitive to the needs of clinical and therapeutic situations.

It was natural to seek supporting objective evidence from independent diagnostic studies by clinical psychologists. These studies started with the cognitive and projective tests normally used in the psycho-diagnostic work of the Tavistock's adult department, supplementing clinical interview assessment. I have already alluded to the meagre return from comparing the spouses' intelligence levels. It was nonetheless important to demonstrate this fact, as we did by the use of the Hartford-Shipley scale and/or the Raven's Progressive Matrices, in the experienced hands of Herbert Phillipson and later, successively of his colleagues Gerald Staunton and John Boreham. If major discrepancies in 'g' between partners in our large client-population were rare, nevertheless a fascinating minor study might have been made of comparing qualitative variations in the partners' ability and direction of 'g' utilization, but this was never an aim. It was perhaps one of the factors which made for cohesion at Subsystem I and II level in our sample that they were on the whole well-matched in 'g'. We now call for 'I.Q.' tests only if the diagnostician is in doubt, as when the career record or social adaptation of the couple, or one of them, contradicts their apparent level.

The situation was not very different with our use of standard personality or projective tests. These were the Rorschach and the Thematic Apperception Test, and later Phillipson's more relevant Object Relations Technique.[7] These yielded in the main what they could be expected to yield—modifying or confirmatory evidence for clinical judgments on *individuals*. With continuing observation such confirmation or modification could often be made in interviews, especially JI. What we needed most were instruments that could objectively validate *interaction phenomena*. We hoped to achieve this by a combination and comparison of (1) predictions from interview data, (2) psycho-diagnostic procedures, and (3) the therapeutic test. The programme was planned by the therapeutic team in collaboration with Herbert Phillipson and Peter Hildebrand.

There were as yet no dyadic interaction tests. We therefore proceeded to design new ones, to test and objectify the two areas in which we were chiefly interested: (i) Sub-System III, the deeper bonds of unconsciously shared internal objects with their mutual transactions in projective identifications, etc., and (ii) Sub-Systems I and II, the levels of the cultural and the personal values, conscious expectations and rôle norms of the couple. For each of these Phillipson and Hildebrand designed simply administered, if lengthy, tests, which we called respectively the Self-Object Perception Test (SOPT) and the Marital Rôle Involvement Questionnaire (MRIQ) already mentioned earlier in this chapter. Both were to be given to the presenting couple *before* the clinical interviews, to secure freedom from transferred bias of the interviewers, and to stimulate the clients' mental processes about the areas to be explored. Our team used both these tests only for a few trial runs. Their administration, scoring, statistical analysis and evaluation in adequate numbers of cases would have required full-time research teams whom we did not have. The designs are summarized mainly for interest. Obsolete designs may embody principles others could adapt to good purpose.

(i) *The Self-Object Perception Test.* This test consists of a check list of 100 adjectives (or brief phrases) selected as typically used by our patients to describe significant people in their lives. The test is based on our assumption that in a conflictful marriage the partners' unconscious perceptions of each other are influenced by the residual internal object relations at Sub-system III level. These introjects may be thought of as forming an 'inner society' of the marriage. Thus we asked the spouses, separately from each other to check the 100 adjectives seven times, as they would respectively describe (a) *Self*, (b) *Partner*, (c) *Mother*, (d) *Father*, (e) *Ideal Self*, (f) *Ideal Partner*, (g) *Self as thought to be seen by Partner*. The seven sheets to be checked list the 100 adjectives in randomly changed order. A copy of one arrangement of the list appears as *Appendix I*.

In order to facilitate the analysis of data, the adjectives were chosen to test six categories.

We planned to compare the adjectivally condensed profiles given by each partner to all these figures. These categories were selected empirically to fit our concepts of interplay of conscious and unconscious object relations and of the different significance of regression as a prelude to maturation as against regression determined by rigidity of fixation (see Chapter III). The categories under which we ordered the adjectives were: (a) *Ego-Supportive*, (b) *Ego-Interactive*, (c) *Primary Need Gratification* ('libidinal ego' needs of later terminology), (d) *Anxiety Expression*, (e) *Super-Ego* ('anti-libidinal' ego),

(f) *Neurotic Defence Regulation.* The words belonging to these categories are all obvious to the psychologically trained reader.

In our preliminary work with this test two methods of using the data were employed:

(i) In terms of the six just-mentioned categories it was possible to discover, from the 14 sets of ratings (self, partner, ideal self, etc.)—seven by each partner— the concordances and discrepancies in any two records, or in any two groups of records, of the way in which the various objects were perceived. This enabled one to obtain estimates of the area and extent of positive and negative identifications with past objects now transferred and operating within the marital relationship. Such an estimate, independent of the clinical assessment, would provide confirmation or amendment of the major hypotheses mentioned in Part I of this book, notably:

(a) That mate choice in a disturbed marriage was based more on the attribution to the partner of characteristics derived from or sought in an identifiable persistently cathected past love object (e.g. 'bad mother' or 'ideal father'), than on perception and cathexis of the real personality and needs of the partner; thus creating rôle conflict in both self and the partner.

(b) The object relation sought and lived out in such a conflict-laden marriage will come to resemble the relationship with the early object represented by the partner to a varying degree.

(ii) A method of factor analysis developed by Sandler[8] was to be used to explore the nature and quantifiable intensity of marital interaction at object relations level, as revealed by the 14 SOPT records. These factorializations would show:

(a) What objects in the 'inner-society' of the marriage contribute to the key themes in the marriage and what these themes are;

(b) What particular qualities in these objects are excluded (or denied) from the themes, or are dominant;

(c) The degree of libidinal and ego involvement, and of flexibility/rigidity in the transactions at Third Sub-system level, by reference to the six categories by which our 100-word check list was classified.

The same list could also be used by the interviewers to rate each partner after single and JI. In the phase of development when SOPT was tried out, there were two interviewers, so that a consensus rating could be used to check against the clients' own appraisals of themselves and their partners on SOPT. These two scores could then be compared with each other and with the parental and the 'ideal' ratings.

As mentioned, the SOPT was not fully exploited or validated. It should be mentioned, however, that the procedure we added last, namely 'Perception of Self as thought to be seen by Partner', has formed the point of departure for a new, more rigorous technique of marital interaction assessment by Laing, Phillipson and Lee.[9]* Developed in the context of Laing's work with disturbed families, this technique relates the perspective of each person to a 'meta perspective' ('my view of your view of me') and a 'meta meta perspective' ('my view of your view of my view of you').

I do not propose to go further into a discussion of tests I have not used. Recent research developments in Britain and the U.S. aim at methods by which the propositions and clinically won insights about dyadic interaction could be tested and measured in situations which would show up latent regressive behaviour after failures to live up to the required rôle or task norm of the shared experimental problems, and how the couples coped with it. Because we also perceived this close connection between shared rôle performance and deeper motivations as sources of stress in marriage we devised the second test, the MRIQ which merits description.

(ii) *The Marital Rôle Involvement Questionnaire.* This probe was based on our assumption that the attitudes to, and involvement in the main rôles taken within marriage were *manifest representations* of what went on deeper—in the 'inner society' of the dyad studied in SOPT. At the same time, the way in which a couple handled their rôle behaviour, including its complementary and conflicting aspects, was evidence of how they maintained the equilibrium of the marriage and attempted change and growth within it. We argued that within the broad framework of rôle involvements in what I called 'the areas of co-operation', the maintenance of healthy equilibrium in the growth of dyadic (and subsequently family) relationships depends upon the libidinal involvement as well as on the ratio of rigidity versus flexibility in the rôle assignments which each couple evolve to regulate their marriage—Haley's 'rules'. These vary in social and cultural groups, as well as from family to family. This was shown for example in the work of Florence Kluckhohn and J. Spiegel[10,11] and of Elizabeth Bott[12] which influenced our design for the MRIQ. The two first named writers demonstrated variations in the rôle patterns at cultural, anthropological level as between different ethnic subgroups in the Eastern U.S.A. Miss Bott documented the inter-family

* In that book there is a chapter on recent developments in dyadic test procedures.

differences on a culturally homogeneous sample of marriages in London. Of particular interest in Elizabeth Bott's findings is the observation of two major tendencies in marriages. One tendency is that towards *sharing* of tasks—highly flexible, not strictly sex-rôle linked. This is apparently the solution of conflict by something like the 'all-in-all' method, and found in those whose extra-familial networks (kin, friends, etc.) are scanty. The other tendency is that towards *rôle segregation*, found in couples with richer extra-familial connectedness. Here the expectations of how much and which of a person's skills and involvements must be shared inside and what can be left outside the marital involvement are less all-inclusive. It is not difficult to see that tensions may develop in a marriage between offspring of families with these contrasting marital norms.

In Chapters II and III, I discussed the importance of the differing norms and rôle models both in respect of sexual identities and 'inherited' rôle assignments which partners in the new marriage have to reconcile, either by rigid adherence to one of these 'inherited' models, or by working out a new domestic 'culture' of their own.

In the MRIQ we sought to supplement clinical information with more systematic, scorable and independently collected data testing the above assumptions. It is also a check-list questionnaire given to each partner, covering five out of some eight or nine possible areas of co-operation: (a) financial arrangements and decisions; (b) household tasks and responsibilities; (c) child care and control; (d) leisure pursuits; (e) social relations outside home, such as with extended family, neighbours, friends, etc.

In my original list of areas of co-operation I had included the much more 'sensitive' areas of sexual fit; mutual affection and respect; and ethical and religious convictions. None of these, though vital, were judged suitable for questionnaire methods of study, and had to be ascertained in the interview situation.

A copy of a small part of the questionnaire pro forma and a score sheet providing the key to the rating of answers are provided at *Appendix II* and *IIA*.

It will be noted that the MRIQ enquiry is divided into two parts in respect of the five areas which appear as sections.

(i) The first part is concerned with the *expectations* the partners hold in regard to their marital rôle norms and how these conflict with each other. It consists of a series of statements typifying social norms in British culture, i.e. common attitudes to involvement and responsibility within the area. Here each partner is required to indicate which statement among the selection would be agreed by *Self, Partner, Own Family of Origin, Partner's Family, Own Friends, Ideally.* The answers would provide the data on which the psychologist can compare attitudes to a person's own rôle participation in the marriage, with the home background, current social and 'ideal' culture norms of each partner.

(ii) The second part is a list of *actual tasks* and rôle assignments within the areas. In this portion of the MRIQ each partner is required to make *six judgments* about their own rôle playing per item. These relate to his or her degree of participation, enjoyment, anxiety or concern about the way it is done and the motivation to make changes in it. The partners are also required to make *five further judgments* referring to their *perception of the partners' rôle involvements*, under the same headings. Lastly, each partner is asked to record whether he feels the given item to be a source of conflict or not.

It will be seen that already in 1957 both the MRIQ and the SOPT embodied the 'meta perspective' ('I think he thinks') of projective identification in measurable form, as well as including the retrospective comparison with parental norms and the partners' notions of ideal models and what their social group did. The two tests together could provide a research design by which to assess and compare varieties of marital conflict solutions in disturbed and in normal control populations, and as a check on clinical data and ratings. In fact, two interviewers once or twice used the same method for scoring their clinical assessments of the 'sensitive' sexual, tenderness and religious-ethical areas, excluded from the MRIQ. We had also planned to use the two tests as objective follow-up records on any changes in mutual perception, perception of parents and relation to ideal expectations after therapy. The initial test data would be compared with the test data at the end of treatment, and also with the clinician's assessments of changes at the end of treatment and after some fixed number of months. Had we succeeded in carrying out this total plan, the present volume would have had to be two or three, with a string of co-authors! As it was, we at least found that spouses did not resent these combined interview and test methods. I feel that a break-through towards designing a normative method of studying dyadic marital involvements was achieved as a prototype even though I have no worked out tables of correlations to offer.

5. HOW DO WE COLLATE DATA INTO DIAGNOSIS?

The description of the next step is one which I would have preferred to evade. It should be written by an outside observer trained in philosophy of science, cognitive psychology and group-decision processes, who had watched our team at work, forced us to think aloud while working through the data elicited in the given case assessment. I should emphasize that the following account applies only to my personal way of working which may be useless as a model for others.

(a) I will begin with the easiest part. This is *exclusion* of active organic disease and of identifiable psychotic disorder, gross psychopathy, addiction and sexual perversion in both or one spouse. It is unnecessary to describe the well-known routines by which this is done. It still requires decision about what to call 'gross', what to label 'psychotic', what degree of bodily infirmity to consider as contraindicating marital therapy, that is, treatment in which the focus is on the stresses produced by being married to each other in both partners (the establishment of which diagnosis is itself the core of this section's content). If organic disease is chronic and irreversible, e.g. blindness, an old paralysis or a war wound, diabetes, etc.—and contributes to the complexity of dyadic interaction, I would not bar it. The regressive demands of the handicapped partner and the guilt and reparative feelings of the healthy partner may be essentially in our defined area, like ageing or the menopause, realities to be accepted in the marriage. The supervision and ongoing care of the chronic organic state as such is left to the normal medical attendants. The so-called stress disorders—e.g. asthma or liability to peptic ulceration, I would regard as 'grist to our mill', in which we need to collaborate with physicians skilled in dealing with acute episodes.

Exclusion from marital therapy is well-nigh automatic in cases where the organic or mental illness diagnosed is such as to create different priorities for medical intervention even though marital stress is part of the general picture. The person with active organic disease from reticulosis to cerebral tumour, general paralysis, or other dementing process is not for us to help, though his disturbed behaviour affects his psyche and his communication with others. The young schizophrenic or the depressive or manic of riper years are in need of urgent personal treatment. We are left with the task to direct them to such help and hope that the hospital will deal adequately with the spouse's stress. It can sometimes be evident that the fact of marriage to the particular husband or wife has been a big factor precipitating or re-activating a psychotic illness. In such cases I would leave open a return to me for review, in the hope that later marital therapy might help prevent recurrence. I am here discussing very rare occurrences. Family diagnosis and therapy where one member is psychotic is not the field with which this book is concerned, though what it offers may be of help to those who are.

With the remaining group—the psychopathies, addictions and perversions, we are on more debatable ground, involving suspicious

213

mate choices and collusive dynamics, to judge from such cases as we have seen. The wives of alcoholics or inadequate psychopaths have the need to be rescuing, strong and admonishing, while those of violent or gambling and spendthrift psychopaths have ambivalently masochistic and morally triumphant gratifications invested in the marriage. Despite the surprisingly good preservation of dyadic boundaries and hence of solidarity in many such cases, I call them *gross* when acting-out of the manifest disorder overspills continuously far beyond the marital field; when employers, banks, creditors, bailiffs, homosexual blackmail, etc., are involved, with periodic arrests or police charges to complete the picture. It is part of the diagnostic pattern that in a period of quiescence such patients of either sex will accede to their partners' entreaties to consult the marital clinic, as 'the last hope' where they often present a misleadingly co-operative, charming initial façade. *Case One* in Chapter IV was a good object lesson.

By and large, even in milder cases with this sort of diagnosis independent treatment for both partners is the preferred choice. Hospitalization may indeed be the first chance to break the vicious circle of an alcoholic's or psychopath's exploitation of his wife's power need and of his own infantile omnipotent dependence. There is no reason why joint marital help should not be offered for the residual readaptation problems arising from the change in rôle for both partners, by the staffs of the institution concerned.

A more pleasant task of exclusion is that of deciding that a couple do not require treatment beyond the therapeutic component of the assessment procedure. Such a judgment involves the mental processes of *positive* diagnosis in the dyadic field, as defined in this book.

(b) This *positive diagnosis* seems to me to be composed of all the steps described so far. The case illustrations show how what the clients tell us and the manner in which they communicate their complaints is related to the conceptual framework. Each new presenting couple is a unique constellation of the factors which are recognized as part of this framework with its hypothetical Sub-systems, within which I order the raw data. Thus, when Mrs. Ten says: 'When H. did not behave like Father and Mother I was shattered', I think of the possessive, anxious child who had put so much need for parental love and protection into the image of her husband and had felt let down. I gratefully score an instance of Hypothesis One constructed from previous examples. But to do this I must have assimilated the reality of the existence of oedipal needs and of infantile dependence and of their displacements to current expectations from significant human

214

beings in the Here and Now. The patient's statement must reveal its meaning. That meaning, the recognition of relevance is derived from my training and experience. It is the same problem as unheedingly passing over the appearance of silver-wire arteries in the eye fundus or barely audible rustles in the lungs, or being alive to the significance of these quite small findings as meaning respectively hypertension or pulmonary tuberculosis.

Thus, one begins with symptoms and signs, as described in the previous chapter, and asks of them certain questions.

(i) Why does this person come alone and is the spouse excluded from involvement? This offers already a variety of different hypotheses to follow.

(ii) Even if they came together, what are the interpretations for their distribution of rôles within the JI situation: competition, scapegoating, etc., with me as the joint object?

(iii) Dominance/submission can be seen without trouble, but its significance and satisfaction for the dyad must be watched for in the small hints. Which of the two is the paper-tiger? And which does the roaring?

(iv) What does the manner and feeling evinced in describing their sexual disturbances reveal of basic acquiescence and collusive deeper satisfaction, contradicting superficial distress at 'norm' level? Am I being cast more in the rôle of a dangerous representative of the libidinal forces to be resisted, or of the forbidding parental authorities who will not sanction even free discussion of such needs?

(v) The meaning of acting-out phenomena in all their variety in terms of compelling the partner to value the other and to pay attention, or on the contrary, to demean, reject and drive away. In this symptom-presentation the shifting, ambivalent rôle-ascriptions (or transference) given to oneself are crucially important. Do they, in effect, ask 'Please decipher our childish meta communications', or 'Please deliver us from this burden'? Do they, in other words, want my symbolic sanction to love each other or my permission to quarrel and hate—or how much of each?

(vi) For many doctors one of the abiding confusions about diagnosis in psycho-dynamic terms is the way in which people with psycho-analytic and similar training are apt to telescope fact and inference. When the meaning of a piece of communication is clear, this is a convenience of condensation—methodologically baffling to the non-expert. For example, to the analytic observer *Mrs. Ten*'s statement: 'I'd like to take Dr.

Dicks home with me' is part of the total observation of the *phenomenon* of a positive father-transference of which the joking words are only the most obvious part. To the rigorous phenomenologist or pure clinician, they would be a passing pleasantry, not part of the pathognomonic utterance associated with a described 'disorder'. Thus it would have little meaning for him. Transference is 'only' a hypothesis. For me her remark confirms her need for the good parent figure, connecting the historical with the Here and Now motivation. It alerts me to the woman's feelings that the husband does not satisfy this need, and that she therefore wants to steal this good father from the rival-mother who in that situation was Dr. Mary Luff. The unit of observation is the patient's total communication, i.e. the words, the feelings behind them and my inner perspectives are thus operating in that process which is only in small part verbal, and which I take to be described as 'the operational statement of inter-personal relations'. The 'statement' is the verbalization, in technical language, of the fleeting experiental *Gestalten* both of 'my view of her view of me' and 'my view of her view of my view of her' in my rapport with *Mrs. Ten*.

These connections between what I experience and the complex of the couple when they may be simply telling me how they squabble over whose turn it is to take little Johnny to school, are cumulatively built up into interpretations or hypotheses which illuminate the bare facts and clothe them with meaning. The bare facts are always ambiguous: we have seen how even wife-beating, adultery or 'undying devotion' must be evaluated by the relational inference-making sampling of one's own reaction to the total communication. I doubt whether this is scientific method, but I believe it to be psychiatry's most essential tool. It can activate quite a few of the 'inner society' of the marriage during a JI, even with only one interviewer. There is H. and me; W. and me, H. + W. and me; in addition to H.⇌W. displaying much of the wealth of meaning at the 3 sub-system levels which they also test out on me. In the 2-interviewer JI several extra perspectives or lines of force are added. Tests like SOPT and MRIQ only try to catch on paper what goes on anyhow, as a check on the interviewer's meta-perspective or telescoping of observation with prejudice and counter-transference bias. Tape recordings are another way of doing this, because they can be used for later analysis of interview content by the team. Microphones are not always well received by clients. I would personally only feel able to use recording openly with the patients' consent. Such consent was given fairly often. The time and money aspect of tape study and transcribing is a limiting factor.

(c) There is still the task of turning this experience into a *coherent* picture or *report* that can be communicated. There is also the need for a prognosis for the marriage, treated and untreated.

For a general diagnostic 'case note' the case illustrations in this book are in fact usual though I greatly condensed even the 'long' ones. There would be more rigorous recording of verbal statements, on which the inferences are made.

For *assessment of treatment possibilities* and *prognosis*, our team developed a schedule which, if desired, can be scored in terms of intensity. It contains the factors we selected as likely to influence response to therapy, obtained at interviews. I will list these with comments where needed. Each factor is scored for each spouse:

(a) *Age:* Changes in attitude are assumed to be harder to achieve over 40.

(b) *Broken home: before age 12:* Over 95 per cent of our clientele have this factor, on which comment was already made in Chapter IV. The weight of this factor for prognosis is based on general experience in social work as well as psychiatry, and ultimately on object relations theory.

(c) *Serious disturbance in early childhood:* Comment is scarcely necessary in view of wide acceptance of this factor in psychiatric aetiology, on whatever theory.

(d) *Evidence of constitutional (genetic) loading:* Psychosis, Epilepsy, Alcoholism, Other, in Family history. This again needs no comment.

The reader may wonder why the words neurosis or neurotic have scarcely been used in this book. This is because it has been superfluous. In one sense all pathological or disturbed marital behaviour is neurotic; i.e. it uses childish, regressive defence mechanisms in relation to the Sub-system III interactions with objects which sabotage the adult purposes. But contrary to expectation, the discovery in our clientele of more generalized neurotic illness has not been impressive. Either we have to call the total field of our enquiry 'Neurotic Interaction in Marriage' as Victor Eisenstein[13] does, and as Kubie[14] (loc. cit. p. 10) argues in the second chapter, when he speaks of a universal neurotic process in the present phase of the evolution of human culture. Or we may, as Eisenstein does in his own Introduction (loc. cit. p. viii) simply accept Kubie's statement as read and speak of 'the dovetailing as well as the clashing of unconscious emotional needs'. Many diagnosed

217

neurotics have as good marriages as many 'normals'. It is the marriage relation that is neurotic, and the partners focally neurotic within it.

(e) *Monosymptomatic presentation with lack of awareness that other areas of relationship are disturbed:* (i) *focus on somatic;* (ii) *focus on psychological or environmental* (*economic*). This pointer in symptomatology was discussed in Chapter VIII. It means a high degree of splitting of a hysterical nature, involving dyadic scapegoating, and blaming either one partner's 'illness', or else projecting the 'bad luck' from 'self' to 'the stars' for being underlings. This factor is clearly of importance when rating the chances of insight therapy. Here insight and accessibility are poor.

(f) *Lack of maturational achievement and of striving towards it in the present:* Here come such findings as fecklessness, economic dependence and inability to use adult self-assertion. This rubric overlaps with milder forms of inadequate characters (psychopathies) and psycho-sexual immaturity.

(g) *Fantasy-ego balance:* This is a more sophisticated rating of insight, reality sense and the degree of serious internal object relations intrusion, as measured by response to trial interpretation. We had four scores: (i) 'middle distance'* with insightful and flexible features which we rated as optimal for potentially mature re-adaptation; (ii) mid-distance with introjective features: these are the people with a mainly depressive way of handling tensions resulting in 'containment', or withdrawal if communication is liable to disturb the peace; the couples who were 'too kind', reparative, but with a measurable response to trial interpretation; (iii) Mainly projective, extra-punitive, acting-out symptom pictures, implying less ego-control, more primitive (paranoid phase) relational levels. This sub-factor is derived from the concept of ego-weakness, the 'saving' of intra-personal conflict. It has some overlap with (e) (ii) above. The latter covers the dyad's shared sense of their predicament. This present heading relates to their mutual perceptions as rated on each of them.

On this factor we would have scored *Mrs. Ten* strongly .plus, while we would have put her husband strongly plus under the preceding 'introjective' sub-heading (ii).

* This relates to the impression of how 'near' or 'far' from consciousness the dynamic factors of Sub-system III operate.

Lastly (iv). Too close, or confusing. By too close we designated a degree of nakedness of depth material and absence of healthy reticence which one finds in the potentially psychotic. This is also often of such profusion and complexity that the observer himself is drawn into the bewilderment and cannot see the wood for the trees.

The wife in *Case Fifteen* was an example of swamping one with fast, confusing, 'too frank' talk full of pseudo-insight and paranoid innuendo, covering her own aristocratic background, her husband's infidelity, homosexuality, being a foreign agent, her ill-health, sexual conflicts, the laxity and injustice of British authorities and myself as a dangerous man who would fix all blame on her, all in about 20 minutes!

(h) *The wish to achieve mature marital relationship.* This is a fairly obvious factor which can be rated not only from overt expressions but also from devious behaviour. Negative scores would be: always late, forgetting appointments, and so on, including declarations that the situation is so much better since applying they hardly know why they have come. This is, of course, a rating of dyadic resistance to change.

(i) *Potential capacity for change and willingness to work in therapy as shown by response to opportunities at interview:* This heading overlaps considerably with (g) and to some extent with (h). It was made to remind ourselves to record the responses to trial interpretations and the transference phenomena.

(k) *Worker motivated to help:* This rates our side of the assessment interviews—the counter-transference and the impact made on the diagnostician, from warmth and protectiveness to repugnance and cold fury; or confusion and mystification calling for a second interview and a magical hope that the psycho-diagnostic tests would rescue us.

Out of these factors we would construct a résumé or balance sheet of positive and negative forces we had experienced in the couple and in ourselves which constituted the prognosis, with a flexible line at which refusal to treat occurred. The latter would be influenced also by reality factors such as geography, possible attendance times, etc.

6. TOWARDS A CLASSIFICATION

Classification as an aid to knowledge in any field need not be stressed. It helps us to abstract what is genotypical and recurrently uniform from the phenotypical and unique material of our enquiry. Reference to already classified varieties, however provisional, should, for example, help us at least to recognize a given marital tension state as acute and temporary, or chronic and irreversible; benign or malignant for the health and self-respect of the spouses and their children.

Can we abstract from a series of diagnoses made on individual couples common features which would distinguish some of these gross prognostic differences of type? I think it can be done, provided someone makes it his task to scrutinize the symptomatology and social factors, correlates them with the aetiological psycho-dynamic factors discovered in therapy and follows up the course and outcome of each case treated over a number of years. He must also compare by follow-up this group with at least three other groups: similar cases untreated, though assessed by the same methods; control groups of couples rated as 'normal', stable or 'happy' by agreed criteria; and also control groups of couples during and after proceedings for dissolving the marriage. Neither the 'normal' nor the 'broken' marriages come the way of clinics, except very rarely. Our experience, therefore, of assessing cases has lain between the opposite ends of the scale, and indeed within that group with those couples who chose or agreed to consult us. No doubt even the agreement to see a marital clinic means something distinct from refusal to seek help in otherwise comparable problems.

We have not so far attempted the major research project involved in what I have just sketched. It is work for a team with this programme as its primary task and one hopes it is being planned or undertaken somewhere soon. My contribution towards a possible rating procedure is embodied in factors (a) to (k) at the end of the preceding section, applicable at least to the cases and individuals whom we have seen. It may have classificatory possibilities. It would be easy to add other factors—e.g. social class, income group, or duration of marriage or number of children, or any sociological or psycho-pathological variable suspected of significance. Adequate rating requires a high degree of skill.

I know of no literature containing any classification of types of marital interaction based on a systematic conceptual scheme. It may be too early to attempt one.

It is easy to construct a typology at descriptive or symptomatic level with a 'touch' of character-analysis. The late Bela Mittelmann[13] arrived at such a useful list of complementary patterns:

1. One of the partners is dominant and aggressive; the other submissive and masochistic.

220

2. One of the partners is emotionally detached; the other craves affection.
3. There is continuous rivalry between the partners for aggressive dominance.
4. One of the partners is helpless, craving dependency from omnipotent mate; the mate is endlessly supportive.
5. One of the mates alternates between periods of dependency and self-assertion; the other between periods of helpfulness and unsatisfied need for affection.

This is an approach to describing essential interaction as seen at a point in time. No predictive value is attached to the categories. Winch,[15] working with 'normal' couples in furtherance of his hypothesis of complementary mate selection (already discussed in Chapter VII above), arrived at five or more genotypes which he named after literary models, but on similar factors as Mittelmann: (a) 'Mothers and Sons' (b) Ibsenian (i.e. Father—little daughter as depicted in Ibsen's *Doll's House* characters Torvald and Nora); (c) Master—Servant girl; (d) Thurberian: By the last-named Winch means the kind of dyad depicted by the great humorist James Thurber in which the wife is a dominant, active, managing person who needs a gentle, soothing, supportive husband—superficially a father but really a mother figure, hence not despised as in (a), for *he* does the supporting and consoling. In addition, Winch has (e) the Pygmalion thema—not a sex-linked complementarity, but a tendency towards moulding and coercing the partner to conform to the inner rôle model which may occur in any of the a–d types. There are thus female Pygmalions too. Beyond these patterns, all familiar to those who have a professional or even worldly experience of marriages, Winch does not venture. Like myself, he feels, in discussing these types and other cases that do not fit them 'that undoubtedly it will be fruitful to set up more, but that not enough study has been given to the problem . . .' (p. 233, op. cit.).

Teruel, in the already cited paper, proposes, as yet in shadowy outline only, a classification based on the *level of the dominant internal object* or objects. While these are usually related to one or both parents, they can be 'part-objects', such as a breast or a penis. Following Kleinian theory, Teruel links the differentiatedness of the object with the preponderant defence mechanisms of the phase. In other words, he would choose marital interaction at Sub-system III level as the basis of ordering his cases in terms of these phases. (1) The most 'primitive' would be one at which the spouses projected nothing more mature than a part-object—a good or a bad breast, or a phallus. About the latter M. H. Stein[16] has written in Eisen-

221

[stein's book. There would be no sense of the 'other' as a real person, but only as of a cherished or hated appendage, to be caressed or tormented and so forth. The object as well as the ego-functions relating to it would be marked by splitting, the defence by projection, the prevalent undercurrent of feeling by *paranoid anxiety*, the whole covered by rigid idealizations. The wife in my *Case Twenty* came close to such a level of object-relation.

(2) A more mature type which would be marked by the projections of shared internal objects of already whole persons—with consequent guilt, need for reparation, ambivalence, etc.

(3) Unmentioned, but clearly in sequence in such a list in ascending order of ego development would be couples at oedipal levels.

This classification, though quite independently devised by Teruel, has affinities with our factors (e) to (i) in the above-cited schedule for rating the level of insight and maturity. Teruel in fact has spelt out something akin to the theoretical framework underlying this schedule.

These, then, are pointers to possible future systems of classification. For the present, I have limited myself to *groupings according to the phase* the conflict occurs in, and to the degree of hardening of defences. I will list these, with brief commentaries clarifying the sense in which I use the categories:

(a) *Early adaptation trouble.* This covers tensions and acting-out within the first 1–2 years of the marriage, including sexual failures, reactions to the first pregnancy or the new baby. It also includes ego-defensive reactions to discovering the realities of each others' rôle interpretations, deeper norms and idealizations now put to the test of compromise and working out of 'the new rules' and who makes them, to use Haley's phrase. This category has the overtones of a 'life crisis'—hence of being particularly deserving of help because at such great turning points people are said to be accessible to insight therapy. In my experience this is not true without many reservations. The dyad may never consolidate, therefore the prognosis is open. There may be withdrawal from a lasting commitment.

(b) *Acute transitional crisis in stable marriage.* This grouping includes cases which in the previous chapter I would have called benign, however dramatic, because of showing evidence of preservation of dyadic boundaries and of tending towards a more flexible or mature interaction. Except that they are placed in the phase of already established marriages, this group could also be called 'adaptation troubles'—or growing pains. The marital prognosis with therapy is good.

(c) *Acute episode in chronic disturbance.* This term means either the sudden triggering of a breakdown of homeostasis in a long-standing idealization-collusion (e.g. *Case Twenty-two*), or the periodic acting-out of motivations habitually held in abeyance, by which the dyadic boundary is menaced or broken.

(d) *Chronic disturbance*. This is essentially no different from the above definition, but comes for help without the dramatic, crisis element. The symptomatology for which help is sought arises from slow attrition, and the presentation is by psycho-somatic or neurotic complaints, or by some indication by one or other partner that they are no longer able to maintain the joint façade. The diagnosis of benignity or malignancy has to be made on each individual case, with their implications for therapeutic policy.

The systematic study of rôle-involvement and satisfaction in the 'areas of co-operation' is of some assistance in all these categories, in deciding on the viability of the relationship.

(e) *Dead marriage*. This was sufficiently defined at the end of Chapter VI.

Within these five crude and empirical categories, one adds the further distinctions of (i) 'mainly acting-out', (ii) mainly containment and inhibition or (iii) 'mixed'.

7. CLASSIFICATION AND CONCEPT OF CRISIS

The constant use of the idea of phases or stages of development, maturation and so forth impels me to close this chapter with some remarks on the bearing of the crisis concept on a possible classification of marital stress syndromes. At one end we have the general psycho-analytic theory and the evidence of the bearing of early childhood personality development on later capacity for forming and maintaining adequate inter-personal relations, especially in the sexual sphere. This is reflected in many of these pages, but especially relevantly at this point in Teruel's tentative classification according to levels of object-relations. At the other end my own superficial classification uses the notion of crisis in categories (a), (b) and (c). Critical points in the growth process are accepted and authenticated for child psychology, usually ending with the personality changes of adolescence.

In adult psychology we recognize the 'crisis' of marriage, perhaps the birth of the first baby. After that the female climacteric and its vaguer male equivalent linked to 'retirement' from the economic struggle is the next recognized crisis point. A tendency for each such crisis point to be marked by regressive emotional behaviour has long since been noted in psychiatric thought. I referred to it in Chapter III as characterizing courtship behaviour.

223

Work by Peter Hildebrand and K. Rogers on the Tavistock Clinic's marital case records (unpublished), which will be referred to in more detail in Chapter XII, drew our attention to the fact that the statistically significantly greatest number of couples referred to us (45·8 per cent) fell in the 30–40 age group, with a mean duration of their marriages of 8·7 years. The Registrar-General's Report (1956) relating to the 1954 Census, showed a similar bunching of divorces in this decade (40 per cent) which is not to be explained by this being the decade containing the largest number of married couples. This latter in our (England and Wales) population is the 50–9 bracket, which accounts for only 13·5 per cent of the total divorces, and only 2·6 per cent of our sample. The next highest figures are for the 40–9 age groups, both in our attendances and for divorces in England and Wales.

1954 would, of course, catch a high proportion of 'unrealistic' hasty war-time marriages, who by this time had passed through the phases of marital disenchantment and the subsequent mechanisms of dyadic conflict I have described, and to which some allusion was made in Chapter II. It took our sample an average of 8·7 years of marriage to come for help. The mean duration of marriage in the Registrar-General's figures for divorces was 12·8 years. My point in quoting these figures is that they suggest the possible existence of another crisis period, between the early mating phase and the female climacteric, around the mid-point of human life, which is borne out by a goodly number of our case histories. The lower proportions of the youngest age groups in our sample and in the divorce figures of the 1954 census also suggest a possible explanation for this phenomenon.

In the earliest years of marriage, many of the joint tasks can be said to flow from the sub-personal level of meeting biological and social demands and norms. The young man is busy 'establishing' himself in his career. Most of his spare energies go into 'nest-building' and helping his wife to cope with her task of bearing and rearing her babies. The satisfactions come from these defined rôles. Failure in these accounts for the class of difficulties we called 'early adaptation troubles'. It is in the years when these elemental tasks are on the way to being overcome, when the climb together is levelling out, the babies have become schoolchildren, the husband's job secure, more money flows in, etc., that the marriage partners have the 'free energy' to confront each other as persons. At its simplest, we may say they may just have found that they have only had in common the initial social affinities and the shared biological tasks which they had now fulfilled. They have made their new dyad or social atom—now what? Perhaps this *is* another real turning point in human life history—the

224

discovery or re-discovery of one's personal identity one had so generously subordinated to the reproductive cycle. Such a theory would account for the divergent maturation curves of two partners, for a re-activation of some regressive demands on each other for meeting the 'all-in-all' satisfactions hitherto shelved, or secretly already disappointed. Such a theory would help to explain the concentration of nearly half our case material and of a similar proportion of divorces into the 30–40 decade. But just as one meets with slow developers among individuals, so one can discern marriages who take that much longer to pass beyond 'early adaptation' (e.g. *Case Six*). The slow rate of erosion of idealization could similarly affect the '35 year old crisis' and carry its effects into the decade with the second largest figures of marital conflict and breakdown, i.e. the 40–9 year olds. A '37-year-old crisis' has been mentioned by Jung (reference unavailable) and more lately by Elliott Jaques,[17] lending some support to this excursion into another possible way of tackling the classification of marital stress in terms of typical phase and of bio-psychological crisis points.

REFERENCES

1. HERBST, P. G. (1965) 'Life Space Analysis' I and II. Mimeographed memoranda.
2. BOTT, E. (1957) *Family and Social Network*. London: Tavistock Publications.
3. ACKERMAN, N. W. (1958) op. cit., p. 268.
4. DICKS, H. V. (1953) op. cit.
5. GROTJAHN, M. (1965) 'Family Interviews as an Aid to Psychoanalytic Therapy', in *Forest Hospital Publications, III*, pp. 34–40.
6. TERUEL, G. (1966) 'Considerations for a Diagnosis in Marital Psychotherapy', *Brit. J. of Med. Psychol. 39*, p. 231 ff.
7. PHILLIPSON, H. (1955) *The Object Relations Technique*. London: Tavistock Publications.
8. SANDLER, J. J. (1952) 'A Technique for Facilitating the Rotation of Factor Axes', *Psychometrika, 17*, No. 2.
9. LAING, R. D., PHILLIPSON, H. and LEE, A. (1966): *Inter-personal Perception: a Theory and a Method of Research*. London: Tavistock Publications. New York: Springer.
10. KLUCKHOHN, F. and SPIEGEL, J. P. (1954) *Integration and Conflict in Family Behavior*. Report No. 27 of the Committee on the Family, Group for Advancement of Psychiatry, Topeka. Kansas.
11. SPIEGEL, J. P. (1957) 'The Resolution of Role Conflict Within the Family', *Psychiatry 20*, pp. 1–6.
12. BOTT, E. (1957) op. cit.

13. MITTELMANN, B. (1956) Chap. 'Analysis of Reciprocal Neurotic Patterns in Family Relationships', in Eistenstein, V. W. (op.cit.) p. 98 ff.
14. KUBIE, L. S. (1956) Chap. in Eisenstein, V. W. (op. cit.) p. 10.
15. WINCH, R. F. (1958) op. cit. Chapters 6–11.
16. STEIN, M. H. (1956) Chap. 'The Unconscious Meaning of the Marital Bond' in Eisenstein, V. W. (op. cit.) p. 65 ff.
17. JAQUES, ELLIOTT (1965) 'Fear of Death and the Mid-life Crisis' *Internat. J. of Psycho. Anal. 46*, p. 502 ff.

Chapter XI

TREATMENT

1. INTRODUCTORY

In the beginning of Chapter X, I said that it was more difficult on paper to give an account of 'what one does' than it is to state the principles on which action is founded. This applies even more to the therapeutic relationship than to the relatively detached frame of mind of preliminary assessment. Critics of classical psycho-analysis (which the late John Rickman humorously referred to as the 'chair-couch tandem') seldom realize that psycho-analysts themselves are frequently the originators of new techniques. There are many 'deviationists'! Much of group therapy and many shades of 'brief psychotherapy', social case work, and counselling are adaptations of psycho-analytic principles to the realities of clinical life in 'mass practice' by analysts of various schools. Such an adaptation under the influence of psychoanalytic thinking was discernible in the Memorandum issued to probation officers by the Home Office which I described in Chapter I as the best statement of principles of matrimonial conciliation of the period.[1] The memorandum stresses why the therapist must avoid making the couple's decisions for them; the aim of discovering meanings behind symptoms, and the advantages of allowing resentments to be ventilated for therapeutic relief and as an aid to diagnosis. Though the spouses were to be seen separately first, a joint interview was envisaged as a central feature of the method. Thus, the Probation Inspectors' Committee who drew up the memorandum have the right to claim priority in advocating JI at least as a diagnostic method, and in visualizing an inquiry at a level where my Sub-systems II and III articulate; e.g.:

> ... It is insufficient to discover that an assault was caused by the nagging of the wife. Ill-health may be behind the nagging and the ill-health brought about through the husband's neglect. The neglect may have arisen as the two drifted apart. It is the cause of that drifting that the conciliator must seek.

227

The memorandum is able to describe the point at which 'diagnosis merges into mediation'. Of necessity the Probation Service had mainly to rely on brief therapy, closely akin to our earlier efforts to combine investigation with insight-therapy touched on in Chapter X. My teaching rôle in helping new probation officers to approach their task was part of the challenge to develop both theory and practice on the lines of their model if I was to be a lap ahead of my classes.

The growth of therapeutic methods was essentially an elaboration of the observer's involvement in clarifying what marriage partners were 'doing to each other' and why. It follows closely the evolution described in Chapter X of the assessment procedures from which it could never be strictly separated. That is, we passed from the two-worker team, each concerned with one partner, using the JI as a diagnostic aid, to the stage of one worker working by JI throughout. But the other possible combinations were never discarded from our potential armoury. Therefore one can classify the available variations in use as follows:

A. Individual Therapy:
1. 2 workers, one for each partner throughout. JI only as assessment help—initially and to gauge progress.
2. 1 worker for both partners, seen separately. JI as above.
3. 1 worker treating one partner, the second partner having opted out.
B. Joint Therapy:
1. Treatment in 'foursome' setting throughout.
2. Treatment wholly or mainly by JI but with individual interviews interposed as needful, in 'foursome' setting.
3. Treatment throughout by one person, using JI or separate interviews as required.
4. Involvement of other persons, e.g. children.
C. Group Therapy:
Only one variant has been explored in the Tavistock Unit: that of 2 workers using group sessions for 3–4 married couples forming the group.

This repertoire, built on one basic model, namely the 'analysis' of dyadic interaction, allows of great flexibility in different clinical requirements. It goes without saying that there are many other possible models, which I have not experienced or used.

For the training of marriage therapists and case workers, the safe and gradual path is that from A to C above, staying under 'foursome' conditions and switching to one-worker-per-couple methods only when fully experienced. The same safeguards and consequent

228

complications of the student's entry into this field as mentioned in Chapter X will apply *a fortiori* in therapy. These are conferencing, supervision and constant touch with the working mate.

2. THE AIMS OF MARITAL THERAPY

Before going into detail on the variations of treatment techniques, I should pause to clarify the purposes I hold before me in instituting treatment for a married couple, or in refraining from advocating treatment. Such purposes are necessarily heavily charged with ethical and social value judgments of a personal kind. From this section of the book I therefore explicitly exclude any and all my past and present collaborators because they may not share such values or wish to be associated with expressing them in the words that follow.

I mentioned in my first chapter how frequently couples who consult us display the keenest sense of guilt and failure at the breakdown or deterioration of their marriage. I feel that mankind despite the cynical surface deeply values because it needs the full marital relationship as one of its major goals, and that such a relationship answers the need of children for a stable parental dyad united in love as an optimal condition for their personality growth. In a sense, I need say no more. Any doctor or therapist is pledged to promotion of 'health' as a value, to its restoration where possible, and to a diligent search to make the conditions of its maintenance known and its recovery easier. I am satisfied that a marital dyad has reality and that these remarks therefore apply to the health of marriages. It becomes a professional goal to maintain the life and adequate functioning of a marriage, especially if it is the nucleus of a growing family. By analogy with the recent controversy over the medical ethics of maintaining life as long as possible even in the doomed, I take the middle road when applied to the dyadic 'organism'. I would work hard and hopefully with any marriage—if asked to by the parties themselves—to maintain it and lessen its stress, even where I had made an assessment that, on balance, the outcome was dubious. I would do this not because we are in no position scientifically to make omniscient assessments of latent resources for beneficent change. I would do it also when, as far as my private judgment went, I could see little in a marriage but social conformism, fear of change, or maintenance of the outer husk for neurotic reasons. The fact that these things make the couple come is enough to justify my willingness to help them. The motivations springing from social conformity and from anxious dependence even on a 'bad object' are dynamic factors which can be worked with. I might privately think how bad it was for some individuals or their children to stay together, but I would attempt to clarify why they nonetheless did. Then there would come a moment when they would themselves decide to stop coming—an issue which could have several meanings; or they would work through towards a better total relationship or towards a civilized separation. It is their lives, not my reputation as a sharp forecaster or arbiter of fates, which matter.

From the standpoint of social values, the whole point of this work is the discovery that a proportion of unhappy marriages are remediable—some quite easily. We can never know whether we do a given couple a good turn by helping them to maintain their union and thus depriving them of all sorts of experience of the 'might have been'. This makes it essential that marital therapy should only be directed at enlarging the shared insight into their tensions, and never to assuming the omnipotent decision-maker's rôle. By what I do, I hope that either the quality and satisfactions of their dyadic existence is bettered or the manner of their parting is as reasonable as possible, conscious of what is implied for all concerned.

My aim, therefore, is to help maintain and improve as many of them as possible. If, after an honest and sufficiently enlightening attempt at mending the relationship the marriage ends—perhaps even assisted by the insight acquired—that is a limitation and failure of my aim as a healer of marriages. I would like all marriages to be as all Western humans deep down want them to be: permanent, satisfying, enhancing the identities of both partners. It does not happen all that often at present, but I hope it will more frequently when our aetiology and therapeutic techniques are better.

Finally, I aim at leaving the two individuals better adapted to inner and outer reality; to see themselves more objectively, to project less, to manage their aggression and ambivalence in a less infantile and destructive way. This may happen whichever way the dyadic cohesion goes. They may then make a better marriage next time. Where my responsibility is to the dyad, I cannot make this the central aim, but a bye-product of my work with the dyad. It is this shift of focus which distinguishes marital therapy from psychotherapy of individuals. It is a social, public weal focus directed at the smallest unit of society. The therapist who is asked to help an individual, has a different duty. This is well expressed by Kubie[2] in facing the problems I am discussing:

> The psycho-analyst is not a marriage broker, nor a marriage saver, nor yet a marriage wrecker. Wherever he faces a choice between health and marriage, his medical duty is at least to present this issue clearly so that the patient can make his choice in the full awareness of its implications. (pp. 36–7).

The implication for Kubie *qua* analyst is, rightly, that the individual's mental health comes first. This is the traditional medical and psycho-analytic 'value model'. Kubie, continuing this tradition assumes, as we all must, the ubiquity of potential neurotic reactions which may only be revealed after marriage and *in* the marriage. But he does not cross the threshold of opportunity which the *joint handling* of such 'neurotic' manifestations gives for dealing with them direct, in reference and interaction with the very object and situation which provokes them. If the neurotic internal object relations are expressed in the marital relationship, then, even quite apart from any saving of marriages (which, unlike Kubie's *is* my aim, in marital therapy), the chances of resolving or ameliorating these neurotic tendencies are likely to be improved in this setting; whereas they could stultify individual therapy by being continually stirred up in the marriage and by the partner who is not in treatment. Later I hope to discuss the possibilities of help even in the traditional psychotherapeutic model provided its aim is directed to the marital interaction, with the absent partner still in the therapeutic purview. What I cannot concede *qua* marriage therapist, is the 'I'm all right, Jack' attitude of individual therapy going on *as if* the partner 'out there' were an object, not an interacting agent. We shall see—indeed we have seen in the account of one case already—that the results for the individuals are at times as relieving in this setting which uses the therapeutic possibilities inherent in the marital relationship itself, as in the often lengthier techniques conducted in the social vacuum of the 'couch-chair tandem'.

I hope that this short discussion of my aims and values may help to clarify much of what follows.

3. SEPARATE THERAPY WITH EACH PARTNER

(a) *The Foursome*

As already mentioned, this model has been the standard practice for our unit over many years. The 'ideal' on which it has been modelled is, I guess, that of the concurrent analysis of each partner by a differ-ent analyst, the two therapists conferring 'behind the scenes' and thus utilizing the pooled information discreetly in the handling of their respective analysands. I would claim no originality in the shaping of this model which was developed and used with considerable success in the Family Discussion Bureau (Bannister[3]), (Pincus[4]). This 'four-person relationship' which is necessarily created by the technique, is based on almost exactly the same concepts as my own, and thus uses the same kind of therapeutic levers. In fact, after our pilot phase there began a welcome degree of cross-fertilization and exchange of ideas when the F.D.B. joined the Tavistock Institute. To study the method of four-person therapy at its most developed the two books just mentioned should be read as complements to my remarks here. The account of the progress of *Case Ten* in Chapter VI was intended as the main illustration of this method for the present volume. The principle is to use psycho-dynamic insights in what might be called a focused way—the focus being on the marriage. What is dealt with at any given session is what the clients bring or offer for discussion, on the assumption generally current in psychoanalytic practice that such material is unconsciously purposeful, containing both a statement of need and an element of distortion due to the 'interference' of resistance. The latent conflict in the quality and form of this total communication is related to the changing rapport or transference with the therapist. The creation and maintenance of this setting is the task of each therapist and of the clinic or institution they represent. It is a milieu in which the patient or client can activate and feel safe to relive some of the crucial unresolved early relationships in the Here and Now with the case worker. The latter uses his insight and counter-transference feelings to respond to these communications by acceptance and interpretation. What is perhaps central to the technique is the gradual involvement of the therapist in the same kind of transferred or projected object relations conflicts that form the symptomatology of the marital stress. The awareness of the ever-changing transference, shuttling to-and-fro between spouse and case worker was well illustrated in some of the episodes in treatment sessions in *Case Ten*. We had, for example, the working through with Mrs. Williams of the Wife's need for 'getting into her mother', the curiosity, greed and need to be loved and to bring her sexuality slowly and childishly into acceptance (e.g. via the matchbox play). Similarly we had the husband's very guilty relationship with frequent paranoid reactions to Dr. Hildebrand which at a dramatic moment revealed itself as the same defence as the one he used against his wife, when he exclaimed 'God, what does that make us?' in relation to his discovery that his wife at one level represented his angry, controlling father.

Thus, as in all psycho-dynamically oriented therapy, the case-worker fulfills the rôle of a transitional object whose task is not only to accept the projections and unreal expectations by experiencing them on his own person (which can be very trying) but also so to respond to these communications and emotional onslaughts that his comments are enlightening and increase the patient's insight. In this predicament the therapist's greatest anxiety may well be aroused when he becomes perceived as the useless, unloving parent figure, under pressure to show evidence of being helpful and powerful, to take charge and so forth. Only a resolute sticking to the acceptance and interpretation of negative transferences and infantile demands will help in this temptation to abrogate real technical helpfulness in favour of succumbing to the infantile accusations and blandishments that defeat the aim of therapy: the working through of the past in the transference. This allows the patient to internalize a new, different, more adult outcome of the encounter, so like the repeated crises or tensions in the marital situation motivated by the same forces which are now openly displayed in the treatment situation. The relationship to the spouse follows a parallel pattern of growth, as the feelings for the internal objects are released and worked through in the transference. A year or two years of once-weekly attendances is the usual length of time required for the working through the kind of collusion represented by *Case Ten* in this book or the type of case reported in the Pincus volume by the F.D.B. But one often has to compromise with reality—moves to other cities, joint resistances after initial improvements, or other fortuitous changes—which cuts the contacts sooner than one would wish.

From the first there had been an important difference in the conduct of cases as between my Unit and the F.D.B. This was the effect of the JI not only on the couple but also on us. With the F.D.B. the spouses each had an 'unknown' object—the partner's therapist whom they often never met and who was only seen through the partner's and the subject's own fantasies. This could be a valuable source of material relating to infantile fears and hates and jealousies. With my plan of the almost invariable diagnostic foursome JI preceding the separate foursome therapy pattern, there was at least some real image of 'the other therapist' as a person, and of the co-operating, mutually supportive therapists forming another couple. This, as I see it, provided *both*, the scope for fantasies of an infantile character to enter into the subsequent therapy, but a readier correction by reality testing in the light of the experienced actual personality of the partner's doctor. I have already dwelt on the various arguments which can be used for and against such foursomes as the standard method, granted experienced therapists and the need for economy of manpower and time. In this respect our Unit started at the opposite end from the F.D.B. We began with two experienced consultant psychiatrists, trained and long accustomed to independent therapeutic and analytic work. The F.D.B. began with social worker staff to whom this work was in many instances their initiation into psychotherapeutic activity and into the realities behind book knowledge about psycho-analytic theory. For them the case conference and the supervision were essential life-lines for managing the anxieties and stresses of transference-counter-transference involvements. Any training programme should therefore be built on the

F.D.B. model, with slow and easy stages towards simplification and lessening of supervision, withdrawal from obligatory work on four-somes, towards one-person, joint handling of therapy with the flexibility of seeing the couple separately or together as and when seems best.

It is noteworthy that as the F.D.B. have developed highly sophisti-cated levels and their senior staff have, in parallel, acquired analytic qualifications, the JI has become more freely used by them, for assess-ment and latterly also in therapy (Bannister & Pincus[5]).

(b) *Separate Therapy by one Person*

This way of halving manpower and experimenting with the carrying of sole responsibility for a dyad was dictated in the first instance by reality factors. Granted the preceding JI followed by assignment of each partner for therapy on foursome lines, one has had one's running mate ill or on holiday while their client needed to be seen. Clearly it was better to come to the therapist already familiar with the problem and known to the patient than to a totally new 'locum' for a few weeks. Secondly, the situation in private practice often precluded foursome arrangements. I will admit at once that this variant is to me the least satisfactory of the choices, even if one of the most practical and obvious for anyone not prepared to use the JI technique as their treatment method. It permits one to use the well-trodden one-to-one path along which most of a working psychotherapist's skill and experience has been gathered. One can often get more intimate communications from each of the two persons concerned more quickly and identify with their mind or allow them to influence one's feelings in turn. What my objection amounts to—and this may not apply to others using this method—is that it often precludes one from cross-interpretation in-so-far as this runs the constant danger of disclosing what each partner has said to one trusting in one's respect for confidentiality, but without the use of which the interpretation of the other's feelings and fantasies cannot be substantiated by chapter and verse of their communications and behaviour. It seems to me the worst of both worlds. One is treating interaction, but keeps the inter-acting persons separate. The one thing they seldom vouchsafe is what they feel goes on between the partner and myself, or how they use me at Sub-system III level in their day-to-day interaction outside, mis-quoting, competing and envying. Although my theoretical position makes a strong point of the influence of the *shared* object, this particu-lar way of playing the transitional shared object without sampling by direct participation what the sharing feels like to the partner not in the room is burdensome. I find myself having to use material of

234

possibly months ago worked over in a preliminary or intercurrent JI towards which I am inwardly straining as a relief from the semi-secret intermediary or 'double-agent' rôle whom each party clearly feels to be acting for 'the other side', even if they deny it. I feel split in a way which I would not be in the four-person therapy, nor yet if I was sitting with the dyad as the unit to be confronted. It is as if a pianist was forced to perform the scores for the Right and Left hand in succession instead of synchronized. Perhaps paradoxically for the reader used to solo-interviews, I feel much better integrated when the integer of the couple confronts me.

Therefore I decided very quickly not to pursue this combination as a form of therapy, even though I use it frequently for diagnostic purposes, provided always that the couple know I am following the individual sessions with a JI, if they have not begun with it. I do not object to the odd solo interview in the course of mainly JI therapy. I switched over to my present method of choice, the triadic interview, as the staple way of working with marital cases, to be described in a subsequent section.

First I must briefly touch on the possible indications for separate therapy for each spouse by one worker. I do not think there are any clinical ones. Where very strong anxiety or hostility is encountered in the diagnostic JI, I deal with it by almost immediate transference interpretation. In still more reluctant beginnings, I add the reminder that they need only talk of what they can safely express, adding a reassuring remark about my therapeutic rather than judicial rôle if this seems right. The dread explosions simply do not happen with my cases, only plenty of paranoid and hostile feelings are expressed. So if I have to resort to separate therapy it is only for reality reasons, such as I can accept as unavoidable: working conditions, sometimes baby-sitting difficulties for long-continuing regular therapy, etc. With so few persons at present engaged on this form of therapy, I feel it improper to refuse promising cases on grounds of my dislike of a method when it is still much better than any they could get else-where without waiting six months.

There is lastly, one situation which can still be called marital therapy though only one person is attending. This is where it is worth trying to help the willing partner when the other—usually less insight-ful and less suffering—partner has opted out, or cannot attend for good reasons. In one sense this is simple, standard psychotherapy for someone with a marital symptomatology, as old as psycho-analysis and its derivatives. The difference in focus from these is that the absentee partner *has* been involved, and is, as it were, invisibly present. The absentee is not left with the illusion that I am regarding him as uninvolved in the problem of a sick partner. On the contrary

235

the understanding is that the attending spouse is working for both. The content and focus of the therapy is therefore still on the marital interaction, not diffusely on general personality change for the attending partner's sake. Frequently the latter has the main benefit, but not always. If one is dealing with, for example, a very masochistic woman who will goad her husband into attacks of rage that depress him and make him inefficient at work or destroy his domestic peace, he may be the chief beneficiary, whilst I cope with her transference troubles. It remains true, both, that working with one partner can and does change the dyadic collusive interaction, and that this change in the absence of the collaboration of the second partner has a less certain prognosis for the marriage, even though the partner in therapy may mature a good deal. This isolated maturation may be away from the partner and the marriage, at least in part attributable to the absence of reciprocity and dovetailing of the developing insight. Some of the most poignant encounters in this field have been with such 'left out' spouses who had discovered too late that by their original decision to opt out of joint therapy they were now stranded, and it *was* too late. In such cases, or where one is called upon to render help to the mourning process of a broken marriage, one is still having to deal with the invisible presence of the absent partner—the lost love object.

Yet another variant of one-to-one marital therapy, usually brief, is that in which one party has temporarily (but in fantasy 'forever') deserted, and has come for 'consolation' in a state of acute grief and longing for their injured mate, or conversely for the deserting partner whom they have been instrumental in driving away. In this situation one invites both to join in a JI and treatment now becomes that of the dyad.

As I have said, my own work has made little original contribution to the technique of separate therapy, by one or two persons. These are better and more fully dealt with by other writers, among whom I have quoted the books by Bannister, Pincus, et al., and the essays in Eisenstein's symposium. Most of the literature with which I am familiar skates lightly over the techniques, even if there is considerable agreement about the dynamics, aims and assessment.

4. JOINT THERAPY

I will now attempt to set down my experience in the joint handling of dyadic therapy which represents for me an advance in the application of developing concepts to actual practice. This development was sketched throughout the preceding chapters, and much of the argument for its advantages in the case of an experienced psychiatrist or psychotherapist marshalled in Chapter X when discussing the diagnostic JI. In the optimal event where the diagnostician or receiving consultant is also the future therapist, there is scarcely a firm line to be drawn between where the assessment ends and mediation or treatment begins. They merge, as they should in any adequate medical consultation. The feeling that the condition is understood, that a concerned but objective qualified helper will now devote himself to handling it is itself a therapeutic experience, even if the apprehension and resistance to 'What will they do to me?' is also aroused.

(a) *Four-Person Joint Therapy*

Joint Therapy developed from the diagnostic JI and thus began as another form of the four-person relationship, as recorded in my 1953 paper cited in Chapter X. Its potentiality was revealed in some early cases handled by Mary Luff and myself which greatly influenced subsequent decisions to institute joint four-person therapy as a continuous method. I will describe one such case because it conveniently illustrates our approach, the events during JIs and the rapid therapeutic outcome, in a manageable compass.*

Case Twenty-six: The case presented by H. alone, referred with a curt note by his G.P. as follows: 'I would greatly appreciate your opinion on Mr. Twenty-six. He has a history of lack of desire for intercourse. I would like to know how much is psychiatric. Signature.' A standard referral to a psychiatric consultant for a diagnosis. H. himself echoed this modest hope in his application form which read: 'I have been suffering from partial impotence for over 10 years. Treatments prescribed by various doctors included injections, pills and also some psychological effort a few years ago, but my present condition is worse than ever. I should be grateful if you will allow me to attend for a consultation.' The first attendance was thus by individual interview with me, during our pilot phase, some 14 years ago.

H.'s diagnostic interview: Aged 45. Married 20 years. 3 adolescent children, the eldest a girl. A spare masculine man of sad mien, who makes good contact. He says his impotence is now complete, but that is not his worst trouble. He has black moods and irritability continuously at home, directed at W. and children, which threaten his marriage and damage those he loves. He relates how the war disturbed his family and career. It necessitated his prolonged absence, during which the 1940 'Blitz' was raging, and he had to leave W. to evacuate the then young children and her widowed mother to a tiny cottage in a safe area. Here he rejoined them months later. Impotence occurred for the first time when, within hearing of the

* Many Probation Officers who heard my lectures will recognize this case.

237

old lady and the children he attempted coitus on his return, almost an interloper to this unpropitious scene he had not had a hand in arranging. Both he and W. were very upset. It happened again—this time a wailing air-raid siren disturbed them. Since that time he had become increasingly impotent and each attempt at coitus was ruined by his anticipation of failure. 'Possibly W.'s attitude has not been helpful,' he said. 'Every time she got into such a terrible state half-an-hour afterwards, shocking distress and weeping—more than seemed necessary—but then I'm not a woman.' This reaction of hers was part of the anticipatory dread. The need for birth control by condom was another.

H. next stated that W. had always wanted him to have psycho-therapy. He had seen a distinguished urogenital surgeon-endocrin-ologist with strong views on sex functions. His injections had helped 'wonderfully'. But when the identical hormones were later injected by H.'s own G.P. they lost their efficacy. Pills (not specified) did not help. It was then he saw a reputable psychotherapist for a time. 'He tried to dig up the past—childhood and so on—I couldn't help feeling it had little to do with it. I didn't like it and it didn't help.' (This was 4 years before our talk.)

H. described how nice his home was, what a good mother W. was, but how exhausted she became. He had no reason to be unhappy: 'the chief trouble is myself—I get so impatient and have a nasty temper, always with people I'm fond of. I pick on the small things—it is the children—I get at W. by them—if they leave lights on or doors open—I swear inwardly. My way of attacking is passive—I go silent. I don't think the children suffer. I sort of expect them to do as I would. *H.V.D.: 'Does this happen with other people?'*—'No, similar slackness in the office leaves me quite undisturbed.' This, in condensa-tion to essentials, ended the spontaneous statement.

I now say: *Tell me how things used to be* (aiming at earlier marital history). The reply came: 'It was terrible.' To H. my vague invitation meant his family of origin (my rejected colleague of 4 years ago must have achieved something!) He now described his mother as 'worse than me—we were never allowed to walk on the carpets, only on newspapers. Home life was vitiated by mother's love to exert power and her meanness. She had a hard life, sure, because father left a lot to her but no doubt she liked it that way. He was a little businessman but he took life very easy, so her domineering suited him. He stayed out as much as mother would let him, playing cards with his friends, but he was a charming character. He would also become upset by small things, and then he sulked too, mother would even occasionally give in then. But they quarrelled so much and never seemed happy, mother always harping on father's weakness and making him pay for it. It

238

was a place to get out of.' So H. not only stayed out as much as possible but decided to forgo his engineering training at the local college because that would have meant home residence. Instead he came to London and established himself gradually in business—not his choice, but he was bent on not being dependent on his domineering mother. Nor did he stay long in his relative's firm—he wanted to be his own master. He was satisfied but not enamoured with his business—not enough challenge or skill is needed. Later he told me of an older brother—an amiable black sheep, a gambler, always up and down in life who was mother's favourite because a great charmer, who could get away with being dependent on her though he caused a lot of trouble to the parents. (This is inserted here to round off the family picture, and stress H.'s fierce need for not being weak.)

He was invited by me to talk about his earlier sex attitudes. His reply was he was always more interested in sport, joined the Boy Scouts and loved the life of camping and climbing. He had not suffered from adolescent masturbation guilt, and he dealt firmly but kindly with a scoutmaster who tried mild homosexual advances. H.'s associations switched almost at once back to his parental home and its atmosphere, as if to tell me where the source of the trouble lay. Adding further detail to the sketching of its character, he said: 'With me this sulking doesn't work as it did with father. I too make it as unpleasant as I can, but knowing I am in the wrong.'

At this point he was offered an interpretation: '*There seemed to be a similarity between what he called attacking passively and the sexual withdrawal.*' H. replied he saw none. However, his next sentences were: 'You know my wife always had her own way as to times for intercourse. Otherwise she was always tired or something. What I wanted didn't count—that's how I see it!' After telling me how she was the only girl he had loved, and that he was not interested in acquiring any new ones, he praised W. saying: 'I only had the outdoor life—the mountains and that—I have no intellectual hobbies or gifts. My W. and daughter are musical—they play instruments—I don't. I am out of it and can only listen.' The reader will not be surprised that the temptation to add an interpretation more at this point was irresistible, especially as H.'s response to the first had yielded such good material. So I said: '*You do seem to feel very inadequate to W., as if you felt that she had all the potency and power much as it was in your parents' case, and not only in the sex sphere.*' Again came the emphatic disagreement. 'Not at all, W. is not a nagger like my mother. She criticizes me constructively, she urges me to have hobbies, inquires what I am reading—she tries to improve me—(and then suddenly with a burst of feeling)—I dislike it intensely! It has quite the opposite effect. I know I am not likeable like my brother, I have not

239

his wit or manners. I get superficially interested in things—I start several books at once and don't finish them; or I try a bit of carpentry. I would like to take up painting as W. says, but I know I am no good, and I hate to make a fool of myself . . .' This virtually completed the interview, save to get H.'s consent to our inviting W. on the grounds that we always needed to get a balanced view of both partners when there was such an obvious state of marital difficulty. He felt sure we would find her very intelligent.

W.'s diagnostic interview: (a fortnight later) by Dr. Luff. An alert, pleasant woman of high intelligence, aged 45. 'Has come by invitation, to help in the marital difficulties due to her H.'s impotence and irritability.' No specific problems stated. W. began also by describing the situation early in the war, assuring us that he was 'all right' before that. She confirmed all facts, and the two accounts dovetailed, but she initially claimed 'the marriage was very happy' apart from the sexual difficulty of H. Challenged to a little more explanation of this, W. said 'Oh well I do become upset at times and then he is much worse.' She stuck in her spontaneous account entirely to describing H.'s condition: how he has become more and more absorbed in his own problems and has lost interest in outside problems, especially in the progress and concerns of the children. She was presently able to add she could not be tolerant about this withdrawal and tried to talk him out of it and make him be more considerate. Perhaps after all she is not a calm equable person, and gets worked up. Later she said, 'The relationship is gradually deteriorating, though fundamentally we are devoted'—she had even thought at times of separation if he could not pull himself out of it. He was so hard on the children. On holiday he was easier, even a little better sexually. (cf. Case 6 in Chapter V). At this point her own statement dried up and she was asked 'What about your own background?' The data were interesting. W. came from a cultivated home, with a much older brother and a younger sister who died 20 years ago. W. was her father's favourite. He was the 'culture carrier'. She described rather glowingly his deep interest in scholarship and the arts, and how he inspired her to strive for education, his high standards and his strictness in seeing that she did her schoolwork and her music practice thoroughly. She was much closer to him than to her mother, who was described somewhat contemptuously as highly strung, emotional and irresponsible, utterly dependent on the father. The parents squabbled a lot over trifles, and W. was happier at school than at home. The plans for her University career were cut short by the sudden death of her beloved father when she was 17, who left too little money. She had now to take severely practical training to earn her living and help support the mother who collapsed into dependence on her. She had to be the mainstay of the home, though she strove to keep up her intellectual and musical life. She shared H.'s love of wild country and hiking, and was very much in love with this virile, striving, energetic young man. She described a good adaptation to her domestic and marital rôle, with a varied social life and outside networks connected with music, evidently much richer than H.'s.

In sum, a versatile, gifted person with no obvious neurotic trouble, but a strong bond to an idealized father and ill-concealed hostility to the weak mother still to some extent on her hands. W. obligingly agreed to a JI though not sure what she had to do with H.'s defect.

First JI (a week later). Dr. Luff unavoidably absent. The atmosphere one of awkward tension, myself feeling very unsupported. Little fresh information was forthcoming. The partners were very reticent in front of each other, and this was commented upon. H. was very self-blaming and tried to exempt his wife from all responsibility. W. tried gallantly to counter this, by stressing she became so hysterical, and was not this contemptible too. *I comment how reserved they are, and how they try to exonerate each other, as if each had to hold in what they might say in criticism of each other.* They both agree that it would help if only they could establish better communic⁹tion, and they hope we shall do this for them. H. gets close to saying he knows he behaves like his father did at home, as if his family ought to know what he wants without having to say it. There is an opportunity, when they describe the repeated sexual failure, for a comment from me that *they seem both to have settled on a stereotyped and unvarying pattern of trying coitus very consciously, as a test, anticipating failure, inevitably followed by W.'s distress symptoms.*

(Not said but noted by me was that W. was not at this stage insightful, that she had certainly a somewhat childish reaction to sexual frustration, and could not free herself from a conditioned reflex though she knew it was unhelpful to her purpose. In the main, a sticky, rather unsuccessful start to what I visualized as a hard and long case.)

Second JI. It took nearly 4 weeks to assemble the foursome. Both spouses said they had been helped to feel more sympathy for each other by the first JI. After this they fall silent. *We comment that this tense inability to talk with each other must be very central to their trouble.* H. now asks our advice how they should manage their sex life. 'Should we separate our bedrooms or try to face disaster?'—by which he meant the debacles of repeated impotence. *We comment that the wish to make us decide so personal an issue for him sounds as if he were*

241

abdicating his responsibility for his reactions in favour of outside authorities. Should we not rather see how they themselves feel about this?

This quasi-interpretation breaks the ice and there follows a long discussion illustrative of how gingerly and over-considerate they are in criticizing one another (brought into connection with the first JI), or in saying spontaneously what they feel. H. can now say he would like to continue sleeping together for fear of increasing estrangement. But W. differs: it is too great a strain to sleep in the same bed. She sleeps so badly, is always tired, which 'of course is purely physical'. *We remark that these symptoms are of course physical but that they show the strain created by her emotional frustration, which is especially marked in her 'hysterical crying' as she had called it. Could it be that she felt disappointed because H. had let down her expectation of him?* (Note: a venture with my hard-worked Hypothesis I.)

The comment leads H. to say that this must be right—W. is very critical of him and only the best in all respects is good enough for her. W. looks bewildered and unbelieving. We now say something like this: *There has been this great disappointment in H. as a strong, potent man which both of you have felt. W. has certainly felt it in her wish to improve him and make him do things he does not do. For H. this has seemed a driving force making him anxious but which he has also had to resist.* This makes W. say rather spontaneously: 'But he doesn't do enough with his mind. For one so intelligent he wastes his capacities!' She now adds this applies not only to general interests but also to the indifference how his children, especially the older girl, are developing. A free argument develops. H. wonders what all that special interest is—aren't they going along all right? W. tries animatedly to explain. H. concedes that he feels restless at home—no peace for him. He may leave the office cheerful, even look forward to seeing the family; but the moment he turns his front door key a cloud descends and he goes dead, cannot concentrate. 'I know this is irrational but I get the feeling of being constantly nagged and belittled.' The children do not show any respect. They are better when W. is not there. We say: *'Is this not part of the sense of being under scrutiny for better performance and more interest?'* W. says he does not attack her, he is always perfectly behaved. No, it is the children who get all the backwash of his moods, and she fears he will lose their love. He seems to expect instant obedience and alacrity in carrying out his wishes. There follows a long discussion by four parents on the ways of teenagers, their maddening slowness, sloth and so on. W. says at this point that what is wounding is not that H. asks the children to do things which in the end they always do, but the angry, peremptory orders he gives. She now describes H.'s discouraging belittling of their achievements, fault-finding and sarcasm (examples here omitted). She recalls how he

242

got their eldest daughter into such a state over some plans she had independently made, that she was reduced to confusion and tears, and then he was very sarcastic.

At this point we say: *It seems that there is a lot of feeling about exerting power and control in both of you. There is a vicious circle: H. feels W. is trying to run and control him, when in fact he himself clearly has great need to control the family, his children standing for W. But when he does this W. becomes anxious and resentful because she would also like to be the one to run things her way. It looks as if this struggle has invaded their relationship to the extent that it has pushed out mutual affection, and trying to hold these urges to dominate in check produces a lot of strain.*

This is followed by silence. W. who hitherto had been rather detached and accusing, shakes her head and looking rather crestfallen says at last: 'Yes it is me; that drive to control comes from me, not from him. I can see, the way he behaves with the children is because he feels he is being bossed and he lets his resentment out on them. No, he is not the dominant one in any abnormal way.' (*Note:* It is hard to convey the change which took place in the bearing of this woman who at the first JI especially had a very non-involved, unbelieving attitude.)

This was, in our eyes at the time, a diagnostic JI. *We therefore at this stage put the vague proposition 'that their earlier experience with tensions in their parental homes might not be irrelevant to their feelings in the present.'* W. now reviews the history of her feelings of lack of support from her mother whom she despised for her immaturity. The restatement, in front of H., of her devotion to her prematurely deceased father, her need to become the supporter and controller of the weak mother, her identification with the lost father's aspiration for her achievement in the arts and education, her feeling of frustration, were eagerly followed by him. 'Of course, then, when I married H. I felt that would make up for it all and we would do these things together.' We now gave a *longish interpretation to her but meant for both. W.'s feelings must be very complicated not only about H.'s sexual difficulty but about his own feelings as the 'weak' one. She had looked for strength and support not only for the satisfaction and vicarious experience of them for herself, but also because she now saw him not being the interested, inspiring father for the children, especially the eldest daughter in whom she saw her own needs mirrored.* She suddenly interrupted with much feeling, saying how she now recalled that for all his lovingness, her father had been very demanding and had used the worst weapon of all on her—sarcasm—so intolerable to her in H.'s dealings with his children!

We took this up: *Perhaps W. had not seen the similarity before between*

243

her feelings for H. as resembling her father, hence her great unhappiness about his not living up to the loved image but disappointing her in having some of the weaknesses too which she felt she must somehow control, because she could not bear them. (Hypothesis I again!) The word 'weakness' was now seized on by H. who told us with animation how as a child he had a very strong will and always compelled his mother to give in to him. He quoted an occasion when aged 8 or so he came home from school where he had heard a violinist and there and then badgered his mother for a fiddle. Though the shops were closed he made her go with him to a music dealer they knew and have him sell them the child's violin there and then. There was a smirk of triumph as H. related this tale. Yes, he was more determined than his spineless, wheedling brother who was the mother's boy! (We never learnt how he had changed, and could only surmise that his suppressed anger and tension with the mother made him reject his parental home so early, determined not to be like the despised father, but also inhibited from attacking his mother openly.)

We work through this with him in a free exchange of talk, winding up with a comment: *This strong-willed, determined part of H. was no doubt what W. liked about him. Having seen his father oppressed by the mother, he was going to be strong and self-directing. But because of his fear of weakness, the failure in sex which might have happened to anyone in the circumstances when it did, he was quite disproportionately cast down and self-contemptuous as the sequel to it.*

It seemed we could understand now why H. had felt so downcast by his sexual failure and why he had to react with so much compensatory need to assert himself in the home. He felt like his weak father, and therefore reacted defensively like his father had, and felt wife-dominated like father had. But W. on her side had attached all her aspirations of success and strength to him, and so she also had felt a quite disproportionate disappointment at H.'s failure because it cracked her fantasy that he was like her father. So she had at this moment again lost the supporting strength of him. We knew her reaction in the past—when faced with someone weaker she has to take control and run them. (We do not press the change of her perception of H. as the weak mother figure.) Thus they had shared an expectation of strength in him, and neither could bear to face its absence.

This dyadic interpretation seemed to produce a sense of closure in our foursome. As we had been about 2 hours, it was decided to stop, and a further appointment for a JI foursome was fixed for a week or two later. The couple departed thoughtfully.

Our note added: 'We agree that W. had lacked insight and depth as compared with H.'s sensitive depth of feeling. 'But this looks now a hopeful case for continuing, by contrast with H.V.D.'s first JI working alone.' We also recorded our belief that such JIs required a partnership of interviewers, 'because of the strain of participation and yet keeping track of content, whereas in a team the rôles can be exchanged and insight of one can reinforce the other's.' It was the period of learning for us. Well, the couple did not come but let us know they had gone on a holiday instead. We did not see them until 2 months after the JI just described.

Third JI. Both partners report that since their last visit their general relationship had been 'infinitely better'. W. announced eagerly that H.'s 'sexual response' (*sic*) had been better, he had been completely potent 'on a number of occasions'. This had helped but both agreed that it was the removal of the tension between them which had so changed the whole situation, including the attitudes of the children who no longer avoided home or dodged their father's presence but were gay. H. adds that W. no longer nags him and that they have more understanding for each other. When we remark that perhaps this has shown that we could be of help if we continued, H. becomes very firm: 'Last time produced enough help'. W. agrees. Both feel they do not require to come any more, time will complete the cure. It becomes a quite sticky social occasion, fishing around for topics of useful conversation. Our JI terminates long before expected, amidst good wishes and our understanding that they would contact us again should further difficulties occur. We never heard again and a follow up letter 12 months later remained unanswered.

The lesson of this dramatic and unforeseen effect for us was not, and should not be for anybody, that marital psychotherapy is rapid or easy, even though this is not the only case of its kind. It was the realization of the change that came in this marriage, and in the man's chronic and hitherto resistant impotence (often a very difficult condition to remedy in medical practice) when for the presenting symptom in one partner we substituted the dyad as the focus. We visualized the factors operating in this 'brief therapy' to be (a) a correct hypothesis of the interaction between the partners in their dove-tailing projections of parental images; (b) the communication of this insight to them in terms that they could assimilate; (c) our acceptance of their withheld active resentments towards each other while not discrediting their loyalties; (d) not taking the quasi-somatic symptoms (his impotence, her insomnia and tiredness) as more than they were. Whatever the levers, here was a powerful technique. Something changed quickly and as a sequel to our words and actions. What rôle exactly was played by transference in the stricter sense was not very clear. The attempt on H.'s part to make us into arbiters of his sex life was clarified and thus his unrecognized dependence made conscious, to the point that his old autonomy need reasserted itself, and he became the spokesman for the dyad in dismissing us quickly. As a model of this type of 'investigation merging into therapy' the case is eloquent enough. We do not know how long the effect lasted. The case also shows how a hypothesis is used in actual exchanges with patients.

Longer Therapy. In our experience only a certain proportion of marital cases have so dramatic a response to a few interviews. Both partners in *Case Twenty-six* had good personalities, and their idealizations were built on their response to whole objects. H. was of depressive type with plenty of reparation-need, while his wife had a pretty full range of libidinal energy available and had regressed only to the mildly 'phallic stage' of her mainly good and loving father-identification. Where the internal object world is more ambivalent and 'primitive', with much paranoid feeling between the partners, things do not go so fast or smoothly. But just this kind of paranoid, projective marriage most needs the JI method of handling for reasons I have made clear, although it is chiefly in relation to such cases that the warnings of earlier workers, 'not to let them loose on each other' in a JI chiefly apply. Where suspicion and jealousy run highest, it is most necessary for the therapist to have a relationship which is at reality level perceivable as open towards both contestants, rather than increase the scope of paranoid fantasy by separate interviews. Acting-out will occur during the intervals between interviews in any case. When the dimensions of such acting-out can be delineated in JI one can at times even forestall it, or positively forbid it, so that the angry interchanges and rivalry come to be focused within the interviews.

I will now endeavour to illustrate these points with a case we treated for over a year by the *JI foursome method*. The sole exception was of separate reception interviews, due to our need to exclude individual psychotic illness in each partner before deciding if we could help, in view of the gravity of their trouble as outlined in the referral letter.

Case Twenty-seven: Referred by a consultant psychiatrist of a teaching hospital. H. aged 44, W. 38 when first seen; one adolescent child. The couple had been for some time running an educational establishment with religious connections in which W.'s rôle was important. Their need to co-operate at Sub-system I and II level was part of the reality situation. W. was received by Mrs. Judith Stephens and H. by myself. The same two therapists conducted treatment as a foursome. When one of us was on holiday the other therapist would take the JIs alone.

Great condensation will be necessary to keep the note from becoming a volume.

W.'s and H.'s personal data: (combined from separate interviews). H. short, slightly podgy man with jovial, ingratiating manner, full of clichés, not too well educated, tries to give impression of sophistication and raciness. Only child of doting parents who projected their unfulfilled 'messianic' aspirations into him. Elderly father died when H. was 13. Admiring, over-solicitous concern of mother for her son to be the vessel of God's work. Growing up in an impoverished area of Britain during the industrial depression he jumped at the chance of his sectarian community offering a teacher training for which he had now to profess a somewhat phoney vocation and play the dedicated rôle, helped by histrionic talents and by ambition to shine and be acclaimed. These qualities attracted W. who had a great security problem of her own. She was brought up in a similar background of lower middle-class evangelism. She learnt at puberty that she was adopted and that her real parents were of upper middle class origin. This information changed her aspirations and she made a mental barrier against her whole background. She left the family and entered professional training that carried her into a different part of England. She had to deny that 'she belonged anywhere' and became rather self-contained and detached until she met H. in a church setting. They 'clicked' at once over their value systems, and he was greatly attracted to this vivid, strong and handsome girl, as she still remained when we saw her. They married when he was 27 and she 21. He relied a good deal on her mental resourcefulness, and she admired his inspirational fervour and eloquence. H. was very insistent that she was the only woman who had ever attracted him and still did. But sexual relations were troubled from the first by religious scruples over contraception and H.'s poor performance, so that coitus occurred rarely, especially after one failure of *coitus interruptus* resulted in W.'s pregnancy. 'We must be hot stuff,' he joked. Their sense of deterioration of their relationship followed her discovery of his dependence and his inability to satisfy her sexually; and his discovery of her sensitiveness to slights from third parties which ruined many good social and working contacts for him. He also felt irritated with her frequent illnesses, and this he showed by spiteful tempers. This hurt W., and when during one such illness he imported his mother into the home, the loss of her idealization became manifest. Four years after marriage H. developed severe Graves' disease, and was off work for a year, partial thyroidectomy settling him and enabling him to resume work, but in a new town, rougher and with more difficult pupils. It was now W.'s turn for surgery. At 28 or so an innocent adenoma led to unnecessary radical mastectomy, the results of which both partners tried to deny but which had a devastating psychological effect. W described H. as angry and unkind instead of supportive, leaving her all alone. He characterized this experience as 'being left all alone to carry the burden, the child and all, but pressing on regardless. At first I bent over backwards to reassure W., but to no avail. I began to lose confidence, my work lost its glow.'

From this period there developed a paranoid relationship close to a *folie à deux*, each regarding the other as the originating partner. W. seems to have flared with a paranoid defence (à la Jay Haley, see Ch. VII) of rationalizing H.'s lack of potent support by his interest in other women, even scenting homosexuality if he went to a committee or took boy pupils in class. When he argued she would become vituperative. Each had to deny that the other had become a damaged and unlovable object. We have no exact record of the ups and downs of the 7–8 intervening years, except that with another change of job to a pleasant neighbourhood there was a lull and an improvement in health for both. At the time of our involvement the following picture of their marital interaction presented. On account of depression H. was referred by his G.P. to the teaching hospital psychiatrist, to whom H. said 'I need help in dealing with W. . . . That's what it really is . . . I'm supposed to be the patient . . . she attacked my life and work—even playing the piano was supposed to mean signalling to the woman next door,' etc. W.'s spontaneous complaint was: 'My personality is being torn to shreds . . . he has been savage and violent . . . he ought as a Christian to value human personality—he doesn't value mine!'

Both confirmed that the last 5 years had been hell, for themselves and their adolescent child 'who idolizes us both'. Each was adducing psychopathological grounds for the other's behaviour. W.'s paranoid taunting of H. with infidelity and sexual intrigues continued. He on his part would forbid her to go out alone as she was so attractive to men. Nights would be marked by his wooing of her in a rather obscene sadistic way which she would reject, followed by his physical and verbal violence. Each felt the other was destroying them. Yet both also protested their loyalty to each other, to their shared religious faith and their guilt and shame over their joint behaviour. *Joint Therapy* was decided on in view of the paranoid difficulties and the need to supply a father and a mother figure whom each had missed and who could form a new model of reasonable co-operation. 21 joint interviews were possible over 14 months. Their journey took four hours each way. From the first we noted W.'s ascendancy and better social persona—she *could* have gotten another man—as against the slightly ludicrous figure of H., warmer and humorous, cut out to be a comic rather than a leader, confused and ambivalent, with W. flashing at him from a more austere and principled sense of contempt for one who needed mothering, who was a fraud, who had shut her out from his work. Hope came when we had the statement 'We both act like spoilt children.' *Our early interpretations stressed the support each had needed and the other had been unable to give—like a loss of secure parents, who must not be ill or make demands.* H. was the first to verbalize his anger that she was no 'damned use to him' ill and depressed and 'out of sympathy with him'. A repeated interpretation *was of how they shared the need for a good parent and how the anger at this disappointment took the several forms they had reported. This pointed to a likeness as if they felt each other's feelings* (identification). *H.'s illness had changed his appearance—so he feared W. would turn to other men; W.'s operation had damaged her, so she felt he would prefer undamaged women, etc. Each now felt unlovable.*

During the early sessions they recognized their mutual projections, though W. could not so easily see herself as a childish person. Transference at this stage by both partners treated H.V.D. as the perfect father-figure and ignored the mother-figure, Mrs. J.S. (who made more, and more apposite, interpretations!) After 3 sessions they both reported feeling quieter and depressed. H. was now working through his loss of his elderly father, his ambivalent dependence on a mother who would not let him be a man—'perhaps a bad man'—idealizing him and demanding so much. This is what he now felt W. was doing, and he had to try and control her, and resented her control of him. *We interpret the split in their object between idealization and persecution with loving sex left out.* W. said H. had always had a spiritual problem —he really wanted to be an actor. She now begins to be able to show us that she really was the spiritual leader—he is barren—no real fire. *We find ourselves having to defend H.,* but her attack is pressed home.

Longish holiday intervenes. We find W. has, with H.'s half-hearted approval, joined an archaeological society—'interesting people'. H. makes a great self-abnegatory speech of giving up selfish possessiveness of her—'out of emptiness comes creativeness', religious strivers have these crises, etc. Both partners feel we (the therapists) are selfless and good, as a couple. There is much discussion on the value of developing distance, differentiating their lives, after which *we interpret the possessive sense of being rejected when one has something the other has not, the envy of our 'superiority'. It is hard to let others be, e.g. over H. loving to play the piano in his school, alone, and not at home.*

H. who had before attending us been on sick-leave because of his depression, is now back on full duties, and we note how anxious W. is to comment on H.'s confusion, 'the mess he's in' when in fact he seems to be working through some of his infantile anxieties and coping well in his work. It is clear to us she wants him 'down'. She has a phase of hostility to us: 'she may not be a psychiatrist but her faith works'. We interpret this and how it is related to her need to have H. 'like herself', feeling left out if H. becomes successful on his own account. Yet she also feels he is restricting and excluding her. Hence her assertion of her own independence from H.V.D. as the source of wisdom just as she has 'unmasked' H. as useless. Her parents were not her real parents, she had to reject them.

The next session, the 7th, brings W.'s very fully stated masculine protest against her way of life and subordinate status as 'only the Head's wife', at everybody's beck and call, and a real mourning for her lost femininity since mastectomy—how she envies men! Both affirm they are better friends and more tolerant of their differences. Soon comes a reversal. H. is violently jealous of W.'s happy week-end away, when he could not bear even to meet her at the station. She breaks and attacks him, he hits her, calls her homosexual, she calls him mad, the doctor is fetched, calls them incompatible. Is she safe from being murdered? We treat this by re-interpreting the destructiveness of being envious of the other's otherness or separate experience. This regression becomes a crescendo. He fears her withdrawal into separateness, she fears being excluded from his work—'nobody talks to her now'. These feelings lead to scenes of violent fights in the night, H.'s taking a sexually sadistic form, as his only way of exerting power: e.g. ripping the bedclothes off her, calling her a whore, etc. H. had a very upsetting interview with his chairman who criticized him for not enough public contact. When W. took his account of it, full of self-pity, rather complacently, he accused her of siding with the enemy and bullied her till she 'blew up'. This was related to us by W. with the introduction: 'I can't take any more.' For when he had goaded her into anger he could triumphantly say 'You see you are against me', and then abuse her. In the session this was used as an attack by both partners on us as useless and interpreted as the terrible sense of being abandoned by the needed good object to be a prey to hate and fear.

In the next phase W. does a good deal of working through of this, along the lines of what a sham, and how narrowly restrictive their religion has been. H. does all these good works but has no kindness. She is repeating the need to break away from the foster-parents, and needing 'outside interests'. This feeling has two prongs: one attacks her useless hypocritical H., the other H.V.D. as an unkind critic for trying to pin hate on her instead of loving her. This is interpreted. At another level this also represented a healthy search for her separate identity. The feelings came out strongest during a session (the 13th) when H.V.D. was absent, though interpretation by Mrs. J.S. of the anxiety this occasioned for H.V.D.'s safety was denied. But W.'s acting-out of this theme was reported: H. had to go to a school concert and didn't take her. When he did not return at the time she expected she was impelled to go and bring him home, with a terrible quarrel resulting. *Our interpretations repeat the theme of mutual projection of hostile intent and rejection by the needed object so that each one's aggressiveness seems only a wish to compel acceptance and justified defence. Her search for H. showed how much she needed him.*

There was now a turning point. Up to this period sexual activity and working co-operation had been virtually non-existent. Now both revived, though the touchiness and scenting of belittlement and condemnation by the other remained. Their need of us as good figures to keep them in order and interpret their childish anxieties was very marked at this stage. W.'s projection was marked after coitus, as if she had to repudiate his (and her own) sexuality as demeaning. She was frankly embattled, and as the result could say: 'I feel disentangled and much healthier.' She participated in his life but also gave him hell. H. was less integrated, or at least differently split: all tolerance and sweet reason by day, but very retaliatory and sadistic at night, leading to the sequel of her rejection and withdrawal and his guilty contrition. The pattern was of a *'Mother-guilty boy' type, interpretation which H. could accept.* It was pointed up by the incident of one of his pupils making a 16-year-old girl pregnant. He felt identified with this bad boy, and could also *feel* the damage his own sexual sadism caused W., as if becoming aware of his primitive need to possess and attack his love object. *We underline this potential insight by our comments. W.'s rejection and belittlement makes him anxious. We press interpretation of his need to make her feel lonely and depressed because then the scales are even.* Thus H. became very persecutory and unpleasant when, after his brief absence, he found W. looking well after her week's freedom. He did not, however, accuse her of infidelity.

The co-operation at Sub-system II level improved. At Sub-system I, W. emancipated a good deal from her narrow religious outlook. Her general bearing became more self-confident, her dress more elegant and attractive. At this period H. had the offer of a better job in a distant city, and our contact came to an end. He was pleased because W. would have more to do in the large city to which they were going and be less dependent on him. H.'s promotion helped (a) to demonstrate how localized can be the operation of a near-psychotic personality factor to the marital sphere and (b) give him back some sense of worth.

I have purposely chosen this difficult and equivocal case to illustrate what goes on and emerges with a continuous JI technique, in a setting where despite very destructive behaviour, divorce or separation could not be countenanced by either party. The benefits for this paranoid dyad were an improvement of working co-operation, greater tolerance of rôle and leisure differentiation, sporadic sexual closeness, and 'survival' after angry scenes. It was not the result of a *Case Ten*, but it seemed worthwhile in a very unpromising diagnostic picture. The explosions which had marked both these people's presenting symptomatology were not aggravated by JIs, but on the contrary lessened and their impact on the daily co-operation of the partners changed as they gained at least a modicum of shared insight. We had no doubt that the experience of these shared sessions and of another 'couple', a man and a woman, able to offer at times interpretations of critical import to each of them, helped them to modify parental introjections, making acceptance of infantile defence reactions easier to tolerate in self and partner. Our own hesitancies and at times uselessness in providing masterly solutions, and our refusal to play omnipotent rôles was probably also a good model to assimilate. It was significant though not brought out in the above account, that after an initial omniscience-transference to myself, the father figure, and a virtual exclusion of Mrs. Stephens, both partners in the latter part of the work expressed much confidence and affectionate dependence towards this maternal figure of the team, and faded me out in proportion.

Reding and Ennis[6] have helped to spell out the advantages and therapeutic moments of such a foursome, despite the seeming complexity of the six-some transference currents: i.e. therapists A and B to each other, couple A^1 and B^1 to each other, plus AA^1, AB^1, BB^1, and BA^1. A good therapeutic team can become very relaxed and open, can even take sides, and give more spontaneous responses. Reding and Ennis also comment on the rapid degree of learning. The dyad's *shame* at their infantilities in front of the therapists' couple is held to be part of this assimilation process and to help bring the marriage partners closer. I would add that it could provide a motivation to grow up.

In sum, the original foursome pattern of JI, preceded by individual assessment, offers a very promising model: each partner originally seen and 'identified with' by a therapist 'of their own', and then the four—or rather—sixway ongoing relationship in which the therapists struggle with the *same* forces as the patient couple, accept and reject one another's insights, can differ, and also accept the patients' shifting transferences towards the two therapists. The difficulty is, of course, that such stable, well-run-in staff partnerships are rare in out-patient clinics. I suppose the ideal team is a married couple who have shared training and skills in psychological medicine and social case-work. Prague already has the Drs. Knobloch. Venezuela is to have such a team in Dr. and Mrs. Teruel! It could also become a model for a type of private practice partnership, provided the two co-operating partners, not necessarily married or even of opposite sexes, preserve some independent cases and professional lives as well. Few cases of the severity of *Case Twenty-seven* are likely to be encountered. But if they are, this is the therapeutic model for this type of paranoid-level symbiosis.

(b) *One-person Joint Therapy* (*Triadic Therapy*)

The practical arguments, reinforced by some theoretical support, in favour of simplifying marital therapy down to JIs with one therapist have been stated. From the therapist's (that is my own!) standpoint joint handling is preferable to separate handling by one therapist, and solo JIs preferable to foursomes with a 'casual' partner with whom one is not 'run-in'. Here again, then, the indications are opportunistic and practical rather than based on a nosological classification of the type of case. It is probable that such a concept as that of the dominant shared internal object is based on reality, as my observations and Teruel's have shown. But the internal population of any dyad inevitably contains many others: at least two fathers and two mothers who may be split into good, bad and ideal objects, and part-objects in addition. Even a foursome cannot distribute these in clear transferences. What has to be sacrificed in triadic therapy is thus not so much a neat apportionment of split transferences, but a model of a co-operating quasi-marital dyad to match the patient dyad. Once granted that the single therapist has to carry additional transferred valencies, all the rest of the procedure is much simplified. The results do not seem to be greatly affected one way or the other. If the therapist is also fortunate enough to be a member of a team of experts and experts-in-the-making, conferencing, supervision and informal discussion of the difficulties encountered still remain available to him. The chief qualifications for undertaking what many would still regard as a daring and difficult departure are a certain sensitiveness to the changing climates of transferences to oneself from the dyad and from the spouses as separate beings; and to be able to correlate the joint and individual fluctuations in this tri-partite interpersonal system with what is going on between the couple. This skill is developed by experience with many joint therapies, and with many different clinical pictures. Some case material may help to illustrate how varied problems call for flexible adaptation of the above rationale.

253

(i) *Long Cases*

My first illustration is chosen because it represents a transition: a case assessed by the foursome individual-cum-JI method; also because I have already described its diagnostic picture. It is a case in which 'early adaptation trouble' threatened to turn into a 'chronic disturbance'.

This is, in fact, *Case Twenty-one* (see Chapter VIII, p. 158), which presented as a non-consummated marriage, characterized by much tension and struggle for dominance. Annulment was constantly in their minds. On our assessment we had estimated them as having strong bonds in Sub-systems I and II as well as sharing an anti-libidinal mother figure alternately projected and introjected, based on some objective reality in both partners. There was a good level of rôle sharing, but also some rôle conflict in leisure interests. The couple's motivation to mature together into a full relationship in our estimate barely outweighed their resistances expressed as fear of commitment, of babies and of loss of freedom of action. They both wanted the line of retreat from marriage left open to them.

The decision to take them on by myself was purely practical—I alone did late sessions when they could attend after work in a distant suburb. On an average the couple attended once in 2–3 weeks.

The general setting of JIs was already accepted by them as the result of the assessment (q.v.). The notion of shared and projected feelings was familiar from trial interpretations. Both had accepted that they were always out of step in their erotic approaches to one another; that while they liked the *idea* of love-making and could accommodate it in their value system, in practice they were terrified when either behaved amorously, and quickly angered with the other for not picking up their too timid cues. W. had in addition displayed much evidence of a rather Victorian, feminist resentment of male 'lust' (as she called it) which was 'purely selfish' and devalued her as a person.

The situation at assessment conformed to Haley's observation: both partners worrying if the other really loved them or was merely putting up with them because they had to. The earliest JI treatment sessions continued to develop these themes, with W. slowly revealing her hidden aggressiveness, which she started acting out at home in belittlement of H.'s passivity. H. is discovered unable to be aggressive not only with W. but also in resisting his boss's call for more output, yet afraid to take the plunge and become a freelance in his job. There came a moment after working on these themes, about a month after starting once-weekly JIs when following a short holiday H. and W. both felt attracted and had some sex play with H.'s partial erection

. . . and then returned to work and their inhibited state. But W. had allowed the sex play because she felt he now put her first and had mended his late home-comings. But she also attributed all the reluctance and squeamishness to him, while he stuck to the joint defence of not having enough free time, being so busy, etc. Interpretations were aimed at the joint resistance: '*I wonder if you weren't just frightened that things were going too well—so you invent a new cause for getting furious with each other*', but from the way they were now voicing their problems, I also made the comment: '*You are now talking in terms of "we"*.' I then proceeded to interpret the mutual attribution of insufficient love (à la Hypothesis I): ' *You are both very suspicious and want to be sure that the other really loves . . . Always on the alert for little signals that you are not wanted or put first—as if you had demanded a lot from each other, and have fallen short—so this whole business is now sour grapes to you both (etc.).*'

This enabled W. to express her fear of pregnancy instilled by her mother, and shared by H. who regarded her as very frail and petite—in fact *his* mother had told him W. was much too small to bear children. W.'s reluctance to attend was freely ventilated, as a resentment of joint discussions. In fact they managed a $2\frac{1}{2}$ months' respite over holidays and suitable joint dates. When they came, they reported being back to the *status quo ante* each blaming the other for the relapse. H. showed his need for a sanctioning parent; thus: 'I'm wondering why I am not active (in sex advances), what an older person would do trying to woo their wife . . .' When asked what he imagined such a senior male would do, H. in effect put the onus on the woman to respond to general affection. W. criticizes his approach as crude and immature and also wanting a more paternal, sophisticated wooing, and feels sure he is dreaming of being free again and angry at having been trapped. H., honestly admits he gets a longing to 'wander'. but this is balanced by his longing for the love nest and W. as 'the only woman', but realizes he gets petulant and won't try to do the foreplay her way. We spend a great deal of time eliciting details of their genital fumbling and lack of know-how, which I repeatedly *interpret as the anxiety in each if they find the other sexually aroused, leading to automatic bodily checks: her rigidity, his loss of erection. She will not let him make her his plaything; he will not dance to her tune.*

We now get material showing that W.'s resentment of H.'s conscientiousness and overwork is a projection. She values and shares his 'responsible' attitude, but resents that it brings him home so overtired. H. in fact had corrected this. A report that he had come home, fresh, sexy, gone to bed early to make love—but he was 'drawn magnetically to a book he should be reading for his professional work.' *This was interpreted as his inner persecution for relaxing, not doing his puritan duty.* The reaction was a confession of his great self-blame for masturbating as a boy. It brings W.'s agreement that she shares this inner drive—it makes her too hard-working, house-proud, overtiring herself. *It enables me to enlarge the interpretation to say how they really share this nagging bad conscience—clearly shown by H. but animating W. also, to reject his bad, lustful, 'selfish' aspect and really encouraging him to be a striver like herself. Almost any criticism she makes destroys his confidence but relieves her guilt. She is his conscience, he is her guilty sexual self. That is why she rejects both his sexual excitement and his passivity.*

The reaction to this work with their shared but polarized guilt is a marked release in H. of his boyish, shame-faced gaiety. He now dresses colourfully and is livelier. Concurrently he expresses his inadequacy fears: 'I haven't that quality (of masterfulness) . . . I've either been in the state where I depend on her more than normally and it has given her the mother instinct . . . at other times I upset her and put her off . . . Then she is very disapproving.' But he also voices his counter-identification with the solid, steadfast 'insured' citizen, not least because he feels W. is more loving when he is down and she is in the ascendant. When he is uppish and playful he is rejected. She rejects horseplay, she wants a stuffy old man sitting by the fire! So he goads her to have her school-ma'm disapproving expression and then he can laugh inwardly. The only fun he gets . . . if he ever had another woman it would be a dumb blonde who does what *he* wants! W. is too 'intelligent' for his simple boyish fun, and they haven't laughed together since courting days. W. feels he has become childish, and she can't take this—he is peculiar, even eerie then. *I interpret her fear of this puckish, March Hare element as so unsafe—might lead to anything uncontrolled.* As the sequel to this uncovering of polarized rôles, both partners not only begin to lead more differentiated lives but ask for separate interviews. These are conceded as a 'temporary' move, 3 each. The material in each is amazingly dovetailing. She talks of her mother rôle, he talks of her disapproval and his need of her to control him, how he fears her vicious aggression, and is now apt to retaliate. By and large he is more spontaneous and quite tough but not resentful, and W. feels much more warmth—plans to go part-time in her work so as to 'be fresh for him'. It is noted she is much more attractively dressed and coiffed when she sees me alone. 'Knows' she is ready for him if only he could be potent and not use her as a masturbation object in such cold blood. He complains she won't let him use foreplay by which to rouse her and himself. No clear transference deduction; probably each wanted a sex-tolerant parent figure to themselves, instead of the feeling of doing everything unselfishly together.

JIs resumed. H. much less confused and not so evasively deferential.

256

He can now say how she puts him off by her demand for his behaviour to match her expectation of the moment, and how he refuses to do this, capping it with an impassioned attack on all her female kin—so intolerant, demanding and controlling, and W. returns similar criticisms of males. I note (but do not interpret) the change in W. Feminine and vivacious in single interview, she is hostile and complaining in JI. But H. now has a less downtrodden hang-dog attitude, much gayer and more confident. In the 10th month (and about the 14th interview including solos) they reported a change: W. had become much more active sexually. She also displayed a more participant and less defensive behaviour in the JI. While the failure to consummate is now in H.'s court, W. is on his side. For he is now in the anxious process of leaving his slave-driving employer and setting up on his own. Discussion of the anti-sexual collusive element brings spontaneous allusions from both to their mothers. They pool their insights: how W.'s mother nearly died in childbirth with this, her youngest daughter, and all the female horror stories with which her youth was filled, while never explicitly enlightened. H.'s mother always disliked W.—warned him she was too small and would probably die in child-birth. His real hell-fire fear of being naughty, aggressive, etc., came from two old maiden aunts with whom he was evacuated during the war (aet 3–9). He can now tell her a dream in which his erotic fantasies were centred on 'dressmakers' dummies and table legs', and how he had to struggle against his masturbatory impulses. Another dream comes up in which he and W. try to go over a five-barred gate together but she injures her face and he has to bathe it. *I interpret not only once again their shared maternal anti-libidinal attitudes, but how W. has rightly felt that he had to tie sex to an inert, non-responsive object like a piece of wood, to avoid the dread of hurting a real living woman who was also so threatening. This was the hurdle to overcome: their shared fear of damaging her by his bad penis.*

The result of these events was not at all 'the happy ending' in coitus. It was a more intense but conscious rebellious independence on the part of H. and a more overtly security and control-demanding W. living out her strict, nagging mother. She says 'If I had a real husband instead of a guilty giggling child . . .' to which he responds: 'And don't you know just how to make me feel like that with all your fears and no encouragement to be otherwise . . .' There is a lot of very insightful and meant-to-hurt aggression flying round, which at least H. in a subsequent JI can relate back to his mother's hard driving and the religious fanaticism of his background. Like the husband in *Case Twenty-seven*, H. had been dedicated by the kinship group to a missionary future. Though he had rebelled, the puritan guilt had remained.

257

The mood soon cleared. They knew that they were fond of each other, they didn't really quarrel now; but weren't they 'letting Dr. Dicks down' if they did not have sexual intercourse? H. was clear that he wanted to stay a child—why shouldn't he if that is what he felt. W. was able to see that it was largely conformity with social norms (an idealized image of the perfect marriage) and some envy of her age-peers who had babies that was expressed in this attribution of pressure to be 'normal' to the psychiatrist. This is played back to them: *their fear of failing to be adult both ways: not having sex, but also letting this bad, puckish demon get out of hand. Why shouldn't they enjoy their lives and their home-building and tennis and so forth rather than strive to live to some external 'adult' norm they think I have for them as representative of the world of elders?* At this point the summer holidays once again interrupted therapy.

On their return they said they had a carefree, happy playful time visiting various relatives of H.'s. He had quite lost his childish awe of these people and both had felt accepted and welcomed. There had been no coitus, but both agreed they liked living their adolescent love life together and did not wish to force the issue of babies and intercourse by worrying all the time. Neither blamed the other, they had lost their compulsiveness. 'I wonder,' said H., 'how long it will take us to get rid of that deadly sense of sin?'—but with humour. Both looked relaxed, are gaily dressed, and report that his job change to independence and hers to part-time has not affected their earnings adversely. This was in fact the last JI and the couple have not shown up for any further visits which we offer as a matter of course. A follow-up letter 12 months later remained unanswered.

Something quite different from a 'cure' of the symptom happened to the young *2Is* during their therapy. They had formed a dyad with a common purpose and a new value system of their own by acceptance of regression. Their relation to me had resolved a double-bind type of feeling about sexual freedom and the rôle of adults as on the one hand demanding 'Now you must have babies', yet also not allowing them to build a genital mutuality on their sensuous, masturbatory excitement. They had reached adolescence; no longer frightened children anxiously and compulsively trying to sexualize their relation in order to be textbook adults. H.'s terrifying elders had become nice, welcoming people. At this point they stopped coming. The change effected was a manifest increase in mutual enjoyment and satisfaction in their total relationship. If they were to develop their erotic life, it could only be on this basis, never on the 'borrowed' know-how of elders such as H. had tried to get out of me.

Ascending the age scale and length of therapeutic contact, I should

258

next like to report another case of sexual failure—this time *secondary*. Treatment also began as a JI foursome but was carried by me as a JI threesome after the first few therapeutic JIs for the same reasons as *Case Twenty-one*: times of attendance from a distance.

Case Twenty-eight: A self-referred couple in the lower professional stratum, H. 38, W. 40 when first seen. W. had previously had help from the Tavistock when single, and persuaded her G.P. to refer them together after 6 years of marriage. It was group therapy during their long courtship which had enabled them to marry, as she had improved by becoming less aggressive, impulsive and 'tom-boyish'. Her marriage to a man not of her faith and ethnic background had been an act of asserting her 'free identity' in face of her family.

The presenting story was of an intense, fully sexual and highly satisfying unmarried relationship 'more often in bed than out' together, which had turned into tension, H.'s complete loss of sexual drive and violent paranoid outbursts of rage on W.'s part almost from the moment of their marriage ceremony. Both had for several years tried to deny the relevance to their total relationship of this dramatic change and had blamed pressure of his job, the presence in their not self-contained lodging of a snooping dominant landlady, and the insecurity of a marriage against W.'s family's clannish and financial objections. It was only when they acquired their own house that they could no longer blame these external factors.

Assessment data: W. casts herself in the 'patient rôle'—her ghastly temper outbursts have destroyed H.'s love, 'he rejects and despises her'. She is a handsome, intense characterful woman with ready emotional response to interview (single first consultation). She described insightfully how she had revelled in mothering H. and in 'having a cosy home', how she called him pet baby names and he called her Mummy—managing him in all things with his acquiescence except his responsible, rather remote technical job which she could not understand even when he told her about it. 'So now he is impotent,' she said. In the last year or two, since the purchase of their home, her temper tantrums had revived and H. was their exclusive target. 'He is too forgiving, can't be aggressive. The tempers come because I want someone to belong to . . . I get his devotion, he loves home, but as a child would' . . . It seemed that she had gallons of feeling that had to be poured into H.'s pint pot of emotional capacity. She related her symptom to her lasting sense of exclusion from her large family, mainly of brothers who made her feel stupid, babyish and unwanted for being only a girl, with a remote, scholarly, latterly irritable father whose early death cut her education by comparison with the older sibs. Her mode of getting 'in' was by temper tantrums when the brothers and parents would have to quell her. She thus knew the attention-getting, masochistic purpose of her infantile symptom. As a spinster she had interesting and varied jobs, partly abroad, and was not lacking in sexual experience à la *Mrs. Six*, with one or two disappointments and heart-breaks that attracted her to H., the model of kindness and steadfastness. H. was a sternly brought-up working class man, by now distinctly donnish and intellectual. Gentle and soft in manner he described how before marriage he had loved W. 'as a little lonely girl' whose rages he not only tolerated but knew how to assuage by passionate love-making. But her (previous) treatment had changed her—no longer the little girl—'it is a different fondness which precludes sex.' 'She feels I am punishing her but I can't see it.' His background data showed that his father was a cautious, over-protective disciplinarian, creative as a craftsman, but very discouraging of adventure, risk and high spirits. Mother gayer but toeing father's line, and there never was a quarrel. The sexual history reflects H.'s general subjection to the anti-libidinal father, in which early sex ventures were fraught with danger and anxiety. W. had reconciled his image of the enterprising, gay and sexually inviting girl with the protective and home-security offering woman.

H.'s attitude to JI is mixed: he knows how psychotherapy has helped W., but now he is chary. He joins in a spirit of scientific inquiry. (First interview by Mary Williams who also took part in the early JIs.) There being a decision to treat, JIs are from the first therapy-oriented. Even in the first JI the *shared object* in the guise of the intrusive landlady appeared. This parent figure forbidding sex and turning H. into a son in the house, made W. feel jealous and inadequate as a wife, and was also seen by both as relating to H.'s rigid, fussy parents who had predicted this trouble because of different class and ethnic origins. W. had two natures: one 'cosy' and motherly, the other an angry, demanding girl. The contrasts in 'voltage' between these two people became very obvious: W. intense, passionate, tearful, H. placid, conciliatory; it is as if W. had tried to compress herself into the 'cosy' parent (half father) figure H. had expected, house-proud, 'insurance'-conscious; he had become the hard-working provider to be cosseted. *We interpreted that they 'had become Mum and Dad',* *hence sexually taboo-ed.* In the next interview W. explicitly saw how she had taken over H.'s father's rôle. H. could not see this, but praised W. for her 'responsibility' and sense of order. From the over-protective, inquisitive landlady to his parental model, H. was shown to be back in boyhood, with W. feeling wildly deprived and excluded but trying to model herself on, and outdo, her own over-protective pessimistic mother—so like his father. This idyll was punctured from time to time by W.'s infantile, uncontrollable outbursts which H. now treated with contempt and with withdrawal, as 'he could never see any sense in them'. Then she would feel totally rejected as in her childhood. 'He could not even attempt to make love then', because unlike pre-marriage her mood was so totally unyielding. described by her as a 'too late now' attitude. Retaliation even to restrain her violence, was to him 'unforgivable'—though W. had seen it as a gleam of light: he had reacted as a man! To him it was 'At least one of us is rational and civilized.' *We can interpret the way in which the partners are re-enacting their respective childhoods: she tries to 'get in' by the only way she knows; he keeps this bad, aggressive child out, and does so by passive, rejecting methods.* We can also see that H.'s influence is to make W. try to be too cosy, never ordinarily critical, since she hates quarrels too, and that the tantrums are a bursting of a dam, in complete contrast to her rôle aspirations. We all agree that the over-solicitude and avoidance of heat leads to such explosions. W. enlarges her picture of her parental home as a perpetually active, quarrelling, arguing group, with her brothers both ganged up together and fighting each other—very alive, with W. only longing 'how nice to be in such a relationship'. H. confirms that she was treated as an explosive, idiot child by these brothers, and nobody was on her side. Soon we discover that W. herself has a great contempt for her 'horrible little golliwog' personality and thus shares her H.'s attitude towards herself—*needing him to be both totally accepting and totally rejecting because she then gets the satisfaction of thorough, total expression of her hate and destructiveness.* 'If only someone would stop it,' W. sighs.

This leads to commenting on the *scapegoat function her outbursts play in the marital relationship. H. is her brothers, 'rolled into one' and can feel controlled and rational, patronizing and smug. That makes her the kid sister and him the big disdainful brother. She is using her marriage to work this out of her system, and he has, of course, not seen this. Before they lived in their own house, her tempers were 'just temperament', now they are a battle for power, for getting compliance from the unresponsive father–brother figure who belittles her.* We suddenly hear of W.'s wish to be a dancer, which was sternly discouraged by her father: he wanted her to be a teacher; only bad girls went on the stage—another blow at her female identity. She longed for her father's approval.

All this rich thematic material emerged in the first two Jls with its vista of multiple projective identifications and displacements of bad internal objects between the partners and from W.'s own parents to the landlady and H.'s parents.

Therapeutic stages. By the third JI a dynamic change had occurred. H., in coping with another violent onslaught by W. had lost his temper —he was so angry she just 'slunk away'. H. brought us a drawing of a nightmare he had had in the following night, of two prehistoric, red-eyed monsters rising from the sea. These are *interpreted as their shared hate feelings*, and we spend much time on W.'s pleasure that H. has been able to deal with her like this, though H. was very anxious. We hear of W.'s anxiety when her mother could not cope with W.'s tempers at age 4. W. had a dream concerned with fear of doctors —smothering her, etc. This was interpreted as *her fear of her identity obliterated by us, like it had been at home when she suppressed her own girlish self and buried herself in her hated-envied aggressive brothers' lives.* Reistance to our treatment now affected both partners. H. was still apprehensive of the effect his rage had had on W. 'I've never seen her run away weeping before.' So he decided to conceal from her a bank overdraft—'to spare her worry'. This, needless to say, led to a severe paranoid reaction by W. who felt excluded and not trusted. She was the 'poor little idiot', as well as a 'dangerous bit of dynamite for H'. H. now expressed real anxiety, and feared W. would walk out, linking this to an early memory of his mother threatening to leave him if he wasn't good. H. had wept over this memory—'but it re-lieved a lot of tension, and discussing it with W. had made them feel close and loving towards each other'. H. now relates memories of rebellion, stealing, etc., and being punished by maternal rejection. Much material, including more dreams, showed how he had with-drawn to 'stay in the dry' by repressing his aggression and becoming an aloof 'scholar'. He now felt shame at this policy of avoiding trouble —like 'I'm all right Jack'. W. is glad H. is involved in the therapy. She relates how anxious and envious his detachment has made her: she had always felt it as his rejection of her. *All this is interpreted.* H. now concedes W.'s as the more 'normal' standpoint, but continues to be very anxious about the change in him which he likens to being dissected. W. concurs: her home influence was to urge her not to be emotional, 'babyish' but objective, logical. *The shared model of the rational relationship that controls the infantile is interpreted.* The partners can see they had lost a great deal by avoiding lively, heated discussion. We now find W. 'feeling a shutter has come down inside her—as if the change in H. had taken the wind out of her sails'. H. calls it being 'out of phase', and there being two W.s—one sweet and loving, the other vicious. A long and subtle work-through of the relation of their feelings to their parental influences. W.'s father becomes less rejecting in her memory, H.'s stricter. W.'s father himself is seen as remote and unhappy—outside the circle—like herself, belittled by the mother and brothers. H. confirms this of his mother-in-law, and realizes how, unwittingly, he has played the same rôle for W. This change towards her father is closely mirrored in the partners' transference—laughing at proposals made by another doctor that she should be treated by calming injections, and H. by trying himself on another woman! *One can criticize doctors, they are fallible, we remark.* The notion that W.'s reactions are somehow 'not her', but an impersonal evil affliction is thoroughly worked through and rejected. She realizes they expressed a need for a relationship which H. can also see—hence their ability to prefer my approach to the other doctor's.

The sixth JI brought news of another row, 'the worst ever' that 'provoked H. into losing his temper very badly . . . but it seems to have had an effect on him . . .' 'Yes,' adds H. '. . . she struck me and then I saw red and struck her . . when it all cooled down we felt very friendly and had sex for the first time in many years!' (after an incubation of 2 days). They associated sexual re-awakening rather explicitly with the permissive parent feelings about us (Mrs. Williams returned for this particular JI). W. could now even accept the kindly feelings her in-laws had for her, which she had rejected, and H could see that (like the husband of *Case Twenty-six*) he had passively hit back at W. by withholding his sexual love—'almost to the point of sadism' as he put it. He is now the one to express his resentment at his smothering, unmanning father, with W. contributing evidence of how H. had revelled in being 'babied' by his parents and how she had despised him for it. (This was, of course, something she only learnt after marriage and on entering H.'s family.) A much clearer picture emerges of his passivity and her tom-boy identification with her brothers—not previously realized by either partner. We get a clear view also of how W. suffered this 'idealized' contented 'Peter Pan and Wendy' life under the eyes of the landlady who had to be kept sweet. Only when this figure disappeared did W.'s real demands and frustration break surface as desperate, quasi-dissociated attempts again to get a passionate response from H. as a man. When her long attempt at playing the indulgent mother broke, H. withdrew from this horrible golliwog who now emerged and who wasn't his nice little girl he could indulge by projective identification, and who so cosseted him. There was little need for interpretation—the partners worked through this themselves. W. had shed her awe-struck identification with her brothers: she now felt just as intelligent as they are —'silly over-indulged Mummy's boys!' She finally had a dream at this stage, in which she rescued a little boy in a bus who was squashed by an immense fat, unconcerned man: cuddled the little boy and felt very happy. *This was interpreted as her own squashed masculine tendencies (her little 'animus' in Jungian terms) as well as her own tender maternal feminine needs to protect the infantile in herself, in H., in life.*

She was now experiencing a great access of self-confidence and sense of worth, discovering her *mind*, discarding her brothers' views and conceit. H. had brought to the same session a recurrent dream of being in the centre of a circle of 'orientals' all with their backs to him. They glowed with colour, but he felt ostracized, excluded, yet 'buried' or stuck on this spot. Our work on this dream together leads to the interpretation *of H.'s inner isolation, a central self of unrealized possibilities he vaguely mistrusts but which represent a different life and culture from his narrow technical persona. We link this to W.'s dream of the squashed little boy—her need for more self-expression—and here is his version.* She agrees—his work is lonely, complex and unsociable—she has to jolly him out—like getting blood out of stone—getting him to parties, concerts, etc. She accepts her cultural, human values as complementing his. Next session H. brings a further dream of imprisonment in a pirate ship from which a woman rescues him. *This was interpreted both as a recognition of how his mother rescued him from his father's narrow severity and as a pointer to his need to accept feminine values for releasing him from his male mental prison, just the task W. can do for him, if he will 'let her in'.*

The partners are now getting on 'better and better'. W. says she still fears bossing him, but he has 'come out a lot'. He shouts if she flies off the handle and it quietens her at once. No new themes over the next few Jls which are spent working over the material so far described, especially the over-determined significance for them of the rather mannish, male-depreciating landlady figure—their shared object—who made them both feel like naughty children, evoking W.'s envy and anger over H.'s compliance, and H.'s detachment—'all that mothering going over his head'. I interpret at a suitable moment *that they felt this woman's hostility to them as a happy couple—not as individuals—a person who did not like them getting on well together and tried to separate them and inhibit their sex.* This switched the work-through to H.'s parents as a source of inhibition to both of them, ending with my saying: *'In H.'s home aggression was taboo, in W.'s affection was taboo'—so that both had to try to find these in the partner and were afraid to express the feelings themselves. It had flattened their post-marriage relationship into a very tame business. The tantrums were needed to express passion, colour, feeling not otherwise represented in their busy workaday lives.*

This is followed by a constructive work-through of the important theme of W.'s ambivalence and preoccupation about H.'s parents on behalf of both partners. She recognizes that for her one or other of them was always either totally bad or totally good, and how she switched these and also involved H. in this. They are 'rigid', 'unloving', 'false', and we point out how H. always defends them against her while criticizing them freely himself. W. accepts that deep down she has always doubted if people's love for her is genuine. She now volunteers to stay with her in-laws for a week, to H.'s surprise! The sense of this phase, with rapid interchanges by all of us, re-interpretations, etc., is the re-introjection and acceptance of parental internal objects, hitherto projected. After 2–3 Jls devoted to this task, W. as the expressive partner is now able to express her hitherto carefully hidden negative transference to me: the treatment will not work; H. is tired of her—men need change. This is at once interpreted as *'at least she can have two feelings about the therapist—love and rejection —at the same time'*. W. said perhaps she didn't really care if she stayed married. The likeness to her feelings about her brothers and H. is accepted. *'Better to feel nothing than hate.'* H. says: 'Strange—our sexual relations have been better than for years in the last weeks.' W. is now depressed—her tantrums are scarcely in evidence. H. says it has helped him to be more sexual instead of coping with her rages, but she feels his sex is not loving. *Evidently, I remark, the cure of their sex failure was not what they came for—but rather her need for total love she could never feel she had.* She complains not only that H. seems now to criticize her, but with Dr. Dicks, too, 'it is always *she* who is blamed—just as in my family!' This is the beginning of a long working through of her 'shan't be good' reaction to educators, parents, etc., and involves H. who has been telling her memories of his childish aggressions and how they were quelled by his mother. He can now tell us how he wished his parents dead around age 8–11. *We end up by seeing how attractive W.'s spontaneity and rages must have been to H. who had felt forced to deny and control his. Now that W. no longer does this for him, he can become aware of these feelings in himself.* (I did not interpret the meaning of W.'s depression as a maturing towards coping with her primitive hate; nor her negative feelings as an acceptance of her identity.)

This is very reassuring to W., and she can more positively attack men such as the author of *Women, an Analytic Study*—clearly a substitute for myself. In the heat of such remarks H. tells her not to shout so much—a vivid demonstration of their old rôle distribution. A revealing new factor enters in W. bringing a dream to the 14th Jl—of an undisguised incestuous wish for her eldest brother whom she had always hated consciously. From the working-through of this key to her symptom: *rage substituted for sexual excitement*, the marital situation begins to settle very rapidly. The partners now have heated but lively discussions, as equals, sharing all manner of problems. W. says 'I start to get bothered—but something has clicked—so I don't go on'. The next few Jls are all about working-through fantasies of the treachery of fathers and the unsatisfactoriness of mothers

265

(including the absent Mary Williams), the harm parents do. Slowly her paranoid, 'rejected by father-figures' attitude is internalized as her own masculine envy and hate, and a transient Lesbian preoccupation is worked through.* But work with W. is mainly the uncovery of her split about good and bad males—oscillating between me and H. and between the (now) loved eldest brother and her bad, cerebral, belittling young brothers. The hate of the latter becomes her own fear of hurting and castrating. This, unexpectedly, turns out to be the source of the recent depressive mood: 'had her attacks on H. damaged him so that he ceased being potent, just as mother had accused her of causing her father's heart attack by her tantrums as a child?' (This could only come out after the return of sex life.)

An elder sister's visit from abroad provides W. with a reality test of the alleged solidarity and closeness of her family group into which she had always longed to get accepted. To her great sorrow but ultimate relief she discovers this to have been a fantasy: they are all individuals, by no means a solid front, least of all against herself. But the long-absent sister's attitude confirms W.'s worst paranoid fears and convinces H. that W. had really suffered—he is protective and fights her battles angrily. We work over this very painful loss of the dependent love ties that bind her so powerfully to these (largely internal) figures. I point out *'This lets you off—you too can now be just yourself'*. W. on tranquillizers at this point and really disturbed by the discovery of her current family background as a war of all against all, with the aged mother stirring them all up. W. is hostile to all of them in turn, hates them for never allowing her to be small and dependent. H. vigorously defends his parents who also come in for her vituperation. *My interpretation is of her fear of growing up and becoming an individual*, which W. promptly projects to H. as 'he is still afraid of his parents'. This work occupies 2 JIs in 2 months. The marital atmosphere is now low tension, cheerful. H. scores a notable success in his work, and stands up firmly against W.'s continuing childish preoccupations with her bad objects. W. is contemplating a job, and able to resist her sister's moral blackmail that had stirred her guilt of killing her father, and of being heartless towards their mother, who now lives with this sister. It is still painful to resist the ambivalent pressures of her childhood ties, but W. can now tolerate them. H. is very helpful to her, and has responded to W.'s work-through of her paranoid anxiety by showing us quite a different side of his own past: the rebel adolescent who worked through his own emancipation from his stuffy, oppressive parental milieu by leaving home and living in picturesque, 'beatnik'-like disarray after his war service—sandals, artists, pubs, long hair. In fact it was then he met W. dressed 'in a

* It will be recalled that W. in *Case 10* also worked through this.

266

grubby mac' distributing political pamphlets. Somehow these early, highly protesting but lively links seem to bring them together in a rather relaxed, loving way. She now chooses becoming clothes instead of 'little girl' patterns, she is no longer in need to read what her ideological brothers would approve, and H. has started painting. They can both accept that they now like solid comfort and that neither are missing children. W. has taken a full-time interesting post in her old line of skills. The last JI of 27 over as many months related to another attempt by the older sister to recapture W. by a gift—H. had to be the whipping boy for not taking the decision to send it back for W. He retaliated with a phase of headaches. But the tension was short lived. I discharged the couple with the usual 'open door' proviso.

A year or more later W. came alone for one interview to work-through her guilt and mourning over her mother's death in the sister's adopted country. Her floral offering was not passed on to mother's sickbed by the sister. So W. worried whether the dying mother ever knew that W. had loved her and forgiven her as an adult, like H. had been able to do with his parents. (The possible links with Mary Williams' break with conducting this case was not taken up, nor the need to express W.'s love for me as the lost object, which was simply interpreted and left at that.)

Initially the JIs were weekly, but were then allowed to spread over longer intervals to suit the partners' distant work. A great deal of 'homework' always occurred in this couple, and they may be said to have done the greater part of the therapy themselves.

Discussion on Long Therapy: It is, as I have stated, very difficult to convey the full picture of a long therapeutic relationship in condensed form, and I would not blame any reader if he was bored or disappointed with the accounts of these long cases, abstracted from tape-recordings or page-long details of each interview. In these contracted accounts the spirit of collaboration and the to-and-fro of rapidly shifting interchanges of feeling, with the need for alert catching of nuances of meaning, is missing. Only major phases or changes can be reported, and how insight wavers to and fro. It is a much more active technique than that of classical psycho-analysis, and the re-play or reading of tapes of such JIs reveals a large amount of small comments, requests for clarification and partial interpretations by me, many unnecessary. The discipline and self-training of hearing oneself and pruning away inessential intervention by the therapist is the larger part of improvement in technique. Yet analysts reading these accounts may see a lot of obvious cues not interpreted!

There are two chief aspects to long therapy shown in the above case descriptions. One is the rapid emergence of the main dynamics of the dyadic interaction; the other is the working-through phase. As in a symphony, the chief themes are stated early, the rest of the movement is occupied with their development and working-out, ending with a restatement. It is the working-through period which takes the time. In the cases quoted we have tended to give quite major interpretations early, almost in the assessment phase. The objective of an interpretation is to facilitate the emergence of fresh material, forgotten or repressed or ignored, and to mobilize feelings hitherto anxiously denied. These are likely, but not certain, to be expressed in transference. If this happens, acting-out (in mood, words or actions) outside the consulting room diminishes and the JI becomes now the main arena of conflict while the actual life of the couple improves, and the two personalities also feel better. This can be seen in the last record: the couple report better relations but have tense angry sessions with us. The therapist(s) thus becomes the catalyst and mediator, and also serves as a new, more adult, transitional object to be internalized. Apart from this function as a symbolic object first feared and idealized, then denigrated or attacked and finally seen more realistically, the actual job of the therapist is quite repetitive: to reinforce the early interpretations by further glosses, by reminders of what had already been said, using different words or new variants of the older material. For a time he becomes a 'counter-dyad', the dyad's joint auxiliary reality-ego assimilating the meanings of what they externalize towards each other and towards him. He feeds it back to them as interpretations and re-interpretations. There is a difference from individual psychotherapy or analysis in that the terminal phase of marital treatment leaves the dyad in a better position than the single patient. The anxiety over losing dependence on the therapist with all its variants of denial and rejecting over-compensations, is softened by their having each other. The working-through goes on all along with the real partner, is being integrated during the JI sessions and can continue after the end of attendances, since the partners have shared and can go on sharing the insights provided by the therapist now internalized as their 'joint-ego'. This hypothesis may explain why the vast majority of our couples 'disappear' once treatment is ended. The terminal analytic mourning phase is much less marked. The mediating figure of the therapist fades out. This, I think, is as it should be. The bearing of this point on follow-up studies will be alluded to in the next chapter.

I imagine that I share with the majority of psychotherapists the aspiration for methods that are economical in time and effort for patient and doctor and yet sufficiently effective to permit subsequent constructive working-through—maturation if you like. David Malan, for example, has devoted much effort in pursuit of this goal with individual patients.[7] I am therefore concerned to raise the problem (without being able to provide an answer) of the differences in the marriage partners or the nature of their interaction that make for long or for short cases. This, I think, can only be solved by systematic, rigorously controlled research. Such research would have to investigate such factors as the nature of the shared bad as well as good objects that operate at sub-system III level; consequently the amount of undertow from unrecognized and counter-invested hate the couple have to contend with in maintaining their dyadic boundaries; the rigidity and stereotypy of their joint resistance to change by the defences of shared idealization, exclusion of anger or sexual spontaneity and so forth. Equally, I think, such a research programme would have to take account of the explicit or unconscious attitudes of the therapists, governed by their training and personal background as well as by their theoretical evaluations of the given case. The retrospective study of post-therapeutic results is part of such an effort at prognosis and choice of therapy.

(ii) Shorter Therapy

I have now reached a point when I use the JI assessment phase as if it were part of therapy, whenever I have decided by explicit or implicit pointers to continue with the case. Then, after letting the dynamics and social structure of it impress itself on me as spontaneously as possible without my intervention, I interpret to the limits of my insight and discretion, and see what happens next time the couple come—and they usually want to come. I do not offer time limits but rather say that the number of weeks or months required cannot be foreseen—it will depend on how we get on. And this is no more or less than the truth as far as my power to predict the speed of therapeutic effect goes. It should be understood that I am here speaking of those couples whom I believe myself capable of helping after assessment by reason of the 'benign' nature of the dyadic condition and a sense of my insight. I can also say that the length of therapy has shrunk as experience has grown.

As illustrations of this current policy in the search for shorter treatment I would like to report, fairly briefly, two cases in middle-aged couples, both presenting as serious acting-out crises by adultery. They demonstrate, incidentally, the variety behind a common presenting situation, also shared with *Case Twenty-two*, and the as yet uncertain prognosis.

Case Twenty-nine: This couple were sent as a near-emergency privately. I saw them in JI. Married 26 years with three adult children, these

269

people of 54 and 52 respectively were in great distress: H. in agonizing conflict over whether to leave W. there and then for his latest mistress (of a series) who was his true soulmate; W. desolate because this seemed the final recurrence in serious form of what previously she had suffered and condoned knowing she was frigid and H. an incurable romantic. It had always been lonely, unhappy girls he could not help rescuing—not mere sexual attraction or beauty or youth. At once W. says: 'We are both orphans'. She lost her mother at 3, her father at 9. H. lost his father at 6 and hated his hard, unloving mother who 'drove father to death' on a long well-paid job in the tropics because she needed high income and was an ambitious snob. He never knew him but was the unhappy victim of this hard possessive mother driving H. since tender boyhood to success. 'We had no parent models' she adds, and in her depression also adds that her children are all problems. This had been a marriage of idealization regarded as 'a model' by all friends—no quarrels, but with tensions underlying apparent patience and 'understanding' by W. punctuated by H.'s periodic acting-out in these infatuations, a mixture of knight-rescuing-damsel-in-distress and Pygmalion. H. had never let W. into his inner world. A creative writer, he revelled in classical music in his den into which she must not come. 'Even on honeymoon she only wanted to lie on beaches, I wanted to see old churches,' he said.

During this initial JI information simply tumbled out, showing how H. had been drawn to W. because she was strong, popular and practical (also very nice-looking) in contrast to 'his snooty, intellectual self-containment' (his words) which made him despise the road of possible commercial success and prefer high-brow work with small rewards, secretly envying the big-income men in his profession. H.'s depreciation of W.'s interest in 'culture' seemed to have little real foundation—she was well educated and versatile, but not so precious or intense. It was the war evacuation with her young children which made him feel abandoned and unloved (he was an only child), seeking for suffering, lonely girls he could pour his affection out on and identify with. W. at this stage became for him the strong, uncultured, hard woman, not least resented because accepting his needs. *These I now interpreted: W. as the autonomous, withholding mother-figure, not responding to his need for 'all in all', so that he had split this off to seek needy, lonely women who are like himself* (note: the use of the projective identification hypothesis). H. said: 'It happens so quickly'—the present lady, aged 36, had worked in his organization for 8 years unnoticed by him. Then she was abandoned by her man-friend—'it clicked'—'just a sitting duck for me—I befriend her, take her out—we discover common tastes—she uses me as a solace—doesn't really want me—only hoping for her man to come back—but I become devoted, and

270

unbearable to W. . . .' To this W. adds: 'But it hurts—I want the cherishing, not the deceptions and lies'. H. can't bear to hurt W.—this is the horror of it all. He only wants to snatch romance and happiness—he missed adolescent romance—'always so lonely and could not make male friends, always easier with women'.

The next JI is very soon after the first because H.'s distress has risen to suicidal intensity: if he leaves W. then *she* will be the lonely unhappy woman and the situation would turn inside out—he must kill himself to escape the dilemma. In this very tense situation W. comes to have more say. She is the more controlled and frustration-tolerant of the two. She gives more detail of how she came to be so undemanding and competent, how H. had not appreciated that she had to make her own way. We hear of vague psychosomatic suffering as her way out, and we hear of her childhood dominated by deaths, of being brought up with strict maiden aunts, longing to see her mother's grave, but hiding her own feelings because she was there on sufferance—other people's values and norms had to be accepted. 'If you ask me what I want, I hardly know . . . I always want what H. wants' was a telling sentence. She had acquiesced in being the admiring Galatea (or Eliza) to his Pygmalion, feeling despised and low-brow, but also deep down regarding this intellectual preciousness and snobbery as a little boy's antic—she just comforts him now in his misery and fetches the milk and codeine, etc. 'He always needed looking after.' *The picture, more complex than this, was in its essentials interpreted to them: how both partners had expected to be compensated for their orphaned feelings by each other: H. longed for a very tender mother who also constantly admired his cleverness. W. needed a very protective, stimulating father-figure whom she could revere. The opposite feelings—namely of the disapproving, critical, controlling mother, and of the belittling man treating her as a Cinderella but concealing his romantic dreams from her had invaded their marriage from the past. So she could not share his excitements, because each had mistakenly attributed 'bad parent' intentions to the other and this had made them too insecure to enjoy their evident good friendship and devotion, etc.*

The report after this encounter was most encouraging. 'The wall had vanished'—H. felt completely relieved and suddenly flooded W. with his intense love feelings. They resumed sexual intercourse, with a closeness and completeness 'never before experienced in all their 26 years'. His obsession with the other woman vanished completely. The positive aspects of their relationship reasserted themselves. There were in fact only two JIs; the working through came over the next two years, with a very contented H. revelling in being close to and cherished by W., but becoming less potent. His satisfaction came partly from W.'s developing an obscure 'allergic' condition which made her a 'poor little thing' to feel protective and loving about. She concurrently worked through a great dependence need (agoraphobia unless H. accompanied her). H. could identify himself with this 'dreadful feeling of another person's loneliness' . . . 'I had thought W. had everything and was so strong that I forgot about her and did what I liked'. While he was working through his inadequacy, covered by his feelings of 'being a very special, paraded little boy', W. could show him how much she really needed him and express much more participation in his varied cultural enthusiasms he had always felt she rejected. In a few individual interviews over nearly 2 years the sense of being hemmed in by her beholdenness to the object and consequent denial of her identity was worked through. The last experience in the case was a liberation of H.'s and W.'s ability to quarrel without bad consequences. This was epitomized in a scene reported as follows: W. said 'I really knew I was as strong as he. Well, I don't want power, but when he did his usual act of knowing better, I suddenly shouted like a fishwife: "don't tell me what I ought to think and feel!" H. was surprised and our little granddaughter was quite startled. Well I have had no tummy pains or fears since.'

An interesting feature of these people's attitude to their problem was that even at the height of their respective suffering they never accepted drugs, 'knowing' it was a relational problem.

The essential marital therapy was brief—the working-through was long; largely in the hands of the couple themselves and their fully briefed G.P. who would know when the couple or one of them needed another session with me. These were mostly individual visits. Initially I gave the prognosis of 'long therapy'. But in effect this never needed to be taken up. I would retrospectively classify the case as 'Crisis in stable Marriage'. It did not look it on first contact!

The next case illustrating my search for 'essential' brief therapy, had an even more ominous aspect on presentation, fraught with unhappiness and the sense of 'this is the end'.

Case Thirty: A couple on limited U.K. leave from H.'s academic post abroad. H. aged 52, W. 56 when seen, with children ranging from 24 to 17. To begin with, extracts from the referring psychiatric colleague's summary of the symptomatology:

'Increasing marital incompatibility. Already separated. Their accounts not discrepant but the implications not hopeful' . . . 'H. emerges from his self-portrait as an intelligent, sensitive, guilty but somewhat bored and reluctant husband, whose interest in his wife and his marriage has progressively declined, although his interest in himself and in other women has not. W. is an intelligent, anxious, vulnerable, articulate neurotic whose reaction to feeling superfluous

and actively unwanted (though still a source of anxious responsibility to H.), has been to become depressed and periodically hysterically explosive and recriminatory. A vicious circle: the more resigned
and remote H. becomes, the more distressed and self-destructive is
the behaviour to which W. finds herself driven. Their grown-up
children seem fond of them both but are helpless in face of their
parents' impasse. H. while in many ways no less involved . . . is less
likely to seek treatment on his own account, though his attitude is
. . . pathological in its . . . self-centredness.'

The couple met for the first time in weeks in my room, anxious and
defensive. A culture gap was obvious in his superior 'Oxbridge'
manner and her warmer, spontaneous but more provincial personality.
I decide to let things happen without asking any questions. It was not
a 'virgin' case; it transpired that there had been a past attempt to
consult the Marriage Guidance Council, and the recent meeting with
my colleague had 'taught them more about each other than they had
ever managed before to share'. I intimated I knew a little of the
problem from his notes, would they speak freely please. W. raised at
once her mounting anxiety at H.'s 'opting out' and blamed this on
his contempt for her, whereas she is very competent—with reference
to her past career, recently resumed. H. counters this by saying he
regards her as intellectually as good as himself. W. flares angrily at
being called intellectual. Her mother wanted to make her that, to
become a cultivated lady. H. also speaks of his overpowering,
snobbish, intellectually ambitious mother, so cold and ungiving. Thus
we alight at once without prompting from the therapist on the shared
anti-libidinal or rejecting object—a driving mother (H. lost his father
young; W's father was ineffective and withdrawn—her only relation
to him was contempt and rebellion). It became at once possible to
interpret this shared object: *W.'s projection of her despising, scholastic
success-demanding parents to H., and his projection of the snivelling,
little love-starved child to W. which aroused his haughty defensive withdrawal.* Both partners were quite mixed up in split, incompatible
self-images: H. was touched by W.'s good handling of their children,
her straightness and lack of snobbery, but highly critical that she could
not fulfill the 'public relations' aspects of their status abroad. She
admired his intellect and aloofness and dignity, but hated his lack of
spontaneity and warmth. A crescendo of mutual accusing of the other
of withholding themselves. Both weep, W. flounces to the door as if
to leave—she cannot tolerate this. *I interpret this as resistance to facing
the issues of mutual involvement from which she had withdrawn by leaving
him abroad alone and separating, but also show her we need such spontaneous expressions which their marriage had lacked.* H. accompanies
this by weepy contrition over letting her down (but I feel he is moved

273

by identification with his 'victim' in sado-masochistic terms). Sat down again, W. discusses their empty marriage which made her leave him, then suddenly changes to describe her own tenderness taboo: during H.'s illness she was always horrid and unloving—as if he were her mother who would demand compresses from W. for her headaches. At the end of this first encounter I wrote 'Try a few Jls' on my case record. The main themes were displayed and the complex interplay of projective identifications discernible. Both were disappointing ideal love-objects, turned into similar rejecting figures; each felt the other had the warmth to give but withheld it; both needed yet also despised the affective, tender side of life. Instrumental and expressive rôle distribution was highly polarized and mutually resented. W. was the sensitive vulnerable child, H. the successful careerist she rebelled against because her mother had imposed this rôle on her, cheating her of a feminine identity.

There were 10 more Jls. The second enlarged on W.'s history of initial attribution to H. of intellectual superiority, in a Pygmalion situation, which she could only challenge in the area of child-rearing. She now saw him as insufferably bossy; H. had always hoped his bluff would be called, but with W. there were never any encounters between equals, only mounting, suppressed irritations, once the children were out of the house. My rôle was *to keep interpreting her envy of his superiority and career rise and her own domestic isolation, 'only good with children', which she had played in a dog-in-the-manger, accusing way:* By the third meeting, the partners had resumed cohabitation. H. showed us how much he had valued W.'s contrast with his mother: so natural, affectionate, unstuffy. He had felt she had supported his self-advancement, which now emerged she had resented. I could interpret *W.'s confusion when she felt H. to be her critical belittling mother and when she felt an attacking, hostile woman herself,* which helped H. to see a similar mechanism in himself, lecturing her how to be independent, efficient and 'spontaneous', when he should have been kind. The work-through of this took a little time. W. felt almost depersonalized at the fourth session, as if repudiating these startling vistas of herself and her projective attributions to H. And no wonder, for the most traumatic episode was about to be revealed: the joint decision around age 38, to have her Fallopian tubes tied after her last child. She could now release the flood of resentment and deep grief about what she had always felt was done without her inner consent, to help him economically and save his 'couvade' anxiety over a difficult pregnancy. A lot of the mutual recrimination that had underlain their model co-operativeness of the child-bearing period was ventilated—essentially, I thought, a response to my original 'projective identification' interpretation. We now experience together the

274

source of W.'s deep sense of inadequacy, 'like a gelded cat'—as if this had been the reason for H.'s philandering (hardly mentioned hitherto!) 'You didn't suffer any loss in your creativeness!' she exclaimed at him. 'She could have had other men in safety but she was faithful.' She also expressed much general hate for his smugness and smooth 'organization man' qualities, leaving H. quite demolished. At the 5th JI he reported that after the last meeting she had wanted to murder him, he was so cerebral and inadequate. But she had slept— he hadn't. He just had not imagined that she had secretly resented this operation for some 18 years, but now her tantrums and rages suddenly made sense. The most important event in this session was W.'s capacity to accept her dominance, i.e. her re-integration of the bossy woman—ultimately her own sin against her femininity she had blamed her H. for despising. It was now H. who explained how he 'could never win', and how this made him withdraw more into his lofty intellectualism. The 'all-in-all to each other' theme was ventilated, with the slump in the original idealized expectations of healing all the splits and finding the missing bits of themselves; the dovetailing belittlements of childhood: 'not being Mother and Father as we wanted them to be'. W.'s father ever resented she was not a boy; H.'s mother was always talking of 'little' H., his father had joked how small H.'s penis was, etc. It was a great swapping of explanatory atrocity stories of what the projected objects had done to them.

At this point the acting-out adultery by H. became safe to talk about. The pattern of this conformed essentially to what I described in Chapter IX as the benign kind, i.e. its purpose turned out to be an intra-dyadic challenge, not a rejection. The stage was set by each partner feeling the other to be unfriendly, critical, and unsupportive. It transpired that there had been two 'unimportant' affairs while W. was not with him owing to illness of one of the children. She felt 'It had changed him'—he now had no use for her. She never knew until now of the last, and most important one which was behind the change. She felt so unwanted that she came alone to England, in a sense deserting. All this emerged amidst tears, for H. had many letters and photographs of the 'transitional object' which, he confessed, he could not yet bring himself to destroy, and which W. found only since they began to see me. H. quite deservedly, was now forced to face his evasive, cold and calculating attitude, W. comparing him to nasty little boys who pull flies' wings off, and puncturing his pompous façade. Here occurs an opportunity to re-interpret her rôle for him of a critical, cold mother whom he had to defy and cheat while being outwardly a model boy and feeling justified by W.'s attempts to force him to pay attention to her. She had hit back in self-defence by leaving him, *but also because she had to have him depreciative to chime in with her own secret feelings of 'gelded, ageing cat'.*

By the following JI a lot of 'home-work' had been done, enabling H. to express much more feeling for W.'s essential warmth, fairness, etc. He could feel relief in accepting her own wish to de-idealize him and cut him down to size. With this climate, he can also disclose how her inferiority feelings had led to a false 'meta-communication': he felt she felt that he wanted her to be like the rest of bitchy, smart, under-employed intriguing expatriate wives who all slept with each other's husbands on the campus. She confirms this, and he now saw that his 'lady-friend' was just such a snooty woman. 'Yes—I can see what is meant by the differences—the complementarity—in the past I always wanted W. to be just like me.' His praise for her had been lip-service: 'I thought I valued W.'s sense of loyalty and devotion— but I am really a bastard.' *I could now point out how the submerged resistance of both to the other's idealized rôle expectations had emerged. Here we were both asking W. to be a good girl, to accept a sadistic, cold bastard as her husband while we were asking him to be a good boy to a belittling bitter cat: really both to act as feathers in their unloving mothers' cap.* We now hear, in indirect response that both H.'s brothers had married 'terribly destructive' wives as if they could not shed their bad mother. Both partners now pool fresh information on how their respective mothers were over-protectively depriving: both were reared on the legend that they were delicate and only survived by their mothers' constant devotion and control. *I interpret their projective identifications of each other as the dominant, unloving mother and as the hated dependent baby. While W. did this by rebellion against being this aspiring intellectual, yet always feeling inadequate vis à vis H. as the mentor-superior being, H. had not married a bitchy sadist mother-figure like his poor brothers; he had tried to defeat his mother by taking her inside him and in effect lived just as she had bidden him, aloof, precious and patronizing.*

This interpretation 'shattered' H.—the horrid little boy who went scenting out weaknesses in others and then bullying them—at work he couldn't do it so it was all let out on poor W.! The latter said 'Yes and I asked for it because I had to be the good baby who never made a fuss, I was a proper masochist. But if only H. had let off natural anger, not this aloof superiority', etc.

The 9th JI had them arguing frankly: W. expressing her doubts whether he can love her if he still keeps souvenirs of those women he now openly shows. H. equally can say they gave him happiness, he does not propose to destroy but let them fade out. After all W. ceased loving him before any of it happened, tore up her will, returned his rings. What do I think, they both ask? *I reply that at last they are*

276

open with each other, accepting each other with their difficulties which largely came because both carried the fear of offending their dominant mothers. It seems to me that they already see how they should deal with each other; not as if both were unconsciously at the same time a frightened child and a bad attacking mother, using the same methods of coercion and control through anxiety which leads to secret defiance and hate. They respond by agreeing that they have both been afraid and anxious to be 'clay' in the partner's hands. W., a few moments after my interpretation, discusses the effect of meeting an old confidante of H.'s had on her; a kind of subverter of H.'s morals who received much of W.'s hate. H. had worried she would attack that man, but she carried the meeting off with adult self-control. 'But you can see he (H.) treats me like a child!' My response was: 'If he didn't treat you as a child he'd be afraid you would treat him as a child.' This produces a flood of examples of mutual humouring—'never knowing what one's words would produce', each liable to be hurt or snub the other and having to treat each other like raw eggs, and how both had longed for straightforward affection. H.: 'I had seen too much hollow kissing by father and mother. I said to W. that I will never be the kind of husband who meaninglessly pecks you goodbye.' To W., early in their marriage, this had been deeply wounding: 'In my family they were much too puritan to kiss each other—your saying that meant that again there would be no love for me.' The 10th JI was taken up with the working-through of mutual suspicion and resentment. H. could angrily say W. had wronged him by never expressing her distress of being sterilized but instead withdrawing her love, and so causing him deep resentment, not least by neglecting her personal appearance, refusing social engagements, humiliating his status and self-esteem in this way. The development of these themes offers the opportunity to interpret their *mutual narcissistic projections: each needed the other to be just right and perfect and could not tolerate any departure from their ideal expectations* (once again, dear old Hypothesis I!). H. had then turned to a search for a simple, unassertive but smart substitute female, whereas W. had revived her adolescent scorn for 'cheap women who only set out to please'. All the secondary narcissism was now in H. after W.'s was so damaged by her operation.

H.'s home furlough was drawing to a close. Though W. was still afraid to go with him, both partners were sure they would go together. The last JI was spent in a kind of summing up of consequences which had flowed from rigid idealized expectations that the other would be just as one's fantasy required. One further piece of new insight came from W. who could see that she provoked H.'s temper because, like with her father, it was better than being ignored as a stupid little girl. She saw very clearly her conflict between need for

277

love and her fear of this being in a form that negated her identity. We did not have a very definite 'parting transference'. It was only clear that communication and mutual frankness were much improved.

As W. could not go with H. immediately, having taken a job when she first deserted him, I saw her twice alone during the month she remained in London. She looked gay, charmingly dressed and younger. Her talk was mainly about the beginnings of her own conflict: her tremendous awe of H.'s handsome and scholarly personality from which she at first drew much inspiration. Before his appointment abroad he had been such a participant father. It was with the increasing rôle differentiation that she felt cut off and diminished to a 'mere child minder'; her own previous career achievements useless, and H. trying to force her to be a hostess and glamour woman which meant she was just a 'feather in his cap'. She could see this as an 'inverted male envy'. Thus the vectors converging towards her reaction to sterilization became very clear. We finished on the theme she started with: her projection of her own self-depreciation into her H., who was at the same time her 'beau ideal' and her rejecting parent. A year later, as I revise this manuscript, I hear that the partners could not maintain their insufficiently worked-through insights and had again separated, H. taking all the blame. It does not follow that they will stay apart.

I quote the case as a corrective against optimism and a demonstration of the uncertainty of prognosis as to the length of working-through of the attitude changes. It was a very advanced case of chronic difficulty—18 years long. It showed what I do and how quickly potentially helpful changes occur. Had they not had to go abroad after a few weeks, these might have been consolidated. The case shows that the decision between 'long therapy' and 'short therapy' must be based on a correct estimation of the pace of working-through, and on the assessment of the capacity of the partners to continue it on their own. This apart, the rate of work-through is likely to depend on how much of paranoid internal object relation is mutually projected. In long term therapy we may not, in fact, see the couple so many more times, but we maintain a regular series of JIs over a long period to stress our continuing mediatory rôle as a transitional shared object and to keep the working-through within the triadic system. When the Sub-system III relationship is at a depressive or oedipal 'whole-object' level the working-through takes place faster, and the partners themselves let us know when they can manage without further help and 'drop the pilot'. We should, also, not underestimate or ignore the findings in Sub-systems I and II.

Teruel, working along the same lines, but with a more rigorous scrutiny of transference phenomena, has also shown how quickly the interpretation and the testing out of the shared fantasies on a third object in the person of the therapist can modify projective identifications and permit the projected parts of the internal object world to be re-internalized (loc. cit., Part II). The difficult task is to know after what length of work-through they will stay there!

5. OTHER MODELS OF THERAPY

This book is an account of marital diagnosis and treatment as conceived and carried out on one model. It does not set out to be a compendium of other people's theories and work in this field. I do, however, want to stress that the variety of models of therapy will depend not only on the personal and theoretical background and skills of the workers, but also on their social setting and opportunities. The university research department of psychiatry or psychology will have different aims and resources from a private analytic practice or a social case-work agency. Even where the conceptual framework is common to such differing settings, the application is likely to vary in accordance with the time-scale of the possible, with the socio-educational level of the clientele, and with the primary task of the workers. As will be seen in Chapter XII, the client population at the Tavistock Clinic (and *a fortiori* in private practice) has been relatively sophisticated, of middle, upper middle and upper working class couples, well above the median in intelligence. Through my contact with the Probation Service, I am well aware that less intelligent and socio-economically favoured people lack the verbal and educational resources for reacting to interview situations in ways illustrated by my case reports. We have to modify not our conceptual framework or interpretation of the phenomena but the techniques we employ to help insight and co-operation of different populations. We have to accept cruder transference-manifestations; use simpler words and be prepared to play more overt parental rôles. I have discovered no essential class-difference in the dynamics of marital interaction. While acting-out in lower social strata tends to be more florid and less inhibited, the sub-culture tolerance for such behaviour and counter-behaviour will also be greater. Economic realities will often furnish incentives for maintaining the dyad at this social level which idealizations and ethical values provide at the higher levels. In the uninhibited the authority-rôle may need to stress control of childish acting-out. In the more sophisticated the opposite has often to happen: a more permissive, aggression-and-libido tolerating 'super-ego' figure has to be incorporated from the transference experience, allowing greater latitude to the expression of ambivalence.

Thus, the English Probation-service model, based as it is on the conceptual scheme derived from the Tavistock units, is likely to stress, within that scheme, the rôle model of the case worker as fairly active guide and authority-figure deriving from his connection with the Law, and using this to strengthen the ego-structure at Sub-system I and II levels, in so far as the service has to deal with sub-median or otherwise handicapped populations.

In this service, as in the child psychiatric units of the Health Service and analogous units in the Education services, and in family case-work agencies, there are modifications imposed when the children of the disturbed couple are the presenting members, including young delinquents. One of the chief modifications of technique in the child psychiatric world is the multiple JI, in various combinations of two or more members of the professional team with parents and disturbed child plus or minus other siblings or one of the parents, who may also have 'straight' marital JIs or individual interviews. I have no personal experience of this valuable form of family therapy, in daily use by the Tavistock's Department for Children and Parents and elsewhere in Britain and the U.S.A.

It is worth stressing the existence of much agreement in other centres with us. Theoretical orientation similar to our own appears to underlie the work of Ackerman[8] (op. cit.) in its emphasis on the *Family*, with marriage as a part of the total primary group constellation. The services described by Goodwin and Mudd[9] and by Llewellyn,[10] working in various centres of the United States also are close to ours. As with our techniques, there is considerable flexibility as well as continuing debate over the advantages of one or two therapists and individual versus joint handling. Though I do not know how Dr. Ackerman, in particular, deals in detail with his marital cases, I found his orientation confirmatory to my own current viewpoint:

> The treatment is for the interaction and takes account not only of pathological elements but also of the malleable parts, the strengths and the capacity for change and integration. (p. 153.)

This supports my feeling that in the benign case, where the dyadic boundary is intact though threatened at presentation, one can often rely on the work-through towards maturity and free communication to take care of itself.

Readers will have gathered that I have been greatly stimulated by Haley's way of describing marital interaction phenomena. In the same paper[11] he also analyses the rôle of the marriage therapist in the interaction pattern of a couple. Haley's views, too richly condensed to enlarge on here, come to this conclusion:

Although a marriage therapist typically emphasizes to a couple the need for self-understanding, there is little evidence that achieving understanding causes a change in a marital relationship. More apparently, marriage therapy offers a context where a couple can learn alternative ways of behaving while being forced to abandon those past procedures which induced distress . . . (p. 234 loc. cit.).

Haley's model of therapy is a different one from say, that of the F.D.B. or those of the above-mentioned American colleagues. It emphasizes the use of paradox and almost *reductio ad absurdum* in the handling of dyadic resistance to change and in the perception of their relationship and their own rôles in it. Haley's model appears to lean on learning theory, and to be geared to brief joint treatment by one therapist.

Cognate to the theory of marital and family-interaction in the production and alleviation of many psychiatric ills is the active school of Dr. F. Knobloch and of his wife Dr. J. Knoblochova in Prague.[12] These Czech pioneers use most of the concepts developed in these pages. Their flexible and varied methods are based on the interaction theory of neurotic illness leading to the need for family therapy. This ranges from the kind of methods I have just presented to concurrent or subsequent group therapy and community therapy, with emphasis on the norms of social responsibility and economic independence of both spouses prevalent in the social values of their country. There seems to be a corresponding variety of institutional settings for dealing with patients, according to the nature and phase of the symptomatology.

The mention of *marital groups* prompts a reference to recent developments at the Tavistock Clinic, based on the work of my Unit, but in which I have only played a watching rôle. The work was initiated by Dr. G. Teruel for one, 30+ age group of 3 couples in collaboration with Dr. W. Brough and for a second, younger group in collaboration with Mr. Stephen Cang of the F.D.B. The theoretical approach is to regard couples as the units—as individuals are the units of therapeutic groups. The aim is to observe and influence the changes in dyadic as well as total group interaction in the complex transference relation to the therapists' dyad. It is to be hoped that the findings will soon receive publication. In experimenting with marital groups the Tavistock organizations had hesitated for a long time before this departure, despite their great collective experience with analytic group therapy. The dyadic concepts needed establishing first.

In the U.S.A. Wilfred C. Hulse,[13] among many others, advocates group therapy for marital difficulties, but warns of the dangers of acting-out in life situations if spouses (or other family members) share in the same group. Groups in which the partners are split are preferred. Almost every conceivable combination of foursome, concurrent analysis of both partners by one, or by two collaborating analysts, and groups of couples or groups containing only individual partners of disturbed marriages, are to be found. The dread of treating couples together is generally still prominent.

The therapeutic moments of group and joint therapies are usually thought to be catharsis; self-participation; greater reality closeness and super-ego relaxation; and a mutual re-educative or learning process from vicarious experience of mechanisms first identified and tolerated in group peers, and gradually perceived and accepted for the self. Schools who reject the concept of inter-personal relation have yet to publish their approach to marital therapy.

Lastly, as touching upon the work here described, I should like to refer to an interesting form of therapy specifically directed to one group of problems—unconsummated marriages presenting as the young wife's phobia of penetration. This is a method developed by Drs. Sylvia Dawkins[14] and Rosalie Taylor,[15] Drs. Stephen and Jean Pasmore[16] and some others, on the basis of routine vaginal examinations incidental to contraceptive fitting in their work for the Family Planning Association. This work explores and interprets the woman's fantasies and denials concerning her reproductive organs, her conflicts about sexual feelings and activities. It relies, quite consciously, on the female doctor's rôle as an initiating, permissive mother figure, allowing the anxious and resistive girl to own her sexual organs as well as feelings and clarify her hitherto unchallenged unconscious sado-masochistic fears. Drs. Dawkins and Taylor conclude that though this technique cures relatively simple cases by relieving a marital impasse, it does not help in more deep-seated dyadic trouble, as these authors themselves foresaw. They also stress the advantages for results in seeing both partners in the context of such an examination. The technique presents a great advance on the purely mechanical therapies of insightless 'surgical' defloration and dilatation, on which I have already commented through the statements of some of the women themselves in Chapter VIII.

REFERENCES

1. HOME OFFICE (1948) 'Memorandum on the Principles and Practice in the work of Matrimonial Conciliation in Magistrates' Courts.' London: H.M.S.O.
2. KUBIE, L. S. (1956) Chap. II, in Eisenstein, V. W. (ed.) op. cit.

3. BANNISTER, K., et. al. (1955) *Social Casework in Marital Problems: the development of a psycho-dynamic approach.* London: Tavistock Publications.

4. PINCUS, L. et al. (1960): *Marriage: Studies in Emotional Conflict and Growth.* London: Methuen.

5. BANNISTER K. and PINCUS L. (1965) *Shared Phantasy in Marital Problems: Therapy in a Four-Person Relationship.* London: Tavistock Inst. of Human Relations. Codicote Press.

6. REDING, G. and ENNIS, B. (1964) 'Treatment of a Couple by a Couple' *Brit. J. Med. Psychol. 37*, p. 325 ff.

7. MALAN, D. H. (1963) *A Study of Brief Psychotherapy.* London, Tavistock Publications.

8. ACKERMAN, N. (1958) op. cit.

9. GOODWIN, H. M. and MUDD, E. (1964) in: Nash, E. M., Jessner, L. and Abse D. W. (eds.) *Marriage Counseling in Medical Practice*, University of N. Carolina Press, Chapel Hill, pp. 276–82.

10. LLEWELLYN, CHAS. E., Jr. (1964) ibid. pp. 283–97.

11. HALEY, JAY (1963) op. cit.

12. KNOBLOCH, F. and SOFRNOVA, M. (1954) 'Notes on the Technique of Family Psychotherapy' condensed English version of paper in *Neurologia a psychiatria czeskoslovenska*, XVII-4; pp. 217–24.

13. HULSE, W. C. (1956) Chap. 'Group Psychotherapy' in Eisenstein, V. W. (ed.) op. cit. pp. 303–10.

14. DAWKINS, S. and TAYLOR, R. (1961) 'Non-Consummation of Marriage'. *Lancet*, Nov. 4, pp. 1029–33.

15. TAYLOR, R. (1963) 'Coitus Disorders' Chap. in *The Encyclopaedia of General Practice*, ed. Abercrombie, G. F. and McConaghey, R. M. S. London: Butterworth, pp. 472–83.

16. PASMORE, J. W. D. and H. S. (1964) 'Premarital and Marital Problems'. *Medical World.* October, November, December numbers.

Chapter XII

WHO HAS BEEN HELPED?

It was indicated repeatedly in various contexts that the couples who came to our marital unit did not represent all possible kinds of marriage troubles. I delineated the categories whom we excluded from ranking as 'marital' cases.

It now behoves me to define more clearly those who did come and were the sample of population this book is about. These couples were 'helped' at least in the sense of a diagnosis, a report to their family doctor, as well as at times by actual therapy. The estimated results of treatment will be presented, including some reference to what was learnt about the effect on the children of dealing with their parents. I will also take up the problem of long-term follow-up in marital work, as the ultimate criterion of its value.

A. THE SAMPLE

In this section I have the modest aim of placing our clientele in some sort of sociological perspective in relation to the population of England and Wales. This study of 'numbers' is not made with the purpose of deriving or proving any hypotheses. I do not even know if any statistically minded reader will find these data useful.

There were two numerical scrutinies of our cases since the Marital Unit of the Tavistock Clinic was set up. The first tables were made by my then collaborator, Dr. H. P. Hildebrand, with the help of Mr. Kenn Rogers, circa 1957 on a sample of 157 consecutive couples seen by us. The second was made by myself around the turn of the year 1964–5 on the much larger number of cases on our files. The data scored came from routine case records, i.e. no special questionnaires or interviews were used. I will begin with my own figures because these are a sample taken from the total case material passing through between 1949 and 1964. I will compare them with Hildebrand and Rogers's figures where appropriate. They themselves made certain comparisons with the National Census and with an F.D.B. sample.

Marital case records coming through my unit were from the

beginning filed separately from other records of the Adult Department of the Clinic. Husbands' and wives' case papers together with joint interview records, etc., are bound together and stored in alphabetical order. At the end of 1964 there were some 2,000 such files of 'processed' and 'closed' cases, which did not include the 'current' patient-load of our team. I took every twentieth folder up to a total of 100 and abstracted the data which follow on to large tables. The figures obtained I will now list hereunder. I do not append the bulky tables themselves. They unnecessarily complicate book production. They are columns with ticks under the headings.

TABLE 1

1. *Sources of Referral*

General Practitioners	42
Psychiatric Consultants (other hospitals & clinics)	28
Social Agencies (incl. M.G.C.)	13
Probation Officers	10
Self-referred	7
	100

TABLE 2

2. *Age Groups*

Here I will insert comparisons with Hildebrand & Rogers's figures and with the Registrar-General's figures for the 1954 census of age-distribution of married couples.

Age Group (by husband)	My sample (N = 100)	Hildebrand & Rogers (N = 157)		1954 % in England & Wales	
				Total married population	Divorced population
		%	N		
20–30	27	22·6	35	12·1	18·1
31–40	42	45·8	71	23·2	40·0
41–50	29	29	45	25·3	28·4
51+	2	2·6	4	39·4	13·5

The ages of the second and third column related to time of referral. The age of wives was not significantly different by 'age-group' in decades and need not be separately shown.

285

TABLE 3

3. *Duration of Present Marriage* (100 cases).

Under 2 years	14
2–5 years	25
5–15 years	45
15–25 years	15
Over 25 years	1
	100

Hildebrand and Rogers found 59·6 per cent of their sample falling into 3–11 years' length of marriage.

4. *Previous Marriages* (out of 100)

Only 8 husbands and 9 wives of my sample had been married before, and in only one case was there a previous marriage of both partners.

TABLE 4

5. *Children now dependent* (100 cases), including those by previous marriages.

None	26
One	29
Several	45

6. *Socio-economic level of patients*

This was scored by me according to the six categories of the Registrar-General's Returns, and these refer to the husband's occupation at the time of referral. We knew more about the social background of our couples, who often showed marked upward social mobility compared to their parents' educational and occupational levels, but these were not scored. The first category included full-time students for the learned professions.

TABLE 5

Occupation Category	My sample (N = 100)	Hildebrand & Rogers (N = 157)	F.D.B. Sample	COI Social Survey
1	17⎫			
2	32 ⎬70	76%	36%	23%
3	21⎭			
4	21	23%	46%	56%
5	9	1%	18%⎫	21%
6	None	—	—⎭	

Hildebrand and Rogers, by way of amplifying their figures in Table 5, reported that of 168 patients (husband and wives, not couples), who were tested at the time of their survey, 112 patients scored IQs of 118 or better. 79 out of 259 persons passed G.C.E. or possessed a University degree. 80·7 per cent of the sample of 157 couples in their sample lived in their own homes or rented unfurnished houses or apartments. 71·6 per cent described themselves as living adequately or better than adequately. In terms of upward social mobility Hildebrand and Rogers found that of 127 husbands seen 76 were occupationally in a higher group to their fathers'. This is a more pronounced upward trend than the social mobility scale published by David Glass (1954) quoted by these workers.

7. *Previous History of Psychiatric Treatment*

I alone made this inquiry in my own sample of 100 cases, specifying the factor as 'seeking psychiatric help before this marriage, and other than for the present trouble in the marriage'. In 38 couples one partner had sought such help; in a further 5 couples both partners had seen psychiatrists otherwise than for their marriage difficulties. 57 couples had no history of individual psychiatric illness prior to consulting us for their matrimonial stress.

In no case had there been admission to a psychiatric hospital. I should add that our refusal to handle 'mentally ill' persons in the Marital Unit or as 'marital' was not based on past history but on current clinical assessment at preliminary scrutiny of application or at consultation. Since we took long histories as well as collecting write-in questionnaires of previous history, it does look as if in more than half of our quite disturbed cases it was only marriage which had activated 'neurotic reactions'.

8. *Non-consummation of Present Marriage*

This item of my sample was already referred to in Chapter VII. To score this factor I defined the criterion as 'no penetration by the husband's penis either before or after the marriage ceremony'. It will be recalled that on this criterion 7 per cent of my sample had definitely not consummated while a further 8 per cent had to be scored as 'unproven' either way, but most likely not consummated, and too ashamed or afraid to confess such failure unequivocally. I cannot compare this directly with Hildebrand and Rogers's figures. Of 157 couples they had found 50 couples childless, and only inquired of these couples about non-consummation. They found 10 couples out of the 50 (or 20 per cent) with non-consummated marriages of 1 to 8 years' duration, and a further 21 couples (or 42 per cent) with an 'inactive sex life' that may or may not have included some further cases of primary sexual failure. Pregnancy without penetration is not unknown. My figure, in contrast, is derived from a random sample of the total case material.

9. *Proportion Treated by Tavistock Marital Unit*

This heading occurs only in my survey. Of the 100 random cases, 36 were taken on for marital therapy, i.e. for the sorts of methods described in this book. It does not mean that no help or treatment was offered to the 64 per cent not so treated. They were referred to the general services at the Tavistock or transferred elsewhere. Both suitability on assessment and the manpower factor played their part in this proportion of selection and rejection of 64 per cent after diagnostic assessment. As regards the non-accepted cases, an excerpt from my table will give some impression of these: 'Wife refused'; 'Consultation and Report for Child Guidance Clinic only'; 'Went abroad'; 'Case of alexia and backwardness in H.'; 'Temporary crisis in good relation'; 'W. pregnant'; 'H. refused treatment'; 'Sterility? to F.P.A.' I have already referred also to those where one or both partners needed psychiatric and/or psycho-therapeutic help in their own right. This fraction amounted to 32 couples. 7 suitable couples were transferred to the F.D.B. for marital treatment, owing to our lack of vacancies. The 36 cases treated will be dealt with below, and their relation to my illustrative cases scattered throughout this book defined when I come to the section on results.

10. *Other Data*

Before leaving this Section, I should like to mention the factors statistically evaluated for significance by Hildebrand and Rogers and not repeated by my survey, as well as those I decided to omit from my own survey after due consideration.

First I will cite my colleagues' 1957 report:

We analysed various other categories such as: position of patients in their parental family; age differential between the spouses; children by previous marriage; geographical mobility; number of siblings, etc. However, none could be shown to contribute significantly to marital tension.

A little further in their report they also state:

An attempt was made to discover differences in educational and intellectual background between spouses but none could be found.

288

Clinically speaking, no couple cited intellectual and educational differences as contributing to marital disharmony.

This statistically checked inquiry broadly confirmed Winch's 'homogamy' hypothesis of mate selection or opportunity for encounter at roughly social peer levels. It does not, and cannot delineate the wealth of contrary data about the sharing of, or boredom with, partners' intellectual interests, nor the differences of tempo, practicality, etc., which do indeed constitute 'bones of contention' in marriages. These factors we hoped to catch and score for large numbers in the MRIQ (Chapter X) Test, not yet invented when the first survey was done. It was not practicable to use the MRIQ on a statistically worthwhile scale, for reasons given in that Chapter.

What Hildebrand and Rogers did do with considerable refinement and diligence, was to draw up figures for *parental home background*, in the psychiatric sense of providing emotional security or the contrary for their sample of couples. I have alluded to the significance of an individual's perception in his clinical self-description of his primary group relations for the theory of rôle models and internalized objects, with its bearing on our topic. Hildebrand and Rogers defined two separate factors: (a) broken homes and (b) emotionally disturbed ('poor') homes.

By broken homes we understood all those marriages of the patients' parents, in which one or both parents disappeared from the patient's life from any cause whatever: death, long hospitalization, divorce, separation, desertion, before the patient's seventeenth birthday. This would include those brought up in orphanages or foster-homes, etc., but not those adopted in the earliest weeks of infancy (although we all know that the later disclosure of the fact of adoption may have quite severe results on the emotional life even where the adoptive parents have been exemplary in their rôle performance). We may call these historically factual data.

By 'poor' homes we meant that the description of the parental home life by the patient or the spouse included such items as constant quarrelling between parents, or one persecuting the other who withdrew; temporary 'walk-outs', desertions, threats or gestures of suicide; known adultery without break-up; drunkenness; chronic economic hardship attributed to ineffectiveness or mismanagement of the parent-figures: and of course also parental cruelty, arbitrariness, fecklessness or irresponsibility to the patient or his siblings when dependent children. In sum, these definitions were based on the repertoire of subjective statements in patients' self-descriptions applied to the parent generation.

Of the 157 couples (or 314 patients), 299 individual case records were adequate enough to allow the observers to make the numerical scores for either 'broken' or 'poor' homes in the Table 6 below. Of these 299 individuals 239 were judged to come from parental milieus reported as grossly disturbed by our patients.

TABLE 6

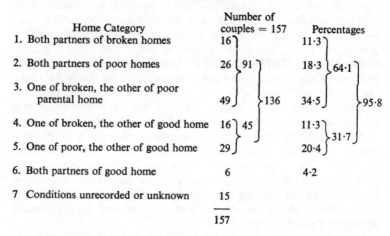

Home Category	Number of couples = 157		Percentages	
1. Both partners of broken homes	16 ⎫		11·3 ⎫	
2. Both partners of poor homes	26 ⎬ 91 ⎫		18·3 ⎬ 64·1 ⎫	
3. One of broken, the other of poor parental home	49 ⎭ ⎬ 136		34·5 ⎭ ⎬ 95·8	
4. One of broken, the other of good home	16 ⎫ 45 ⎭		11·3 ⎫ 31·7 ⎭	
5. One of poor, the other of good home	29 ⎭		20·4 ⎭	
6. Both partners of good home	6		4·2	
7 Conditions unrecorded or unknown	15			
	157			

I think that most readers would regard this as a staggering figure which requires some comment and also comparison with a control population. First, it should be stressed that the childhood recollections of people whose infantile feelings are activated will be coloured to varying degrees by 'retro-projection' of either predominantly good or predominantly bad internal object relations. People at the paranoid (and hysterical) end of personality types will tend to blacken, but depressives and obsessionals to exculpate and overpraise their parent figures. One would have expected more people at initial interviews either not to be aware of, or to wish to conceal the stresses and nasty aspects of their parental homes. The ratings in Hildebrand and Rogers's table above were made from such initial interview records. One could be sure only of the 'broken' homes fraction because these recorded facts of death or other physical absence of a parent. For the 'poor' homes the defences might have worked to distort the figures either way. But they all point one way.

My two colleagues made an effort to obtain some measure of comparative information on couples who had not been in marital trouble. It was possible to enlist the kind help of a number of family doctors who set a simple questionnaire devised by our Team to couples in their care whom they rated as 'happy' or 'normal'. From the completed questionnaires of those who co-operated we found that the combined figure for 'broken' and 'poor' parental home back-grounds was 54 per cent. This figure is significantly different from 95·8 per cent of our patient sample. But as the method of obtaining the data differed greatly also, it is not permissible to draw major con-clusions from this discrepancy. For while it is wellnigh proven by child studies and so forth that poor or broken homes do cause damage to their progeny, we also know that the ambivalence of all children to all parents peoples the deeper layers of the psyche with both persecutors and idealized figures. I feel that the figures are meaning-ful: not only objectively but perhaps even more so subjectively, i.e. for the inner worlds of unhappily married persons. This sort of intriguing uncertainty besets many attempts to quantify, or make superficial mass surveys of factors the meaning of which can only be ascertained by clinical study at depth. I hope to return to this point in Chapter XIII.

11. *Omitted Data*

For my survey I considered whether to try and score such factors as (a) Housing and other geographical moves; (b) 'culture distance' —religious, class, educational or ethnic; (c) relative I.Q.s; (d) dominance of Father or Mother in spouse's parental background. I decided that the series was too small, and the information therefore too unreliable to be of value. The variables listed are obviously of considerable relevance, but the leisure needed to study and analyse a large series was lacking.

B. TREATMENT AND ITS RESULTS

I now return to para. 9 of my own sample survey of 100 random cases. Before I reproduce and comment on the Tables below I want to clarify the relation of the cases quoted in Chapter XI to this sample. *Case Twenty-six* was not picked from this sample. The findings, like those in *Case Ten*, represented a 'turning point' for me and *Twenty-six* was specially chosen to illustrate this element of discovery. *Cases Twenty-nine* and *Thirty* are both from my private practice, and more recent than the survey. The rest are 'luck of the draw' from the relevant categories in the records of the 100 couples.

1. *Number of Therapists*

Of the 36 cases that happened to be included in the sample, 7 couples were treated by one worker, 29 by two workers. The years of reception for the 7 former cases were all 1961 or later.

2. *Method of Therapy*

Individual Interviews with own therapist	31 couples
(But of these 15 couples had occasional foursome JIs interspersed.)	
Joint Interviews throughout (2 workers)	5 ,,
(This figure includes Cases 21 and 28 who *began* as foursomes but continued with one therapist.)	

3. *Number of interviews rated as therapy*

Less than 10 interviews	20 couples	
10–25 interviews	10	,,
25–50 interviews	1	,,
More than 50 interviews	5	,,

4. *Outcomes of Therapy*

Good	6
Satisfactory	17
I.S.Q.A.	11
Break in marriage	1
Unknown (went abroad)	1
	—
	36

Good: included not only such subjective assessments by the partners as 'we have never been so happy before' or 'Life is transformed since we came to you'. It would have to include evidence of substantial change in the dyadic interaction towards full communication at all levels: resumed and satisfying sexual life, the fading of transitional 'adulterous' object attachments; the integration of ambivalence, hence of capacity to quarrel in adult fashion; the strengthening of identity in each partner with consequent higher regard for self and other; the tolerance of differences, with better reality perception of the partner and a fading of projective identifications. Case Ten would be so rated.

Satisfactory: would be defined as a lesser degree of 'good' above. 'We are much happier now' or 'we can bear our troubles' or 'we feel we can make a go of it', might be subjective summings up. Objectively, this rating would be based on evidence of change in several areas of co-operation towards fuller sharing or tolerance of disagreement, more insight into the dynamics and precipitating situations for symptoms, but not necessarily the loss of all symptoms.

Examples: Case Twenty-one; Case Twenty-nine.

292

In Statu Quo Ante: is self-explanatory, and means here that objectively we judged there to have been no significant change in intra-dyadic dynamics, even though we might be thanked for the help given, or told 'We understand better what it is about'; or 'I suppose it is the best we can do'; 'We still get these awful periods of tension—it doesn't seem to have made much difference'.

The Break in Marriage was in a case who from the beginning came to clarify the issues and who needed the reassurance for their considerable social consciences that they 'had tried everything' before deciding on a 'reasonable' divorce.

The proportion, then, of 'positive' results for the marriages we counted as 'treated' was 23:13, or 63·8 per cent of a random sample including cases from our earliest years of work. By less strict criteria we could have included some of the 'I.S.Q.' couples. It is of help to some people to recognize and accept the nature of their predicament. But the criteria I used were based on my definition of marriage. We were looking for affect-change which follows certain kinds of insight-giving experiences, not for intellectual insight as such which the people in our sample frequently brought with them.

There is, to my knowledge, only one other, comparable numerical presentation of treatment results. This is contained in a footnote on p. 9 of the F.D.B. book by Pincus. I quote:

> . . . from a preliminary study of a consecutive series of 100 cases, 'marked' or 'considerable' gains were shown in:
>
> | | | |
> |---|---|---|
> | Short-term cases—by 20% of marriages, | | 20% of individuals |
> | Medium | 41% | 65% |
> | Long-term | 53% | 82% |

This study also showed clearly associated gains in the individuals' physical health, in the adjustment of the children and the effectiveness of the partners in their work life. These findings supported the results of an earlier unpublished study.

These figures are for 100 *treated* cases; mine for 36 treated cases in a random series of 100 couples passing through our diagnostic process. It is therefore of some interest to compare the F.D.B. figures with their high emphasis on the benefits to individuals accruing as the result of marital therapy in that centre's 'classical' form, with my figures for the results stressing the marriages as the focus. The F.D.B. do not state in their just quoted table what are their criteria for short, medium or long term cases. Their results for the marriage improve as the length of therapy increases. My figures show that only 5 couples of my sample received what I would call long-term therapy, i.e. over 50 interviews (which means a year or more of attendance). All the rest were short (21 couples) or medium length treatments (11 cases). I therefore looked at the results of the 23 couples whose results were rated as 'good' (6 couples) or 'satisfactory' (17 couples) at discharge from marital therapy, in terms of the length of therapy.

TABLE 7

Results	Number of interviews			
	Less than 10	10–25	25–50	50+
Good	3	3	—	—
Satisfactory	10	5	—	1

I said I would not use these scant and mathematically unvalidated figures to advance or support hypotheses. But I will permit myself the comment that there may be a connection of these figures with my use of joint assessment interviews in contrast to the rigorous emphasis on 'one client one therapist' at that time current in the F.D.B. Our more rapid grasp of the interaction by the regular use of the JI in assessment and in subsequent therapy by the JI foursome technique (in 15 out of 31 cases) may help to explain our better figures by short methods. They do not alter my conviction that longer methods are essential for adequate and lasting affective working-through in serious marital conflict. Perhaps our selection for easy methods is unconsciously better than we can yet explain!

5. Results of Assessment Techniques only

The above figures relate only to the 36 cases we set out to treat. A case such as No. 26 showed us that there can be a therapeutic effect comparable to the results of longer treatment even after a few diagnostic sessions. Such 'unlooked-for' results happened, additionally to *Case Twenty-six* (which was not part of the 100 sample) in 2 cases in my sample after assessment interviews only. In one case (also included as *Case Twelve* in Chapter VII) we had the opportunity of learning some five years later that the improvement (not cure!) in their marriage had lasted. This case will be referred to in the next section. In other cases one hears of the help the couple had felt from being seen in a crisis, but it is hard to systematize such information. In contrast to such pointers in the direction of the value of short-term JI techniques in helping marital relations, the mere undergoing of diagnostic appraisal, even by the JI technique, does not automatically alleviate serious marital stress. Thus, whereas only one couple treated (with fewer than 10 individual interviews by 1 therapist for both partners) were known to break their marriage subsequently, 13 assessed but untreated cases of the 100 were known to have gone to divorce. These, of course, were cases which on assessment, including always an element of therapeutic trial, we had not accepted for treatment. It may be of interest that they prompted such recorded entries as: 'Pygmalion case', 'The executive and the Nymph'; 'Lady Chatterley'; 'Middle-aged crisis in H.'; 'H. psychopath'; 'Culture-distance'; 'H. psychotic character' (3); 'H. fetishist, W. hysteric'; 'W. adamant, refuses treatment, H. repents too late' (2).

C. EFFECT OF PARENTS' THERAPY ON CHILDREN

With the aim of this volume to provide a certain conceptual frame-work for the approach to marital conciliation, I feel impelled to comment at least briefly and inadequately on such glimpses as our preoccupation with the troubles of the parents has allowed, of the repercussions of our work on the children—small or in some cases grown up. If this book is, as I regard it, a contribution to the wider field of family and community psychiatry and mental health work, total exclusion of the children from purview would seem too one-sided, even though I feel that systematic investigation of this effect would require a special programme, possibly best done by a Child or Adolescent psychiatric unit. I had included such a project as an additional aim in the application for a research grant to certain Foundations.

The effect of our work with the parents on the children falls into 3 broad categories. (1) Positive or directly relieving; (2) Negative, or aggravating the children's mental condition; (3) Unknown. The last category includes the majority of our cases in so far as no systematic data have been collected.

1. *Positive Results*

In some of my longer case descriptions there have been passing references to the change for the better in family atmosphere as the parents' tensions have diminished. In the daily work with marital therapy we hear a much greater volume of comment on this theme than my condensed accounts have portrayed. We hear of young children no longer waking or crying terrified in the night or insisting on coming into their parents' beds. We hear of older children, whose school work had suffered and who were listless and angry, becoming easier to handle and livelier. We did have an unusually good oppor-tunity to test the hypothesis of the relation of child behaviour to parental attitudes and moods in a case which I should like to cite more fully. It provides a bridge between strictly marital work and the wider purposes of family psychiatry, with incidental sidelights on twins.

Case Thirty-one: This couple are not part of the sample of 100 discussed above. They were treated by us at the request of a Child Psychiatrist at a London teaching hospital, who wrote the following in asking us to take on 'this poor young couple' . . . 'We have been seeing their twin boys aged $4\frac{1}{2}$ . . . for faecal retention and overflow. I felt . . . that this was very much bound up with the early mother–child relationship . . . exacerbated by their twinship. At the moment the marriage is in a very precarious state, but both are . . . anxious to keep it going because of these enchanting small boys. The twins' I.Q. is in the region of 125 . . .' etc.

H. was 35 and a small entrepreneur after several false starts; large, 'lazy' and easy-going. W. was 31, petite, compact, feminine, precise and incisive. There was a considerable class and educational difference: W. had the 'better background' and schooling though she did not go through with full training for an unfeminine profession. Both partners gave the Child Guidance doctor's opinion 'that it might help the children' as their reason for coming.

In brief, this was a family situation in which all four members unconsciously wanted to be indulged babies, continually gratified and trying to devolve control to someone else only to defy it. It was also clear that the twins were winning in this contest since they embodied the secret wishes of their parents. The therapeutic task was to try and stop this unconscious craving for total indulgence, resentment of control and identification of the parents with their uncontrollable twin boys. These had reduced their mother especially to a wreck, which in turn endangered the husband's livelihood as he was required at home to cope with the chaos she helplessly created there.

The picture after first individual interviews was somewhat as follows: Both parents were Jewish. W.'s parental background was of a loving, unsuccessful father who never became independent but 'had a good time'. He was indulgent to his children but resentful and irascible in the manner of a henpecked husband (cf. Case 26) with the loving, anxious, over-protective and controlling mother who wanted all her children to be clever, educated and genteel. W. was the fourth —the baby girl—more indulged than any, and she was followed by two 'terrible' young brothers with whom she fought and played—in fact she described tom-boy tendencies and counter-investment of feminine interests, like dolls. She took full advantage of many illnesses, and though clever, preferred an easy life, working in her father's office and becoming a good administrator. 'I am like Daddy, and Mum is sorry for H.' She was allowed to marry H. despite the social distance because the parents had earlier refused her engagement to a tubercular man whom she loved. Before marriage sex was good, but after marriage she described (and H. confirmed) herself changing away from sex, and the emergence of a managing, striving disposition towards H. She said 'When we married after his Army service he was drifting . . . we thought of sending him back to school . . .' ('we' being her parents who ran this marriage). 'He would just sit—I gave him hell —I had to get him to explode before he would act . . . Well he did what we told him (then describes how he began to develop his now growing enterprise) . . . then he said he couldn't manage—so I took over, managed all the books and money—when in trouble I went round to Dad for advice . . . he wasn't a good businessman either but he did provide well . . .' Finally, she infected H. with 'the bug' and H. deployed his dormant energies, but by this time it was to stay out at work and come home exhausted and uncommunicative, nagged by her for dozing off, rarely volunteering an outing and then letting her decide where to go—'not her idea of how it should be'. W. knew she had robbed him of his peace and thought he was the nicer, warmer person. But contrasting herself with her Mother-in-law who always 'upped and said all she thought', W. said 'No—I hold back till I am fit to bust.' (The 'anal' figures of speech in this statement need no emphasis.)

H. came from a much less complicated background of fat, merry East-Enders with no social pretensions and many financial ups and downs. 'Dad and I are the same—placid, easy to get on with.' Mother was the 'explosive' one, but H. always got on well with her and confided in her. H. left school early, passed no exams, 'drifted into the Army', enjoyed the invasion of Europe, did not even bother to claim a pension for a leg wound. He confirms W.'s picture of the march of their relationship. 'I have been very frustrated but I've grown used to it.' 'She wants me to be ambitious and yet get home early! I think she is most upset by finding she can't manage the children—she had such great ideas from her mother about upbringing and keeping control . . .' 'I am the one to manage the boys—they fight her but are good with me: she gets worked up and screams at them. She can't stand them making a noise and then screams at me because I can stand it. She stays awake worrying and resents that I can sleep and not worry.' 'But I am not patient as I used to be. I am reasonable and W. isn't, but we have incessant quarrels—about the kids, about my hours of work, about going out—she is always comparing me with her family—her mother is the paragon, my people aren't any good—she can be very spiteful.' 'As a boy I used to be obstinate.'

The twins were described as dissimilar: A. large, gentle and slow like his father, B. quick and lively. W. became very dramatic as she said with an obstinate pout of her lips: 'B. had to be taken into hospital—no bowel action for 10 days, now he leaks! He *won't* have a motion, and he objects if we help him! A. began it but B. copies him

297

deliberately. A. has stopped and come on a bit. B. doesn't like his new school, but A. does. But now since B. has had a lot of attention, A. has gone back to holding his bowels . . .'

It also emerged that the marital situation deteriorated greatly some 18 months after the twins were born 4 years after the marriage. W. had a 'breakdown'—withdrew, was depressed, would have nothing to do with the babies—she had a course of E.C.T. from a psychiatrist. This was her comment: 'I now think this was wilful on my part —I didn't have to do anything and everybody wrapped you in cotton wool—I was aware I was doing it a bit consciously—mother and eldest brother (a physician) have always run me and protected me— it would have been better if they'd left me to develop my own backbone—anyway I decided to get better because I wanted to keep an eye on things' (she meant H.'s business)—'You'd think I'd be like mother, good with children, but I never wanted them.' She was furious that she had been 'talked out of her job' (as the brains of H.'s enterprise) because the twins needed her attention. It was at that point that H. had taken over and developed his ambition, while W. had steadily become more dependent, self-depreciatory and resentful, trying to put the entire burden of disciplining the children on H., to prove how weak he was.

The treatment was by JI throughout, as a foursome with Mary Williams and myself. We had also done and collated the first interviews. There were six such 2-hour foursomes, spaced December 14; Jan. 25; Feb. 22; March 14; April 26; June 27. The marital interaction aspect can be summarized fairly concisely by citing a progress report written after the first three JIs: 'They report considerable easing of the domestic situation from which the twins seem to be benefiting, especially the defecatory habits. The situation emerged of a gentle, easy going, warm-hearted chap who had married a very over-indulged baby daughter of better class people. She was surrounded by boys and identified with them to the point of resistance to the feminine rôle, including sexual anxiety and disappointment. It became clear that she equated femininity with babyishness as things to be rejected, all the more as her earlier life was punctuated by many illnesses, for example pyelitis with urinary retention, involving urethral stretching. Being small and 'cute' she had become her father's pet, always at his side, learning his business skills and never imagining that in that prosperous life she would ever have domestic duties. She brought to her marriage with this easy going apparent replica of her father also her mother's ascendancy, and proceeded to create an inverted Pygmalion situation. She set about moulding H. into something more acceptable to her expectations and status needs, but also discovered that he simply let her take over more and more, and especially the management of home and the babies when they came, when she abdicated pro tem. The little twins somehow stand both for her filthy, uncontrolled little brothers and for her now buried tomboy self. The very success of her Pygmalion efforts on the H. raised the spectre of losing control over him, so she now began demanding his constant presence and help. As he became more successful so she felt more inadequate, her primary rôle perception undermined, her maternal capacities poor; and deeply envious of H.'s capacity to have a good relation to the children who did not try on things with him. He has managed to be a better mother than she. These things have already become clear to H. and W. and their friendly ventilation has helped. Particularly interesting was W.'s acceptance of her alleged depression as an escape into illness from facing unpleasant realities in the shape of babies. She became the baby for whom everything was done by the devoted family group. She soon saw that under her need to control the so lax and undisciplined husband she was just like her little sons who did not need to control their defecation so long as anxious and devoted parents could be relied on to run after them, but who just in this way used their bowels and other rebellions to control the parents.'

To H. it was a revelation that his so business-like, superior wife might need him to control her—to let her be more of a baby; as exemplified by her exclamation during the first JI: 'If only he would take everything off my shoulders for a month or two so that I could pick up again!' We compared this wish with the policy of the child psychiatrist who had hospitalized twin B. bottle-feeding, etc. in order to let him regress. W. could see, the next time, how before marriage she was not aware of dependence—the family were 'just there' behind her. She blamed them for 'not making a man [sic!] of her', able to stand on her own feet. So when H. was not a parent figure but rather dependent himself, she began to feel she had to control the baby in him, that despicable quality which she has now to experience in herself before she can become a real woman.

From here on W. begins to shed some of her idealization of her family of origin. She copes better with her twins, now both home. She tolerates her H.'s slow tempo of doing things; and he comments 'she leaves everything to the last moment'. He can now help in the foursome, describing W.'s food anxieties: because she fears the children will be late for school, she forces them to eat; when they resist she gets into a panic. Her 'favourite' nightmare is trying to get somewhere and not succeeding—being too small to control events. The anxiety about time, delay, being methodical is revealed as now projected by her less to H. than to the children who must be like miniature adults. Her shouting at them is always also a scream of help to H. to rescue her from these terrifying creatures who are beyond control. H. can admit now that he has often joined the twins in baiting her, purposely provoking her, and enjoying her childish helplessness, in retaliation for her earlier attempts to master-mind. By the next JI the partners can objectively see how the little determined twin B. overawes his bigger slower twin A., and makes him do what he wants; and *we apply this to the interaction of the spouses. H. is forever asking her for business advice only to have his optimism destroyed—just like little B. overturning A.'s endeavours to be a big boy.*

The fifth JI brings a good work-through of W.'s extreme panic at the destructiveness she has projected into her children; with H. reassuring her on 'little boys naturally run wild' lines. Part of the therapeutic effect of these sessions was the demonstration to H. of the strength of his essential tolerant loving-kindness and his power to deal now with W. as he had handled his children, but had not had the confidence to apply to her because she had been his 'superior'. We get the full expression of W.'s despair at the whole insoluble problem of resisting this terrible childish aggressiveness, which can only be indulged and appeased. She can see how she, for example, offers them alternative menus and wonders why they play up; just as her mother would always intervene when she was in a scrape to prevent her father from chastizing her. We alighted on a deeper internalized 'perfectly loving' mother, who never denies or punishes. *We interpret at some length the nexus between her infantile need to keep the authority away from the reckoning with the fiendish little monster—hence to keep the father's anger at bay—hence her resentment of H. having the authority in his hand, as she is so much mixed up with the little boys' rebellion and seeing how far they can go.* H. says she cannot really deny them anything unless she is in a flaming temper, and we get a vivid image of this woman's hitherto insoluble ambivalence: she *is* them, yet she is also the perfect, indulgent mother, and she hates them and fears their monstrous power over her. Left alone they would destroy the whole house. She despises herself when she descends to their own level in fighting with them and always losing, and H. not believing it because not there to see it. Yet to deny them anything is cruelty. This mix-up of her warring internal object world is finally *interpreted to her in terms of the mother who never punished but looked sad when W. as a lively little tom-boy defied her. She felt there was a devil inside her stronger than herself, about which she felt so guilty because she had passed it to the children—she felt she was them.*

'All I want is for them to be *reasonable* . . . now they are getting it at school—oh they get slapped—the school won't have them because they refused lunches', etc. W. now said, with relief, how much children less close to her obeyed and respect her. With them she could be adult. We discovered that she doubted her love—she only felt fear of failure and defeat. When she sees that reproachful look in her twins' faces she melts—it is as if she is the bad, cruel one—not their mother at all . . . 'I want them to be adults, so that we could talk the problem out . . .' She felt that her mother controlled her by moral appeal. Her own hate of the children seemed such a horrible contrast to her wonderful mother. It came as something of a revelation to be told by us *that while she felt her own ambivalence, she only saw her mother but didn't know how she felt when W. was naughty. H. has not this problem to the same extent because he could see his mother flaring up and yet be loving. This is why he was not so troubled by calling the children to order and they felt reassured by knowing their limits.* Gradually W. could see how she had projected her own inner struggle into the family: 'the situation was so explosive', she said. 'Terrible things happen . . . I remember the same with my brothers when they were left alone.' She could finally laugh when it was pointed out that none of them were now in gaol, but were rather fine people. But she once more rose to the attack to include H., this time to accuse him of playing too roughly with them . . . it 'all ends in tears'. W. saw not only how she had imported her childhood conflicts into the marriage, but also that she only felt like this in the marriage, not elsewhere. Her husband, children and home had to be perfect so that these conflicts should not be awakened. To this she could now link her insight into how unhappy her little boys were so much of the time, because 'they don't know where they stand . . . I can see they want me to make a stand —they look at me all the time to see how far they can go . . . they are on me all the time instead of playing. Other children don't follow their mothers about . . . that's because I say to them all the time: if you carry on like this Mummy will have to go away. So they make sure I'm still there and test me if I can stand some more . . .'

By this time the marital situation was peaceable, W. could accept H.'s good feelings and rational, relaxed attitude and make use of his influence with the children. The Child psychiatrist reported very great improvement in the behaviour, play concentration and amenability to control of the 'terrible twins'. We made no further appointments but left it to the couple to contact us.

Some comment must be added about H.'s initial resignation and passive resistance. He had withdrawn to where he let W.'s cries for help and leadership go unheeded, absented himself, was irritable and sided with the twins. There was, it is true, a better internal object world that could allow 'maternal' irrational fears and furies to pass over his head. W.'s anal-compulsive character stood out: she was herself, and had produced, horrible faecal babies.

301

In this case the material emerging during marital therapy was focused on the children, who were seldom absent from the transactions of the foursome though we never set eyes on them. The mutual interaction between the parents' (in this instance mainly the mother's) object relations and the childrens' freedom to grow towards maturer ego-strength seemed to show up very clearly. The mother's ego-split involved her in constant repudiation of her own 'uncontrollable libidinal ego' by an idealized but essentially rejecting maternal anti-libidinal, anti-infant ego which constituted her inner model for her marital and parental rôle. These antagonistic ego-divisions were dealt with by projective identification of her children and partly her husband with her rejected but secretly cherished untamed libidinal ego. This libidinal ego itself therefore had to be controlled and mastered (which became focused on the lazy, self-indulgent 'inferior' husband), thus carrying into the present W.'s apparent compliance with the benevolently coercive maternal ego-alignment. The libidinal ego must, as the same time, not be crushed since it was highly valued as the powerful, defiant core of her identity. Even disregarding H.'s own ambivalent attitudes to maternal control, the behavioural cues streaming out to these children from their mother must have roused almost maximal anxiety and confusion. Every encounter with their mother raised their omnipotent-defiant fantasies and prevented the internalization of her as a safe, controlling object for which both she and they were crying out. Any attempt by the father to play this safe rôle was sabotaged by their mother who ambivalently defied and belittled him both as a competing male and as a 'failed' idealized and potentially threatening punitive parent-figure—a projection which he played back to her. It was a very marked example of the 'double-bind' situation of incompatible cues for all four of them. The father's contribution to the children seemed reassuring partly because of his open siding with 'boys running wild'.

But his behaviour towards W. was also of a passively resistant, authority-sabotaging, dependent-defiant quality, as if saying to the children: 'let her natter, you see how I just laugh at it—it all goes over my head—take no notice, she can't do anything!'

In this case the clarification of the unrecognized inner worlds and consequent sex rôle conflicts of the parents produced a diminution of double-bind and conflict with the children. The enhanced security permitted them to proceed on their developmental road towards greater ego strength. Perhaps this picture of the dynamic interconnectedness of the childrens' predicament with their parents' similar unresolved conflicts fought out inside the dyad, allows us insight into the Why? and How? of the quite universally accepted commonplaces that parental discord hinders and distorts their children's personality development. By what our child-psychiatric colleague did for these twins and we did for their parents, relief was given. Analogous family tensions and mechanisms are likely to be at work in all such marital situations, however much the parents try to hide their conflicts at conscious level from the children.

The question of how permanent such relief is to the children of our clientele presents itself. The figures in Table 5 seem to point to a strong connection between 'broken' or 'poor' homes (and all the cases cited in this book qualify for the latter category in one way or another) and the later capacity to assume adult marital and parental rôles in the now married children of such homes, at least in the relatively economically secure backgrounds of our sample population. Like Slater and Woodhead[3] I think that the damage to personality is not through a break as such but through the emotional strife of parents which is internalized as potential conflict. It is impossible without longitudinal studies to know whether our efforts are in time, especially with children at or over latency age.

2. Negative Results

Not infrequently, as our material shows, the sequel to the improvement in the parents' marital relations is a disconcerting and unwelcome outbreak or aggravation of emotional or behavioural difficulties in their children. In my view this phenomenon can have two distinct meanings.

(a) It can be a 'release' effect on children previously emotionally paralyzed by the fear of finally driving their parents apart by their naughtiness. With a sense of *greater security* they can 'permit' themselves to express their hitherto inhibited aggression, demandingness and similar impulses which need to be acted out in development. As the parents become less inhibited and more communicative, so the children also communicate their discontents and hate of the parents for their past traumatic behaviour. A variant of this phenomenon is the greater awareness in the parents of their children's emotional needs and hurts to which during the period of their dyadic clinch they had been blind, or which they had used destructively against the partner in fact or fantasy. They now focus their guilt and reparative feelings on the child who is felt to be the victim of their bad actions and requires help. The child feels 'entitled' to have his revenge, as it were.

(b) The manifestations of emotional disturbance are an effect of the past history of the family, unrelated as far as can be perceived to the improvement in the parental marital relations. In the childrens' neurotic or behaviour difficulties of this category there need be no immediate connection in time with the changes in the parents. Such troubles in the children do not form part of the transactions in our interviews. There is the feeling that the offspring's illness is a separate chapter, the inevitable later sequel of what had happened perhaps years earlier.

Between these categories there is something of the difference between 'benign' and 'malignant' that was made for the parental symptomatology. One almost welcomes the (a) type of release symptoms: 'the poor little chap has come alive, he has the confidence to assert his anger—things are better, so he can now work through his disturbed parental relations'. An example of this type were the reactions of the two children—the teenage girl and the little son—in *Case Ten*. At her age level the girl began to act out sexually at the height of the parents' difficulties, but with their improvement they could take emotionally effective action to release her from her entanglements with exciting libidinal father-substitutes, that could be related to unconscious two-way identification with her mother's similar fantasies and projections. This young girl may be said to have shown a direct positive effect from the amelioration of the parental difficulties as they became free to perform their adult role towards her. The little boy, on the other hand, was a good example of the benign, apparently aggravated disturbance (enuresis) which caused W. in the case to discuss it. But at the final JI both partners could see that his defiance was part of his greater security, liveliness and independence.

A similar shift of focus occurred with a young professional class couple whom I had helped to the point of 'satisfactory' in a series of triad JIs. The eldest son, aged 7 or 8 had borne the burden not only of two younger siblings, but his mother's ambivalent displacement to him of her husband's 'selfish, defiant' qualities, as well as of her fantasies that this little boy should be 'more like her family', sensible, controlled, an example to his 'terrible' little siblings. When the parental relations eased, the boy became more disturbed and the parents now asked for therapy for him. The whole case, parents and child, was transferred to the Department for Children and Parents where both aspects were now treated.

As examples of the more independent longer-range effects of past parental conflicts and hence of contradictory influences on their childrens' personalities, I should like to refer to the two young sons of the couple I briefly cited as *Case Twelve* in Chapter VIII.

These children were both unintended post-war reminders to their mother of her helpless slavery and her sexual attachment to H. He had played around while on active military service, but she took him back and then proceeded to castrate him psychologically, but not before they had conceived these two children. The man's reaction was to withdraw, to dodge her wrath by taking no part in any domestic decision-making or controlling the children. He was thus expressing his ambivalence towards his strict mother who had been deserted by a harsh as well as adulterous father. W. had had an inadequate father because of war-wounds whom she only remembered as bed-ridden. Her disappointed idealization of H. as the man who would supply the controlling leadership led to her rejection and persecution of him. This was one of the cases which we were only asked to assess, in view of the distance from London. But an individual interview with each, followed by a foursome JI, produced marked change, especially by the interpretation of H.'s counter-identification with his father, and W.'s need for just such a gay, strong and unanxious man to impose limits on her own aggressiveness. The full record was sent to their local Probation Office who had originally referred them to us. It was therefore possible to keep in touch with the longer-term effects of our brief intervention. This showed that while not symptom-free, the couple had maintained a better level of communication, and had only occasionally needed to contact the Probation Officer who was their marriage counsellor.

But some five years later the couple was in Court not for mutual violence, but for the school truancy, petty thefts and 'being beyond control' of both younger sons now aged twelve and thirteen. Though our services had no hand in assessing the aetiological factors, the local diagnosis, correctly in my view, connected the past history and lack of father-authority with the pubertal outbreak of active delinquency. The parents had become more united and did more for their family, but it was too late to undo the effect of the earlier damage in the ego-development of these boys.

An analogous sequel, unrelated to the immediate change in parental relations, was the appearance in my consulting room of the now married daughter of the couple described in Chapter XI as *Case Twenty-nine*, later to be followed by her somewhat unwilling husband. She really only came to seek sanction to break her marriage on which she had already decided with her mother's active prompting. This handsome, vital young woman, it transpired, had done all the courting with her pathologically passive, withdrawn and taciturn work-centred husband. Her personality was an interesting compound of her father's need to rescue lame ducks and to avoid being dominated, with her mother's unrecognized need for a really warm and cherishing man hidden behind a strikingly autonomous and un-demanding exterior. This was the only case in which I have been able to get a direct, two-generation insight into the internalizations of parental attitudes and conflicts as later shown in the mate choice and marital destiny of a child. Obviously, my help to the parents could not affect these—except perhaps in the sense in which her mother, the long-frigid wife and emotionally inhibited woman, now intervened to prevent her daughter from a similar fate of playing a controlling, long-suffering, quasi-maternal rôle to a very introverted (and I confirm schizoid) man, whom the girl had insisted on marrying in the teeth of her mother's opposition. Somehow that young woman had to work through a repetition of the parental rôle model, refusing dates and mating opportunities with all kinds of young men whom she attracted.

We can conclude that positive effects of marital therapy on the children are directly seen where their insecurity reactions have taken the form of regressive and acting-out behaviour. This appears most clearly in pre-latency age-groups. They are indirectly helpful to the children, despite their *apparent* negative appearances, where the childrens' insecurity reactions have been of a cowed, submissive and over-reparative nature; they can now allow their more spontaneous ambivalencies to come into the open to be worked through, with or without some professional assistance which the more insightful parents can now feel less resistant to seeking. The true negative effects are not related to the parents' marital improvement, but are the manifestations of conflicts in the children resulting from the stresses preceding therapeutic intervention in their parents' troubles.

It may be that these open declarations of disturbance which are temporarily linked to the changes in family dynamics are symptoms of disequilibrium. A child had had to adapt to parental quarrels and tensions with certain defences to maintain its homoeostasis. When its external love-objects no longer supply the behavioural cues that give potency to these mechanisms of adaptation the defences fail. It is fair to compare such reactions to seasoned front-line soldiers' return on home leave. They slept well in foxholes under gunfire, but became anxious and sleepless in the peace of their now unfamiliar surround-ings. This suggests that marital therapy could be expected to lead to disequilibrium in the total family pattern which requires an additional effort and period for re-adjustment. The good or satisfactory termina-tion of marital treatment would seem to be a favourable moment for extending such help to the whole family when the insights and wish for reparation are fresh in the parents' awareness.

D. THE PROBLEMS OF LONG TERM FOLLOW-UP

The validation of therapy has been a besetting anxiety and pre-occupation with all investigators in Medicine. It is difficult enough in the sphere of organic disease where there are rapid objective measurements by physical and chemical tests. Even here there is always loss of contact with a proportion of the sample population tending to make the final figures dubious and subject to statistical conjecture. What proportion of such loss of contact is due, even in the organic field, to ill-defined transference phenomena has not been worked out. The pain has gone, the function restored. People just cannot be bothered to go back for re-examination or to reply to letters.

In hospital psychiatry the problem is more difficult than in, say, orthopaedics or cardiology. But still, in remissions of severe mental illness one can use fairly gross behavioural criteria to assess results. Gainful occupation, social participation, disappearance of obvious disorders of conduct can be ascertained and scored. The follow-up can be an integral part of the extension of the hospital's networks into out-patient and community services. 'On paper', a psychiatric social worker can report back on her brief meetings with the former in-patient or his relatives. Even with this 'so simple' scheme, it requires constant expenditure of effort, time and funds. Relatives are by no means reliable informants in all cases.

Such difficulties are magnified when a patient-population only attends an out-patient clinic, and when they do not even accept for themselves the rôle or description of 'patients' with its socially institutionalized obligations and limitations (cf. Talcott Parsons,[4] pp. 274 et seq.). Except in a small minority of couples in whom vivid acting-out by violence, temporary desertion, adultery, etc., has been symptomatic, the behavioural criteria of change in sociological terms scarcely apply to an evaluation of the post-therapeutic changes in personal or marital state. It is, as I have found by trial samples, the exception rather than the rule to receive replies, after 1–5 years, to personal, carefully worded letters signed by myself, enquiring about the present conditions of the ex-clients' lives, even when the letters are not returned through the dead-letter service of the G.P.O. This experience has not encouraged us to organize an expensive systematic house-visitation by a social worker, even where she might have been one of the therapists in the case. From the description of our client population it will be gathered that we were dealing mainly with a socially successful middle-class group who mostly hated and resented the evidence of personality failure disclosed by their marital difficulties. The exercise of medical authority with its sanctions for exacting attendance after the felt need has passed, or for subsequent intrusion by domiciliary calls by a follow-up worker, has been felt by us to be very dubious. The relations such couples form with us are very much those of transitional objects. We fill a passing need, and it is in the nature of such transferences that they are resolved, or at times repressed or put into cold storage. It is sheer wishful thinking for any psychiatrist to assume that his erstwhile patients will be maintaining their gratitude. From the statements of those who have attended colleagues before being seen by me, it is clear that the break in doctor–patient relationship leaves highly ambivalent attitudes even where the help given by the former psychiatrist has been acknowledged and obvious to the observer. The same resistance is going to be felt by the client who ends his treatment with me. It may be that in a case of full analysis such transference residues are finally dissolved. This is not possible in marital therapy even where it is conscientiously attempted. There is therefore here a very subtle problem of continuing contact with the couple which they themselves deal with as I have already indicated: they want to be left alone, and in a sense this is precisely what therapy is designed to achieve for them.

Nor is it any more promising to rely on the referring agency for follow-up data. Contrary to idealized images of the family doctor's intimate knowledge and contact, the actual replies are apt to be: 'They left me several years ago' or 'Have seen nothing of them so I suppose they are all right'. This goes *a fortiori* for other psychiatric clinics and consultants who had off-loaded the case on to us, and for the Probation Service who can barely keep up with their current responsibilities, although they are the most co-operative.

I repeat, at the risk of being thought precious, that the answers obtained to a few 'common-sense' questions would not greatly advance the validation of this work. 'Are you still together' may get the answer—'of course, we always have been'. If we are told they quarrel much more than before it is difficult to assess if this is an advance or a deterioration. Nor, if they no longer fight, whether they have no bones of contention or whether they have ceased caring. And so on. Answers to elementary questionnaires or re-interview by someone at less than the needed depth will be coloured by the wish of the clients either not to hurt the people who tried to help, or by the opposite wish to show that it didn't do any good, and in both cases by the joint dyadic resistance to further intrusion.

As I said in Chapter XI, the evaluation of results, such as the comparison of short and long-term cases and the retrospective making of indications for their respective application, is a most complex and expensive procedure. The carry-forward of such a project into a meaningful follow-up after a number of years is, for the various reasons mentioned above, even more difficult if reliability in the assessment of our type of data is aimed at. (1) It would mean our being able and permitted by a statistically representative and significant proportion of a random sample to conduct depth interviews. These ought to be done by the people who treated the couples originally, for only they can really compare the 'feel' of the data. Scientifically inclined critics would then be likely to suspect such follow-up interview data as biassed. (2) It would therefore also be necessary to administer the same test-procedures as had been given the clients at their diagnostic assessment, also preferably by the same clinical psychologists. (3) Independent clinical assessors would have to rate the combined scores of both tests and interviews and compare the scores with those of the original assessment before therapy. I can see no other way to obtaining such data as, for example, the changes in ego-integration and in projective identifications, the satisfactions and involvements in rôle sharing or in greater rôle differentiation, the quality of conflict-resolution or of sexual commitment and gratification.

Had we in 1958 been able to finance a team for full-time work in this field, we might have been able to design a validation procedure, such as we had already in operation as a pilot on the Sub-system II and III levels. Here we planned to put every couple who had undergone therapy, through the initial appraisal (if they agreed) a second time. The aim was (1) to obtain a fuller retrospective picture of the marital interaction to modify or confirm our original propositions and hypotheses, i.e. our power to predict; and (2) to assess the changes in terms of inter-personal perception and in rôle taking. For the latter purpose we had hoped to compare changes at Intake and Re-assessment in treated couples with a matched control group of couples who had passed the Intake procedure but who had not during the intervening period undergone marital therapy. But even this elaborate design only covered the assessment on cessation of therapy. A full-time endowed research team would still require to repeat the essentials of psycho-dynamic and socio-psychological assay at some longish intervals to establish the permanence of results or the contrary. This is what ideally requires to be done. Half-measures would fail to command respect, and would be shot to pieces by any critic on the grounds of sampling, bias and large unknown factors. This is why, in Chapter IV and elsewhere in these pages, I have stressed the hypothesis-finding status of this work so far, and the inconclusiveness of its therapeutic value *in statistical terms*.

On ordinary human and clinical grounds on the other hand, I have no doubt that we have helped many couples through critical phases of their marriage, hence quite a number of young children from suffering the traumatic exposure to worsening parental tensions and broken homes. A fair number of medical and social work colleagues has gained a better understanding of what these tensions are about, by sharing in our diagnostic and therapeutic findings.

REFERENCES

1. GLASS, D. V. (1954) *Social Mobility in Britain*. London: Routledge & Kegan Paul.
2. PINCUS, L. (ed.) 1960 'Marriage', op. cit.
3. SLATER, E. T. O. and WOODHEAD, M. (1951) *Patterns of Marriage*. London: Cassell.
4. PARSONS, TALCOTT (1964) *Social Structure and Personality*. Glencoe: Free Press.

Chapter XIII

CONCLUSIONS AND PERSPECTIVES

Before ending this volume I want to try and relate its specialized purview to the wider perspective of Mental Health development which has been an implicit aim of my work. This may be a more valuable exercise for a final chapter than a mere 'Summary', especially as I had abstracted my working hypotheses at the end of Chapter VII.

While I should like to think that I have made some contribution to my primary task of medico-psychological method I am aware that my topic has received parallel development over the last few years by other workers, to some of whose work I have referred. It is a heartening thought that the main lines of theory and practice are so concordant. Sager[1] has ably summarized the lines of growth in a review article. I can now turn to my secondary aim.

1. MARITAL STUDIES AND THE BEHAVIOURAL SCIENCES

My ideas owe much more to the behavioural sciences than to neuro-physiology or pharmaco-psychiatry. This is, perhaps, not surprising when we consider that these disciplines exhaust their applicability at the somatic boundary of individual human beings.

Constitutional and physiological aspects of persons in interaction are not irrelevant in studies of interaction. The capacity for orientation towards objects and goals, to cathect other persons and non-personal (for example symbolic or abstract) objects can be influenced by physiological events in past and present, endogenous or exogenous. Marital strife can in a proportion of cases be demonstrated to be correlated with neural or other organic damage, from anaemia of tired wives to cerebral changes in older husbands.

Apart from technical findings elicited by physical examination, the most striking and poignant phenomena even in such organic disorders, are, however, in the sphere of human relations. Both the patient and his loved ones suffer the most when the pathways and

311

powers of meaningful communication are impaired. We strain at the bedside of a comatose friend for a sign of returning recognition; we suffer with the aphasic and the withdrawn, because they have become *alienated*, cannot give to us, and doubtfully take in what we offer. In like manner we wait, more joyfully, for a baby's first smile or babbling word.

Mental illness is *always* social, while *sometimes* also organismic. Its manifestations are largely described in behavioural terms. These include statements of how the mentally ill behave to their surround, and also how they affect us, the professional observers. 'Does not know his name' or 'does not recognize his mother', and also 'says I am going to kill him' are commonplaces in our descriptions of the encounter with mental illness. Sullivan so wisely saw 'the operational statement of interpersonal relations' as the heart of psychiatric methodology. Most of what we know as professionals has been learnt by the operational use of inter-personal communication, verbal and non-verbal, and by the later exercise of ordering recurrences of like encounters into 'reaction types'. Personality is the social face, the totality of impact of a given individual on his human environment and of the latter's response to it, cognitive and counter-cathectic.

To this operational statement I am in this book adding an extensive experience with marital dyads in disorder. This step I regard as an important innovation (without claiming that I am its inventor) in psychological medicine. If 'personality' only manifests and grows in interaction, then a dyad is the irreducibly smallest meaningful unit of description in psychiatry, psychology and the *other* social sciences. For example: an account of the phenomena of post-concussional ('organic') states lists the positive and negative (or absent) personality responses by reference to a yardstick of healthy culture norms. Clinicians are in effect saying to their readers: 'If you tried to enter into communication with such a patient in our systematized way, you would find such and such changes from the behavioural norm.' The statement tacitly postulates a two-person system—the observer and the observed. But the factor of the observer is left out, not only for verbal economy, but because by analogy with physics he is 'outside' the system he observes. Then the systematizing of what are in essence descriptions of recurrently met inter-personal encounters becomes a list of abstracts—'disease entities', existing in themselves. This may be appropriate in that small area of psychiatry where the fault in social communication has been localized in some part of the somatic mechanism which allows classification in terms of a 'cause'. We can, with some sense of closure, speak of 'the arterio-sclerotic dementias' or 'frontal tumour syndrome'.

Yet it is only a minority of conditions to which this justifiably applies. A sulking husband who has not spoken to his wife for a month is, for her, as truly alienated as if he were in organic stupor. In fact she hopes that it is an 'illness'; she *prefers* him to be ill rather than hateful. To me, a different 'other', he may respond with quite different manifestations of personality. Then do we 'localize' his illness in the cortical representation of his wife?

There are many gaps to close between the opposing psychiatric theories of behaviour as physically determined or emotionally conditioned, and analogous pro-psychodynamic and anti-psycho-dynamic sociologists' views, the latter ignoring the human actor as an entity with its own dynamic, rooted in living nature. Any analysis of human behaviour or 'action' if it is to deal with the world as it is, must be broad enough to include the spectrum of Man in nature, culture and society. It must be poised at one end in biology and its medical techniques for understanding the genesis and disorders of man's relating to his human environment, and at the other end on the reciprocal study by social techniques of the ways in which Man's own creations, culture and social institutions—society itself—shape that relationship.

Concrete systems of action—that is personalities and social systems—have psychological, social and cultural aspects. For one thing, the state of the system must be characterized in terms of certain of the motivational properties of the individual actors. The description of a system of action must employ the categories of motivational orientation: cognition, cathexis and evaluation. Likewise, the description of an action system must deal with the properties of the system of the interaction of two or more individuals or collective actors—this is the social aspect—and it must note the conditions which interaction imposes on the individual actors. It must also take into account the cultural tradition as an object of orientation as well as culture patterns as *internalized patterns of cognitive expectations and of cathectic-evaluative selection* [my italics—H.V.D.] among possible orientations that are of crucial significance in the personality system and in the social system. (Parsons & Shils,[2] p. 7.)

In inter-action we find the basic process which, in its various elaborations and adaptations, provides the seed of what, on the human level we call personality and the social system. Interaction makes possible the development of culture on the human level, and gives culture its significance in the determination of action (ibid., p. 17).

Psychology is in large part the study of the internalization of society and culture within the individual human actor (Edward C. Tolman, ibid., p. 359).

These almost random quotations from the most consistent effort I know to integrate the sciences of man in a dynamic theory of behaviour, read like a definition of what I have tried to say in relation to marital conflict. Without deliberate design my conceptual framework appears to fit in with these condensed statements by a multi-disciplinary group of behavioural scientists. My theme and its working-out may serve as a practical application within a medical setting of this broad theory. The Parsons-Shils theory itself is as relevant to intra-personal as to inter-personal and intra- and inter-group relations and dynamics. My work could be an exercise equally in conflict research or in 'intra-group relations', as Teruel regards it.

The psychiatric helper in the field of family relations is in an unusually privileged position to observe the entire gamut of personality in raw conflict and in social interaction. By the complexity of its levels of communication, which I called the sub-systems through which personalities relate to one another (positively or negatively), a marital dyad (with or without dependent children) is certainly a micro-social system. It is an institutionalized body of the society in which it is embedded, and which imposes its functional rôles and conditions on the dyadic system. The dyad itself has the task of integrating the personal need systems of two actors with two sets of culturally structured expectations derived from the rôle models of their families of origin. Here the culture of the society may provide an orientation to be aspired to as the common goal of the marriage, or to be resisted by the personal, now internalized, patterns of object-relations. These object-relations themselves are, for each partner, a system, an inner world, or society of loved and hated figures. On the stage of intimate dyadic relations these three levels can be seen to blend or clash, imposing greater or lesser frustrations (by the degree of fit or its lack) on the primary or archaic need-systems which their cultures had taught the bearers to structure more or less well into the patterns demanded by the wider social system. In marital stress the 'traumatic triggers' are the failed behavioural or rôle expectations, within a given sub-system or all of them. Failure of the need to have one's personality and its tacit assumption of values affirmed and complemented by another, from one's taste in church cantatas to one's sexual quirks, can activate regressive defensive movement as surely as neurological disintegration—and *sometimes as irreversibly* —but only in relation to one object.

The analysis of the localized, focused regression limited to a group of two is thus of great significance to psychological medicine as one of the social sciences. The regressive change in adult, civilized, educated people under our eyes when 'in the ring' of a Joint Interview; the display there of observable acting-out of mechanisms

314

predictable from the diagnostic phase, linked to known or ascertainable parental relationships; and last, but not least, its reversibility in a few interviews (not necessarily permanent); these leave little room for a simplicist mono-factorial neuro-psychiatric interpretation. We see interaction simultaneously as the magnetic field inducing the 'disorder' and also acting to limit it to within the equilibrium of two systems in constant interchange.

Most psychiatric reaction-types, except the severest and completest regression, appear transiently in relation to the love-object and in transference. Even my sparse case illustrations show how, in the limited arena of the marital conflict, the spouses can manifest clinically and interchangeably gross hysteric, depressive, paranoid or aggressive behaviour disorders which are not conspicuous in their extra-marital lives.

Marital conflict illustrates the dovetailing of love, power and self-preservatory needs in the smallest social unit, which is also a biological and 'natural' primary group. Its study is more revealing of inter-personal dynamics than a psychotherapeutic group, artificially assembled for an *ad hoc* purpose. The study can be extended to include the children or the social nexus of the married couple, according to the focus and interest of the researcher. The family is the 'end organ' on which social trends and economic pressures have their final impact, where culture patterns are transmitted and also subtly changed from generation to generation by the educative actions and goals of the parents responding to the 'Zeitgeist'. The family is the workshop that moulds the expression of biologically given needs of infants into the model recipes for impulse regulation of the parental culture patterns. This primary group experience produces not only idiosyncratic personalities, but also modal characters, typical of the culture.

The sub-systems I delineated at the end of Chapter VII as relating to marital interaction are thus useful concepts in analyzing the dynamics of other social systems. In my work on 'national character' (Dicks [3-6]) I applied a similar conceptual framework to an interpretation of how the micro-social culture of a family helps to condition macro-social political and ideological attitudes.

The theory of object relations bridges the intra-personal and the social systems of action. It enables us to visualize the constant two-way feed-back between personality and culture. In marital cases, it receives its most conspicuous confirmation. We literally hear at first hand how the two families of origin had transmitted the culture norms and social permissions and prohibitions to the intra-personal world, how the culture norms 'got inside', how their cultures clash at the inter-face between the spouses. We also observe how the indi-

315

vidual in living out his life re-externalises this 'inner population' back into his inter-personal and inter-group relations. His primary rôle-repertoire will determine his attitudes and his object-cathexes towards the secondary social percepts, through symbolizations and projective identifications. The culture climate of any social grouping or system is in the last analysis the product of the reprojections upon the extra-personal, shared social environment, of the internal object percep-tions and expectations of its members who had also shared many of the culture's learning experiences for life in that group. A culture saves conflict by providing a set of ready-made good and bad objects, of favoured and of rejected values and norms to be striven for. The most heavily charged heritage transmission seems to be by the parental unconscious that contains the grand-parental models, more powerful than conscious rebellion against them.

Marital rôle models are one such manifestation of the effect of group authority in moulding cultural *mores* and norms. The spouse is, as it were, a mediating figure between the inner and outer worlds. Hence we can see the malaise and stress in marriage as a particular circumscribed example of Freud's 'Discontent in Civilization'. Marriage contains within its boundaries the forces which in other configurations could become psychiatric illness or more diffuse anti-social behaviour. Regressive movement here finds a limited field of action, with the spouses acting for each other as 'lightning conduc-tors' and as projection figures for all the bad objects of their culture. Often, nonetheless, they manage to help each other to reconcile these conflicts within the framework of a close bond resembling the parent–child relationship, with its possibilities for maturation and integration of the two warring forces: primary needs and rôle models.

2. MARITAL STRESS AND CULTURE CHANGE

The major themes in marital stress situations follow closely the growing pains in the surrounding culture of which they are reflections. Thus, the lamented frequency of stress in the contemporary marriage can be seen as a testing ground in the re-appraisal of our society's dominance-subordination pattern. In Chapter III, I cited two abstract paradigms of this contest between primary needs and the social stereotype of male dominance and female under-privilegedness, the cultural components of which stand out clearly. In the case of the man we could substitute any other scapegoat figures for wife and children —such as lower classes, foreigners, pacifists, artists or what not. For the woman, male authority figures and 'meek' females might form such alternative figures. It is the deeper, unrecognized projective identifications with the scapegoats which create the insecurity and the need to deny the bond, to de-humanize the relationship with the projected part of oneself and repress the guilt of doing this. I see aspects of wider social conflict in these subordinate-superordinate mutual projections, with denial of equality of rights or status of the actors in their respective assigned rôles in the division of labour. The more severe the social polarization based on the social projections of these primary inner worlds, the more extreme the possible recourse to regressive, paranoid mutual perceptions in a micro-system or macrosystem. Recent history shows how the traditional power balance of our society has become undermined by the inter-action of the aggressive drives of the under-privileged with the guilt feelings of the powerholders. It becomes intelligible by the object relations concept of mutual projective identifications, seemingly polarized, but essentially one and the same. The trend which drives the young towards finding their identity and autonomy in every generation is paralleled by social processes towards re-integration of the split—whether in class mobility, or in the emancipation of women, or in the revolt for political freedom. Is not this movement the vector behind what we call 'social change'?

At the end of Chapter II, I expressed my optimistic interpretation of such events in social history. The content of 'history' is the struggle between the need systems of one set of actors and the opposition of another set of actors representing the defence of the socio-cultural *status quo*. This goes for the renaissance, for the revolt of the French middle class, for womens' right to the vote, or for any young Mary's fight to stay out till midnight, and to wear a mini-skirt.

The evolutionary process seems to me to have two major built-in vectors. One is the tendency towards growth, maturation and differen-tiation, as in the acorn's inherent power to become an oak tree. The other is the trend towards integration, the ordering of discreet or isolated systems into harmonious interaction, as shown in Coghill's and in Sherrington's famous work on the evolution of the Central Nervous System. Nature's 'invention' of sex-differentiation of one gamete or partner with suppression of the potentially available characteristics of the opposite sex, and the mating drive towards reunion with the contrastingly differentiated gamete or partner—is a model of the two basic trends in operation. If there were not the differentiation by maturation towards the capacity to mate, there would be no drive towards the new integrate—the mating dyad—whether thought of as the resultant biological zygote or as the new social unit. It is when the polarized, even antagonistically differentiated, dynamic systems dovetail and produce a synergism of their energy resources that integration ('resolution of conflict') occurs. Intra-personally, this

317

happens not only in child ·development but also observably in a successful analysis. Previously split antithetical object-relations flow together in a new synthesis, with strengthening of the central ego and the disappearance of projected threats from the person's world of external objects. He can now unfold his powers, no longer sabotaged by the archaic forces of former, infantile safety-mechanisms, which also distorted his world image.

The advent of psycho-analysis and the social sciences can be regarded as necessary cognitive tools to aid the evolutionary march of human beings towards the goal of personal differentiation and integration: to be themselves and to belong together. These disciplines are part of the emerging need to understand and control more of ourselves as social change breaks up the old sanctions and traditional norms in regard to piety and conformity towards group authority. To be sure, this advance is patchy and uneven, full of glaring contradictions. The Russian revolution, while savagely overthrowing a highly 'polarized' traditional social system swung to the opposite pole, by initially sweeping away matrimonial restrictions. Within a decade or so, we witnessed a great face-about, not only towards a new authoritarianism, but more specifically towards a return to almost nineteenth-century mores and norms of family regulation. Radical and conservative forces both contribute to the graph of development in the personality and in social processes.

What, then, is the possible evolutionary meaning of the widespread malaise in our society's marital and family life? I would tend to regard it as a manifestation of the pain and maladaptation inseparable from growth towards a higher level of differentiation/ integration. I am helped in this viewpoint by J. C. Flugel's thoughts on the criteria of moral progress.[7] The full list of these interdependent categories, can be found in Chapter XVI of his book. Here I select some that are especially relevant to my theme. (1) From Egocentricity to Sociality, (2) From Unconscious to Conscious, (3) From Moral Inhibition to Spontaneous 'goodness', (4) From Fear to Security, (5) From Heteronomy to Autonomy, (6) From Orectic [Emotional-moral—H.V.D.] Judgment to Cognitive (Psychological) Judgment. Flugel applies these to both individual and social development. It is a movement from primitive, or infantile object-relations towards a reality perception of one's own and one's society's mutual relations and rôles. At one level this was what I described as the Klein-Fairbairn progression from the schizoid-paranoid to the 'whole object' stages of a child's personality growth.

Another model I like is that suggested to me by my late friend, G. R. Hargreaves. It is the evolutionary change from the external skeleton or carapace, such as that of molluscs and arthropods, to the internal skeleton of the vertebrates. The analogous development in social relations is still new and precarious—a few hundred years. The tight control of man's immaturity by the external skeleton of authoritarian, parental institutions and sanctions, secular and religious, is in dialectical conflict with the urge towards differentiation and free assent, both inside and outside the individual, as I tried to show in Chapters II and III. It is even necessary for there to be this resistance of the tutelary, guardian forces of the *status quo*, as a necessary brake regulating the tolerable speed of change. All this has a bearing on how we may assess the stresses in marital and sexual mores.

What is happening in the field of marital relations is not only an abrogation of old values, but an insistence on the autonomous right to try the new values of free covenants, freely maintained. The contemporary emphasis in marriage as I defined it (see Chapter I) is on the 'voluntary agreement to satisfy the emotional, biological, etc., needs of each other', to the detriment of the traditional mores and social coercion implied in the legal contract. The current mores declare that the sanctity of the bond is in what is felt inside, not what people outside say one should feel. If there is no sanctity, then sex is a passing incident. What we are witnessing is, I think, the evolutionary trend towards greater integrity and a more autonomous interpretation of freely chosen and continued marital allegiances between persons. These are required to be capable of healing the split between differentiated needs and historically more infantile conformity with highly ambivalent 'authority' objects. The pressure is towards 'spontaneous goodness' away from moral inhibition, to use Flugel's term. This is the new value. Such big trends take time to work through. Regression is a prelude to new integration. As already mentioned, the revolution in acknowledged social status of women, and all it means, is barely fifty years old. That things go wrong when a new integrate or model is being evolved is not surprising, though it it as alarming as any other revolution. It is interesting to note the conflict between these trends reflected in the current search by the legal and religious guardians of social and moral values for new formulations that shall incorporate this alarming value change into the code. If it can be accepted that we live on the unconscious of our grandparent generation which our parents transmitted as our cultural heritage, then it may take a hundred years from now before the new values will be worked into established social norms. These are unlikely to be as rigid as the medieval 'exoskeleton' that contained our social and marital stability. With optimism we may hope for a system which will be more flexible because it recognizes the instability of biological and social equilibria in growth processes. We may see it resting more on assent than on guilt or shame-determined conformity.

The helping professions will certainly need all the insight about primary love and object seeking, about the nature of ambivalence and its maturation, and about the effects of its frustration, if we are to take a helpful part in steering these changes. Our knowledge will have to be better value than what it replaces: the older idealist and moralist systems built upon the archaic projections of ambivalence into a dualistic 'polarized' world-image. In putting forward my conceptual framework of marital theory and practice I have endeavoured to illustrate one facet of this mediation or catalysis of a natural growth process striving towards greater differentiation and coalescence—in this case of the two sexes, the very symbols of dualism and the severance of parts that are in need of union. Our mediating function has many other facets at micro- and macro-level, from individual child psychotherapy to the essays in controlled social change in industry and other large systems.

3. IMPLICATIONS OF THE NEW MODEL
FOR HEALTH SERVICE POLICY

The consequences of my position in the field of human interaction involve advocacy of new policies. While aware that I have many allies, I also know that proposals of major changes in practice, institutional development and relevant training of personnel, will arouse the criticism and resistance in many among the present psychiatric élite, in many physicians and scientists who are investing their sincere efforts in the substantiation of neuro-physiological, genetic and biochemical hypotheses and/or pharmacological correctives for the phenomena which, as I have here argued, belong mainly to the sphere of object-relations and inter-personal dynamics. The resistance to full acceptance of 'Sullivanian' psychiatry has been one of the main troubles with developing appropriate institutions and therapeutic models for the early recognition and relief of neurotic disequilibria. Neither the staffs nor the built milieux have become available, largely because the hitherto prevailing concept of mental illness rests on the genetic, organic theory. Except in the structure of Child Guidance units and a few 'deviant' models, such as the Tavistock Clinic and the Cassel Hospital, the point of view and the time and staff allotments for out-patient or in-patient services are such as to exclude the proper attention, let alone the understanding, to the meaning of inter-personal and object-relational factors in mental stress. 'Turn-over' of cases—so beloved by administrators as proof of 'activity'—e.g. 10–20 out-patients per doctor session, has reduced much of this work to the equivalent of general-practitioner 'surgeries'. It is then an obvious advantage to justify this practice by an appropriate theory which ignores, or even rejects most of the corpus of knowledge accumulated by the use of dynamic (psychoanalytic and related) concepts and methods and the people using them. The anti-dynamic, organic theory was already castigated by the late Bernard Hart,[8] when he said that 'the quaint notions of the Victorian philosophers concerning the reality of nervous energy and the futility of ideas are not entirely extinct even in the medicine of today'. The applications of psycho-analytic and related theories to practice appropriate to institutions and centres dealing with large populations has not been helped by an analogous culture lag in the analytic schools. In their dread of tampering with Freud's original model of therapy and the high aims of analysis as the one road to radical transformation of the personality, analytic training and technique have tended to stress the 'chair-couch' tandem of the thorough, intensive treatment by the full analytic procedure. This fundamentalism has resulted in a marked mistrust of clinical methods that fall short of their desideratum because they 'only scratch the surface'. We have, therefore, had the undesirable situation that the National Health Service psychiatric clinics have been staffed by people with little or no training in analysis. The skilled analysts, often not medically so well qualified in the eyes of the organicist psychiatric élite, have been driven to the self-perpetuating cycle of private intensive analytic practice, with few appointments in the public health services. It is almost a collusive situation. The public need is just the other way round. It is in the flexible adaptations of psycho-dynamic concepts to economically manageable intensities of psychotherapy and to preventive work that the most skilled and versatile analytic contributions are required. Such versatility is not, at present, acquired in psycho-analytic training, but only in the out-patient and community health services.

Between the extreme views of the organic-chemical schools on the one hand, who would, if logical, treat even marital and similar interaction problems by drugs or E.C.T., and the 'old Vienna' or 'old Zurich' schools* of analysts on the other hand, who would have every disturbed couple undergo full separate analysis, there are, fortunately, emerging new models of service. I have alluded to several such models in Chapter XII, as well as offering the one that has grown out of Mary Luff's and my own endeavour in this volume.

---

* Geoffrey Goper has aptly commented on aspects of this 'cultural conserve' in his Chapter in *Psycho-analysis Observed* (Charles Rycroft (Ed.), Constable & Co. 1966).

(a) *The place of Marital Services in Mental Health provisions*

How, then, on a nation-wide scale, can we hope to meet the demands for diagnosis, and especially therapy, in the field of marital stress that radiates its destructive influence on the next generation, and into the general social connections of the affected parties? Are we to proliferate, at great cost, new centres *sui generis*, or can we incorporate the new approach and consequential skills into existing provisions? I am not by nature a social planner or administration builder and therefore answer my own questions in a very tentative spirit.

Institutions either remain static and faithful to the intentions of their creators, or they accept and use innovation within their sanctioned functions. It is the scope and the social approbation they give to the free working of new ideas and skills of their technical staffs which matter. Society has provided and sanctions medical services that could, if they allowed it, be adapted for the marital work I have described. There exist on the Statute books in Britain general practitioner services, psychiatric hospitals and clinics (now tending towards close linkage with general hospitals). There exist, also, provisions for extended community care for mental health, including child guidance, well-baby clinics and domiciliary nursing and social work, to name the most relevant. The Family Planning Association, originally founded by voluntary effort for another, though related, purpose, is the one medically operated body alert to the psychological problems underlying a proportion of their clientele's troubles with contraception and infertility, and is moving into medical marriage therapy. It promises to render good service to those many couples whose presenting symptoms are sex failure.

In the United States about whose marital services I only know what the vanguard in the field has published, the situation seems similar to Britain. It is capable of more active growth because the teachers in psychological medicine and its related disciplines have had less difficulty in embodying psycho-dynamic concepts into their thinking and training—much to the ill-tempered chagrin of opponents on both sides of the Atlantic. As in Britain, the impetus for creating marriage therapy seems to have come from the 'laity', not from Medicine. Thus, Dr. Nash Herndon, in his foreword to a book, to which I am a contributor, writes[9]

It is unfortunate that most physicians have largely ignored the medical implications of marital conflict . . . Most physicians simply accept the depressing statistics on the rates of illegitimate pregnancies, forced marriages and divorces as social problems, without considering that perhaps the medical profession has some

322

obligation for prevention of such personal disasters . . . (pp. vii and viii).

Little does it behove us, therefore, to decry or criticise the initiatives of the 'amateurs'—clergy, social workers and public-spirited citizens —who have taken up the campaign which our profession—and that includes psychiatrists—had neither vision nor the breadth to see as its own, as relevant to many problems of mental, psycho-somatic and social ill-health. With the exception of the Tavistock Clinic and Institute, such 'lay' counselling has been nearly all that the population of this island could turn to, however willing and even wealthy. In the absence of adequate professional research and development which affect training of future personnel, the efforts of these voluntary agencies themselves have necessarily remained at a relatively static level of competence. But these pioneering efforts can, as A.T.M. Wilson saw,[10] only be regarded as stop-gaps that have held the line until the professionals could replace them. And the professionals are now *potentially* able to make this proper medical sphere their own, because at least models for conceptual approach, assessment and therapies have been created.

The implementation of marital diagnostic and therapeutic services will be as slow or as fast as personnel can be, first, persuaded of the importance and feasibility of the techniques and their underlying rationale to incorporate them, and then trained, in their clinical scope. With the help of the staffs of the Tavistock Clinic and Institute, the Probation services in Britain have so far advanced their training and skills that their professionalization of marital conciliation is now possible. This service has its own specialist tutors and supervisors from among their members who have undergone advanced training at the Tavistock. There is thus a good precedent which doctors and social workers could emulate. Of necessity the Probation service, with its relation to the judicial system and a public fantasy image to match, is likely for a long time to have to deal with late acting-out stages. Unless this image and rôle can be modified this fine Service is unlikely to become the 'general' service. The central mass of marital work requires settings less connected in fantasy with crime and punishment, and more with mental health agencies directed to family life. This suggests locations within the community ('public') health services. I do not mean by this places where just only ascertainment of the existence of marital stress is made as, for example, in the case of mental subnormality. The need is for skilled treatment which creates confidence in potential clients. I have in mind the consolidation, now much under discussion, of many as yet dissociated medico-social *treatment services* under the joint aegis of Regional Hospital

Boards and local authorities, to whom, in the United Kingdom, the mental health of their areas has been confided. Some of us here have, for many years, seen the future of preventive and early treatment services in the growth of the comprehensive 'family health centre', linked to the psychiatric services, to family practitioners and to the already existing public health programmes of domiciliary visiting, school and mother and infant welfare and including child guidance in its most developed form. Here family stresses of the parental relationship, and of the child's or adolescent's home, school and work life could be handled by integrated staffs in whatever form they present. The early treatment of marital stress before it becomes chronic conflict is an important additional preventive measure against the next generation's liability to neurosis, character disorders and repetition of marriage difficulties. These centres could also be a place where, as in Prague, certain ex-hospital patients, with a marital stress factor preventing full rehabilitation, would be referred.

Howells[11] has described his own model at Ipswich with admirable clarity and conciseness. For some time to come clinics based on the psychiatric in-patient hospital are likely to appear to those with marital or family stress as too forbidding despite all the educational work that has begun to change that image. The Family Health centres, where mothers bring their well babies, where the family doctor and the public health nurse are trusted figures, carry much less fantasy threat to the average person. It is for similar reasons that a proportion of couples prefer to take their marital problems to non-medical and non-psychiatric sources of help. This would seem to point to the wisdom of maintaining agencies such as the F.D.B. in which the psychiatric-medical component is unobtrusive. The same professional groups, then, who are now doing child guidance, social case work and psychiatric follow-up work in the community services, are the obvious people to carry the new functions—and doubtless there will have to be more of them. But a change of focus on interaction can unify many apparently separate tasks. With the training aspect I shall concern myself in the next section. The professional workers who will be engaged in family and marital therapy will require the supervision of psychotherapeutic, probably largely psycho-analytically qualified, consultants, who are, at the time of writing, slowly becoming recognized as specialists in their own right within psychiatry. The model for this work has been described, e.g. by Pincus, et al.[12] and by Sutherland.[13,14] Such consultants are likely to be drawn to begin with from more specialized centres which must also exist as the bases for trainin and research. They should, themselves, have the highest skills and xperience in this developing field. It is the supply and training of tuese future experts that chiefly concerns me. For the more sophisticated section of our population, well informed and critical, the best professionalism will be needed. These are the clients who cannot be fobbed off with drugs or psychiatric platitudes delivered *de haut en bas*, in this as in other matters of mental ill-health. They will care less whether their family therapist is medically qualified and an F.R.C.P. than whether he can help them by his methods. These valuable but often demanding citizens in trouble will be among the clientele of future specialist centres in the desert of qualified psychotherapeutic help for them which is, with few exceptions, the whole of Britain outside London, and, I would guess, much of the United States outside certain cities. No British teaching hospital or professorial department of psychiatry (except Aberdeen as I write) has, to my knowledge, yet begun to teach and offer marital treatment. The lack of psychotherapeutic training among consultants in general and even in child psychiatry in Britain has had the consequence that this skill is played down by many senior psychiatrists as being a kind of second-class activity—like massage—to be delegated to 'ancillaries', usually psychiatric social workers. Their psychiatric chiefs are—let us face it—incompetent to supervise their work at technical level, only empowered to criticize or praise it. But this also is a culture lag which the younger generations can remedy by their insistence that training and institutional planning shall meet the needs of the greater part of mental stress, and not, as hitherto, be centred on the numerically smaller, if more obvious, challenge of psychosis. Howells's point on this topic is well taken (op. cit., p. 7).

It is my contention that the treatment of individuals 'in vacuo' by whatever method of in-patient or out-patient handling, is an obsolescent concept. Unless we are dealing with an isolate, the meaningful unit of therapeutic action is the presenting individual's primary group: parents and siblings, spouse and children, sometimes also the work group. If this be granted, then the approach to diagnosis and therapy in large areas of psychiatry demands appropriate new techniques for analyzing such interpersonal networks which all intending psychiatrists and psychotherapists (including analysts) should possess. I will go so far as to assert that they do not know what opportunities for rapid insight and critically decisive help they are missing daily in their work by not having this conceptual and operational equipment.

Without the prior training and emergence into senior medical responsibility of psychiatrists and psychotherapists so trained and capable of becoming the teachers, there is little point in decreeing and crash-programming a large multiplication of the sort of service I have envisaged. Such proliferation on the lines of 'everybody's doing it now' would be as A. T. M. Wilson (loc. cit.) pointed out, a hollow sham. People not already versed in psycho-dynamic concepts and methods cannot suddenly undertake to apply these 'from the book' either in practice, or in teaching and supervising others.

(b) *Training of Therapists*

It is obvious that adequate conceptual tools and the personal skills to apply them are the first essential requirements. These can be effective in dingy premises whereas incompetence in gleaming clinical palaces can only be camouflaged temporarily by high medical prestige. It is time that the skills and the prestige coincided. I shall not repeat the prescriptions for detailed training courses proposed by highly qualified bodies and individuals for this or that aspect of psycho-therapeutic and social work, which are in practice indivisible and continuous. I agree with all those who, like A. T. M. Wilson, have been arguing and pleading for the broadest holistic training with many shared teaching events for doctor, social worker, clinical psychologist and nurse on a psycho-dynamic basis. Training, like the orientation of research, must be in terms of problems that are significant to human beings in their search for unfoldment and belonging. This must include the students' own capacities and problems in meeting stress and ambivalence—their own growth. Holistic concepts do not only cover psycho-somatic unity. They also refer to the continuity between child and adult; between the 'geological layers' formed intra-personally in the course of transition from the one to the other and the relation between culture and personality.

I here only want to stress the *additional* training needed for the skills in handling marital interaction problems, after the above groundwork is done. This again points to the need for special institutes of advanced studies and research in Family Psychiatry, where the future specialists can receive their education in this field and to whom they can turn for supervision and consultation on difficult problems. Three such institutes for Britain would be sufficient: one of them already exists but without teaching status. I hold that while it is optimally in the tradition of *medical responsibility* for the leaders of this training to be physicians (psychiatrists), this is not *technically* essential. Dynamic psychiatry owes much, in creative thought and in training to the 'non-medicals': Anna Freud, Melanie Klein, J. C. Flugel, Susan Isaacs, Jean Piaget, Erik Erikson, to mention but a few of a distinguished band. In some respects clinical psychologists and psychiatric social workers have because of more relevant education less medical school culture lag to catch up when turning to the field of psychotherapy and group relations. In the current climate of psychiatry in Britain, it is still a considerable risk to his career for a bright young aspirant to be identified as a psycho-analyst. But even among such we cannot assume fitness to turn to marital work without additional training. The sequence of clinical experience such doctors regularly undergo, if they also hold posts in the hospital service, is from intensive *personal* analysis in the one-to-one relationship to the much diluted, somewhat imprecise, and highly anxiety-provoking experience of superficial out-patient counselling. The anxiety may reach a new level with assignment to therapeutic groups. In both these situations the *individual* remains the focus of treatment, even if the group, sociologically, has inter-action study devoted to it.

It is a moot point whether the future consultant psychotherapist in training should first gain some mastery of general group dynamics by supervised treatment of small groups of neurotic patients, and then proceed to study and therapy of married couples in distress, or the other way round. The former is the pattern of historical develop-ment. The latter is a more logical step in view of the closeness of the phenomena of marital interaction to what has already been experi-enced in the graduate's own analytic training and in the constant references of his individual patients to significant objects in their past and present. In the training programme of the Tavistock Clinic the sequence has been to familiarize the future specialist with the feel of groups, and then, while he continues with group therapy, to add the marital field.

I have already, in reviewing my own changes of technique in Chapters X and XI, mentioned the desirability of gaining experience of marital tensions in the following progression: first the trainee is partnered by an experienced marriage therapist, each receiving and investigating one spouse separately, and so continuing treating several couples in individual sessions. The co-ordination is done by frequent and detailed conferencing outside the therapeutic sessions. The skilled partner is, or can be, the learner's supervisor. Next, the trainee takes part, with his 'senior' partner, in joint diagnostic inter-views, also in the occasional therapeutic joint interviews that occur during mainly separate therapy. The third stage is similarly partnered foursome therapy, in which post-interview conferencing is particularly vivid and meaningful. A fourth stage is the partnership of two trainees, now already having some case experience, both in individual and in joint handling of the diagnostic and therapeutic situations. Frequent supervision by a senior marital therapist, optimally after every weekly interview with the couples, becomes now especially valuable.

For the development of the overall grasp of the dynamics of a given case, the regular two-hour case conference as a more formal

327

teaching event, attended by the trainees as well as the senior staff, is a good method. The trainees here have to present synoptic accounts of the main vectors, psycho-pathological as well as social, diagnosed as underlying a given clinical picture. These accounts are criticized, questioned and illuminated by other members of the seminar, junior and senior. Selected tape-recordings of key sessions or moments of interest can be played and discussed. At such Case Conferences or seminars the senior staff members should, from time to time, similarly present their cases, and be subjected to open, critical discussion with their students and each other. There should also be overlap and two-way traffic between the teams concerned with marital therapy as their primary task and the teams mainly handling child and adolescent disturbances, and using joint family or parent interviews. After some considerable experience in these ways the trainee may now wish to try single handling of both partners in individual or joint interviews. Supervision, i.e. detailed discussion and ventilation of counter-transference anxieties and difficulties after every meeting with the patients, continues. It is desirable that this, say, four-year period of psychotherapeutic training should be devoted not only to marital work, but cover many other aspects. The supervisors should be changed from time to time. This will give the trainee bases for comparison of individual variations in approach and technique.

I have written as if this kind of intensive training for family and marital interaction techniques were to be confined to the medical profession. Of course, the same programme is entirely suitable for the other disciplines in our field. Some of the finest senior therapists in this area are psychiatric social workers or clinical psychologists by basic training. I wrote of psychiatrists because, in general, their education in these skills is largely non-existent before coming to post-postgraduate training, and they should no longer suffer the ignominy, however disguised by status, of envying their 'ancillaries' superior technical know-how.

(c) *Research*

Scattered through the preceding pages have been references to the need for systematic research—an activity which follows the setting up of institutional and operational models, and is necessary to their proper growth. Such a research component should be built-in and budgeted for in skilled personnel and time in the kind of special institute here envisaged. Nevitt Sanford[15] has pleaded for the setting up of institutes '. . . for the study of human problems . . . defined in terms of their human significance rather than any existing academic speciality; for example alienation and demoralization of youth;

328

freedom and authority . . .' etc. Scientists, he claims, are very chary about envisaging large, interdisciplinary studies. As the result they are apt to stick closely to the patterns of the physical sciences in which human beings are not involved, or in which they can treat them as undifferentiated units. This is actually bad science when applied to living beings.

Marriage and the family is just such a large scale human problem. There is no reason why an assemblage of the relevant skills and interests which is given the necessary means, should not achieve the same kind of research results that Sanford and his co-workers accomplished in their chosen area of authority and freedom, widely known as the study of the Authoritarian Personality.[16] It is in the borderland between academic disciplines that the urgent human problems are often hidden. We obviously cannot study the 'whole condition of mankind' in one giant programme. In study of the primary, nuclear family group, however, we are likely to make an immense contribution to the understanding of the processes on which I speculated in the earlier sections of this Chapter. The wedding of dynamic psychiatry, clinical and social psychology and social science with their statistical ancillaries could in concert cover some or all of the following, and many projects not here envisaged, *in the course of therapy.*

(i) *Clinical projects:* Here I want only briefly to refer to the kind of proposals which my colleagues and I had hoped to do if time and money had been available. To most of them I have referred in the relevant contexts: classification; comparative studies on couples who consult us with the kinds who do not, i.e. the 'normal' families and the grossly disturbed who go to divorce; and also the whole problem of validation and follow-up results in the treated as contrasted with those merely assessed.

For a start, a research team might well apply more rigorous methods of testing the efficacy of its own clinical services, diagnostic and therapeutic. It could, similarly, go into comparisons of the results of other marital clinics, on the obvious variables of man-hours, techniques, frequency and length of contact with patients and so on. Such a study ought to be a preliminary to large scale new institutional development. The validity of my own and other people's hypotheses would be an important research task, since methods and training are related to basic concepts and require different instruments to validate them, and different places to apply them in.

Statistical and epidemiological expertise is a necessary check on the generalizations of analytic and similar insights even on large numbers such as I have argued from. The design and validation of clinico-psychological techniques by such methods, and the subsequent use of such validated instruments on clinical research all hang together. Contrariwise, there is the need for the psycho-dynamically skilled and experienced to supply the meaningful variables which are often woefully lacking in large scale epidemiological studies, and which alone give them status above mere accumulations of demographic data. As clinicians we want to know what kind of events inside and outside people make them behave in certain ways, and what forces make some of them unable, others able to benefit from the help proffered. From such large-scale study by the combined skills of analysts and sociologists I would look for a rich harvest of criteria with which to assess the significance of social and cultural factors in the shaping of the intra-psychic events determining mate-choice, the use and failure of defence mechanisms and the appearance of regression in marital and family interaction.

(ii) *Sociological projects:* While to my mind there can never be a clear demarcation between clinical and sociological terrain, the use of the clinical situation for clarifying wider issues is a distinct facet of such studies as I hopefully visualize a specialized multi-professional team could undertake. Here I have in mind trans-cultural studies such as Florence Kluckhohn and John F. Spiegel have pioneered[17] in our area. As they have shown, different value systems and rôle ascriptions to marital behaviour result in different solutions to conflict. But perhaps the most valuable function of serious research would be to replace present conjecture and 'orectic' judgments by rational assessments of the broad trends in societies in a maturational or in a regressive direction of emotional life and sexual mores, as Flugel defined these.

(iii) *Methodology:* When discussing the difficulties even of clinical follow-up techniques, I alluded to the need for finding ways into sampling at depth of populations whom we were not asked to help but whom we needed both as 'controls' and as important sources of new medico-social knowledge. Here, Elizabeth Bott[18] and J. H. Robb[19] need to be studied for their contribution to methodology, essentially antropological, which can achieve acceptance of observers in the 'normal' family. It would be a methodological breakthrough to gain a comparable position *vis-à-vis* our 'divorce court population' and similar inaccessible carriers of the severest degrees of conflict I have written about. This is only one aspect of devising ways of gaining knowledge without offending the canons of respect for the person. Another is the integration of the skills and concepts of the various disciplines concerned into a consistent socio-technical unit. This is in itself a problem in interactional dynamics and model-making, and no one should underestimate the difficulties. In our scientific culture of today clinical and psychoanalytic insight must ultimately come to be validated or corrected by rigorous tests of significance, and the insight must be so formulated in working hypotheses that such tests can be applied to them in manageable size projects. Here, indeed, is a need for a marriage between the maternal 'expressive' skills of the depth-psychotherapist and the 'paternal', 'instrumental' rationality of the skilled research-designer. Such marriages inside a single human being are the exception. They are infrequent even in our psychiatric and sociological institutions. I fervently hope that this potentially epoch-making union can be effected by the provision of a handsome dowry from the M.R.C. or other wealthy sponsoring parent.

4. SOME CONCLUDING REFLECTIONS

It is not only in the Western world that the technological revolution has brought about great changes from the traditional order and is threatening the destruction of the old certainties of marital and family authority. Dan Lerner[20] in his study of Middle Eastern society, describes some aspects of these vast and rapid events with their disruptive effect on kinship systems and culture patterns much more compelling and less individualistic than ours. Lerner and David Riesman, who writes the introduction to his book, emphasize the immense potential conflict and hazard in introducing the externals of socio-technical innovation in newly 'developing' countries, without changing present intra-familial patterns. The changes may indeed suffer shipwreck on the culture-lag of unsurmounted unconscious oedipal rivalries, jealousies and maternal possessiveness in their emancipating generation now required to make very sudden breaks in cultural continuity, to 'Westernize' in the technical disciplines, live in industrial centres, trying to bridge an immense gap between the educational and mental horizons of the young men and their sisters who scarcely share this development. The stresses in inter-sexual adaptation at this tempo will be of an order of magnitude which should alarm the few social agencies and mental health experts available to study this problem before it reaches full spate, and by comparison with which our own problems of sexual and cultural revolt may come to look like a storm in a teacup. Our change since the Renaissance has been slower, more organic and based on a value system more consistent with individual responsibility, the notion of the worth of the person and the desirability of autonomous development. Can we hope that the new emerging societies will catch up with us and nonetheless avoid our painful growth by extensive use of the lessons the Western behavioural sciences could teach? We ourselves are none too sure of where we should aim, so we may be too late to help the newly industrializing countries by example and theory.

What was accomplished by Europeans over the centuries since the Renaissance allowed men to try the power and adventure of using their mind fully, has not yet fully occurred outside our Western world. But the Renaissance of women's full exploration of their potentialities has hardly begun. True, our women have come out of the seclusion that is elsewhere symbolized by veiling and *purdah*. But have we got much beyond the phase of feminist revolt against the man-made split between anti-libidinal and libidinal female images—the frigid good woman and the warm beckoning harlot, with their antagonistic rôles in the balance of sexual economics? And the hidden, mother-tied homosexuality behind the so-admired masculine virtues with their ramifications in every sphere where men need to co-operate rationally but mostly compete jealously and paranoidally? Need we really deplore the present ferment?

Is not the current demand for sexual autonomy and equality an attempt, a crude beginning of the fusion between the good and the sexual woman, and an essay in the greater tolerance of ambivalence and 'ugliness' than the receding world of double standards knew? And are not our deprecated young non-heroes turning on the man-of-iron values that produced totalitarianisms, those monstrosities of male savagery, debunking them with jazz, ridicule and still rather shocking assertion of the primacy of libido, of Eros over Mars? These, at least, are not the boys who are likely to blow up the world with H-bombs.

I will quote one last clinical example to make this point. This was not a patient, but a loyal young sailor of Hitler's navy, whom I interviewed in 1943.

> After telling me how his parents had brought him up too softly, he related a youthful visit across the Rhine to Strassburg. 'There were all these slouching young fellows with long hair, with their arms round girls, idling their Sunday away. I felt a pang as I recalled our Führer's motto for us German lads: "Tough as leather, hard as Krupp steel, fleet as a greyhound!" How weak of me to envy those French boys! Yes—I was weak, I must curb my animal spirits.' And he forthwith volunteered for service of his Fatherland. 'I joined the Service where I would have this weak will beaten, where I would be hammered into a man. We are a proud cultural nation like Sparta. The Armed Forces are our school—without it we would be weak and divided.'[21]

To me the whole pathos of Christian history of values lies in this boy's story. There, across the river, was the Devil and the temptation of St. Anthony. He flees to become a man of iron, to sacrifice his identity in a great power machine, his hair well cut! Is this what our young men should be doing?

To the pious guardians of the medieval order also the resurrection of the pagan world and its sensual beauty was no renaissance but the coming of the Anti-Christ, the dissolution of all values and restraints. One of its effects was the full-scale collective paranoia of the witch-hunts to counter the threat of woman's power to control men's libido. The battle has fluctuated since then roughly in centuries of libidinal and anti-libidinal predominance, at least in England, but the musty odour of St. Paul and St. Augustine of Hippo has lessened progressively as we have shed the constricting carapace of the medieval world view and let in the fresher air of natural science—even on the mysterious ways in which mankind is always trying to heal the inexorable division into two that need to unite to create new life. Eros, for all his tricks and disreputable goings on, is at least the God of Love.

REFERENCES

1. SAGER, CLIFFORD J. (1966) 'The Development of Marriage Therapy: A Historical Review' *Amer. J. Orthopsychiat. 36*, 3, pp. 458-67.
2. PARSONS, TALCOTT, and SHILS, E. A. (eds.) 1951 *Toward a General Theory of Action*, Cambridge, Mass: Harvard University Press.
3. DICKS, H. V. (1950) 'Personality Traits and National Socialist Ideology' *Hum. Rel. 3*, pp. 111-54.
4. DICKS, H. V. (1952) 'Observations on Contemporary Russian Behaviour', ibid. 5, pp. 111-75.
5. DICKS, H. V. (1960) 'Some Notes on Russian National Character' in Black, C. E. (ed.) *The Transformation of Russian Society*. Cambridge, Mass: Harvard Univ. Press.
6. DICKS, H. V. (1966) 'Intra-Personal Conflict and the Authoritarian Character' in De Reuck, A. and Knight, J. (eds.) *Conflict in Society*. A CIBA Symposium. London: Churchill.
7. FLUGEL, J. C. (1945) *Men, Morals and Society*, London: Duckworth.
8. HART, BERNARD (1929) *Psychopathology*. Cambridge University Press, p. 25.
9. HERNDON, C. N. (1964) Foreword to Nash, E. M. Jessner, L. & Abse, D. W. (eds.) *Marriage Counseling in Medical Practice*. Chapel Hill, Univ. of N. Carolina Press.
10. WILSON, A. T. M. (1949) 'Reflections and Suggestions on the Prevention and Treatment of Marital Problems' *Hum. Rel. 2*, No. 3, pp. 233-51.
11. HOWELLS, J. G. (1963) *Family Psychiatry*. Edinburgh and London: Oliver and Boyd.
12. PINCUS, L. (ed.) 1960) *Marriage: Studies in Emotional Conflict and Growth*. London: Methuen.

13. SUTHERLAND, J. D. (1952) 'Psychological Medicine and the National Health Service'. *Brit. J. Med. Psychol. 25*, pp. 71–85.
14. SUTHERLAND, J. D. (1956) Chap. 'Psychotherapy and Social Casework' in Goldberg, E. M. et al. (eds.) *The Boundaries of Casework*. London: A.P.S.W., pp. 22–5.
15. SANFORD, NEVITT (1964) In *Saturday Review*, Jan. 18th.
16. ADORNO, T. W., FRENKEL-BRUNSWIK, E., LEVINSON, D. J. and SANFORD, N. (1950) *The Authoritarian Personality*. New York: Harper.
17. KLUCKHOHN, F. and SPIEGEL, J. (1954) op. cit.
18. BOTT, ELIZ. (1957) op. cit.
19. ROBB, J. H. (1953): 'Clinical Studies in Marriage and the Family, IV. "Experiences with Ordinary Families" ' *Brit. J. Med. Psychol. 26*, pp. 215–21.
20. LERNER, D. (1958) *The Passing of Traditional Society*, Glencoe, Ill.: The Free Press.
21. DICKS, Lt.-Col. H. V. (1944) *The Psychological Foundations of the Wehrmacht*. Restricted. Research Memo No. 11/O2/9A., Directorate of Army Psychiatry. War Office.

Appendix I

(Part of SOPT as specimen.)

Name......................

Please consider how well the following words describe your IDEAL SELF, and indicate as follows:

Please put a ring round ++ if the word fits *very well*
                          + if the word fits *fairly well*
                          − if the word fits *hardly at all*
                         −− if the word fits *not at all*

hard-working	++	+	−	−−
couldn't care less	++	+	−	−−
understanding	++	+	−	−−
frivolous	++	+	−	−−
generous	++	+	−	−−
spiteful	++	+	−	−−
high-minded	++	+	−	−−
indulgent	++	+	−	−−
unselfish	++	+	−	−−
shallow	++	+	−	−−
calm and confident	++	+	−	−−
artificial	++	+	−	−−
courageous	++	+	−	−−
careful	++	+	−	−−
emotional	++	+	−	−−
cold	++	+	−	−−
spoilt	++	+	−	−−
cruel	++	+	−	−−
lazy	++	+	−	−−
tender	++	+	−	−−
irritable	++	+	−	−−
steady	++	+	−	−−
prudish	++	+	−	−−
loving	++	+	−	−−
possessive	++	+	−	−−
outgoing	++	+	−	−−
smug and self-satisfied	++	+	−	−−
comfortable and cosy	++	+	−	−−
tactful	++	+	−	−−

335

	++	+	−	−−
dull and stolid	++	+	−	−−
messy	++	+	−	−−
easy-going	++	+	−	−−
self-reliant	++	+	−	−−
self-centred	++	+	−	−−
animal lover	++	+	−	−−
honourable	++	+	−	−−
intelligent	++	+	−	−−
warm-hearted	++	+	−	−−
good manager	++	+	−	−−
sociable	++	+	−	−−
happy-go-lucky	++	+	−	−−
enterprising and go-ahead	++	+	−	−−
detached	++	+	−	−−
good-natured	++	+	−	−−
obstinate	++	+	−	−−
religious	++	+	−	−−
indecisive	++	+	−	−−
manly	++	+	−	−−
womanly	++	+	−	−−
staid and sober	++	+	−	−−
lively	++	+	−	−−
clean	++	+	−	−−
strict	++	+	−	−−
self-controlled	++	+	−	−−
genuine	++	+	−	−−
adventurous	++	+	−	−−
slack	++	+	−	−−
fussy	++	+	−	−−
temperamental	++	+	−	−−
ambitious	++	+	−	−−
nervous	++	+	−	−−
envious	++	+	−	−−
vital	++	+	−	−−
hard	++	+	−	−−
overbearing	++	+	−	−−
suspicious	++	+	−	−−
co-operative	++	+	−	−−
slow and deliberate	++	+	−	−−
romantic	++	+	−	−−
severe	++	+	−	−−
humourless	++	+	−	−−
dreamy	++	+	−	−−
sensitive	++	+	−	−−
vigourous	++	+	−	−−
particular	++	+	−	−−
even-tempered	++	+	−	−−
creative	++	+	−	−−

unkind	++	+	−	−−
passionate	++	+	−	−−
placid	++	+	−	−−
spendthrift	++	+	−	−−
considerate	++	+	−	−−
contented	++	+	−	−−
jealous	++	+	−	−−
timid	++	+	−	−−
anxious and worried	++	+	−	−−
cocksure	++	+	−	−−
restless and fidgety	++	+	−	−−
imaginative	++	+	−	−−
moody	++	+	−	−−
glamourous	++	+	−	−−
matter-of-fact	++	+	−	−−
reliable	++	+	−	−−
greedy	++	+	−	−−
trusting	++	+	−	−−
strait-laced	++	+	−	−−
touchy	++	+	−	−−
zestful	++	+	−	−−
selfless	++	+	−	−−
sharp	++	+	−	−−
childish	++	+	−	−−

Appendix II

MARITAL ROLE INVOLVEMENT QUESTIONNAIRE

(Part of the Questionnaire only, as a specimen.)

Name............................

As a background to your interviews, we would like to have some information about the way that you and your wife conduct your married life, and the attitudes and feelings about the tasks, pleasures and duties involved in being married.

For example, people think differently about how a family should manage money and money matters. We have listed some typical opinions below and we would like you to indicate in the column headed 'You' those statements which you agree with. If you think your wife would agree with any of the statements, please indicate this in the column marked 'Your wife'.

We would also like to know whether your family and friends generally would agree with these statements. If you think your family would agree with any of them, please put a tick in the column 'your family', and if you think your wife's family would agree with any of these statements, please put a tick in that column. Finally, if the statements seem to agree with the opinion generally held in your circle of friends, please tick in the column 'Friends', and if you think that ideally things should be done in this way, please tick the column 'Ideally'.

Note: This specimen only includes two of the five areas to be tested in MRIQ, as described in the text, Chapter X. The other areas were arranged and tested in the same way.

338

FINANCIAL DECISIONS AND ARRANGEMENTS

	You	Your wife	Your family	Wife's family	Friends	Ideally
The husband should have absolute control over family finances						
The husband should have control over family finances, but should discuss them with his wife if he feels it necessary						
Both spouses should have a say in financial matters, but the husband's decision should be final						
Both spouses should have a say in financial matters, but the wife's decision should be final						
The final decision should generally be taken by mutual agreement						
The final decision should only be taken by mutual agreement						

Now we would like to know how you and your wife manage your everyday financial affairs. Please tick which describe the way you take financial decisions, that is 'Husband alone', 'Wife alone', or 'Both usually'. If you are concerned about these financial situations, please tick the column 'Causes husband concern', and if you think your wife is concerned about them, tick the column 'Causes wife concern'. If the matter is a bone of contention to you, please tick the column 'Argue'. If you do not know the way the task is carried out, please leave the columns blank.

	Husband	Wife	Both usually	Causes husband concern	Causes wife concern	Argue
Rent, Rates, Mortgages, telephone, wireless and T.V. licences, insurance on house						
Coal, gas, electricity						
Food, laundry, cleaning materials						
Newspapers, magazines						
Re-decoration, renewal of big items, e.g. furniture						
H.P., holidays, presents						
Children's clothes						
Children's toys and entertainments						
School fees, fees for special lessons						
Entertainments, cinema, theatre, outings, etc.						
Personal toilet articles						
Cigarettes and drink						
Own Clothes						
Partner's clothes						

People also have many different opinions about the best way to run the household. Please indicate with a tick those statements you agree with in the column marked 'You'. If you think your wife would agree with any of the statements, please indicate this in the column marked 'Your wife'. If you think your family would agree with any of them, please put a tick in the column 'Your family', and if you think your wife's family would agree with any of these statements, please put a tick under that column. Finally, if the statement seems to agree with the opinion generally held in your circle of friends, please tick in the column 'Friends', and if you think that ideally things should be done in this way, please tick the column 'Ideally'.

HOUSEHOLD TASKS AND RESPONSIBILITIES

	You	Your wife	Your family	Wife's family	Friends	Ideally
Household tasks should be the wife's job alone						
Household tasks should be mainly the wife's job, but she should be able to call upon her husband for help						
Household tasks should be shared as much as possible						
Whoever is available should do household tasks whether they feel it is their job or not						
It is easier to get someone from outside to help with the household tasks than to ask one's partner to do an extra job						
Who does what task is something which should be discussed in the household						

Below are some of the usual household tasks. We would like you to indicate who does these tasks in your household. Would you put a tick under 'Regularly', 'Sometimes' or 'Rarely' under the general heading 'You' according to how often you do that particular task. If you enjoy doing it, would you put a tick under 'Enjoy', and if you worry about it, under 'Worry'. If you think there should be a change in the way it is done, put a tick under 'Change'. Under the general heading, 'Your wife' would you put a tick under 'Regularly', 'Sometimes' or 'Rarely' according to how often your wife does these tasks. If she enjoys doing them, would you put a tick under 'Enjoy' and if you think she worries about it, under 'Worry'. If the task is a bone of contention between you, would you put a tick under the column headed 'Disagreement or conflict'.

HOUSEHOLD TASKS AND RESPONSIBILITIES

| | YOU | | | | | |
	regu-larly	some-times	rarely	enjoy	worry	change
Getting the morning tea						
Getting meals						
Laying the table						
Washing up						
Cleaning and tidying the house						
Shopping						
Laundering						
Cleaning shoes						
Lighting fires						
Fetching coal						
Tending the boiler						
Locking up at night						
Getting up first in the morning						
Repairs						

	regu-larly	some-times	rarely	enjoy	worry	change
Decorating						
Mending clothes						
Planning meals						
Peeling vegs.						
Lawn mowing						
Weeding						

HOUSEHOLD TASKS AND RESPONSIBILITIES

	YOUR WIFE					Disagree-ment or conflict
	regu-larly	some-times	rarely	enjoy	worry	
Getting the morning tea						
Getting meals						
Laying the table						
Washing up						
Cleaning and tidying the house						
Shopping						
Laundering						
Cleaning shoes						
Lighting fires						
Fetching coal						
Tending the boiler						
Locking up at night						

343

| | YOUR WIFE | | | | | Disagree- |
	regu-larly	some-times	rarely	enjoy	worry	ment or conflict
Getting up first in the morning						
Repairs						
Decorating						
Mending clothes						
Planning meals						
Peeling vegs.						
Lawn mowing						
Weeding						

Appendix IIA

A. *Satisfaction in area*
1. Sharing within area with satisfaction
2. Sharing within area without satisfaction
3. Differentiation within area with satisfaction
4. Differentiation within area without satisfaction
5. Inverse differentiation with satisfaction
6. Inverse differentiation without satisfaction
7. Rejection of co-operation

B. *Libidinal involvement in area*
a. Complete involvement in area
b. Very strong involvement
c. Ordinary involvement
d. Reduced involvement
e. No involvement

C. *Acceptance in area*
v. Complete acceptance
w. Good acceptance
x. Ups and downs
y. Partial repudiation
z. Complete repudiation

D. *Conflict*
m. No apparent conflict
n. Little apparent conflict
o. Everyday disagreement
p. Minor overt conflict
q. Strong latent conflict
r. Strong overt conflict

* For Staff use only.

1. *Money: Decision and control*

	Husband		Wife		Joint
	1 2 3 4 5 6 7		1 2 3 4 5 6 7		m n o
	a b c d e		a b c d e		p q r
	v w x y z		v w x y z		

2. *Household Management*

	Husband		Wife		Joint
	1 2 3 4 5 6 7		1 2 3 4 5 6 7		m n o
	a b c d e		a b c d e		p q r
	v w x y z		v w x y z		

3. *Child Care*

	Husband		Wife		Joint
	1 2 3 4 5 6 7		1 2 3 4 5 6 7		m n o
	a b c d e		a b c d e		p q r
	v w x y z		v w x y z		

4. *Special Interests inside the Home*

	Husband		Wife		Joint
	1 2 3 4 5 6 7		1 2 3 4 5 6 7		m n o
	a b c d e		a b c d e		p q r
	v w x y z		v w x y z		

5. *Relations with In-Laws and Kin*

	Husband		Wife		Joint
	1 2 3 4 5 6 7		1 2 3 4 5 6 7		m n o
	a b c d e		a b c d e		p q r
	v w x y z		v w x y z		

6. *Friends*

	Husband		Wife		Joint
	1 2 3 4 5 6 7		1 2 3 4 5 6 7		m n o
	a b c d e		a b c d e		p q r
	v w x y z		v w x y z		

7. *Social Outlets*

	Husband		Wife		Joint
	1 2 3 4 5 6 7		1 2 3 4 5 6 7		m n o
	a b c d e		a b c d e		p q r
	v w x y z		v w x y z		

8. *Special Interests: value systems*

	Husband		Wife		Joint
	1 2 3 4 5 6 7		1 2 3 4 5 6 7		m n o
	a b c d e		a b c d e		p q r
	v w x y z		v w x y z		

9. *Special Interests: Artistic, Scientific and other*

Husband	Wife	Joint
1 2 3 4 5 6 7	1 2 3 4 5 6 7	m n o
a b c d e	a b c d e	p q r
v w x y z	v w x y z	

Please ring appropriate symbol.

347

INDEX